MW00780984

THE PIRATE MENACE

OSPREY
PUBLISHING

DEDICATION

For my parents, who knew they were raising a pirate,
and for David Nicholl, for all the tea and biscuits.

ANGUS KONSTAM

THE PIRATE MENACE

UNCOVERING THE GOLDEN AGE OF PIRACY

OSPREY PUBLISHING
Bloomsbury Publishing Plc
Kemp House, Chawley Park, Cumnor Hill, Oxford OX2 9PH, UK
29 Earlsfort Terrace, Dublin 2, Ireland
1385 Broadway, 5th Floor, New York, NY 10018, USA
E-mail: info@ospreypublishing.com
www.ospreypublishing.com

OSPREY is a trademark of Osprey Publishing Ltd

First published in Great Britain in 2024

A catalogue record for this book is available from the British Library.

ISBN: HB 978 1 4728 5773 6; eBook 978 1 4728 5777 4; ePDF 978 1 4728 5774 3;
XML 978 1 4728 5775 0; Audio 978 1 4728 5776 7

24 25 26 27 28   10 9 8 7 6 5 4 3 2 1

Uncredited images in main text and plate section are from The Stratford Archive.

Maps by Nicholas Buxey
Index by Richard Munro

Typeset by Deanta Global Publishing Services, Chennai, India
Printed and bound in Great Britain by CPI (Group) UK Ltd, Croydon CR0 4YY

CONTENTS

ACKNOWLEDGEMENTS

I'm extremely grateful to everyone who's helped me with this over the years. This book took months to write, but decades to research. So, it would be impossible to mention everyone. You know who you are though, and I thank you for it. This book would have been the poorer without your help. So, I'm going to limit my thanks to a few key institutions and a handful of individuals. Most of my research was done in the National Archives in Kew and the National Maritime Museum in Greenwich. Their archivists patiently taught me the ropes. I also used the National Library of Scotland in Edinburgh, and the National Archives in Washington, DC.

Next, I want to mention a few museums: the Mariners' Museum in Newport News, VA; the North Carolina Maritime Museum in Beaufort, NC; the Mel Fisher Maritime Museum in Key West, FL; the Whydah Museum in Provincetown, MA; and the Pirate Museum in Nassau, Bahamas. All freely helped me with my quest. The staff of the *Queen Anne's Revenge* Conservation Lab (QAR Lab) have greatly advanced the knowledge of piracy through the study of the artefacts they've preserved. For academic institutions I must mention the East Carolina University, which has really pushed the innovative boundaries of the subject.

Finally, I'll limit my personal thanks to a few individuals. Over the years their help and support has been vital to the development of this project. Maritime archaeologist and historian Dave Moore has helped by being my piratical pilot for over a quarter of a century. Thank you, bubba. Fellow pirate historian Benerson Little has also been a very patient sounding board. Every historian needs one of those. I should also thank Baylus C. Brooks, genealogical researcher and historian, whose multi-disciplinary approach has opened new vistas. I should add Charles R. Ewen, of East Carolina University, for his binding together of various academic strands, to produce a much stronger thread. Finally, though, it's got to be that eclectic group of curators from the National Maritime Museum whom I mention in my introduction. Some of them aren't with us anymore, but essentially this one's really for you.

LIST OF ILLUSTRATIONS IN PLATE SECTION

St Croix, where that the pirate Jean Martel was ambushed.
(Getty Images)
Cape Coast Castle, the site of the largest pirate trial of the era.
(Getty Images)
Marconi Beach at Wellfleet, MA, where the *Whydah* was wrecked.
(Getty Images)
The Spanish Treasure Fleet of 1715 sailed from Havana in Cuba.
(Getty Images)
In the early 18th century, Nassau was a thriving pirate haven.
(Getty Images)
Ocracoke Island in North Carolina's Outer Banks was once
Blackbeard's lair. (Getty Images)
Harbour Island, off Eleuthera, was an entrepôt of pirate plunder.
(Getty Images)
Edward Thatch acquired his cognomen 'Blackbeard' thanks to his
wild-looking beard.
Sebastian Inlet, FL, where some of the Spanish Treasure Fleet was
wrecked. (Getty Images)
Governor Woodes Rogers tried to bring law and order to the
Bahamas.
A French slave ship of around 1720. These vessels were well suited
to the needs of pirates.
Governor Alexander Spotswood of the Virginia colony was no friend
of pirates.
New Providence's harbour, Nassau, boasted a commodious protected
anchorage.
The buccaneering movement started on the island of Hispaniola.
Charles Town in the South Carolina colony was a major trading
port.
Blackbeard knew that intimidation was a powerful piratical tool.

A NOTE ON TIME, NATION AND DISTANCE

During this period two types of calendar were in use at the same time. Until 1582, for the best part of 1,600 years, the Julian calendar was used in Europe. Created by Julius Caesar, it ran on a cycle of 365 days, with a leap day added every four years. This, though, created a slight discrepancy between the calendar and the seasons. So, in 1582 Pope Gregory XIII solved this by leaving out a leap year on three out of every four centuries. This was all it took to bring the calendar and the seasons back into step. The New Year was now celebrated on 1 January, rather than 25 March. This Gregorian calendar was quickly adopted by most European countries, along with their newfound colonies in the Americas. Unfortunately, as is often the case, the British didn't play ball.

Instead, they stubbornly stuck to the old Julian calendar until 1752. By that stage there was a ten-day difference between the two calendars. That meant that when the British – and their American colonies – finally adopted the Gregorian or 'New Style' calendar, 4 September 1752 was followed by 14 September. While some people missed their birthday that year, there was some consolation in having two New Year celebrations in nine months – one on 25 March 1752 and the next on 1 January 1753. This of course gives historians something of a problem. While a British source gives one date, a French, Spanish or Dutch one gives another one ten days later. Both, though, are referring to the same day. For much of this book this hasn't been an issue. In a few cases, though, where say French and British sources are used, we have a problem.

So, as most of the sources here are from British records, we've stuck with the old-style Julian dates. If we've used new-style Gregorian dates, from say French records, then for the sake of consistency I've changed these so they match the British date. However, to avoid confusing the modern reader too much, I've changed the year on 1 January rather than 25 March, in line with our modern Gregorian-style calendar. In fact, this isn't as radical as it sounds, as during this period many letters and documents written between 1 January and 25 March were dated using both years. So, you'd get a letter dated 14 February 1717/18. Even the British of the period recognized that the whole dating game was a little confusing.

So, for example, Governor Woodes Rogers first landed at Nassau on 27 July 1718. In today's calendar, it would have happened on 6 August. Similarly, Blackbeard fought his last battle on 22 November that same year. In our modern calendar, that would've been on 2 December 1718. So, if you want to bring all the dates into the modern style, then please feel free to add ten days to them all. Sticking with the dates used at the time makes things a little easier to follow. A place where we've modernized is the start of the day. Officially, at sea the day began at noon. For us, though, we've followed the modern style, and have our days starting just after midnight.

I have two other things I should mention before we begin. Until 1603 England and Scotland were independent kingdoms. Then, following the death of Queen Elizabeth I of England, the English cast about for a successor to 'the Virgin Queen', and settled on King James VI of Scotland, the son of Mary Queen of Scots. So, on July 1603 James was duly crowned King James I of England. This created a union of the Crowns. The two countries remained independent, but there was now a unity in some areas, such as international diplomacy. Then, on 1 May 1707, the Act of Union came into force, and for better or worse Scotland and England became one country – known as Great Britain. In this book, I've used the labels 'England' or 'English' before 1707, and 'Britain' or 'British' afterwards.

Finally, this book is all about pirates – who clearly operated on the high seas. So, throughout this book, when we mention miles, we're speaking about nautical miles. In the period, this meant a meridian arc the equivalent of a minute of latitude (a 60th of a degree) at the equator. Today this has been simplified to a distance of 6,076 feet (or 1,852 metres). That means a nautical mile is a little over 2,025 yards long, making it the equivalent of just over 1.15 land miles (or 1,760 yards). So, in the book if we refer to miles, we mean nautical miles. On the very few occasions we talk about events on land, we'll use land miles. I hope that makes sense.

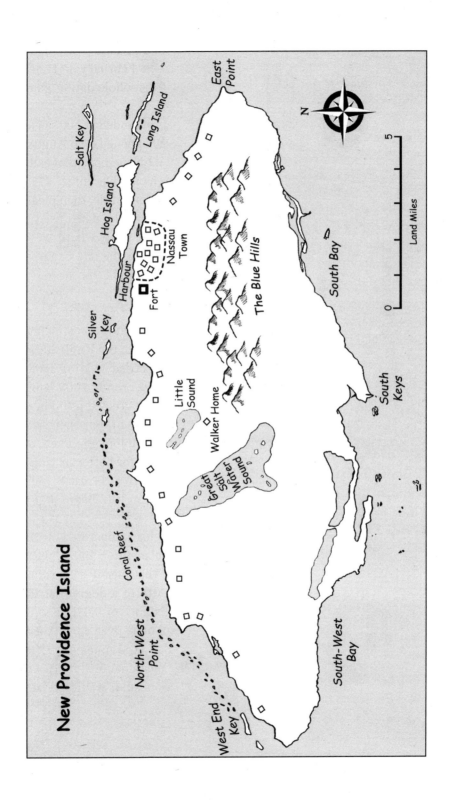

New Providence Island

Salt Key

Long Island

East Point

Hog Island

Silver Key

Harbour

Fort

Nassau Town

The Blue Hills

South Bay

Little Sound

Walker Home

South Keys

Great Salt Water Sound

Coral Reef

North-West Point

West End Key

South-West Bay

N

0   1   2   3   4   5

Land Miles

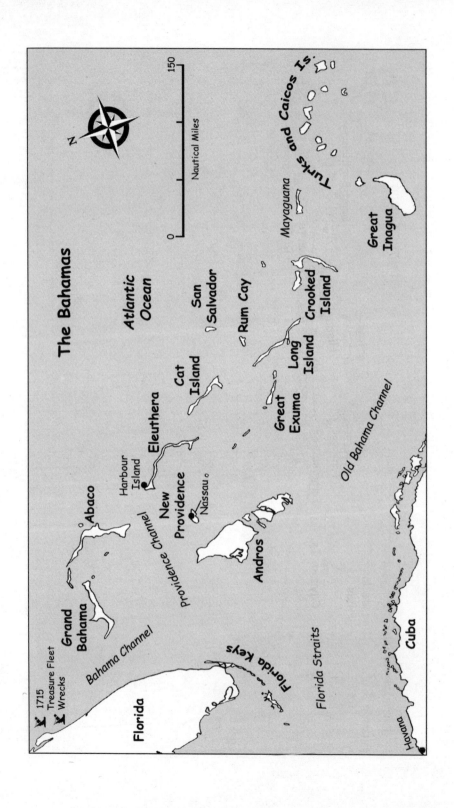

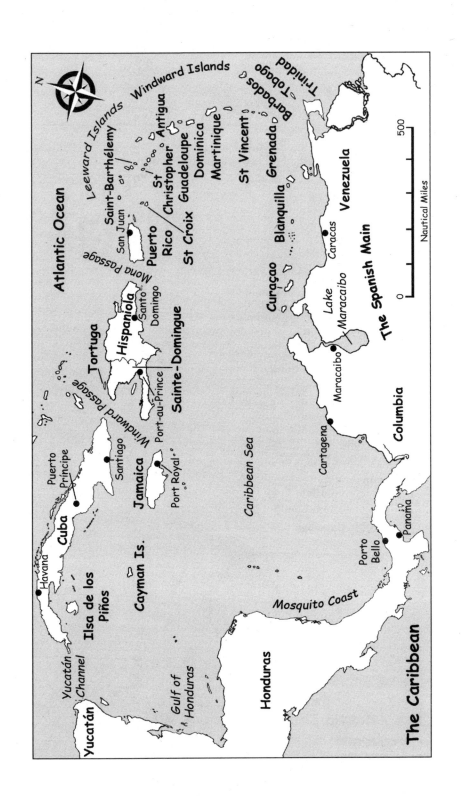

The Caribbean

Atlantic Ocean

Windward Islands

Leeward Islands

Saint-Barthélemy

St Christopher

Antigua

Guadeloupe

Dominica

Martinique

St Vincent

Grenada

Barbados

Tobago

Trinidad

Blanquilla

Curaçao

Venezuela

Caracas

The Spanish Main

Lake Maracaibo

Maracaibo

Columbia

Cartagena

Panama

Porto Bello

Mosquito Coast

Caribbean Sea

Honduras

Gulf of Honduras

Cayman Is.

Jamaica

Port Royal

Santiago

Puerto Principe

Cuba

Ilsa de los Piños

Havana

Yucatán

Yucatán Channel

Windward Passage

Tortuga

Hispaniola

Santo Domingo

Sainte-Domingue

Port-au-Prince

Mona Passage

San Juan

Puerto Rico

St Croix

N

Nautical Miles

0   500

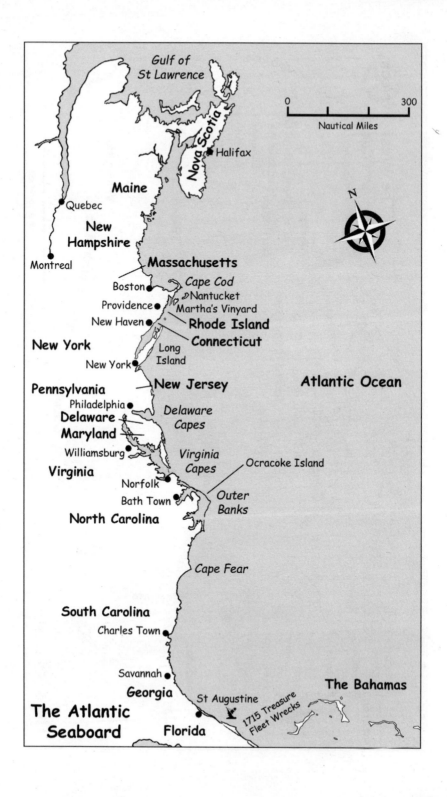

Gulf of
St Lawrence

Nova Scotia

Halifax

Maine

Quebec

New
Hampshire

Montreal

Massachusetts

Boston

Cape Cod

Nantucket

Providence

Martha's Vinyard

New Haven

Rhode Island

Connecticut

New York

Long
Island

New York

Pennsylvania

New Jersey

Philadelphia

Delaware
Capes

Delaware

Maryland

Williamsburg

Virginia
Capes

Virginia

Ocracoke Island

Norfolk

Bath Town

Outer
Banks

North Carolina

Cape Fear

South Carolina

Charles Town

Savannah

The Bahamas

Georgia

St Augustine

The Atlantic
Seaboard

Florida

1715 Treasure
Fleet Wrecks

Atlantic Ocean

N

0   300

Nautical Miles

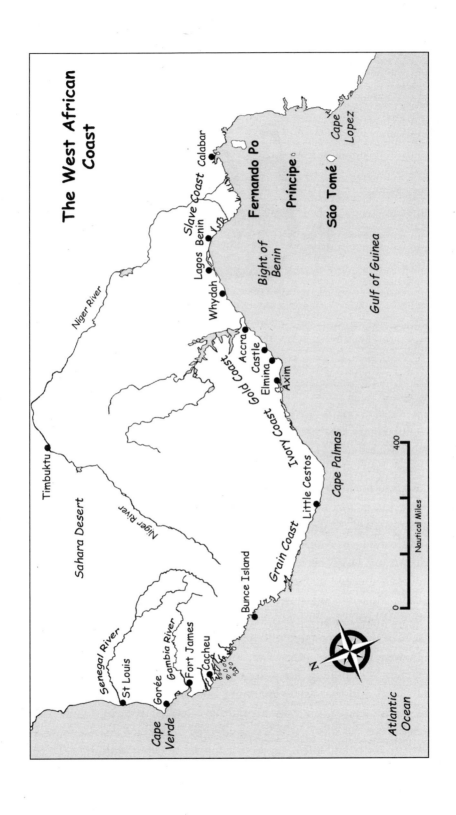

The West African Coast

Timbuktu

Sahara Desert

Niger River

Niger River

Senegal River

St Louis

Gorée

Gambia River

Fort James

Cacheu

Cape Verde

Bunce Island

Grain Coast

Ivory Coast

Little Cestos

Cape Palmas

Gold Coast

Axim

Elmina

Castle

Accra

Whydah

Lagos

Benin

Slave Coast

Calabar

Fernando Po

Príncipe

São Tomé

Cape Lopez

Bight of Benin

Gulf of Guinea

Atlantic Ocean

N

400

Nautical Miles

0

PROLOGUE

The steady north-easterly breeze filled the topsails of the small 20-gun frigate HMS *Rose* as she slipped cautiously between two scrub-covered islands – Hog Island to larboard (port) and tiny Silver Key to starboard. Once past them, she was in the sparkling blue waters of Nassau harbour's main channel. Captain Thomas Whitney wasn't taking any chances though. His guns were loaded and run out, and the gun crews were at their posts, with matchcord burning in the tubs next to the carriages. Ahead of them, across the harbour, lay a stone-built fort, while a large French-built merchantman lying at anchor flew the flag of St George at her masthead. Behind her lay dozens of smaller vessels. Most of them were mere sloops, some flying the black flag of piracy. Whitney only had eyes for the fort as he ordered his topsails braced, to bring the frigate to a gliding stop.[1]

It was now just after 6pm on Monday 25 July 1718. Captain Whitney was hoping for a signal – any sign – that his arrival was welcomed, and the pirates manning the fort weren't planning to open fire. As he waited, his crew would have looked around, taking in the stench from the shore, which was covered in wooden shacks, makeshift sailcloth tents and a few, more substantial wooden buildings. To their

left, along the southern shore of Hog Island, the bleached bones of
dozens of vessels lay rotting in the early evening sunshine. Even the
sparkling water and white sands couldn't hide the shabbiness of the
pirate haven. It was a tense moment – within seconds Whitney and
his men could be fighting for their lives. Suddenly a gun cracked out,
and smoke billowed. Surprisingly, it didn't come from the fort, but
from the merchant ship, which had now hoisted a black pirate flag at
her mainmast. Seconds later a fountain of water erupted off their port
beam. They were under fire.

In all, three shots were fired at them, over the space of several
minutes. Whitney ordered the longboat lowered and sent over his
First Lieutenant and some marines to find out why he was being fired
at. They returned quickly to report the crew of the ship – pirates to a
man – were mostly drunk, and under the command of a pirate captain
called Charles Vane. When asked why he'd opened fire, Vane replied
that he'd do his utmost to burn them that night, together with all the
vessels in the harbour. It was an ugly incident, but it seemed an isolated
one. So, when nothing else happened, Whitney ordered his own guns
to be fired – a signal to the transport ship waiting outside the harbour
that it was safe to enter.

Less than an hour later, four vessels flying the British flag dropped
anchor in Nassau harbour, and three more outside it. Three of them
were warships – including the 32-gun frigate HMS *Milford*, commanded
by Captain Peter Chamberlaine, the acting commodore of the convoy's
escort. Inside the harbour was the 20-gun sixth-rate frigate HMS
Rose, and the tiny ten-gun sloop-of-war *Shark*. Anchored behind them
was the *Buck*, a small armed sloop, looking little different from the
pirate vessels farther inside the harbour. Last was the *Willing Mind*, a
300-ton transport ship, her decks crammed with colonists, eager for a
first glimpse of their new home. The largest of the newcomers, though,
was the *Delicia*, a 460-ton armed merchant ship. She snugged down for
the night at anchor just outside the harbour entrance, accompanied by
the *Milford* and a second small armed sloop, the *Samuel*.

On board the *Delicia* was Woodes Rogers, the future governor of
the Bahamas. The tall, broad-shouldered 39-year-old was no stranger
to the sea. In his younger days he'd been a celebrated privateering
captain. Now, though, as he surveyed the harbour, he would have been
preoccupied by concerns about what would happen the following

morning, when he finally set foot on the shore, and claimed the island of New Providence – in fact, the whole of the Bahamas – in the name of King George I of Great Britain. Until that moment, Nassau had been little more than a pirate haven. From the moment he read out his royal commission, the Bahamas would be brought to heel, as a place of law, order and decency.[2]

Others, though, wanted no part of all that. In the months before Rogers' arrival, the Nassau pirates had been torn between accepting the promise of a royal pardon, absolving them of their past crimes, or refusing to bow to the yoke of authority. Leading this last group, known as the 'die-hards', was Captain Charles Vane. That evening, as the sun set just before 8pm, he was busily preparing for a grand gesture of defiance. Once darkness fell an hour later, he set about transferring men and stores from the French merchantman – a recent prize. He had her 24 guns loaded and double-shotted, some filled with partridge or scatter shot, for maximum havoc. Old sails, barrels of tar – indeed anything that could burn – were piled on her decks. By midnight everything was ready. That was when Vane made his move.

Two pirate ships – a sloop and a schooner – had already rigged towlines to the Frenchman, and after cutting her anchor cable they turned her head around until she pointed down the narrow harbour. Directly ahead of them was HMS *Rose*. Then, at Vane's signal, the French ship's sails were hoisted, and her skeleton crew set her ablaze, before scrambling over her side into a waiting boat. Charles Vane, the leader of Nassau's remaining pirates, was about to unleash terror on the forces of the Crown. As she began making way, the fireship headed directly towards the unsuspecting frigate. Roused from his cabin, Captain Whitney instinctively ordered his men to chop through their thick anchor cable. Seamen raced to raise jibs and sails, as the captain and crew of the *Rose* desperately tried to escape the flaming horror coming towards them.

As the blazing fireship reached the frigate, seamen stood ready to fend her off with oars, boathooks and spars, while others busily pumped water over the sails, to reduce the risk of them catching fire. It was just as well. Sparks were now showering the frigate. The fireship's guns began shooting off, adding to the chaos. Miraculously, all four of the British ships in Nassau harbour narrowly avoided the fireship, but it was a close-run thing. Watching all of this was Charles Vane, while his pirates cheered the fireship on. Eventually, the blazing hulk ran herself aground on the south side of the channel, and the crisis passed. There she burned furiously all the way to the waterline. By morning there was nothing left of her but a few charred, smoking timbers.

When Woodes Rogers eventually set foot on the beach at Nassau he was met by a group of extremely apologetic ex-pirates. They all assured him of their loyalty, and that they were horrified by Vane's attack on a king's ship. They also reminded their new governor that they'd all signed a pardon and were reformed characters. They were pirates no more. Woodes Rogers should have taken some solace from that. However, in the back of his mind was the image of the hatred shown by Charles Vane and his men, who had escaped from the harbour amid the confusion of the night. Governor Rogers now realized that merely hoisting the Union flag over the pirate haven of Nassau wouldn't mark the end of piracy in the Americas. This was only the start of a bitter fight against the pirate menace.

INTRODUCTION

AUTHORS OFTEN CLAIM JUST how long they've taken to research or write a book. For me, the writing part of that is easy – about three months from start to finish. It helps, of course, that you've got a rough idea what you're writing about. Although I'll never claim to have the whole story, I've been researching and writing this subject for a very long time. My first pirate book, *The History of Pirates*, was published in 1999 – almost a quarter of a century ago. It was something of a best-seller back in the day, which taught me just how little I really knew about the topic. I'm a little embarrassed by it today – I got a few things wrong, and there were places where I could have told a better tale. So, I set about trying to find out more, and gradually, over the years, I did.

I'd like to say my whole interest in pirates began as a child, with my grandparents giving me a copy of *Treasure Island*. It did of course – and I loved the story – but apart from spawning a lifelong interest in maps and charts it didn't really lead to anything. In the Christmas of 1967 my dad gave me a copy of *The Valiant Book of Pirates*, a beautifully illustrated book for kids, which kept me entertained for hours on end. I still have it on my bookshelf over half a century later. It looks battered, and has lost its spine, but the illustrations are every bit as vivid as I remember them. That still didn't fire up my passion for piracy though. At the time I was more interested in modern ships, especially ones with guns. That's probably why I joined the Royal Navy and landed up on a frigate in the Caribbean, going to many of the exotic places mentioned in this book.

That still didn't do the trick, although it really helped later, when I came to describe little islands in the Caribbean that I'd been to, or the appearance of the Bahamian coast. No, the enthusiasm came much later, when I had another job of sorts, working as a curator in a national museum, the Royal Armouries, which at the time was based in the Tower of London. I say 'of sorts', as I'm still amazed someone would pay me for turning up to work there and getting to play with arms and armour on a daily basis. The stores – then in medieval round towers in the Tower of London's outer walls – were like a string of Aladdin's caves, with racks filled with swords, muskets and pieces of armour. I learned a lot there, particularly about weapons, which by then was my speciality. In the Navy I only got to wave a sword on a parade ground – here I could wave them about every day.

In 1988 the National Maritime Museum down the river in Greenwich decided to stage a major exhibition called *Pirates: Fact & Fiction*. I was summoned by a group of the museum's curators and told they wanted to borrow objects from our collection which had some sort of pirate provenance. We'd just done something similar with their major exhibition on the Spanish Armada – it being its 400th anniversary. The pirate theme, though, proved much tougher to work with. The trouble is, very few objects in our collection had any kind of pirate provenance. The best we could do was to lend objects which were from the right period, and were of the kind used by pirates, or the government forces ranged against them.

During the planning of the exhibition, I had several meetings with the curators at 'the Maritime', many of which ended up happening in a pub outside the museum's gates – the Plume of Feathers, which was their curators' watering hole. It was there that I got to discuss the subject of pirates with the likes of Teddy Archibald, David Cordingly, John Falconer, David Lyon and Alan Stimson, all superb company on what the Navy would term 'a run ashore'. From them I learned that these curators – all experts in their field – were also struggling when it came to tying down historical piracy, and separating pirate fact from pirate fiction. In the end, that's exactly where David and John went with their superb exhibition – an exploration of the way the facts have now been largely obscured by decades, or rather centuries, of romanticism, embellishment and downright nonsense.

In the end the exhibition was a roaring success, and David Cordingly went on to write several wonderful books on historical piracy, which developed this theme of fact versus fiction. An excellent scholar, his books were groundbreaking and offered me – a whippersnapper of a historian – a reliable entry point into the world of Blackbeard, Black Sam Bellamy and John 'Calico Jack' Rackam. So, my spur to launch myself into pirate history wasn't that copy of *Treasure Island*, or a pirate picture book, but came from sitting in a pub with some real old-school scholastic curators and letting their enthusiasm for the topic wash over me. I landed up reading whatever I could find and visiting the National Archives in Kew in my spare time. Gradually, as the years passed, my grounding in the subject grew, and my grasp of the facts became more solid.

Winding the clock on a bit more, in 1995 I took up a new job as the chief curator in the Mel Fisher Maritime Museum in Key West, Florida. When I joined we were just pulling together our own major exhibition called *A Slave Ship Speaks*. It dealt with the poignant finds from an English slave ship wrecked off the Florida Keys in 1700. So, it was back to the archives, to play my part in filling out this superb story. In the end the exhibition was another rip-roaring success, and when it went on tour it landed up in the Smithsonian. After that we wanted to do another exhibition, and I rashly suggested one on pirates. It was then that I remembered just how little I knew. So, it was back to the archives again, and we fleshed out the bones of the story, tying it in with the many period objects in our collection, from Spanish treasure to early 18th-century cannons.

It was here I first recognized the importance of the Spanish Treasure Fleet of 1715 to the story, as it was a major cause for the rise of the pirate menace in the years that followed. Fortunately, the museum had a huge collection of treasure from the wrecks – enough to make a pirate like Henry Jennings happy. *Pirates!* the exhibition was so popular that we sent it on tour as well. After it finished, I kept up with my research, with the added advantage that once again many of the places featured in the tale of piracy were within reach – a puddle-jumper flight to Nassau for instance, a yacht trip to Cuba, or a drive up to North Carolina's Outer Banks. It helped, too, that I was British, which meant annual flights home, and yet more visits to the archives in Kew.

So, my first pirate book was duly commissioned and published. That, fortunately, wasn't the end of the story, as by then I'd decided to 'drill down' into the world of Blackbeard – Edward Thatch, or Teach. One impetus for this book then, is to bring his story up to date.

One final thing. The subtitle of this book is *Uncovering the Golden Age of Piracy*. Over the years this phrase has become a sort of shorthand for this period of pirate history. Historians rarely agree, and this is one of those areas where everyone has their own opinion. I'd say this so-called 'Golden Age' lasted for a few short years, from about 1714 to 1723, by which time the 'pirate menace' was most definitely over. Others add a few years to either end, but generally everyone is speaking about the same thing – the spectacular upsurge of piracy in American waters during this period. That, then, is the subject of the book – the rise and fall of what was widely seen as a major pirate menace.

This was the era of the likes of Sam Bellamy, Howell Davis, Benjamin Hornigold, Henry Jennings, Walter Kennedy, 'Calico Jack' Rackam, Bartholomew Roberts, Edward Thatch and Charles Vane – notorious pirates to a man. It also saw the women pirates Anne Bonny and Mary Read make their brief appearance in history, showing that piracy wasn't just a man's game. As for where the phrase 'The Golden Age of Piracy' came from, I can't really say. I've asked other pirate historians – yes, there's a very small but select band of them – and so far they haven't come up with a definitive answer either.

I suspected it was a late 19th-century or early 20th-century thing. That was the time when artists like Howard Pyle and Frank Schoonover were painting such evocative images of pirates, or the likes of Raphael Sabatini were redefining the swashbuckler novel and paving the way for Hollywood's pirates of the silver screen. This, of course, lies at the root of the 'pirate fiction' which David Cordingly talks about – the way these fictional strands have all but hidden the historical roots of piracy amid a welter of romanticized and often wildly inaccurate flimflam.

The closest I've heard to a 'Golden Age' definition comes from the excellent pirate historian Benerson Little. He reckons that it probably was coined by the American historian and philosopher John Fiske in the 1890s, while writing about American colonial history. The late 19th century was a time when 'the golden age' was often used as an expression, when speaking about everything from pirates to Latin literature and Flemish painting. So, the phrase gradually slipped into general use and has been with us ever since. Benerson pointed out that, by 1953, when one of the first real pirate historians Patrick Pringle wrote his book *Jolly Roger*, the phrase was already firmly established, although Pringle called it 'The Great Age of Piracy'. So, we should embrace its value as a useful shorthand for a truly fascinating period in history – a time when pirates really were the terror of the seas.

Angus Konstam
Herston, Orkney, 2024

Beyond the Line

THAT MORNING, DAWN CAME to Port Royal just after 5am. It promised to be a sultry, humid day, with not even a breath of wind. The growing light over the tops of the Blue Mountains revealed a cloudless sky, while the clear waters of the harbour were mirror still. The only movement came from the ripples of fish breaking the surface, or the occasional splash of frigate birds, diving for their prey. For the plantation owners and smallholders in Jamaica's interior, the recent rains had brought everything back to life. After five months of drought, May's tropical rains had transformed the verdant island, and the crops were now thriving. The rains lasted for a month and had stopped abruptly a week before, at the start of June. They were replaced by a stifling stillness, where the Caribbean sun blazed down, with no cooling breeze coming from the sea.[1]

That Tuesday morning of 7 June 1692, the usually thriving harbour of Port Royal, Jamaica, was as languidly inactive as it had been since the rains stopped. Without wind the ships in the harbour couldn't put to sea.

It was the same for every sailing vessel there, from the sleek privateers to the smallest, meanest fishing boat. They were trapped there, and their crews were forced to endure another day of inactivity and airless discomfort. It wasn't just the humidity though. The recent rains had brought out the mosquitoes, and with them the growing threat of yellow fever or the bloody flux (now less spectacularly known as dysentery). It was almost as if the airless heat had sapped the soul out of the usually vibrant, wild and freewheeling atmosphere of Port Royal.

The place certainly had a reputation. It had been a boom town, which sprang to life after England's conquest of Spanish-owned Jamaica in 1655. Oliver Cromwell's 'Western Design' – his military expedition to invade the Spanish New World – might have been a bungled, half-hearted venture, but it did win England an immensely valuable prize – a secure base in the very heart of the Spanish Caribbean. As there was little chance of military support from home, Jamaica's early governors turned to the buccaneers for help.[2]

Buccaneering transformed Port Royal and earned it the label 'the most wicked city in the world'. It was also probably the richest port in the Americas. While this was heaven for most buccaneers, some elements of Jamaican society were less impressed. In 1682, one visiting clergyman famously said of Port Royal, 'This town is the Sodom of the New World.' He described its population as made up of 'pirates, cutthroats, whores and some of the vilest persons in the whole of the world'. Inevitably, he soon decided, 'I could better preach the word of God elsewhere.' He left Jamaica on the same ship that had brought him to Port Royal.[3]

He probably had a point. Another visitor claimed that, in 1690, one in every four or five buildings in Port Royal was either a brothel, a gaming house, a tavern or a grog shop. It was the archetypal boom town, where a fortune could be made almost overnight by merchants, smugglers or privateers, and it could be blown just as quickly. While the boom times might have been over by June 1692, thanks to a renewed need for privateers, Port Royal was still one of the busiest ports in the Caribbean. This was all about to change. In fact, it all came crashing down. There are those who might have viewed the catastrophe as God's judgement on such a vile and wicked place. That, however, was little consolation to Port Royal's 6,000-strong population.

In late spring 1692, upwards of 16 privateering men-of-war were operating out of Port Royal. That meant at least 1,500 seamen were involved in privateering, serviced by a port which was well versed in the needs of privateersmen, and in the semi-legal sale of their plunder. Still, this never quite rivalled the rise in trade, despite all the risks involved in shipping cargoes across the Atlantic in times of war. Unlike buccaneering, privateering in late-17th-century Port Royal was little more than a major sideline. Now, though, more than 500 merchant ships a year used its busy and spacious harbour. The port's wharves and warehouses bustled with trade – or rather they would have that June morning, were it not for the unusual stillness and utter lack of wind.[4]

The anchorage itself was well protected by five stone-built fortifications, one of which was called Fort Morgan in honour of the great buccaneer, and another, Fort Carlisle, had been built under Morgan's supervision. Now, though, trade was the key to Jamaica's future, and the harbour that was once crowded by buccaneering ships was full of merchantmen. The port itself was still a lively sailors' town, full of taverns and brothels, but there were signs of gentrification. St Peter's Church, for example, towered over the other buildings, and there were even plans afoot to replace its bell with a larger one, shipped from London. Its spires loomed over the crowded buildings of the port, many of which were stone built, giving Port Royal an air of permanence.

The largest of them included the Governor's House, currently the home of the acting governor John White, who had recently taken over the post after the Earl of Inchiquin succumbed to yellow fever that January. Close to it was the Custom House, where official business was transacted, and the Exchange, the bustling centre for mercantile transactions. Other official buildings in Port Royal were the Court House, where the Admiralty court met to try pirates, and two prisons, one each for men and women. While the colony's official seat was in Spanish Town, around the bay, Port Royal was the real hub of the island. This crowded port, arguably the busiest harbour in the Americas, was crammed onto the club-shaped end of a narrow spit of sand. Past Port Royal's eastern defences – Fort Rupert and the Palisadoes – the sandy spit curved around the anchorage, and the firm road running atop it linked the port to the Jamaican mainland, and on to Spanish Town, 25 miles away across what is now Kingston Harbour.

On Tuesday 7 June 1692 it was business as usual in Port Royal. Cargoes were loaded, taverns and brothels opened for business, traders arrived from Spanish Town and merchants swapped news in the Exchange. The lack of wind meant that no ships could enter or leave the port, but most thought the stillness wouldn't last. For those who could read the signs, however, there was a growing unease. Many knew that this kind of weather often preceded an earth tremor, something that happened almost every year. Port Royal, after all, was built on sand, and even a minor tremor could cause serious damage. Most, though, went about their business amid the growing heat of the day. Then, just before noon, cataclysmic disaster came to Port Royal.

One of the port's merchants, John Uffgress, described the moment his whole world fell apart: 'Betwixt eleven and twelve noon, I being in a tavern, we felt the house shake, and saw bricks begin to rise in the floor.' Outside in the street the warning cry of 'Earthquake!' rang out. Uffgress continued, 'Immediately we ran out of the house, where we saw all people with uplifted hands begging God's assistance. We continued running up the street, whilst on either side of us we saw the houses, some swallowed up, others thrown on heaps. The sand in the streets rose up like waves in the sea, lifting up all persons who stood upon it, and immediately dropping them into pits.' The horrified merchant watched: 'And, at the same instant, a flood of water breaking in, rolled those poor souls over and over.'[5]

The lucky ones were able to grab on to the torn beams and rafters of houses, but many were battered to death or simply drowned. Uffgress was one of the lucky ones: 'The small piece of ground whereon 16 or 18 of us stood (praise to God) did not sink.' Other survivors had equally terrifying brushes with death. Doctor Heath, the rector at St Peter's, was sharing a tobacco pipe with Acting Governor White on the porch of the Governor's House: 'Before that was out, I felt the ground rolling and moving under my feet, upon which I said, Lord Sir, what is this?' The governor felt it was an earthquake but assured the clergyman that it would soon pass. When they saw the church tower fall, they decided to make a run for it. They became separated, but White made for Morgan's Fort, which he thought the safest spot. He continued, 'As I made towards it I saw the earth open up and swallow a multitude of people, and the sea mounting in upon us over the fortifications.'[6]

In the end, he made it to the Rectory, where he and passers-by knelt and prayed for salvation. Then the tremors eased. He and his group were extremely fortunate. That morning, Port Royal had a population of around 6,500 inhabitants, living in a bustling community of upwards of 2,000 buildings. The earthquake struck at 11.43am – the time verified almost three centuries later by the discovery of a pocket watch, which had stopped when the earthquake hit. By noon, around 5,000 of these people were dead. The shock itself was felt throughout Jamaica and caused major damage in Spanish Town, 10 miles away as the crow flies. In nearby Liguanea – present-day Kingston – all buildings were flattened. It seems that not only had Port Royal been built on a bed of sand, but it also lay astride a tectonic fault line.

During the quake the sand liquified and appeared to flow like water, swallowing buildings and people, or else sweeping them into the sea. Sinkholes opened up in the sand, then closed again after people were swept into them. The water itself drew back up to a mile, then came roaring back as a tsunami, which broke over the town. At least 20 ships anchored in the harbour were ripped from their anchors and carried along, only to be wrecked on what remained of the fort, or cast back into the sea as wreckage. One of these was the frigate HMS *Swann*, which was being careened on the edge of the harbour. After being carried over the buildings of the port she was left smashed and stranded amid the remains of the buildings.

In all, two-thirds of Port Royal had been lost in a matter of minutes, the northern and western sides of the harbour and town being reclaimed by the sea. All of its wharves and warehouses had vanished, and what remained above water had, with few exceptions, been reduced to rubble. Bodies lay everywhere, floating in the harbour, buried under homes or half-swallowed by the very ground itself. Within hours these began to smell in the heat. After the disaster came the horror. Port Royal had an unsavoury name, and in the days that followed it lived up to its reputation. Starving survivors looted and pillaged whatever they could, and began hauling out rotting corpses, searching for money, and even cutting off fingers to claim wedding rings. It took a while before the Jamaican authorities sent in their militia to restore order, and to do what they could for the survivors.

In Spanish Town, the Jamaican legislature knew who had caused the disaster. This was, they declared, 'An Instance of God Almighty's severe judgment.' In any case, it was the end of Port Royal – or at least the end of the place in its old hell-raising form. What little remained of Port Royal would be rebuilt, but it would never be more than a shadow of its former self. Still, it was simply too good a harbour to be abandoned. The commercial trade, though, which had recently made Port Royal prosper, would now flow into Liguanea across the bay. This tiny fishing harbour was renamed Kingston within weeks of the earthquake and by the end of the decade would become Jamaica's largest port. There was also a war going on, which in turn meant that there was a need for both warships and privateers. So, Port Royal would be reinvented as a small naval base and privateering port. This time around, everything would be rigidly controlled, to make sure there was no return to the old buccaneering ways.[7]

We have already come across the buccaneers of Port Royal, but as they lay at the root of much that followed, let's look at them more closely. The name itself is worth explaining. The first *boucaniers* – a French term for the hunters and curers of wild beef – were French frontiersmen, operating in the forests of Hispaniola. The Spanish saw these hunters as 'interlopers' and did their best to root them out. By the mid-17th century, in response to the Spanish campaign against them, the *boucaniers* had evolved into small-scale pirates, using canoes to prey on passing Spanish trading ships. They established their own haven on Tortuga, a small turtle-backed island off the north-west coast of Spanish-held Hispaniola. By the 1640s they'd largely abandoned hunting and become a buccaneering community, who styled themselves the 'Brethren of the Coast'. The old French term, by then, had largely evolved from *boucanier* into buccaneer.[8]

Most of these early buccaneers were Huguenots – French Protestants – but the community soon attracted others who shared the buccaneers' Protestant faith, including Dutch and English recruits. Many of these had reached the Americas as indentured servants or convicted felons, sent to work in the plantations. Instead, they ran off to join the buccaneers. The seizure of Jamaica in 1655 led to a dramatic increase in the number of English buccaneers. Merchant sailors, naval or army deserters, or runaway indentured servants and slaves boosted their numbers. In Jamaica, the governor Edward D'Oyley actively encouraged privateering as a means of defence, issuing 'Letters of Marque' to buccaneers who were willing to help protect the island, as well as raid the Spanish Main, the Caribbean coast of South America.

The first attacks on the Spanish Main began within months, using English warships and troops. Although success was limited, this encouraged the buccaneers to move to Port Royal, and by 1658 the Jamaicans had enough buccaneering muscle to carry out a series of successful raids on Spanish settlements on the coast of the Spanish Main. Unusually, these often used a combination of naval and buccaneer forces. So, from the very start there was a peculiar symbiotic link between the buccaneers and the Jamaican authorities. By issuing privateering licences, or Letters of Marque, the Jamaican governor had given the buccaneers a veneer of legitimacy, at least in the eyes of the law. Still, these joint naval and privateering raids were unusual, and in 1659 their leader, Captain Christopher Myngs, was recalled to the Admiralty to explain himself.[9]

Despite an official ceasefire in 1660, fighting in the Caribbean would continue for another decade. Jamaica's governors firmly believed that until Spain recognized England's ownership of Jamaica, the colony was still under threat of invasion. The buccaneers were their way of ensuring the security of the island. In the mid-1660s a new governor, Sir Thomas Modyford, tried to develop the island's plantation economy, but to do this he needed his colony's share of the profits generated by the buccaneers. This was gained through issuing Letters of Marque to privateersmen, allowing the Jamaican authorities to keep a fifth of any plunder. For Jamaica, this was a great source of easily earned income. Modyford was a firm advocate of the 'no peace beyond the line'[10] philosophy, where the niceties of European diplomacy meant little in the Caribbean. So, he continued to issue privateering licences. In 1667, one of Modyford's Letters of Marque was issued to the Welsh mariner Henry Morgan, who had served under Christopher Myngs. This promising young buccaneer was now captain of his own vessel.

Morgan was a natural leader and soon gathered enough followers to stage a raid. In April 1688 he sacked the city of Puerto Príncipe – now Camagüey in Cuba – at the head of 700 buccaneers. Then in July he fell on the heavily defended Spanish treasure port of Porto Bello on the Caribbean coast of Panama. Morgan took the city in a surprise attack, and then stripped it clean. He and his men returned to Port Royal with plunder worth half a million pieces-of-eight. Nothing succeeds like success, and more buccaneers flocked to join Morgan. A delighted Governor Modyford even began calling Morgan his 'Admiral'.

This, of course, went far beyond merely protecting Jamaica. It was little more than violent robbery on an international scale. The raids would continue, but back in London the Spanish ambassadors were baying for blood, holding Morgan and Modyford to account.

For the moment, though, the raids continued. In April 1669 Morgan entered the Maracaibo Lagoon and ransacked the area. This time, he had to fight a Spanish naval squadron to escape back out to sea, but he still made it safely into Port Royal with another large haul of Spanish booty. By now, Modyford had been ordered to stop hostilities against the Spanish, as peace talks were finally under way. In Port Royal proclamations stopping further raids were nailed up on the tavern doors. However, the peace didn't last. In early 1670, after Spanish privateers raided Jamaica, Modyford let Morgan slip his leash.[11]

In August 1670, Morgan left Port Royal at the head of a small force of 600 men and 11 ships. He then joined forces with a French buccaneering contingent, and together they sailed to the coast of Panama. In December they landed to the west of Porto Bello and captured the Spanish fort guarding the mouth of the Chagres River. From there, Morgan led his men upriver towards Panama, disembarking halfway across the isthmus. Spanish scouts reported the invaders were no real threat, one officer saying, 'There are no more than 600 drunkards!' At dawn on 28 December, however, these drunkards appeared on the plain in front of the rich but well-defended Spanish city of Panama, on the Pacific coast.

The next day Governor Juan Pérez de Guzmán led his army of 1,400 troops out to do battle. Morgan's men were veteran buccaneers rather than raw militia, and completely outfought their opponents. Within an hour Guzmán's army was fleeing back to the city, leaving 500 dead or wounded behind them. Unable to stop the rout, Guzmán fled to a waiting ship, and hurriedly put to sea. The buccaneers captured a near-empty city but found little there worth plundering. It seemed Guzmán had already loaded his valuables and treasury onto his ships, which were now out of Morgan's clutches. So, Morgan and his men returned to Port Royal with little to show for their efforts.

The largest and most daring of Morgan's raids had ended in disappointment. Worse, on his return to Port Royal in March 1671, Morgan learned that everything had changed. The Peace of Madrid, signed in 1670, meant that the Spanish were no longer England's enemies. So, not only were all buccaneering licences cancelled, but that summer, when the new governor, Sir Thomas Lynch, arrived, Modyford was ordered back to London, to answer for his support of Morgan's raids. Then, Morgan too was arrested, and shipped to London to stand trial. On his arrival, Morgan was feted as a hero by the English public. The English government was well attuned to the public mood, and the charges were quietly dropped. To cap it all, Charles II then recalled Lynch from Jamaica, and replaced him with the younger and more malleable John Vaughan, Earl of Carbery.[12]

For Morgan, the real turning point was his meeting with King Charles in November 1674, who knighted the buccaneer. Two months later, Morgan and Carbery sailed for Jamaica, each with a commission in his pocket. On their arrival, Carbery would be the new governor, while Morgan, freshly dubbed Sir Henry, was now Jamaica's new deputy governor. His job was a difficult one. First, he had to guide the young and inexperienced nobleman through the pitfalls of Jamaican politics. More importantly, he had the unenviable task of dealing with a port filled with buccaneers, whose livelihood had now been taken from them. The danger, of course, was that many of Morgan's old followers would now turn to piracy.[13]

During its buccaneering heyday, Port Royal was a piratical haven, where lawlessness and debauchery were rife, but the port thrived on the fortune in Spanish gold and silver being brought home by these battle-scarred seamen. Most squandered it amid the port's delights, but a few, like Morgan himself, used their plunder more wisely and bought land, and benefited from the status that came with it. By 1675 the greatest buccaneer of them might have turned his back on the sea, but he'd also become Jamaica's deputy governor, a knight of the realm, and a man of wealth and consequence. However, the Earl of Carbery, a man a political opponent described as being 'as ugly in face as in fame', earned an unenviable reputation for debauchery and corruption, while Morgan preferred carousing with his former buccaneering officers rather than seeing to the affairs of state.[14]

Buccaneering ventures were no longer sanctioned by the Jamaican authorities. If any buccaneers attacked the Spanish again, they would become pirates, and so put themselves beyond the law. In April 1675, Carbery issued a proclamation offering an amnesty to former English buccaneers who promised to renounce their old ways. Most ignored this, while Carbery became annoyed at Morgan's reluctance to convince his old followers to accept the deal. Still, the remaining Port Royal buccaneers had two options – to meekly serve aboard Jamaican merchant ships, or to move east, where the French were more favourably disposed to buccaneers – or *flibustiers* as they now called them. Others took themselves off to South America or the Pacific Ocean in search of Spanish plunder. Jamaica, though, turned its back on the buccaneers.

By the mid-1670s the buccaneering movement had effectively moved from Port Royal to the French settlements on Tortuga and the western side of Hispaniola – soon to be the French colony of Saint-Domingue. During this period, the *flibustiers* launched several raids on the Spanish Main, something peace between the two countries did little to change. In Jamaica however, the economy was booming. Colonists were busily transforming the island's hinterland, and agriculture and sugar production soon became the mainstays of the economy, rather than Spanish plunder. This prosperity was built using slaves – many thousands of them – and Port Royal sated this growing need by reinventing itself as a slaving entrepôt. Jamaica was now firmly established as an important leg in 'The Triangular Trade' – the slaving route between Europe, West Africa and the Americas.

Morgan was finally forced to deal with the remnants of his buccaneers. The last of them who hadn't accepted Carbery's pardon or joined the French *flibustiers* had taken to raiding the Spanish colonies in South America, and some even ventured into the Pacific. A handful, though, were still operating as pirates in the Caribbean. By 1678, Carbery's open corruption had led to his replacement by Charles Howard, Earl of Carlisle. He was a very different governor, determined to bring the Jamaican General Assembly under firm control, but he seemed unconcerned about the continued existence of former buccaneers in Port Royal, and the linked increase in piratical attacks in Jamaican waters, and along the Spanish Main.[15]

These continued raids on Spanish settlements led to a string of official complaints from the Spanish ambassador at the court of King Charles II. So, the Earl of Carlisle was recalled to England to explain his tolerance of buccaneers and pirates. Carlisle also faced charges of corruption, following a long-running dispute with the colony's landowners. He escaped prosecution, but he never returned to Jamaica. It was clear the mood in London was considerably less tolerant towards the former buccaneers, who were now regarded as pirates. Sensing this, and to safeguard his own position, Morgan, the acting governor, decided to take action. He duly drafted an anti-piracy bill, 'An Act for Restraining and Punishing Privateers', which he presented to the Jamaican Assembly. What became known as 'The Jamaica Act' was passed in 1681.[16]

Like a poacher turned gamekeeper, Morgan was happy to turn on his old followers. In the past, buccaneers had served a real need, as they provided Jamaica with an effective defence force at a time when the English Crown did little to support the colony. Now buccaneers were deemed a threat to law and order and had become little more than pirates. For many, this act was all too long in coming. Jamaican merchants were developing lucrative trading links with the Spanish colonies, and these piratical attacks were a threat to this new arrangement. So, the Jamaica Act was designed to ensure that buccaneers stopped preying on the Spanish. If they did, they would be deemed pirates and would receive 'the speedy execution of justice'. Even those who supported pirates would be prosecuted – a direct move to prevent the merchants of Port Royal from trading with the pirates.

Effectively, it ended at a stroke the last of the cosy symbiotic relationship between the former buccaneers and the Jamaicans. From that point on, Port Royal would be a closed port to anyone who 'committed treason, piracies, felonies and other offences upon the sea'. This was an important step, as it was the first piece of anti-piracy legislation to be introduced in the Americas. In the British colonies in America, the Jamaica Act of 1681 would lay the groundwork for the far more draconian anti-piracy laws introduced three decades later, designed to end a much more serious pirate menace. Then, the British authorities would turn to Morgan's act, dust it off, and reword it, to counter this new threat.

Importantly, the act gave the Jamaicans the right to try their prisoners in Jamaica, in a Vice Admiralty court. The advantage was obvious. Before this, captured pirates had to be shipped to London for trial. Now, the prisoners could be tried and punished right there in Port Royal. That, Morgan hoped, would deter other former buccaneers from turning to piracy. One of the catalysts for the act was the capture of Jacob Evertsen, a former Dutch buccaneer who had been preying on Spanish shipping. In January 1680, Morgan led an armed party which boarded Evertsen's sloop off Jamaica, and the buccaneer and his crew were captured.[17]

On 14 March, Evertsen and his men were tried in Jamaica's Vice Admiralty court. The evidence was unequivocal, and a verdict of guilty was passed. Morgan balked at holding a mass hanging though. His new law had only just been drafted, and at the time it still had to be presented to the Jamaican legislature, the General Assembly. The last thing Morgan wanted was to inflame his old buccaneers and cause a major revolt. So, Morgan opted for the prudent course. He explained his reasoning: 'I thought it fit not to post them to execution, lest it should scare all others from returning to their allegiance.' So, Evertsen and his men were imprisoned, save for six Spaniards among his crew, who were shipped off to Cartagena to be handed over to the Spanish governor there.

Meanwhile, Morgan's Jamaica Act was completed, and in mid-May it was presented to the General Assembly for approval. It was duly approved, and with a stroke of his pen Morgan turned his bill into law. Morgan's act was officially ratified in Whitehall in 1683, by which time the former king of the buccaneers was a mere shell of his former self. In August 1681 the Lords of Trade in London appointed Sir Thomas Lynch as governor of Jamaica, and he arrived there to take up his post the following May. Morgan's commission as acting governor was cancelled, and soon his allies in the legislature were ousted and replaced by loyal supporters of Lynch. The two men didn't get on, and so Morgan turned his back on island politics.[18]

He also sought solace in drink. When Lynch died in 1684, Morgan didn't even try to replace him. Instead, one of Lynch's supporters, Henry Molesworth, became acting governor. By then Morgan's Jamaican Act had been effective, and Port Royal had reinvented itself as a bustling commercial harbour. In late 1687, when Christopher Monck, the Duke of Albemarle, arrived to take over his appointment as governor, he asked Morgan to serve as his adviser. By then, though, the old buccaneer had almost drunk himself to death, and with his legs swollen by dropsy he was barely able to walk, let alone play an active part in Jamaican affairs. He now preferred to spend his remaining days drinking with his former officers and reliving his glory days. By then, the buccaneering phenomenon he'd help to create was a thing of the past.

Henry Morgan, the English buccaneer who turned Port Royal, Jamaica,
into a lawless buccaneering haven.

A concerned Duke of Albemarle sent his own personal physician to examine Morgan. Doctor Sloane found his patient 'lean, sallow-coloured, his eyes a little yellowing and belly jutting out', adding that Morgan was 'much given to drinking and staying up late'. The despairing physician ordered him to avoid drinking to excess and diagnosed that his patient had severe dropsy. Morgan duly ignored the physician's advice and continued drinking himself to death. Sir Henry Morgan finally died in bed in his plantation house at Lawrencefield in late August 1688.[19]

Albemarle gave him a state funeral and even had the heart to offer an amnesty to all former buccaneers and pirates, so they could pay their respects to their old leader, as Morgan's body lay in state. He was buried in the Palisadoes Cemetery in Port Royal with great pomp and ceremony, while the English warships in the harbour thundered out a 22-gun salute. Nobody at the time could imagine that less than four years later Morgan's grave would disappear into the sea, together with most of Port Royal. It was almost as if the Caribbean was washing the place clean of its last vestiges of the buccaneering past. Morgan's death was certainly the end of an era for Port Royal, and for Jamaica too. Both the English government and the Jamaican authorities had learned their lesson. Never again would state-sponsored pirates be given such a free reign to do as they pleased.[20]

In 1685 Charles II died suddenly, after a fit of apoplexy, and his younger brother acceded to the English and Scottish thrones. So, in April, James II of England and VII of Scotland became the new monarch of the two kingdoms. He continued his brother's policy on piracy, and six months after Morgan's death, a copy of a new anti-piracy law reached Jamaica. 'A Proclamation for the More Effectual Reducing and Suppressing of Pirates and Privateers in America' had been signed by King James II in January 1688, because of complaints by English merchants of an increase in piratical attacks.[21]

Like Morgan's Jamaica Act seven years before, this gave the colonial authorities greater powers to hunt down pirates in their waters, and to administer justice through Admiralty courts sitting in the colonies. It also included a 'carrot and stick' approach. Pirates or privateers who refused to end their attacks would be hunted down without mercy. However, they had a 12-month period of clemency. If the wrongdoers surrendered to the authorities, then they would receive a pardon – if they didn't carry out any more attacks. It was an effective enough policy, as it reduced the number of pirates at large, and bought time for the Royal Navy and the colonial authorities in the Americas to concentrate their resources, ready for a major pirate-hunting offensive from the spring of 1689 on. The trouble was, King James' Act was quickly overtaken by a string of game-changing events. As a result, this pirate-hunting drive never took place.

The reason was that, once again, England was at war. In September 1688, just weeks after Morgan's funeral, a French army crossed the river Rhine, invading the territory of the Holy Roman Empire. A coalition was quickly formed to oppose the French, and this gave the conflict a name – the War of the Grand Alliance. Word of the new war reached Jamaica just before Christmas, but for the moment it seemed that King James II refused to approve the issue of privateering licences. He was no great supporter of privateering, and as he made clear in his act, in time of war it was easy enough to give someone permission to become what was effectively a licensed pirate. It was much harder to revoke this permission when the war had ended, and privateers were ordered to cease their attacks. Many, inevitably, did not.[22]

Then, in November 1688, William of Orange landed on the southern coast of England. The Dutchman intended to claim King James' throne for himself, and in the name of the Protestant religion. He brought a Dutch army with him, and as he marched on London an increasing number of James' supporters abandoned their monarch. In December, bowing to the inevitable, James went into exile in France, and William was free to claim the throne for himself. In April 1689 he was crowned King William III of England and I of Scotland. By then both the Dutch and the English were heavily involved in their war with France, and French privateers were busily preying on enemy shipping in the Caribbean. So, it was almost inevitable that the pragmatic Dutch-born monarch would reverse King James' stance and would encourage privateering.

Although privateering had been frowned upon when the war began, under King William III, from 1690 on, a growing number of privateering Letters of Marque were issued by the Admiralty in London. By the following year, the Vice Admiralty courts in the colonies were permitted to issue them too. In Jamaica, the size of privateering ventures remained small compared to the buccaneering years – little more than a dozen ships appear to have been active.

The real impetus for this was that the new Williamite governor, the Earl of Inchiquin, wanted to form a force that could protect Jamaica, at a time when the wartime Royal Navy was overstretched. He achieved this by limiting the radius of privateering operations, meaning these privateers were kept close to hand, in case they were needed.[23]

Unlike the English, the French keenly endorsed privateering, both in European waters and in the Caribbean. Spain, like the Dutch Republic, had now become an English ally, so for the French the seas were full of potential prizes. For the French, privateering – *guerre de course* – became a lucrative venture. In all, by war's end, around 4,000 English merchant ships had been captured. Inevitably, the shipowners and landowners of Jamaica suffered, and they sought retribution by fitting out their own privateers. This process was heavily controlled by the Jamaican legislature, and both backers and privateering captains had to lay down surety that they would follow the rules. The growth was slow, and investment was hindered by a crippling increase in taxation, to pay for the war. Then, in June 1692, came the earthquake that destroyed Port Royal.[24]

The disaster effectively brought an end to privateering in Jamaica – at least for a while. Even the French privateering efforts abated, largely because by then the Royal Navy was able to spare ships to protect maritime trade in Jamaica and the West Indies. Another factor was the intervention of the French Crown itself. In 1696 a large-scale French expedition was planned against Spain's overseas empire.

This enterprise would involve an unusual mixture of regular warships and troops and the *flibustiers* of Saint-Domingue. In early 1697 this expedition landed at Cartagena on the Spanish Main and laid siege to the great port. When it fell, the *flibustiers* were deprived of the chance to plunder the city. Instead, they were short-changed by the expedition leader, the Baron de Pointis, who sailed away with the loot. Cheated of their reward, the *flibustiers* returned to the now defenceless city and stripped it bare. The war ended shortly after, and for a few brief years, peace returned to the Caribbean.[25]

It could be argued that the man who did most to encourage the pirate menace of the early 18th century was King Louis XIV of France. It was his enthusiasm for dynastic expansion that set everything in motion. This in turn created the perfect catalyst for a generation of pirates to spring up, as if from nowhere. In fact, the first of them came from Port Royal, where for the best part of a decade, the port was a privateering haven – a true throwback to its roistering buccaneering past. It all began in November 1700, when the sickly, disabled and strikingly unattractive 38-year-old King Charles II of Spain died, without leaving an heir. Ever the opportunist, Louis XIV proposed he should be succeeded by his grandson, Philip of Anjou, due to Bourbon family ties to the Spanish royal line. The dying King Charles agreed and named Philip as his successor.

This didn't go down well with Leopold I, the Holy Roman Emperor. He felt his son the Archduke Charles had a stronger claim. So, when Charles II died in Madrid's Royal Alcazar Palace, and the teenage Philip was proclaimed King Philip V of Spain, Leopold was apoplectic. He responded by stoking resentment to the Bourbon *fait accompli* among the European powers. In September 1701, amid growing tension along France's northern border, the old Grand Alliance was re-formed, and war between its signatories and both France and Spain became inevitable. In the end, it was mid-May 1702 before England and France actually declared the start of hostilities. By then, William III had died, and his daughter Queen Anne was the ruler of England and Scotland.

News of this new war reached Jamaica in late July. From that point on, almost ten years after the earthquake, Port Royal became a major privateering base once again. It would remain in business for a little over a decade. This conflict, known as the War of the Spanish Succession, or Queen Anne's War, was a real boon to Jamaica. By lucky coincidence England was at war with Spain as well as France, which meant pickings were plentiful. In 1712 the owner of a small fleet of privateers described the Spanish shipping routes off the Spanish Main as 'the happy region, where gold and silver most abound'. This time, after the experience of the buccaneers, in which the Jamaican authorities were unable to control their own creation, the Port Royal privateers would be closely supervised and their activities heavily regulated.[26]

The whole system was administered by the High Court of Admiralty, based in London. It controlled the number of licensed privateers, and their behaviour, and when an enemy vessel was taken they were able to 'condemn' her – in other words, confirm whether she was a legitimate prize. In return, the court would levy a fee on behalf of the Crown – a percentage of the profits from the prize and her cargo. By the mid-17th century, a series of Vice Admiralty courts had been established in

English colonies in the Americas, including one in Jamaica. The first prize trial there was held in 1660, but it was King William's War before these colonial courts were temporarily given the authority to condemn prizes for themselves. In 1702 this system was made permanent, while colonial Vice Admiralty courts also now officially had the authority to issue Letters of Marque. While these had been issued in Jamaica for decades, this made the whole arrangement unequivocally official in the eyes of Europe's maritime powers.

Jamaica was fortunate, as having a Vice Admiralty court gave the island a real advantage as a privateering base. This meant that any delay or inconvenience in processing prizes could be avoided. There were ten of them in British Colonial America – six in American ports from New York down to Charles Town in South Carolina, two in the West Indies, one in Bermuda, and finally one in Jamaica. Any privateer captain cruising in American waters who held a British Letter of Marque would have to take his prize into one of these ten ports. Given its location, within easy reach of both French and Spanish colonies, Jamaica was the perfect spot for a privateer.[27]

For that privateer, the key to legitimacy was his Letter of Marque. In Jamaica, this could be obtained only from the Vice Admiralty court, although a bribe to the governor or court usually sweetened the process. The applicant had to give full details of his vessel, crew and armament, and post a sizeable sum as surety for his abiding by the rules of privateering good practice, as laid down by the court. These guidelines also covered the details of capturing prizes, and the process of condemning them. Once all this was done, the Letter of Marque could be issued, and the privateer could begin his cruise.

The court could easily deny licences to captains they didn't approve of, limit the duration of the licence, or even revoke it, if the privateer didn't abide by the rules. For the most part, though, the Jamaican Vice Admiralty court tended to encourage privateering, especially if it benefited the island economy and the financial backers of the privateering venture were well known to them. It was a cosy arrangement, and it helped make Jamaica very rich indeed. So, when news of the war reached Jamaica in the summer of 1702, the system to support privateering was already in place. Acting Governor Peter Beckford was happy to encourage privateering, and as an army officer his replacement, Governor Thomas Handasyd, was equally happy to leave Beckford to continue to deal with the colony's maritime affairs. All he had to do was to sign the paperwork.[28]

This was obviously an expensive business, but in Jamaica there seemed a few moneyed landowners and merchants who were willing to buy into a privateering venture. The opportunity of windfall profits ensured that not only were financial backers available, but seamen were too. During the War of the Spanish Succession, the Royal Navy found men were deserting purely to sign on as privateers. Merchant captains also had problems raising a crew, as so many seamen had opted to serve aboard privateers instead. These ventures involved a lot of overheads. First a vessel had to be found – usually a converted merchant one – and a suitably experienced captain and crew secured. The ship then had to be armed and provisioned before it could set off on its cruise. The voyage itself could be long and costly and might incur further expenses for repairs. The profits, however, made it well worth the effort.

When a captured ship was brought into Port Royal it would be quickly processed by the Vice Admiralty court. If deemed a legitimate prize, she would then be condemned, which in turn let her be sold, along with her cargo. The bulk of the profit would then be divided among the privateering captain and crew, and the investors. The government, on behalf of the King, would also get its cut. The crew would spend their money in Port Royal, the chandlers and merchants would benefit from the business of provisioning the vessel, and then the whole lucrative business would start all over again. In other words, in time of war, in a place like Jamaica the opportunities were immense – virtually there for the taking – and there would be enough money coming in to keep everyone happy, from the governor to the meanest tapster or most jaded harlot. Everyone benefited – apart from the French and the Spanish of course.

Essentially, for the Crown this was a cut-price way of harassing the enemy, by disrupting his trade. Some of the largest French or Spanish ships carried a fortune in their holds – a rich haul of cargo such as sugar cane, logwood dye or coffee beans – which would make the Jamaican privateers and their investors rich men. Of course, privateering was a double-edged sword, and enemy privateers were also at sea, preying on merchant ships sailing from Jamaica or England's colonies in North America. As a result, as the war progressed it became increasingly dangerous to transport merchant cargoes, unless the ship formed part of a protected convoy. So, an increasing number of merchants cut back on their operations and diversified into privateering instead. It was, put simply, too good an opportunity to miss.

Fortunately, we know a little about how successful these Jamaican privateers were. A total of 125 prizes were condemned in Jamaica's Vice Admiralty court during the war, making it by far the busiest of all the courts in the Americas. This represented almost a third of all the privateering prizes captured in American waters between 1702 and 1713. Of these, the majority were French prizes, although Spanish ones were captured in large numbers too. Privateers in Jamaica were perfectly placed to cruise the waters of Cuba, Santo Domingo or the Spanish Main. The English also benefited from an illicit trade with the Spanish colonies, and so, by 1707, Spanish ships were issued special passes, allowing unmolested trade between the Spanish Main and Jamaica, and the Spanish Main was deemed off limits to British privateers. The French, though, were considered fair game.[29]

The court records reveal just how busy Jamaican privateers were. The first entry was in October 1702, when the French privateer *St Denis* was captured, together with the French merchant ship *St Jean*, outbound from Nantes – most likely a slaver bound for Saint-Domingue. Danish ships were legitimate prizes too, if they were engaged in trade with the French; so, in 1703 the court condemned several small Danish vessels, which had tried to smuggle goods into Saint-Domingue. The list of prizes was extensive: a French merchantman of 300 tons laden with brandy and wine, a Spanish sloop carrying dry goods, a French vessel with indigo in her hold, and another Spanish sloop bearing cargo of iron, steel and snuff. A few French privateers were also captured. Taken together, it was a significant portion of enemy shipping in the region.

The records also tell us something about the privateer captains and their ships. Typically, these vessels were small – usually sloops or brigs of around 100 tons, and crewed by 100 men, but armed with 12 to 18 guns. A good privateering vessel was fast and nimble, but as cruises were relatively short, they didn't really have to be commodious. Some were smaller, like Captain Charles Gandy's sloop in 1704, carrying a crew of 60 men but armed with just four guns. Some of these captains and ships are mentioned repeatedly in the records, which meant they were particularly successful. One of the most prominent of these was the Jamaican privateer *Charles*, of 18 guns, commanded by Captain

William Tempest. After a decade of this, these ships and their crews had evolved into near-perfect hunting machines – specialists in the trade of legitimized piracy.[30]

Then, suddenly, it all came to an end. In April 1713 a peace treaty was signed in the Dutch city of Utrecht, between representatives of the British and French Crowns. Intermittent peace negotiations had begun three years earlier, on the initiative of Louis XIV. By then, actually from 1707, Queen Anne was the sovereign of a newly formed united kingdom – Great Britain. Her government agreed to these talks, and by October 1711 a preliminary peace deal had been negotiated. The war continued, though, and in January 1712 formal discussions began in Utrecht. That October the discussion had developed far enough for a temporary armistice to be declared. It seems, though, that this had no effect on privateering in American waters – only military campaiging in Europe. Finally, on 11 April 1713, Britain and France signed the document that brought the war to a close. While it would take longer for the Holy Roman Empire to agree to a peace, these pen strokes in Utrecht effectively brought an end to the business of privateering.

When copies of the treaty reached Jamaica in mid-July, the Vice Admiralty court there immediately suspended all privateering Letters of Marque. Jamaica's governor, Lord Archibald Hamilton, then formally announced the end of hostilities. At that instant, the lucrative business of privateering came to an end. For more than a decade, British seamen had signed up as crew for privateers, and many had grown prosperous, if they hadn't squandered their prize money. Most, though, had imitated the buccaneers of old in letting their share slip through their fingers in the fleshpots of Port Royal. Now, at a stroke, they were out of a job. Hamilton announced that a handful of privateers and their crews would be retained for use by the Jamaican authorities, but for the rest they had nothing to look forward to, apart from the poor pay and hard labour of a hand aboard a merchant ship.

For the merchants and investors who had backed privateering ventures, they had for the most part all made a fortune in the business. With the coming of peace, trade could be expected to expand dramatically, and so profits were to be had there; they would not be out of pocket. This, too, provided some consolation to the ship chandlers, riggers, shipwrights, blacksmiths, armourers, coopers and carpenters of Jamaica, who could all expect work to continue, now that peace had come. Even the tavern owners, pickpockets and harlots of Port Royal could still expect to make a living, even though the days of roistering privateersmen with coins in their pocket were over. It was only the seamen themselves who would really suffer.

Inevitably, many of these former privateersmen were reluctant to give up their old ways. Privateering had essentially been a form of licensed piracy. To many, the difference was just a legal distinction. So, while most of these former privateersmen meekly signed on to merchantmen, others found it harder to abandon their warlike trade. As 1713 drew to a close, it became clear that this represented a fairly serious problem to the Jamaican authorities. Already, there were reports of small-scale piratical attacks taking place in Jamaican waters and elsewhere in the Caribbean. It would take time for the merchant trade to expand now that peace had come. In the meantime, there was a growing number of disaffected, hard-bitten privateersmen, who felt they had little to lose by stepping outside the law.

What prevented many of them from taking the step was the threat of retribution from the authorities. Essentially this meant capture, trial in an Admiralty court, and almost certainly execution. Others would have been put off by the realization that once they had crossed that line, legitimate ports like Port Royal would be closed to them. They would have to turn their back on friends, family and home, and live out what remained of their lives on the run. A few of the more intuitive privateersmen might even have taken this a step further. Without a friendly port, they wouldn't be able to sell any of the cargoes they plundered.

What the British government could have done was to come up with a scheme that would offer these men hope, or at least a gentle easing back into the world of the normal mariner. But that didn't happen. Instead, many hundreds of former privateersmen in Port Royal found themselves facing a grim future, and a big decision. The potential for a real disaster for the authorities loomed – one that few fully appreciated. The danger stretched beyond Jamaica, from the ports of New York down to Barbados, where others faced the same future. All it would take was a spark – and that spark was already glowing.

TWO

Henry Jennings

G ENERAL JUAN ESTEBAN DE Ubilla watched the Morro Castle
slip by to starboard as his flagship, or *capitana*, glided out of
Havana harbour towards the open sea. The morning of Wednesday
24 July 1715 was proving to be a fine one, with a fresh southerly breeze
and a clear sky. The Sailing Master Don Antonio Porflits was a skilled
mariner and had everything under control. Capitan Don Luis de
Villalobos was standing on the high poop deck, keeping watch. So, the
Nuestra Señora del la Regla was in safe hands. From the city's waterfront
abeam of them to port, faint cheers could be heard, and figures could
be seen waving as the *capitana* glided past. Drums sounded from the
ramparts of the Morro, where Havana's archbishop stood, in his black
robes, blessing their voyage.[1]

The fort's guns roared out – a 12-gun salute, which on the general's
nod was answered by *la Regla*'s gunners. It was all a highly satisfying
spectacle. Ahead, waiting for them outside the harbour, was the Tierra
Firme fleet, a mixed bag of six ships, commanded by General Don

Antonio de Echeverz y Zubiza. This fleet ranged in size from the mighty *capitana*, the *Nuestra Señora del Carmen*, of over 700 tons, to a patache, a small two-masted tender to the flagship. *La Regla* was leading the New Spain fleet, made up of the *almirante* (the second-in-command's ship) the *Santo Cristo de San Román y Nuestra Señora del Rosario*; a large store ship called the *Santissima Trinidad*; the small frigate *La Francesa*; the smaller sloop *Galera*; three pataches; and a small French warship named the *Grifón*. As they joined the Tierra Firme fleet the combined armada headed north, out into the Estrecho de Florida (Florida Straits), a majestic assemblage of Spanish maritime power.[2]

Almost every year, from the late 16th century to the mid-18th century, the Spanish sent two treasure fleets or *flotas* from Spain to the New World. The Tierra Firme *flota* (known as the Galeones *flota*) collected gold, silver, emeralds and an assortment of trade goods from the Spanish Main. The second fleet, the Nueva España *flota*, did the same from Mexico. Each of the fleets was centred around a pair of well-armed warships, the *capitana* and the *almirante*, as well as a cluster of little pataches that could act as scouts, and usually a cluster of merchant ships, sailing in convoy with the treasure ships. In time of war the escort was strengthened, and the combined fleets were often accompanied by a convoy of merchantmen, grateful for the protection of the powerful warships. The two fleets would then rendezvous in Havana, before sailing home to Spain together.[3]

Usually, the New Spain fleet left Seville in March, while the Tierra Firme fleet followed it two months later. The fleets headed down to the Canary Islands, usually with an escort, which then parted company as the fleet sailed west across the Atlantic. Roughly two months later they would make landfall in the West Indies and would pass into the Caribbean. Once there the fleets headed in different directions. The New Spain fleet would put into Vera Cruz in modern-day Mexico, where it picked up cargo from Central America, as well as goods shipped across the Pacific in the treasure galleons from Manila, then transported overland from Acapulco. The following spring the fleet would set sail for Havana in Cuba, where it would wait for the Tierra Firme fleet to join it.

The Tierra Firme fleet would head to Cartagena in modern-day Colombia, before making a side trip to Porto Bello, on the isthmus of Panama. The ships would winter in Cartagena before heading off to Havana in the spring. Then, after both ships were re-provisioned, they would set out together on their return voyage to Spain. Their route would usually take them out into the Florida Straits, where they would pick up the Gulf Stream. This would carry them north through the *Canal Nuevo de Bahama* (New Bahama Channel between Florida and the Bahamas archipelago). Then, once they were clear of it, they would follow the Gulf Stream east into the Atlantic, picking up the winds which would carry them on to Seville. In Spain the arrival of the combined *flotas* was always a matter for rejoicing. Spain was almost wholly dependent on the gold and silver shipped to it on the treasure fleets. If the fleets didn't arrive, it would be a monumental disaster.

The combined treasure fleet made good time. Their course took them east along the Cuban coast, making around six knots. Then, near the entrance to Cadenas Bay they would turn north-east and aim for the Cayo Sal, a tiny speck 25 miles off the Cuban coast where salt was produced. This was the first of a series of waypoints, usually small islands or rock formations that would guide them safely into the New Bahama Channel. Waypoints made navigation easier, especially in poor weather. When darkness fell, the ships would shorten sail and ride out the dark until morning. Everything went well, and by 3pm on Thursday 25 July 1715 they sighted their last waypoint, Cayo Tabono (Tavernier Key), in the upper Florida Keys, near modern-day Key Largo. That was where they picked up the Gulf Stream, which took them north up the Florida coast and into the channel. So far everything had gone well.[4]

However, that evening the winds became erratic, changing direction and strength without warning. It made safe sailing impossible, so General Ubilla ordered the armada to head farther east, to give the ships more sea room. There they would wait until wind conditions improved. The freakish winds lasted until 2pm on Friday, until a steadier north-easterly arrived. Ubilla ordered the armada to press on, tacking into the wind every three hours, making a series of sweeps from one side to the other as they sailed northwards. It was slow work, and by Sunday afternoon, 28 July, they began to detect ominous signs of a change in the weather. To the south-east the clear sky grew cloudy. The next morning things became steadily worse. The sea developed a rolling swell, and by evening the wind slackened. It was clear that a storm was coming.

That night, rather than reducing sail, General Ubilla ordered the armada to press on. After consulting with his captain and sailing master, he felt the best plan was to try to outrun whatever was heading towards them. With the Florida coast to leeward, they were in a dangerous position if a storm hit. Out in the Atlantic they would be much safer. When dawn came, on Tuesday 30 July, the winds had become erratic again, and the ominous swell had increased. Then, as the morning wore on, the changeable winds were replaced by a steady one, blowing from the north-east. It became increasingly strong, bringing racing black-grey clouds with it. By early afternoon the wind was approaching gale force. On board all the ships, with Ubilla's permission, sails were brought in, hatches were battened down, and safety ropes were rigged across the pitching decks.

By mid-afternoon they were hit by rain squalls, and the waves grew into large, foam-topped peaks. In each vessel the helmsmen struggled to hold their northerly course, fighting to keep as far from the Florida coast as they could. Then the wind increased to storm force. By midnight they were being pounded badly, and the ships struggled to keep from broaching – turning broadside on to the pounding seas. The *capitana* of the New Spain fleet, the *Nuestra Señora del Carmen*, almost did when her sails were ripped out, but she survived for the moment, despite tons of water pouring into her. All the time the rain lashed down without mercy. Sails were reduced to a minimum, and the ships were gradually driven westwards, towards the dreaded lee shore.

Just when the seamen thought things couldn't get worse, the howling wind rose several octaves until it became a constant shrieking roar. By 2am on Wednesday 31 July the ships found themselves in a full-strength hurricane. All notion of operating as a fleet was abandoned. It was now every ship for herself. Many of the ships were soon dismasted and found themselves driven towards the Florida coast. When their masts went, some of the ships broached and were rolled over on their beam ends, people and livestock being thrown across the rapidly flooding decks. Others tried to jettison whatever they could – guns, anchors and stores – in a bid to save themselves. It was no use. One by one the Spanish ships foundered or were cast ashore and torn apart.[5]

The crew of *la Regla* tried to lighten ship, but it was too late. The *capitana* struck the seabed and was ripped in two, throwing everyone on board into the sea. General Ubilla and virtually all of her crew were drowned in the raging surf. The same happened to the rest of the New Spain and Tierra Firme *flotas*. The only relatively lucky ones were the crew of the *Nuestra Señora de la Nieves*, which was torn apart in the surf, but the upper hull held together long enough to carry a hundred crew onto the beach and safety. Ubilla's *almirante*, the *Santo Cristo de San Román*, broke into pieces against the shore, and almost all of her 120 crew were drowned.

Some ships fared better than others. The crew of the *Santissima Trinidad*, also known as the *Urca de Lima*, managed to anchor off a river mouth for a while before the anchor snapped, and she too was lifted by the surf and thrown onto the rocks. The *del Carmen*, flagship of the Tierra Firme *flota*, sank in the shallows but remained intact, allowing General Echeverz and many of his crew to ride out the hurricane and then make it to shore once the winds eased. *Del Rosario*, the *almirante* commanded by his son, was torn apart in the waves a few miles to the south, and all her crew perished. It took eight hours before the hurricane passed, leaving miles of beach littered with wreckage, bodies and cargo. In all, 11 Spanish ships were wrecked, and 700 of their crew lost. Only one ship survived to tell the tale – the fast-sailing French frigate *Grifón*, which had parted company with the armada a few days before the disaster and was safely out of reach when the storm hit.[6]

Afterwards, a survivor, Father Francisco de León – the priest in *la Regla* – told the authorities in Havana, 'The hurricane was so severe and violent that, according to what we heard from old mariners, they had never seen one like it. Such was the violence of the waves that they seemed like arrows.' He added, 'After some of the ships had been cast ashore, the furious rolling back and forth of the waves would drag everything back into the sea, where it disappeared, so that the coast was bare again.' When the storm abated, the dazed survivors, many of them wounded, tried to make sense of the disaster that had befallen them. For Spain, though, the loss of the ships and men wasn't even the worst of it. The combined *flotas* had been carrying the equivalent of 14 million pesos in their holds – the entire year's income from Spain's overseas colonies. The peso was a silver eight-reale coin, which the English called a 'piece-of-eight'.[7]

The place where the disaster happened was a long strip of sandy barrier islands a couple of miles to the west of mainland Florida. This barrier ran south from Cabo Cañaveral (now Cape Canaveral) for just over a hundred miles. The Spanish called this area 'Palmar de Ays', the palm trees of the Ays, a local Native American tribe whom the Spaniards knew very little about. So, the survivors continued to huddle on the barrier islands, scattered along a ten-mile stretch, opposite the modern towns of San Sebastian in the north to Vero Beach in the south. Today this stretch is known as the Treasure Coast. In the summer of 1715, though, it was just a barren wilderness. The survivors salvaged what they could from the wreckage, as the castaways waited for rescue.

With General Ubilla dead, his deputy Admiral Francisco Salmón took command of the men. By early August his scouting parties had met up with the small groups of survivors, and these began coming together into a string of encampments, built from canvas and spars. Foraging parties went out looking for water or shellfish, while hunters combed the islands for game. Salmón knew that the nearest Spanish settlement, St Augustine, was 130 sea miles away to the north. So, a ship's boat was patched up and sent north, carrying a letter from the admiral to Governor Francisco de Córcoles y Martínez. A second boat was sent off to Havana, 360 miles away. The first arrived in St Augustine on 7 August, and de Córcoles immediately sent a relief column. This undoubtedly saved the lives of the castaways.

It was mid-August when word of the disaster reached Havana. The governor of Cuba, Laureano de Torres y Ayala, Marquis de Casa Torres, was quick to respond, and ordered a rescue expedition to be sent out immediately. Accompanying it would be a large body of salvors, armed troops and native divers. The business of rescuing the survivors was now under way. The next priority was to recover whatever remained of the treasure. On 10 September the rescue ships reached the survivors. After unloading the food, water and clothes, they took the survivors out to the ships. That done, the man in charge of the rescue squadron, Don Juan de Hoyo Solórzano, began unloading his hastily assembled cargo – everything from diving bells, grappling hooks, extra-long rakes and chains to many empty chests, ready to fill with whatever specie could be salvaged. So, as the survivors left for Havana, the salvage operation swung into action.[8]

A salvage camp was quickly established for the salvors. Solórzano then ordered the foreman of his divers to start work. Juan Clemente, from the Isla de Margarita off the Spanish Main, was a veteran salvor who'd spent years supervising work on the island's pearl beds. His 30-strong team of native divers had also learned their trade there. Now, though, they would be working in water churned up by the surf, on an exposed coast. Solórzano was disappointed his diving bells couldn't be used, at least at this stage, as the salvage boats carrying them were too large to operate close inshore. Still, after a week of diving, Clemente had a good idea what they faced. Some coin chests were still intact, but others had broken open, and their contents were scattered over the seabed. Given the poor visibility – little more than a few feet – the salvage of the treasure would be a long, hard and laborious business.

They worked on throughout the autumn, and slowly the pile of recovered treasure grew. A storehouse was built, where the coins and specie could be kept securely and guarded. What worried Solórzano was that three months had passed since word of the disaster first reached Havana. By now the bad tidings would have reached Spain. There would be pressure to mitigate the loss by recovering as much specie as possible. Solórzano returned to Havana, to brief the Marquis on progress. He understood there was another factor to consider – one that didn't involve the Spanish at all.

Inevitably, news the fleet had been shipwrecked would have spread through the rest of the Americas. Solórzano and his deputy Juan Clemente knew that meant trouble. With such an incredibly valuable prize lying there virtually unprotected, it was inevitable that 'interlopers' would try to steal some of it. So, Clemente wrote to the Marquis de Casa Torres, asking that the accumulated treasure be removed as quickly as possible, and that more soldiers be sent out to protect the salvage camp. The problem was, by then it was already too late. Not only had word of the treasure fleet disaster reached Jamaica, but an expedition was already being formed there, to set sail for the Palmar de Ays. They intended to steal the treasure for themselves.

Juan Clemente was quite right. News of the 1715 treasure fleet's loss had quickly radiated out from St Augustine and Havana, as trading ships brought word of it to other parts of the Caribbean, and the English and French colonies in North America. When the one vessel that survived the hurricane, the French frigate *Grifón*, finally reached Brest, the news spread quickly across Europe. After all, if this happened today it would be global news. By late August it even reached the ear of the British government, and the court of the country's new German-born monarch, King George I. So, by the time the rescue expedition from Havana reached the Palmar de Ays, word of the disaster had spread across the Atlantic.

The British government was also kept apprised of the progress of the salvage mission. In late September, Governor Alexander Spotswood of the Virginia colony wrote to his superiors in London, adding another juicy morsel of information:

> There is advice of considerable events in these parts, that the Spanish Plate Fleet, richly laden, consisting of eleven sail, are, except one, lately cast away in the Gulf of Florida to the southward of St. Augustine. And, that the *barca* sent from the Havana to fetch off from the continent some passengers of distinction who were in that fleet, having recovered from the wrecks a considerable quantity of plate, is likewise cast away about forty miles to the northward of St. Augustine.[9]

Spotswood added, 'I think it is my duty to inform his Majesty of this accident, which may be improved to the advantage of his Majesty's subjects, by encouraging them to attempt the recovery of some of that immense wealth.' The snippet of information about the *barca longa* – a small single-masted boat used a lot by the Spanish – was nothing more than a rumour, although Governor de Córcoles had offered a flotilla of small boats to move valuable cargo, survivors and their belongings northwards between the barrier islands and the Florida mainland, bringing it in stages to St Augustine. What is more significant here is the rapacious attitude of the governor. It was almost as if he were encouraging British adventurers to go and grab a share of the treasure. There were certainly many who were more than willing to do just that. Gold fever was about to sweep the Americas.

In Jamaica, word of the 1715 treasure fleet disaster sparked intense excitement. First, it was a crushing blow for the Spanish, and no peace treaty could stop a general feeling of animosity for the old rival among the British in Jamaica. In Spanish Town, the island's seat of government, the Jamaican governor Lord Archibald Hamilton was spurred on by the missive from his Virginian counterpart. After consulting with the Jamaican Assembly, he decided to send a couple of hired Jamaican sloops to investigate the wreck site, and see if there was any salvage that could be claimed for the colony. In other words, he wanted to plunder whatever the Spanish salvors hadn't already taken.[10]

Lord Hamilton was an interesting character. The 42-year-old nobleman was the youngest son of the late William, Duke of Hamilton, whose seat was near Motherwell in Lanarkshire. Archibald Hamilton's eldest brother James succeeded his father to the family title, and when he died in 1712 it passed to James' son. For his part the young noble studied mathematics at Glasgow University, and after graduating he attended the Royal Observatory in Greenwich, to study under the Astronomer Royal, John Flamsteed. In 1687, at the age of 14, he went to sea, becoming a midshipman aboard the 70-gun ship-of-the-line HMS *Resolution*. Three years later, the teenager was in the West Indies, attached to the staff of the governor of Barbados. He passed his lieutenant's examination in 1690, and the following year Hamilton distinguished himself in the assault on Guadeloupe. In that campaign the youngster commanded an *ad hoc* battalion of marines, holding a temporary rank as a lieutenant colonel. His superiors noted his 'zeal and honour'.

He seemed to be a young man who was going places. Sure enough, within two years he had his own command, the frigate *Sheerness*, but despite some success he ended King William's War without earning further distinction. When the new war began he experienced further setbacks, but in March 1703 he was given a fresh command, the ship-of-the-line *Eagle*. After the Battle of Malaga the following August he was court-martialled for allowing his ship to run out of ammunition in the middle of the fight. He was exonerated, though – much of it had been expended on the fleet commander's orders, bombarding Gibraltar. Although he remained on the Navy list afterwards, he took a break from sea service, and in 1708 he became a Member of Parliament for Lanarkshire, representing the Whig party, which formed the new government.[11]

He opposed the government over the controversial Treason Act, which rode roughshod over Scottish law – supposedly protected in the Act of Union signed two years before. This split with the Whig establishment may have played a part in his quitting the House, to take up the post of governor of Jamaica in May 1710. It also was in part a desire for a fresh start, after the death of his wife Anne the previous year. Lord Hamilton's selection as governor was supported by none other than John Churchill, Duke of Marlborough, the victor of the battles of Blenheim, Ramillies, Oudenaarde and Malplaquet. Clearly, Lord Hamilton had friends in high places and was viewed with favour by Queen Anne.

At that time the governorship of Jamaica was viewed as a lucrative appointment – one where the holder could earn a small fortune if his scruples weren't too high. Although Hamilton was a religious man – a staunch Presbyterian – it seems he wasn't averse to using his position to his own advantage and to turn a profit. His predecessor, Governor Thomas Handasyd, had endured a turbulent relationship with the Jamaican Assembly, and its President Peter Beckford had fallen downstairs in unexplained circumstances, on the day Handasyd had tried to dissolve the island's governing body. After that Handasyd begged the government to let him resign his post. So, the arrival of a new governor to replace the confrontational Handasyd was viewed with both hope and some degree of apprehension.[12]

When Lord Hamilton arrived in Jamaica in July 1711, he discovered the island's coffers were almost empty. In fact, he even held back payment of his predecessor's unpaid salary, to make sure there was enough to finance his own £2,500-a-year post. His relationship with the Jamaican Assembly was guarded – unsurprising given the situation. Its first clash with Hamilton came over the payment of the island's garrison – the governor wanting the Jamaicans to pay a larger share towards its upkeep. He was given the money, but it came at a cost, souring the relations between the new, inexperienced governor and his Jamaican legislature. Hamilton's solution was to align himself with a group of plantation owners, whose support helped him limit his conflict with the Assembly. It was clear, however, that both the governor and the Assembly needed more money.[13]

So, when a copy of the Virginia governor's letter crossed his desk, Lord Hamilton felt he might have a solution. Still, he only represented the Crown in Jamaica; to do anything, he needed the support of the Assembly. Fortunately, one of his inner circle was Francis Rose, the Assembly's president. He convinced fellow landowner Jolm Blair, the current speaker of the Assembly, to lobby members. As a result, Lord Hamilton had the official support he needed for what was at best a speculative and semi-legal salvage operation. In some eyes, any attempt to loot plunder from the Spanish shipwrecks was tantamount to a diplomatic outrage – or worse, an act of piracy. However, armed with the sanction of the Jamaican Assembly, Governor Lord Hamilton was free to press ahead with his scheme. The Jamaicans were about to go into the salvage business.[14]

The man Lord Archibald Hamilton chose to carry out his bidding was Henry Jennings. In late 1715, when Governor Spotswood's letter arrived, Jennings was the commander of the sloop *Barsheba* of eight guns, which was based at Bluefields, a settlement on the south coast of Jamaica, some 75 miles west of Port Royal. She was probably just a local trading vessel, although it has been suggested she had previously been used as a privateer. A second sloop, the slightly larger *Eagle* of 12 guns, was available to Hamilton. She was commanded by Captain John Wills. Both Jennings and Wills were experienced Jamaica-based captains, and although their sloops might not have been privateering vessels, they had links with the Jamaican landowners and merchants who had bankrolled privateering ventures in the last war. Many of their crew, too, were almost certainly former privateersmen, who could be trusted in a fight. Now they would be serving the governor.

Henry Jennings was born in Bermuda around 1680, in Smith's Parish, halfway along the island, where his family had owned land since the early part of the century. That placed them among Bermuda's earliest settlers. Nearby was the small settlement of Flatts Village. Flatts Inlet, where the island's aquarium now stands, had a reputation as a smuggler's haven, where cargo could be landed discreetly, several miles from St George's, the island's seat of government. Bermuda was also a centre for shipbuilding, particularly small, fast, single-masted sloops like the *Barsheba* and the *Eagle*. Their sleek lines made them popular as both fast trading vessels and privateers. It was probably a Bermudian sloop that first brought Jennings to Jamaica, at some point during the closing years of King William's War.[15]

Interestingly, Jennings' family already had an association with Spanish shipwrecks, as Richard Jennings of Bermuda had been linked with the salvage of a Spanish wreck as far back as the mid-17th century. By the 1660s, the family owned around 250 acres of land, centred around a plantation house at Smith's Tribe, to the south of Flatts Village. He may have had a hand in the smuggling business, as one chronicler wrote, 'At the Flatts, and in other secluded inlets, a considerable and largely undocumented amount of illegal trade took place.' So, even before he reached Jamaica, Henry Jennings had family links to both salvage and smuggling.

Little is known about Jennings until 1710 – five years before the treasure fleet's wrecking. He is almost certainly the Henry Jennings linked to the sloop *Seaflower*, which was engaged in the logwood trade – harvesting the wood around the Gulf of Campeche in New Spain (now Mexico), which was then used as a fabric dye. It appears that Jennings used his earnings wisely, buying land on the island. So, by the closing years of the war he was recorded as owning plots around Kingston on the western side of Jamaica. He has also been linked to slave trading and the shipping of sugar. What he hasn't been linked to directly is privateering, as has been claimed by Captain Charles Johnson, the *nom de plume* of the author who wrote the first pirate best-seller, *A General History of the Robberies & Murders of the Most Notorious Pyrates* (also known simply as *A General History of the Pyrates*), published in 1724.[16]

However, both Henry Jennings and his sloop *Barsheba* appear in custom records for Boston, in early July 1715 – just four months before his commission from Lord Hamilton. So, he might not have been a privateer at all, although many of his crew probably had. Instead, it was Jennings and Wills' arrangement with the governor that gave them the honorary status of privateering captains. It was likely Lord Hamilton had been unofficially issuing Letters of Marque to would-be captains during his previous four years in office. As Britain was at peace, these had no legal justification. He was probably paid well for the service and may even have garnered a cut of any profit. Given his connections with the Jamaican Assembly, it is likely this was done with their passive connivance, if not their active support. It also meant that these 'privateers' could still use Port Royal as a base.

In a way this was all understandable. There was no love lost between the Jamaicans and the Spanish, and in earlier decades Letters of Marque had been issued in times of peace. When he was later challenged on this point by the Admiralty, Lord Hamilton explained his policy. It was, he argued, exclusively 'for the purpose of defending the island's shipping against Spanish privateers'. He argued that when the war ended the Royal Navy had quit the Jamaica station, and so this was a legitimate means of protecting the colony from attack. It has been claimed that he also hired ten former privateering vessels to form a squadron which could properly defend the islands. This has yet to be proved. However, his hiring of *Barsheba* and *Eagle* in November 1715 has been documented, as has his issuing of privateering licences to their captains.[17]

That winter, there were at least two warships in Jamaican waters. The 50-gun frigate HMS *Diamond* was based at Port Royal, under the command of Captain John Balchen. A distinguished naval officer, Balchen was stationed in the Caribbean to suppress piracy. So, he took a professional interest in the dispatch of Jennings' two-ship expedition. Accompanying the frigate was the newly built sloop HMS *Jamaica*, whose commander had recently been approached by Lord Hamilton, sounding out whether he would be willing to become involved in the salvage of Spanish treasure. Naturally the governor's plea was firmly rejected, a stance seconded by Balchen, who was acting commodore of the anti-piracy squadron. The Royal Navy would not become involved in such questionable activities. This, presumably, was when Hamilton cast around for other, more willing captains, and subsequently approached Jennings and Wills.

In May the following year Balchen mentioned Jennings in a report to the Admiralty, stating that Hamilton had officially hired Jennings 'for suppression of piracys'. It was a strange claim, given that Hamilton already had a powerful anti-piracy squadron at his disposal. What didn't sit well with this story was the added note by Balchen that Jennings 'signed on fourteen skilled divers'. He added that both *Barsheba* and the larger *Eagle* were both unusually well-armed. Balchen was no fool. He'd heard of the treasure ship disaster too and knew exactly what Hamilton and Jennings were up to.

The two sloops left Port Royal and headed west, following the southern coast of Cuba until they turned north into the Yucatán Channel. It was over a thousand sea miles from Port Royal to the salvage site, but this route, less direct than the one through the Windward Passage to the Bahamas, was faster, due to the prevailing winds. Sure enough, by late December Jennings was off Key Biscayne – present-day Miami – when on Christmas Day they captured a Spanish dispatch vessel, the *San Nicolas de Vari y San Joseph*. Fearing for his life, her captain, Pedro de la Vega, told Jennings exactly where the two

Spanish salvage camps were located, near St Sebastian Inlet, some two miles apart from each other. Jennings and his men reached the place two days later, having spotted the glow of the Spanish campfires as they approached in the dark.[18]

Jennings now knew a little about what to expect and felt he wouldn't have to face much in the way of opposition. So, any notion of passively investigating the extent of the shipwrecks, or even looting wrecks where the Spanish hadn't begun salvaging, was ignored. Instead, Jennings and his men resolved to plunder the Spanish camps and make off with whatever they could carry. The line from semi-legal privateer to full-blown pirate was about to be crossed. So, that night the men prepared for a dawn attack on the larger and closer of the two camps, the aim being to overawe the defenders and force them to surrender without a fight.

Two days after Christmas, on 27 December 1715, Jennings and his men landed on the Florida coast, near the St Sebastian Inlet. They split up into three armed columns, two from *Barsheba*, led by Jennings, while Wills and another captain, Edward James, led another made up of the men from the *Eagle*. All told, they had around 150 to 180 men under arms. In the salvage camps, Admiral Francisco Salmón had protected them with defensive works built largely from sand, but these were really designed to stop any probing attack by the local Ays tribe – not heavily armed former privateersmen. Some of his musket-armed men were even stationed a few miles away, guarding the smaller camp close to the shattered remnants of the New Spain fleet's *almirante, San Román*. So, Salmón had insufficient men under his command to put up a real defence in the event of a determined attack.[19]

Until that moment the salvage had been going well – with much of the treasure from *la Regla* and *San Román*, which had wrecked nearby. When Jennings and his three columns of armed men appeared on the beach in front of the main camp, the salvors knew they didn't have a chance of resisting. So, Admiral Salmón approached Jennings and held a parley.

He began by asking Jennings why he was there. Jennings replied it was to 'fish' the wrecks, and to claim some of the 'mountain of wealth' there for himself. Salmón told him firmly that it belonged to King Philip V of Spain and wasn't available for the taking. When this didn't make an impression, Salmón offered a bribe of 25,000 pieces-of-eight, if the armed raiders would go away. Jennings, though, wasn't there to negotiate. He and his men entered both camps and held the garrison prisoner while they took what they'd come for. Jennings was there to claim the whole lot for himself.[20]

In his *General History*, Johnson described what happened: 'Captain Jennings sailed to the Gulf and found the Spaniards there upon the wreck. The money ... was left on shore, deposited in a storehouse, under the government of two commissaries, and a guard of about sixty soldiers.' Sure enough, the Spaniards had built a wooden storehouse to hold the salvaged specie, but it was really designed to prevent low-key pilfering, not a small army of well-armed plunderers. Johnson continued: 'the rovers came directly upon the place, bringing their little fleet to an anchor, and, in a word, landing 300 men, they attacked the guard, who immediately ran away. And thus, they seized the treasure, which they carried off, making the best of their way to Jamaica.'

Johnson claimed that the Spanish had already recovered millions of silver pieces-of-eight and transported it to Havana. Still in the salvage camps, he claimed, was around 350,000 pieces-of-eight, with more being recovered every day – until the moment Jennings arrived. Johnson had got some of his facts wrong – a frequent occurrence in his book – but as usual the gist of what happened was correct. It is generally considered that Jennings' haul that day was more in the region of 120,000 pieces-of-eight. Don Juan Francisco de Vale, an emissary of the governor of Havana, who complained to the British authorities in Jamaica, added a little more in the way of detail. He claimed Spanish gold and silver worth £87,000 in English currency had been removed and taken away in the looters' launches.[21]

The Spanish claimed that they also took four small bronze swivel guns or *versos* and spiked three artillery pieces emplaced to protect the camp, rendering them useless. The Spanish later claimed that this rendered the camp defenceless in the event of an attack by marauding natives. To make this worse for the Spanish, when Jennings' raiders put to sea again, they almost immediately fell in with a Spanish merchant ship, which they forced to strike her colours. Again, Johnson picked up the story: 'In their way they unhappily met with a Spanish ship, bound from Porto Bello to the Havana, with a great many rich goods, viz. bales of cochineal, casks of indigo and 60,000 pieces-of-eight more, which their hands being in, they took, and having rifled the ship let her go.'

What happened next is slightly less straightforward. Henry Jennings and John Wills had succeeded beyond their expectations, and probably those of the rapacious Jamaican governor. They decided that rather than heading straight back to Jamaica, they would be better to go somewhere else for a few days, so they could quietly take stock of their haul and divide it up into shares – those for the captain and crew, and others for Lord Hamilton and any other backers the venture might have had. They decided that the Bahamas would answer perfectly. So, the *Barsheba* and the *Eagle* headed across the Bahama Channel and entered the archipelago. They then set a course for the island of New Providence, some 225 miles away from the treasure wrecks.

By January 1716 this small island had already become something of a centre for miscreants. The small, struggling agricultural colony there had recently been joined by former privateers and outright pirates, who used it as a base for attacks on Spanish shipping in the Bahama Channel or the Florida Straits. One of these was the former privateer Benjamin Hornigold, whose privateering sloop *Mary* of six guns was roughly comparable to Jennings' *Barsheba*. However, when Jennings' two sloops glided into the island's main anchorage at Nassau, it was clear the newcomers had the strength to rule the roost in Nassau. It was even claimed that Jennings took over a captured Spanish sloop of Hornigold's, to ease the overcrowding in his own vessels.[22]

In any case, over the next few days the business of dividing the plunder went ahead. Then the two incomers left New Providence, bound for Jamaica, this time sailing there by way of the Windward Passage between Cuba and Saint-Domingue. So, a month after the attack on the salvage camp, on 26 January 1716, the *Barsheba* returned to Jamaica, where a delighted Lord Hamilton was on hand to accept his share of the plunder, supposedly on behalf of the Crown. It can't be proved that Lord Hamilton knew at that stage that the plunder had been stolen directly from the Spanish, although it was glaringly obvious that Jennings and Wills couldn't have garnered such a haul so quickly if they'd 'fished' for the treasure. In any case, the accusation was made soon enough, when Don Juan de Vale appeared in Spanish

Town and presented both the governor and the Jamaican Assembly with the Spanish side of the story.

The official protest by the emissary was only the start of the storm. De Vale was brushed off by Lord Hamilton, who promised to send an expedition to the Palmar de Ays to suppress the pirates. De Vale was aware who had profited from the venture, and he reported back to the Marquis de Casa Torres, the governor of Havana, saying that he'd learned Lord Hamilton had owned a quarter share in the piratical scheme. He also claimed that he had traced some of the plunder to the governor's own residence. Lord Hamilton's response to these Spanish allegations was to ignore them. He did, though, promise de Vale that he'd send out another supposed anti-pirate expedition, to deal with the problem. Inevitably, it would be led by Hamilton's own looter, Captain Henry Jennings.[23]

Inevitably, at this point the true story becomes a little murky. Lord Hamilton's association with the looting of the Spanish salvage camp was an open secret in Jamaica, and it reached the ears of the Jamaican Assembly. Around the time the *Barsheba* returned to Port Royal, the governor was facing the official wrath of the island's legislature. In December he was formally accused of misappropriating funds, which almost certainly centred around the hiring of Jennings and Wills. The assembly demanded an inquest. Hamilton's response in January was to refuse to hold one, and he chided the members of the Assembly for their 'peevish and fruitless enquiries'. This, then, was the situation in Jamaica which the *Barsheba* sailed into, her hold laden with Spanish silver.

The confrontation between Hamilton and his legislature led to the Assembly writing a letter to London, claiming that 'the island has been ill-treated by his Excellency and loyalty alone had induced its representatives not to vote any further sum of money, while his lordship continued in the government.' In other words, the two sides were refusing to govern the island. By that stage Hamilton had even refused to accept correspondence from the Assembly, as it wasn't presented with due deference. It was an intolerable situation, and so news of the looting gave Hamilton's enemies in the Assembly all the ammunition they needed. Inevitably, word of the partnership between Hamilton and Jennings reached the ears of the British authorities.[24]

At that moment, the British government was fully occupied with the threat of a Jacobite invasion. Supporters of James Stuart, the son of the exiled King James, had risen in Scotland in August 1715 – the same time as the survivors of the treasure fleet were awaiting rescue on the coast of Florida. In mid-November the Jacobites clashed with government forces at the Battle of Sheriffmuir near Stirling, but the outcome had been indecisive. In the end, many of the highland clansmen who had risen simply returned home, and Jacobite support ebbed away. Despite another clash at Preston in November, the crisis had passed by the end of the year.

Still, fears of a Jacobite conspiracy had swept both Scotland and England, and several attempted plots and conspiracies came to light. For a time it seemed as if almost everybody was under suspicion. These included the new 5th Duke of Hamilton and his relatives, especially his uncle Archibald in Jamaica. So, any infraction bearing the name of a Scottish-born noble was liable to attract attention in government circles. In fact, Lord Hamilton, a staunch Presbyterian, was no supporter of the exiled Catholic king, and neither was his nephew, the current duke. Both had sworn their allegiance to King George I and stood by their pledge. What unseated Governor Hamilton was his shady dealings, rather than his politics.

By July 1716 the Jamaican Assembly had had enough of their governor. Although he was the representative of the Crown, they forcibly removed him from office, and replaced him with an acting governor of their own, the plantation owner Peter Heywood. At this point they formally arrested Hamilton, arraigned in his own Vice Admiralty court on the charge of involvement in piracy. Four months before, Samuel Page, secretary to the Assembly, had sailed for Britain with a dossier of papers cataloguing the governor's piratical dealings. These included a letter copied to the Admiralty by Captain Balchen of the *Diamond*. The dossier gave an account of Hamilton's involvement in the Jennings raid and included a copy of the official complaint lodged by the Spanish.[25]

Now though, there was a fresh batch of evidence to support it. Jennings had planned to return to the Spanish treasure wrecks, but the political turmoil in Jamaica prevented Hamilton from endorsing the operation. When he went out on a supposed privateering cruise, looking for pirates, there would be no official move to stop him. Jennings was helped, however, by the gold fever that had been sweeping through Jamaica ever since he returned from Florida, with his holds filled with plunder. Now hundreds of seamen wanted to join his band. Even Captain Balchen complained that ten of his crew had deserted, 'being all mad to go a wrecking'. Other Jamaican and Bahamian sailors almost certainly made their own way to Florida, to see what they could scavenge.[26]

In April 1716 Jennings sailed from Bluefields in the *Barsheba*, bound for the salvage camps. This time, he was accompanied by the sloops *Mary* and *Discovery*. Leigh Ashworth of the *Mary* had a Letter of Marque, but James Carnegie of the *Discovery* wasn't an official privateer – he was simply tagging along to take part in the looting of the camps. Not, of course, that these Letters of Marque were worth the parchment they were written on. This wasn't a pirate-hunting expedition. It was theft. Off the western tip of Cuba, they were joined by another Jamaican sloop, the *Cocoa Nut*, captained by Samuel Liddell. In the end, the whole expedition came undone when they came across a French merchant ship, the *St Marie* of La Rochelle, which Jennings captured after a short fight. This was unquestionably an act of piracy.[27]

To compound it, Jennings tried to capture another French vessel, the sloop *Marianne*, which was reportedly some 23 miles down the coast to the east. He sent a force to capture her, but it seems they never reached her. Instead, while Jennings was still anchored in a bay, waiting for his men to return, he saw the *Marianne* sailing past the entrance. She was accompanied by Hornigold's *Benjamin*. It seemed Jennings' rival had got to her first. Jennings gave chase, but Hornigold's *Benjamin* outran her pursuers. However, his prize was left behind, and so Jennings claimed the *Marianne* for himself. As Jennings held a pirate-hunting Letter of Marque, the recapture of a pirate prize was perfectly legitimate. The plundering of the *St Marie*, though, was an act of outright piracy. So, when Jennings returned to Jamaica with his French prizes, he tried to keep quiet about the illegal part of his venture. However, he hadn't reckoned with Governor Michon of Léogâne, from the French colony of Saint-Domingue.[28]

In June, Governor Michon sent a delegation to Lord Hamilton, complaining that while he expected the Spanish to act as pirates, he didn't expect British ships to do the same. He reported the attack by four sloops, commanded by Jennings, Ashworth, Carnegie and Liddell, which took Captain d'Escoubet's *St Marie* and Captain Gardeur's *Marianne*, and took away plunder valued at 50,000 crowns – the French equivalent of pieces-of-eight. This was a real game changer for both Hamilton and Jennings. Hamilton's own pirate-hunting privateer had been caught red-handed. Michon added that he knew some of the 'privateers' had estates in Jamaica, and suggested these be sold off, to 'repair the wrong they have done'. To reinforce the demand, Captain d'Escoubet was part of the delegation, willing to prove his legitimate ownership of the French ship now anchored off Port Royal.[29]

For the Jamaican Assembly this French delegation arrived at the perfect time. The resentment this caused strengthened the resolve of the legislature to remove Hamilton from office. He was irredeemably stained by charges of corruption, and now his accusers had clear proof that he was in league with pirates. It is little wonder that just two weeks after the French arrived, Lord Hamilton was arrested in his own governor's house, and detained. It also gave them a much stronger case with the colony's governing body, the Board of Trade in London. So, in late July, when the 40-gun fifth-rate HMS *Adventure* arrived off Port Royal to relieve the *Diamond*, it gave the Assembly and the new acting governor Peter Heywood the chance to ship Lord Hamilton back to Britain in the returning frigate. Captain Balchen was, of course, happy to comply, and left bearing copies of these new explosive charges.[30]

In the end, Archibald Lord Hamilton managed to wriggle out of his charges. During the preparation for his trial, he circulated pamphlets around London which laid out his version of events, and which stressed his abhorrence of piracy. He portrayed the charges laid against him by the Jamaican Assembly as bogus, and even had the audacity to claim that he had done all he could to suppress piracy in the Caribbean. In the end he was believed by the British government, and all of the charges against him were quietly dropped after a token hearing.[31]

Given the strong feeling against him in Jamaica, a return there was unthinkable. Instead, a new governor, Thomas Pitt, grandfather of the politician Pitt the Elder, was sent to Jamaica, to relieve Acting Governor Heywood, who had never enjoyed an official royal endorsement. Later, Lord Hamilton returned to politics and was re-elected as a Member of Parliament in December 1718, and he re-married. From then on he courted respectability, as far as that was possible for a politician of his time.

As for Jennings, he remained in Jamaica during Hamilton's arrest and removal, but the axe fell for him in August. Then, a ship arrived from London, bearing a proclamation that declared that Henry Jennings and John Wills were now deemed to be pirates. Also named were Jennings' later Jamaican consorts, Leigh Ashworth and James Carnegie. The next day Jennings' controversial privateering Letter of Marque was cancelled by Governor Heywood. This meant that Jennings and the others were outlaws, and the authorities would attempt to hunt them down. By then, knowing what was likely to follow Hamilton's arrest, Jennings had already left Jamaica, bound for the Bahamas. There, out of reach of the British authorities, he would resume his career, this time as a full-blown pirate.[32]

THREE

Piracy in the Bahamas

S o, from August 1716, Port Royal and the markets of Jamaica were closed to pirates. That included looters of Spanish treasure, as well as ex-privateers who still targeted the Spanish and French ships, even though the war had been over for three years or more. The definition of piracy was fairly wide, covering anyone who committed a crime on the high seas, or indeed below the high water mark. Quibbling about how far up the beach the Spanish salvage camps were wasn't the business of the Admiralty. Men like Jennings had put themselves above the law and had to live with the consequences.

So, Henry Jennings and his followers needed a new base – one where the legal niceties of Admiralty law didn't apply, and where they'd be safe from arrest, trial and even execution. There was only one glaringly obvious place for them – one which had already been taken over by pirates. The harbour of Nassau, on the island of New Providence in the Bahamas, made a near-perfect pirate base. It had more than one entrance, so it would be difficult to attack. Anyone landing elsewhere on the island would soon be spotted, which would give the pirates time to flee, or to organize some kind of defence. There was already a nascent trading community there, made up of merchants who had few scruples about dealing with plundered goods or looted Spanish treasure. Just as importantly, Nassau lay close to the busy shipping lanes of the Florida Straits, the Bahama Channel and the Windward Passage, and it was within range of the equally lucrative hunting grounds of the West Indies or the Gulf of Honduras. Nassau would suit men like Jennings very well indeed.

Jennings and his men had put in to Nassau after plundering the Spanish salvage camp on the Florida coast. So, they knew what to expect there. They also knew that they weren't the first lawbreakers to choose New Providence as their haven. When they visited the island that January, they met Benjamin Hornigold, who had already established himself there. When both Hornigold and Jennings arrived on the island they found a local population, eking out a precarious living. Of course, human connection with the Bahamas stretched back much farther than that. The Taino people first settled there a thousand years before Christopher Columbus first set foot in the islands in 1492, but by the time he arrived there the Lucayan people had colonized the archipelago. In the wake of Columbus came the Spanish. They raided these islands for slaves so effectively that the Bahamas were almost entirely stripped of people.[1]

The first European settlers arrived in 1648, when a group of English colonists from Bermuda established themselves on Eleuthera. They found the soil there poor, but the colony survived on the back of what was little more than subsistence farming. Then, in 1666, another group from Bermuda landed in New Providence. This proved a much more fertile place, and the colonists made a reasonable living through agriculture, supported by fishing, salt production and the hunting of turtles. While exploring the archipelago they also came across the remains of several Spanish shipwrecks, which they salvaged for anything valuable or useful. By the late 17th century, the population of the island was over 500. The main settlement in New Providence was called Charles Town, in honour of the English king. Technically these settlements formed part of the Carolinas, but the absentee Carolinian Lords Proprietors weren't much interested in the place, which suited the independent-minded Bahamian settlers perfectly well.

They could have used the protection though. In 1684 a Spanish expedition arrived and burned the settlements in Eleuthera and New Providence to the ground. Charles Town was reduced to fire-charred timbers. Although England and Spain were at peace, this was supposedly in retaliation for the looting of Spanish shipwrecks, which the Spanish saw as the property of the Spanish Crown. Still, two years later a new wave of colonists arrived from Jamaica, and the settlement on New Providence was rebuilt. This time, the island's harbour was called Nassau, in honour of King William's Dutch origins. Governor Nicholas Trott, sent there by the Carolinian Lords Proprietors, even built a small fort at Nassau out of local stone to defend the anchorage, and armed it with 28 guns. So, New Providence had a new lease of life, although the island's economy remained fragile.

Fortunately for the residents then, during the War of the Grand Alliance of 1688–97, a few English privateers used the Bahamas as a base for raids, for much the same reason that the later generation of pirates did. Supposedly, the pirate Henry Every also visited New Providence after fleeing the Indian Ocean before word of his immense and illegally gained haul of Mughal treasure reached the ears of the English authorities. The tale goes that he arrived at Nassau incognito, in early April 1696, keeping his pirate ship the *Fancy* tucked away out of sight. He was taken to meet Governor Trott and introduced as Captain Henry Bridgeman. It was unlikely that Trott was fooled. The bluff, West Country mariner standing before him, with his weathered, tanned but scarred face, was almost certainly the pirate his superiors in the Carolinas had warned him about.[2]

Every's recent capture of the 80-gun Mughal treasure ship *Ganj-i-sawai* in August 1695 became the sensational news of the age, taken after a particularly hard-fought gun duel and lengthy, bloody boarding action in the Indian Ocean. Fortunately for Every, the Mughal commander Muhammad Ibrahim was more concerned with saving himself and his royal passenger – the Mughal Emperor Alamgir's granddaughter – than repelling the boarders. So, he left his men to do the fighting and emerged only after they lay down their arms. Just before he did, he armed a consignment of Turkish concubines for the emperor's harem and sent them to join the fight. The pirates, it seems, disarmed them and spared their lives, but not much else.[3] The next few hours saw an orgy of raping, looting and violence on board their rich prize. When it was over, Every and his men made off with their plunder – a jaw-dropping haul of gold, silver, gems and jewels, which some have valued at over half a million pounds – the equivalent of £350 million today. It included half a million Indian and Arabian gold and silver coins, four times the haul that Henry Jennings made two decades later. Better still, the pirates didn't have governors or backers to share the spoils with. All they had to do was divide the plunder among themselves. The real total might have been less, as these things tend to be exaggerated with the retelling. Still, by any standards it was an impressive sum – probably the most lucrative pirate haul of plunder in history.[4]

Afterwards, Every quit the Indian Ocean, stopping only at the French-owned island of Bourbon (now Réunion) to divide the plunder – each man getting around £1,000 in coin, and a bag of precious gems. Then, after rounding the Cape of Good Hope, he headed for the Caribbean – and then the Bahamas. He knew that the attack would have consequences. At the time, the English East India Company needed the Mughal Emperor's support, and this had been placed in jeopardy by the attack on the *Ganj-i-sawai*. After all, the attackers had all been English. So, while the East India Company recompensed the Emperor Alamgir out of its own coffers, the English government declared Every a pirate and a wanted man – the most sought-after fugitive of his day. It was little wonder Governor Trott knew who he was.[5]

Henry 'Bridgeman' claimed he and his men were slavers, operating illegally off West Africa's slave coast. That region was the preserve of the Royal African Company, and so unlicensed slavers were viewed as interlopers. In return for a temporary haven, and for keeping the news of their presence from the Royal African Company, he offered to pay Trott a small fortune in elephant tusks. After consulting the island's council, Trott agreed to let the *Fancy* enter the harbour. So, for the next few weeks, Every and his wild-looking pirates roistered ashore in Nassau's simple taverns, their pockets filled with money, and the Bahamians officially discreetly turned a blind eye to their antics, the sight of their still-battered ship bristling with guns, and to the influx of exotic coins. This was a first for Nassau – but it wouldn't be the last time a pirate crew cut loose in the port.

*Henry Every plundered a king's ransom in the Red Sea,
then arrived in Nassau with his loot.*

Every didn't even bother patching up the *Fancy*. In the end, when he judged the time was right to leave, he deliberately ran her aground on rocks outside the harbour. Again, this was probably done with Trott's consent. He certainly stood to gain from it – the powder, weapons and shot on board were now his, along with the *Fancy*'s anchors. No doubt Trott and his islanders were happy to strip the pirate wreck clean, in return for keeping their mouths shut.

The reason for this might well have been the arrival of a proclamation circulated to colonial governors in late 1696, demanding the arrest of Every and his men if they appeared in their waters. Trott had no option but to inform the Lords Proprietors of the Carolinas that Every had turned up in the Bahamas. He then gave Every and his men the chance to slip away before they were hunted down. The pirate band split up, some going to the Caribbean, others to North America, and Every, it seems, to Ireland. Although the manhunt for him continued for a decade, Every was never caught, and, despite a lot of speculation, his fate remains a mystery to this day.[6]

Unfortunately, when war returned to the Bahamas in 1702, so did the Spanish. This time it was a joint Franco-Spanish force that descended on the archipelago – a mixture of Spanish troops and French privateersmen – ex-*flibustiers*. In October 1703 two frigates – one French and one Spanish – appeared off the island. After landing on a beach near Nassau, they captured the town and its fort after a brief fight and a wholesale slaughter that left up to a hundred colonists dead or wounded. The invaders then plundered Nassau, razed the settlements on the rest of the island, and left, taking the fort's best guns with them, and spiking the rest before pushing them over the ramparts into the sea. They also took up to a hundred prisoners, most of them slaves from the island's few plantations. One of the prisoners was the Bahamian governor, Ellis Lightwood.[7]

A few colonists managed to escape the invaders, hiding in the island's woods and mangroves until the invaders finally left. What they found when they returned to their homes didn't really seem worth rebuilding. Everything had been comprehensibly pillaged, then destroyed. Hearing of this, the Lords Proprietors of the Carolinas sent out another governor from London, Edward Birch, with orders to restore English rule in the Bahamas. He landed there in January 1704, three months after the raid, having taken passage in a ship to Barbados, and then taken on in a small Bermudian sloop. What he found was devastating. Essentially, there was hardly anybody left to govern. Most of the survivors had already fled to Eleuthera, Cat Island or other nearby settlements, while those who remained were scattered and still in hiding, because they feared the Spanish would return.

One of the surviving settlers, John Graves, said they were living 'scatteringly, in little huts, ready upon any assault to secure themselves in the woods'. Birch remained there for another three months or so, living in the woods with the others, but they didn't seem willing to rebuild their lives or their settlement. In the end Governor Birch quit the melancholy place in the late spring, aboard a visiting sloop from Barbados. While he was there, he hadn't even bothered to read out the proclamation declaring his governorship. So, the Bahamas were literally left to their own devices. The Spanish returned the following year, and again in 1706, but there was nothing left worth plundering. By then the few settlers who remained lived in crudely built huts, and the old plantations of the island had been replaced by subsistence-living plots.[8]

It was against this backdrop of misery that a few British privateers arrived, presumably to use the Bahamas as a watering hole and to seek supplies. In November 1704 a small privateering sloop from Charles Town in the South Carolina colony arrived off Nassau and sought out the Vice Admiralty court there – at a time when no such thing really existed. Still, several Spanish prizes taken by the sloop's commander, Captain Thomas Williams, were unofficially condemned by the Bahamas' chief judge, Thomas Walker. Walker still lived on the island, a few miles outside Nassau, where he and his family – his wife Sarah and their four children – maintained a small farm. They had rebuilt the farmstead after the Franco-Spanish raid of 1703, helped by a small influx of privateering plunder. After the Spanish invasion the court didn't hold formal sessions, but Walker effectively issued rulings as if it still did. He was, after all, one of the few respectable officials left in the Bahamas, and he wanted to play his part in the restoration of law and order in the archipelago.

Surprisingly, over the winter of 1706–07 Thomas Walker himself fitted out a small 20-ton sloop as a privateer in New Providence, and crewed it in Nassau with 35 trusted men. The judge then went cruising off the north coast of Cuba and returned home in January

1707 with five small Spanish prizes. Presumably he condemned them himself, then awarded his crew £50 a head. Undoubtedly, more privateers used the archipelago – it was too well placed not to. However, it seems their captains preferred to take their prizes taken off the Cuban coast or in the Bahama Channel for condemnation in less legally suspect courts.[9]

It wasn't that surprising. After the Spanish raid of 1703 there wasn't much left there at all – a half-destroyed fort, a few shacks and a number of burned-out houses. A mariner, Captain Samuel Chadwell of the sloop *Flying Horse*, left a useful snapshot of the Bahamas in 1707, four years after the raid. He put the whole population of the archipelago at 600 people, half of whom were slaves. These were almost all in either Eleuthera, New Providence, Cat Island or the Exumas. The main income came from harvesting braziletta wood, tortoise shells, salt production and the picking over of shipwrecks. Chadwell reported that around 20 small trading vessels visited the Bahamas each year. It wasn't much of an economy.[10]

However, there seems a lot more to it than that. The fact that there were other signs of mercantile activity in Eleuthera suggests a faint but steady heartbeat of an economy, and at least for some traders a reliable income was there to be made.

In Jamaica, the potential of the Bahamas would have been well known to the mariners of Port Royal. So, one of them – a man who decided he didn't want his privateering career to end so abruptly – decided to make New Providence his home. At some point in the late summer or early autumn of 1713, Benjamin Hornigold and a small group of like-minded followers, all hardened ex-privateersmen, left Jamaica without fanfare and set a course for New Providence. He might well have been there during the late war. In fact, it's probable that he'd been one of the privateersmen who'd used the Bahamas as a watering hole, as he seemed to know its waters.

What Hornigold found there didn't look promising. It was nine years since Nassau was sacked and burned. The blackened remnants of its buildings had lost that fire-ravaged smell but had now been largely overrun by verdant tropical foliage. The ruins of the fort were indefensible; for the most part the walls were still standing, but sections had fallen into the sea. The few guns that remained had been spiked and had their cascabels knocked off, rendering them useless without the specialist attention of a trained gunner and his tools. The church was nothing more than a blackened ruin too, as was the once-respectable wood-built governor's house. In between these creeper-covered ruins was a handful of wooden shacks and cabins, some built using driftwood and ship's timbers. Elsewhere a few of the older, less-damaged buildings had been crudely repaired and re-occupied. Nassau was no longer the up-and-coming settlement it had been in Governor Trott's day. It was now little more than a squalid, makeshift refugee camp. Hornigold would have seen it as near perfect.[11]

Clearly, Hornigold and his men had little to fear from the settlers. They were too busy surviving to bother him, living off vegetables and fish, and the handful of wild pigs that now roamed the island's interior. So, with no governor or any other civil presence on the island, he felt he could pretty much do whatever he liked. He began by either building or reclaiming three *piraguas* (or *periaguas*) – large Caribbean dugout canoes with outriggers, capable of carrying two dozen men apiece. They could be powered by oar, or by one or two masts carrying gaff-rigged sails. The small six-gun sloop he'd left Jamaica in was left at anchor in Nassau harbour, and he planned to use these *piraguas* to lie in wait off Andros or Grand Bahama islands, to the west and north-west of New Providence. Both bordered the Bahama Channel, and these low, fast and difficult-to-spot craft were perfect for darting out and pouncing on passing trading ships.

Hornigold had around 70 to 80 men with him, which meant two dozen could crew each *piragua*. Armed with cutlass, axe and pistol, they would intercept their prey, swarm aboard and loot the cargo. Hornigold led the force from one of the canoes while two young deputies, John Cockram and John West, commanded the other two craft. Throughout that autumn and winter the pirates preyed on passing French and Spanish ships, ranging as far as the eastern coast of Florida and northern shore of Cuba. When they ran short of water they put into some of the smaller islands of the Bahamas archipelago – Bimini was a good watering place, while supplies could be had at Harbour Island, a tiny key off the north-east end of Eleuthera, where there was a small settlement.[12]

They had a successful time of it. The pirates returned to Nassau several times during that period, their *piraguas* laden with everything from textiles – linens and silks – to the local produce of the Caribbean

– sugar and rum. They even retuned with Spanish pieces-of-eight, looted from the Spanish trading vessels they attacked in the Bahama Channel. They didn't just prey on ships. Sometimes they landed on the Cuban coast and plundered isolated plantations and settlements. In one of these they even took 14 African slaves, who were brought back to New Providence to be sold. In all, their haul that winter amounted to £13,175 – the equivalent of around six years' wages per man, if they'd been serving aboard a merchant ship.

Strangely, throughout all this, Benjamin Hornigold insisted he was a *bona fide* privateer, not a pirate. As if to prove it he would flourish his Letter of Marque, which of course had ceased to be valid the day peace was signed. So, he limited his attacks to Spanish and occasionally French ships, as if he were still bound by the contract's terms, trying to cling to the last remnants of order, civilization and legality. While New Providence – far from the eye of officialdom – was his chosen demesne, it was almost as if he craved the sureness and stability of life on the right side of the law. Perhaps, like the buccaneers before him, he was hoping for a pardon. Hornigold would maintain this self-deception for the whole of his piratical career.

One of the main problems with piracy is that regular markets were closed to them. As a legitimate privateer, Hornigold could just sail into Port Royal, Bridgetown or Charles Town, and after his prize and its cargo was officially condemned, there would be no end of merchants and traders willing to buy the cargo from the clerks of the Vice Admiralty court. Now, though, they had a growing pile of cargo worth a small fortune, but no merchants on hand willing to buy it from them. Fortunately for Hornigold, during his provisioning visits to Harbour Island he'd met Richard Thompson – probably the wealthiest man on the small island, and one of Eleuthera's principal landowners. He also owned a handful of trading sloops that made regular voyages around the Caribbean basin, or to the burgeoning ports on America's Atlantic seaboard. Thompson wasn't a man who was overly hindered by scruples.

In conversation with the merchant, Hornigold learned that Thompson had a strong dislike of the Spanish, as they'd taken his ships in the last war, and his island lay under the continued threat of Spanish raids. So, when Hornigold broached the delicate subject of offloading his plunder, he found that, for a profit, Thompson agreed to be Hornigold's 'fence' – his receiver of stolen goods. This was a real breakthrough for Hornigold and his fledgling pirate enterprise. With a guaranteed market for his goods, he could not only continue his attacks, but also have the chance to expand the whole enterprise, taking on more men and using larger vessels capable of ranging farther than his *piraguas*.

As if to underline this union between thief and fence, Hornigold's younger deputy, John Cockram, fell for one of Thompson's daughters in Harbour Island, and in March 1714 the couple wed. At that time Cockram left the pirate business to become his father-in-law's receiver of stolen property. From that point on he was officially Thompson's man rather than Hornigold's and became the master of one of Thompson's trading ships. In this capacity he made regular voyages between the Bahamas and Charles Town, taking his 'fenced' goods one way and returning with a cargo of legitimate 'clean' produce on the return voyage. Later, he and Thompson, who also commanded one of his own sloops, expanded their enterprise to include voyages as far afield as Boston in the Massachusetts colony, and the Dutch colony of Curaçao off the coast of the Spanish Main. For Hornigold, it was a near-perfect arrangement.[13]

By the spring of 1714 Hornigold had begun to recruit more volunteers from among the ranks of Eleuthera's settlers. One of these was Jonathan Darvell, allegedly a former mutineer on a slave ship, who had helped kill the officers and then sell their human cargo to Dutch slave traders on Curaçao. He was now a trader, although not quite as successful a merchant as Thompson on nearby Harbour Island. However, Darvell arranged a deal with Hornigold. He would lend the pirate his tiny 15-ton sloop *Happy Return*, crewed by his son-in-law Daniel Stillwell and assisted by the trader's teenage son Zacheus Darvell. This arrangement gave Hornigold the ability to range farther afield in search of prey.[14]

So, that summer Hornigold used the *Happy Return* to cruise off the Florida side of the Bahama Channel, before ranging down the northern coast of Cuba. This small trial cruise was a great success. When Hornigold returned to Eleuthera he and his men unloaded a considerable pile of trading goods, money and even a slave. When divided up, a delighted Jonathan Darvell was presented with his quarter share, valued at around 2,000 pieces-of-eight. That autumn, while Hornigold remained in Eleuthera, the rest of his small crew made a second cruise in the *Happy Return*. This time, the seas were virtually clear of Spanish trading ships, and they were able to plunder only a few tanned cow hides valued at a miserable 300 pieces-of-eight. So, Hornigold went back to basics. He used a small longboat purchased from one of Darvell's neighbours and returned to the Cuban coast in her with just a handful of men, including Darvell's son.[15]

He literally struck gold. In early December they fell in with a small vessel cruising off Matanzas on the north Cuban coast, accompanied by a *piragua*. On board the craft was a wealthy Spanish merchant, a Señor Pedro Barrihone from Puerto Príncipe. This was a prize that made up for everything. According to Barrihone's deposition to the authorities in Havana – effectively the filing of a crime report – he said the pirates had stolen money and cargo valued at an impressive 46,000 pieces-of-eight. This represented a small fortune, and it was a delighted longboat's crew that returned to Eleuthera that Christmas.

However, in the last days of 1714, a number of disquieting rumours reached the Bahamas. According to news gleaned in Charles Town and Port Royal, the Spanish authorities in Havana were planning to do something about the string of pirate attacks on their shipping. They knew that the raiders had been based in the Bahamas – their *piraguas* weren't really designed for lengthy voyages. So, that probably meant the raiders were in either New Providence or Eleuthera. The word was Governor Laureano de Torres y Ayala, Marquis de Casa Torres, was about to send a powerful military force into the Bahamas to deal with the pirates and destroy any trading facilities there as well as the communities who supported them. Hornigold and his men wisely decided to lay low for a while.[16]

First, they divided up their remaining plunder, which was valued at up to £60,000 worth of specie and unsold goods. This meant that every man got a share of almost £400 – the equivalent of a dozen years' worth of wages for a skilled sailor. The group then scattered, with some heading for Jamaica, and some for the Carolinas, which was, after all, only a week's sail away. Hornigold remained in Harbour Island as the guest of Richard Thompson. So too did John Cockram, who was busy setting up home with his new wife. It was claimed that Thompson had a gun battery defending the narrow entrance to the lagoon covering the approach to the harbour. Then they waited to see what would happen.

In the end the Spanish attack never came. By then, however, Benjamin Hornigold and his local backers Richard Thompson and John Darvell had other problems. At the end of 1714 Thomas Walker, the Bahamian judge and occasional privateer, was probably the closest the Bahamas came to having any form of government. He'd already written to the Lords Proprietors, telling them about the arrival of pirates in the Bahamas. When they didn't listen, he even tried writing a piece in the *Boston News Letter*. In his letter to his superiors, he pointed out that his authority had officially lapsed but added that he saw himself as 'The prosecutor and disturber of all pirates, robbers and villains' in the archipelago. In other words, he was prepared to become a vigilante.[17]

Apart from the illegality of it, Walker was strongly opposed to piracy on two counts. First, these attacks irritated the Spanish and risked provoking another retaliatory raid against the largely unprotected islands. As residents of New Providence, Walker and his family were well aware what that could mean. He also knew that success for the pirates would inevitably lead to more of them coming to the Bahamas. This could lead to the fragile community he had helped establish becoming a lawless, ungovernable place, and the lives of the honest Bahamian colonists would become intolerable. So, he gathered a group of settlers – some of them, no doubt, the crew of his old privateering sloop – and as he put it in a letter, he set off 'to execute justice upon piratts'.[18]

He waited until just after Christmas to make his move, when he thought the pirates and their local hosts would be too drunk to react. In the last week of December 1714 he made the 50-mile voyage to Harbour Island. He was quite right. He slipped past the defended entrance into the lagoon at dawn, before Hornigold and Darvell's men knew what was happening. He'd taken them completely by surprise. The whole of Harbour Island – all just under three miles of it – was in his hands. Walker's vigilantes captured Daniel Stillwell, Zacheus Darvell and another young pirate, Matthew Low. Unfortunately, neither Benjamin Hornigold nor his host Jonathan Darvell was there – they'd been spending Christmas elsewhere on Eleuthera. The rest of their men either slipped across the shallows to Eleuthera or hid in the woods running along the spine of the small island. Still, it was enough. Walker sailed back to Nassau with his three prisoners and the *Happy Return*, which he'd confiscated.[19]

As he put it in a letter to the Lords Proprietors, it was all about curbing the activities of the pirates and bringing rogue settlers like Darvell into line. He wanted to ensure 'Said Inhabitants are made Settlers at Providence'. He added that they 'Will not be Suffered to live upon Ileatheria [Eleuthera] who when they are Guilty Doe fly into the Woods and deffend themselves with their Armes, against the pursuit of Justice.' In other words, he was annoyed that so many of the Harbour Island locals had escaped capture by his vigilantes by fleeing into the woods, then firing at Walker's men from the safety of the trees.

Now, though, he had three pirates, and once back on New Providence he began interrogating them. He quickly found that he could get the teenage Darvell and the inexperienced Matthew Low to talk, and he used their testimony to build up a stronger case against Daniel Stillwell, who was by far the most experienced pirate of the three. This done, Walker decided he needed a show trial. Such a trial, however, couldn't be carried out in the Bahamas, as he had no authority there, and neither did anyone else. He decided to let the two younger pirates off with a warning. He would then ship his remaining prisoner to Jamaica, where he could be tried in the active Vice Admiralty court there. Fortunately, the sloop *Portsmouth* of Jamaica was in harbour, and so Walker convinced Captain Jonathan Chase to transport his prisoner back to Kingston with him, and then to hand him over to the authorities. As well as the prisoner, Chase was handed a large package containing all the legal documents needed to convict Stillwell, including the sworn depositions of the two turned pirates. Chase left for Jamaica on 2 January 1715.[20]

That done, the enterprising Walker then decided to deal with the Spanish. Hornigold's attack on the Cuban merchant Señor Barrihone's boat would almost certainly have goaded the Spanish, and there were already rumours circulating that the Spanish planned to launch another retaliatory raid on the Bahamas. So, true to form, Walker decided to deal with the problem head on. A few weeks after the *Portsmouth* departed, Walker left Nassau too. Ironically, he used Hornigold's own *Happy Return* and sailed her directly to Havana. He was warily allowed to enter the port, and once ashore he requested an interview with the Cuban governor, the Marquis de Casa Torres. When he finally met the governor, Walker told him that several of the pirates had been arrested and would stand trial in Jamaica. The problem, Walker claimed, had been dealt with.[21]

The Marquis not only believed Walker but was grateful for his efforts. He assured Walker that there would be no more retaliatory raids on the Bahamas, then added, 'I return you grateful thanks and likewise all the inhabitants of Providence.' He continued, 'You have taken care to detect such villains who make it their evil practice to rob those who follow honest means to live.' Walker remained in Havana for a few weeks as the guest of the governor. His mission had been a complete success. There would be no Spanish attack, and his negotiations with the Marquis and his staff had greatly eased relations between the Bahamian settlers and their powerful Spanish neighbours.

So, in late February 1715 Walker returned to New Providence in good humour. This buoyant mood was quickly dashed soon after he dropped anchor at Nassau. His prisoner, Daniel Stillwell, had escaped. Somehow, Hornigold had learned of Stillwell's arrest and transport to Jamaica and, although the details are unclear, at some point in the voyage the *Portsmouth* was intercepted, probably in the Windward Passage – the natural bottleneck to lie in wait for a passing ship. Captain Chase was forced to hand over his prisoner, and presumably the parcel with the depositions and other evidence for the trial was thrown over the side. It was certainly never seen again.[22]

As a result, Hornigold was free to continue his attacks. By now, he knew that while Walker was his enemy, the former judge and all-round man of honour lacked the muscle to stop Hornigold. So, when spring came, he resumed his attacks on Spanish shipping. The attacks were overshadowed by the tragic events on the far side of the Bahama Channel. News of the wrecking of the Spanish Treasure Fleet on 31 July 1715 reached the Bahamas within a week or two of the disaster. For generations the Bahamian settlers had augmented their living by picking over the carcasses of ships which wrecked in and around their archipelago. So, it was inevitable that some of them would try their hand on the Palmar de Ays. So too did a growing number of adventurers of various kinds, who were drawn there by the lure of gold. Inevitably, many of these wreck scavengers would establish themselves in the nearby English-speaking Bahamas.

As for Hornigold, he still maintained the fiction that he was a privateer rather than a pirate. To underline the point, he limited his attacks to French or Spanish ships. It was the Spanish in particular who really suffered at his hands, as he tended to operate in the Bahama Channel, the Florida Straits and along the north coast of Cuba, though he also ventured east as far as the Windward Passage between the eastern end of Cuba and the western side of Hispaniola, where the French had their prosperous colony of Saint-Domingue. In times of peace, which these supposedly were, this 45-mile-wide channel was used by ships of all nations. Then, in late 1715, Hornigold's stance changed dramatically. For the first time in his career, he attacked a British ship.[23]

In early November, Hornigold was cruising off the north coast of Cuba in two sloops when he came upon a British-flagged sloop, the *Mary* of Jamaica. She tried to outrun the pirates but was overhauled and captured. The capture of the *Mary* was a real game-changer for Hornigold. He couldn't hide behind his pretence of merely being a privateer anymore. By attacking a British ship he'd stepped over the line into full-blown piracy. Of course, he'd always been a pirate, but by claiming that he didn't recognize the Treaty of Utrecht, at least in his own mind he was still a law-abiding privateer. With that illusion stripped away, he had nothing left to cling to. The likelihood was that Benjamin Hornigold had little say in the matter. It was probably his own crew who'd made the decision for him, after seeing one too many juicy British prizes slip through their fingers.

If you had to capture a British vessel, the *Mary* of Jamaica was a good place to start. She was larger than most trading sloops of her kind. She probably displaced around 40 tons, making her similar to Henry Jennings' sloop *Barsheba*, and had room for 140 men and around six guns plus eight small rail-mounted swivel guns. At last, Hornigold had a pirate ship worthy of the name. Also, off the same stretch of the Cuban coast he captured a second sloop, this time a Spanish one, laden with a cargo of sugar and dry goods. Rather than head back to his usual base on Harbour Island, Hornigold decided to deal with the problem of Thomas Walker once and for all. So, that November, he decided to put into Nassau.

He sailed into the harbour in the *Mary*, accompanied by two other sloops – his original one and the Spanish prize, renamed *Benjamin* in honour of himself. Hornigold now had a crew of at least 100 men under his command, so he greatly outnumbered any force of law-abiding settlers that Walker could muster. When he sent his men ashore they quickly established themselves in Nassau, setting up shelters, occupying buildings and generally making themselves at home.

The harbour lacked any form of jetty or quay, so Hornigold stacked his plundered goods on the beach. For safety's sake he also stationed his own men at the fort, to make sure it wasn't occupied by the island's settlers. Benjamin Hornigold was now the pirate boss of Nassau.[24]

According to the testimony of Thomas Walker's 20-year-old son Thomas the Younger, at some point in that December the young man ran into Hornigold in Nassau. Hornigold asked him where his father was, calling the former judge an 'old rogue'. When he told him he was at home, Hornigold replied, 'He is a troublesome old fart, and if I see him I will shoot and kill him.' Hornigold then threatened that he'd also burn down the Walker homestead and beat and whip the rest of the family. After that, the Walker family kept their distance from the well-armed and hostile pirates. It was now a year since Walker's raid on Harbour Island, but in that time everything had changed. Benjamin Hornigold now ruled New Providence and used fear and intimidation to get his own way.[25]

Around Christmastime, Hornigold and some of his men put to sea again in the *Mary*. They returned just before the end of the year, accompanied by another Spanish prize – a large sloop, which Hornigold also renamed the *Benjamin*. Unlike the *Mary* she was classed as a 'great sloop', and so probably displaced around 60 tons, and had space for up to ten guns and 200 men. A delighted Hornigold duly transferred his men, guns and equipment into her, then sent the *Mary* back to Jamaica crewed by men who no longer wanted to serve with him, since his illusion of privateering had been abandoned. It is possible that Hornigold sent the *Mary* back to Jamaica because he wanted to make amends for crossing the line and regain what he probably saw as his preferred status as a legitimate privateer.

Word of these attacks had also reached London. In mid-December, the Council of Trade wrote to King George to tell him of the disturbing rise of piracy in the Bahamas. They reported that 'through the neglect of the Proprietors, these Islands are in a defenceless condition, and become a refuge for pirates'. The Board's recommendation was that the King strip the Lords Proprietors of the Carolinas of ownership of the Bahamas and turn it into a colony administered directly by the Crown. The Board even suggested that the King appoint a governor, who would then form an administration to govern the archipelago.

The situation had already been flagged up by Henry Pulleine, the acting governor of Bermuda, who as early as spring 1714 had warned the Board that the Bahamas were rapidly becoming a 'nest for pyrates'. At the time, though, he had been ignored. Now, more than a year and a half later, the authorities in London were finally beginning to take notice. This meant that Hornigold was creating ripples in the British corridors of power.[26]

For a few brief weeks, Benjamin Hornigold had everything. In the *Benjamin* he had a fast and roomy sloop with the men and guns he needed to take almost any merchant vessel they came across. The large and growing band of men who had agreed to follow him were a mixture of former privateersmen, Bahamian settlers and unemployed merchant seamen. Hornigold hoped that with a few more successes under their belt, they'd coalesce into a far more biddable crew. They'd even created a name for themselves – 'The Flying Gang'. So, for Hornigold the coming year of 1716 seemed full of opportunity. Then, when January came, it all fell to pieces.

Around 1 January 1716, Henry Jennings and his flotilla of vessels entered Nassau harbour. With his 150 men – many of them former privateersmen – he could easily overpower Hornigold and his Flying Gang if he needed to. That was the moment that Hornigold must have realized that his unofficial reign over the Bahamas was at an end. Now Jennings was the top dog in the pirate haven, and he intended to keep things that way. If only to enforce his superiority over Hornigold, Jennings commandeered one of his Spanish prizes, a small sloop, to help alleviate some of the overcrowding in his own well-manned vessels. For Hornigold, this was a slight he couldn't really do anything about.

Another key figure who witnessed Jennings' arrival and seizure of Nassau was Thomas Walker. With over 250 pirates in the harbour, they outnumbered the locals by at least four to one. It was clear that his colony had been taken. All of his letter-writing to the Lords Proprietors, the Board of Trade and even the King had come to naught. He had already had death threats from Benjamin Hornigold. With this new development, any attempt at confronting the pirates would end in his own death, and probably the murder of his family. Walker was effectively stifled. He was like a homeowner whose house had been taken over by a gang of hardened criminals. A new era had begun in New Providence. It was now a fully-fledged pirate haven.

FOUR

Benjamin Hornigold

Y OU COULD CUT THE atmosphere in Nassau with a knife – and
there were a lot of knives around. Two pirate gangs were in port,
and two pirate captains. But there was only room for one top dog.
The charged situation wasn't helped by the fact that, between the two,
300–400 heavily armed pirates were going ashore in Nassau. With just
a handful of shacks there selling drink, fighting was almost inevitable.
It didn't help that one of the two groups was awash with plunder. These
crewmen weren't exactly the kind of people to shy away from a fight.
It was a certainty that Benjamin Hornigold and Henry Jennings and
their followers wouldn't get on. For the past few months, Hornigold
had ruled the island as a sort of piratical warlord, and the locals in New
Providence had tried to avoid provoking him. Now, in the time it took
for a sloop to glide through the sparkling blue waters of the harbour
and drop anchor, everything had changed.

Before that anchor dropped, Hornigold had spent the past two and a
half years building up his piratical business. Despite setbacks he'd just

reached a point where he had the ships and manpower he needed to take his enterprise to a new, more effective level. With a well-crewed and powerfully armed great sloop like the *Benjamin*, he could undertake extensive cruises throughout the Caribbean, venturing as far as the Spanish Main or the West Indies. He could also range up America's Atlantic seaboard, and prey on shipping off busy ports like Charles Town, Philadelphia or New York. Until now, his insistence that he was still a privateer had tied his hands slightly. Clearly, Hornigold still wanted to maintain this illusory status – his recent return of the captured sloop *Mary* to Jamaica demonstrated that – but if his crew forced him to attack British shipping too, then his potential for prize-taking would expand dramatically.[1]

The arrival of Henry Jennings in early January 1716 completely scuppered Hornigold's plans. Where before, Hornigold had the muscle to control Nassau and use New Providence as his own personal base, he now found himself overshadowed by this new rival. If it came to a fight between the two crews – Hornigold's 'Flying Gang' and Jennings' treasure salvors – the newcomers not only had numbers and probably experience on their side, but Jennings appeared to have been the more ruthless of the two. So, he would have no qualms about using violence to overpower his newfound rival. The prize, of course, was control of Nassau. With it came the use of a reasonably well-fortified base, a small but growing community which was willing to support and trade with the pirates, and the ability to operate in a place which was effectively beyond the reach of the authorities. Now Jennings rather than Hornigold would be the top dog in Nassau.[2]

Hornigold was certainly no fool, and he made his peace with Jennings. It is unclear whether they knew each other, as they had been in Jamaica at the same time. Although they were both mariners, they moved in very different circles. Henry Jennings was a landowner and had powerful connections among Jamaica's elite circle – the men who made up the Jamaican Assembly. It seems he also had the ear of Governor Hamilton, a man who, just a few weeks before, had acquired a substantial stake in Jennings' salvage expedition, and then gave it a veneer of validity by granting Jennings a Letter of Marque as a pirate-hunter. Hornigold, on the other hand, had only a Letter of Marque as a privateer, which had become invalid following the Peace of Utrecht signed almost three years before. Hornigold was also self-made – a largely uneducated sailor from East Anglia who'd worked hard to get where he was.[3]

It's hard not to feel a little sympathy for Hornigold. Jennings' arrival not only usurped his authority in Nassau, but it also risked dividing his own men – his self-styled Flying Gang. After all, they were now officially pirates, while Jennings and his men were pirate-hunters, and had a Letter of Marque to back it up. It would have been inevitable that some of Hornigold's gang would desert him and side with Jennings, just to stay on the right side of the law. The tension in Nassau during those days in early January must have been high – and ready to boil over. Fortunately for Hornigold, it soon became clear that Jennings had little interest in bringing pirates to justice. His whole aim was to use Nassau as a secure base where he and his men could divide their plunder without interference from any authorities, and then finish the last part of their arrangement with Lord Hamilton. Starting a piratical civil war was in nobody's interests.

So, from the start of 1716, Henry Jennings was the *de facto* ruler of the pirate haven that was Nassau. And, after assuring his dominance over Hornigold, Jennings must have told his men to avoid needless confrontation. Instead, the two crews fraternized, seemingly without any major incident. Meanwhile, Jennings divided the plunder from the Spanish Treasure Fleet between his men, setting aside the share for Lord Hamilton and the other backers in Jamaica. Around that point Jennings commandeered a small Cuban-built sloop from Hornigold, a Spanish prize he'd captured late the previous year, but hadn't manned. Poor Hornigold couldn't even show his indignation for fear of losing his best vessel, the newly acquired sloop *Benjamin*. That at least left the Flying Gang the wherewithal to go out hunting again.[4]

After two weeks in Nassau, Jennings left for Jamaica in his sloop *Barsheba* with a crew of around 50 men. The rest stayed in Nassau. In the *Barsheba*'s hold was a small fortune – the Jamaican governor's share of the Spanish treasure. Jennings' legal status as a privateer was highly questionable, as was that of his partner, John Wills. After all, they'd stolen treasure in plunder from a foreign power, and had done it at gunpoint. Their privateering licences as pirate-hunters said nothing about stealing from the Spanish – but that was covered in the private arrangement between Jennings and Hamilton. So, as he made his way back to Jamaica, Jennings fully expected that the governor would be supportive.

The Spanish were less understanding. When the *Barsheba* was off the northern coast of Cuba she was spotted by a pair of Spanish vessels. She was clearly recognized, and the Spaniards shadowed her as she headed east into the Windward Passage. They kept tailing her all the way to the entrance to Port Royal and Kingston Harbour. They only turned away when they came within range of the gun batteries protecting the anchorage. This meant that not only was the *Barsheba* a marked vessel after leading the attack on the salvage camp, but now the Marquis de Casa Torres in Havana knew exactly where she had come from. As the *Barsheba* had entered port without being stopped, the Spanish understood that she'd been operating with the full connivance of the Jamaican governor.[5]

When the *Barsheba* arrived in Port Royal Jennings and his crew were safe from arrest, and the crew set about drinking and whoring their way through their share of the plunder. Jennings and Wills sought out Lord Hamilton and arranged the delivery of his substantial share of the plunder. It is very possible Jennings and Wills didn't tell Hamilton the exact details of how they'd acquired their loot. Even Hamilton would have been suspicious because they'd returned so quickly. If they'd actively been salvaging the shipwreck, then the whole process would have taken much longer, and an awful lot of hard work. Others in Jamaica would also have had their suspicions. This would have been particularly true of the members of the Jamaican Assembly, who were busy building a damning case against the governor. They must have been watching him like a hawk and would probably have known about his association with Jennings, and his newfound haul of specie.

The truth would come out soon enough, when the Marquis de Casa Torres sent his official letter demanding justice against Jennings and his pirate band who'd robbed the Spanish of the treasure. This, as the Marquis pointed out, amounted to theft from the King of Spain. Jennings was aware the other shoe was about to drop, so he badgered Hamilton for permission to leave on what he ironically claimed was an anti-piracy cruise. He actually hoped to have another crack at the treasure and be well clear of Jamaica when the real story emerged.

At the time, though, Jamaica was being swept by gold fever, as news of the attack on the salvage camp had spread through the island like wildfire.[6]

So, after a little over a month in Jamaica, Jennings sailed off again on 9 March in the *Barsheba* armed with his pirate-hunting Letter of Marque. His official privateering status was shared by Captain Leigh Ashworth, commanding another of Jennings' vessels, the 50-ton sloop *Mary*. The likelihood was that Lord Hamilton told Jennings to quietly leave Jamaica before the inevitable diplomatic storm broke. Besides, the Jamaican Assembly had already accused Hamilton of being in league with pirates. So, having Jennings out of the way was probably a good idea. Also accompanying Jennings were two other ships whose captains had no Letter of Marque to shelter behind: Samuel Liddell and the *Cocoa Nut*, and James Carnegie in the *Discovery*. In all, then, Jennings had four sloops under his command and around 200 men.[7]

Although Jennings planned to raid the Spanish treasure camps, he wasn't immune to temptation either. On 3 April they rounded the westernmost point of Cuba, Capo San Antonio, and turned north-east, following the line of the Cuban coast. This led directly to Jennings' capture of the two French vessels *St Marie* and the *Marianne*, outlined above. This was almost certainly an impulsive move by Jennings, but it was one that would cost him dear. The full story, however, was a little more complicated. They weren't the only predators in the area who were keen to capture the pair of French merchantmen. Indeed, they weren't the only ones who'd been raiding the Palmar de Ays.

The first of these predators was Samuel Bellamy, a native of Devon, who together with another salvor, Paulsgrave Williams, had gathered a band of men and went off 'wrecking'. From late January on they spent a few weeks picking through the wrecks of *la Regla* and the *San Roman* together with several other British salvors. On 22 January 1716, when Spanish reinforcements arrived from Havana, they were forced to stop their pillaging. So, Bellamy and Williams headed south to the Gulf of Honduras to gather their own reinforcements from the British logwood men who operated there. They fitted out two large *piraguas* and used them to capture two vessels – one Dutch and the other British. Bellamy and Willliams had moved from salvage to piracy.[8]

The British vessel was a sloop commanded by a Captain Young. The pirates forced him to take them to the Palmar de Ays. They headed north but had only got as far as the north-western coast of Cuba when they encountered Jennings and his four sloops. Jennings easily overhauled them, at which point Bellamy and Williams both jumped into the *piraguas* and paddled away upwind where the sailing ship couldn't follow. That left Young and his sloop for Jennings to deal with. Jennings simply took Young prisoner and added the sloop to his fleet. They then continued up the coast, and with the wind freshening, they headed for the safe anchorage of the Bahía Honda (Deep Bay), some 50 miles west of Havana. It was a remote spot, and its onion-bottle shape made it the perfect place to ride out the blow.[9]

That was where Jennings came upon the French merchant ship *St Marie* of La Rochelle. There was some dissent – after all, Carnegie and Liddell were there only to salvage the Spanish camps, not carry out acts of piracy. In the end, Liddell didn't join the others as darkness fell and they planned the attack. However, a little way out to sea Bellamy and Williams had been watching and realized these were fellow pirates not pirate-hunters. So, they rowed over to join them. It was soon decided they'd carry out a joint attack, with each *piragua* towing a sloop behind her. In the end, the mere sight of the pirates approaching was enough. After the attackers fired a volley of musketry, Captain d'Escoubet hauled down his colours.

So, it was an easy victory – and a clear act of piracy. This, though, was only the start. After a night of looting and drinking the pirates began interrogating the Frenchmen, who revealed that d'Escoubet had hidden a pay chest ashore. This was quickly recovered. At that point, in the late morning, a canoe was seen entering the bay. She glided up to the *St Marie*, and her crew of 19 men were taken prisoner. It turned out they were from another French ship, the sloop *Marianne*, which was anchored in Mariel Bay to the east, halfway between the Bahía Honda and Havana. They'd come to trade and exchange news with Captain d'Escoubet, but instead after a forcible interrogation they were pressed into service as guides. Jennings decided to capture this second French vessel.[10]

So, a *piragua* was crewed by Jennings' men, and it set off up the coast with Carnegie in command. This was all too much for Liddell, who quit the expedition, sailing off out of the bay in the *Cocoa Nut*, before heading back to Jamaica. He was distancing himself from this new and flagrant act of piracy. After Carnegie set off, Jennings and his men waited in the Bahía Honda for their shipmates to return with their prize. For just over a day, nothing happened. Then, that evening, they saw two sloops pass the entrance to the bay, heading west. One was the *Marianne*, which was identified by one of the French prisoners. The other was familiar to Jennings too. It was Benjamin Hornigold's great sloop *Benjamin*. Jennings' juicy prize had been taken by his rival.

A furious Jennings immediately ordered the *Barsheba* to cast off and get under way. It took time to make it out through the bottleneck-shaped entrance to the bay, but once in the open sea the *Barsheba* put on all sail and gave chase.

Benjamin Hornigold hadn't had an easy time of it after Jennings left Nassau. There was already a slow but steady stream of newcomers arriving by trading sloop, canoe or longboat. The onset of gold fever, though, had changed this dramatically. After Jennings' arrival in Jamaica with some of his plunder the floodgates opened in earnest. Now just about everyone who had use of a boat of any description, or could steal one, headed to Florida. Many came from places like Jamaica and Bermuda, or even Saint-Domingue, but others made the trip down from Britain's North American colonies – including men like Bellamy and Williams, who encountered Jennings off Cuba in early April.

Then, in late January, Captain Ayala Escobar arrived off the Palmar de Ays with troops to protect the salvage camps. Patrols were sent out to deter the wreckers, and in early February, when a second contingent of Spanish troops arrived, the wreckers were forced to abandon their salvaging. Inevitably, they then pitched up in the Bahamas. Equally predictably, most of them descended on Nassau. The small waterside shanty town was gradually transforming itself into a sort of boom town, not unlike those that sprang up in California during the Gold Rush of the mid-19th century. Many of these new arrivals were mariners of various kinds, including deserters from the Royal Navy, logwood cutters from the Gulf of Honduras, or men who had walked off their merchant ships to join the treasure hunt.[11]

Others had no real connection with the sea. These included runaway slaves, criminals, indentured servants, and even shopkeepers, clerks, labourers, apprentices and army deserters. They shared the same dream – they were adventurers all, in search of Spanish gold. What they found, though, was a string of lucrative wreck sites which were far too heavily guarded by the Spanish to let them hunt for treasure there among the surf. Instead, they hung around Nassau, looking for work of any kind, or an opportunity to make easy money, legally or otherwise. After all, they'd all travelled there to loot and steal from the Spanish. It wasn't a particularly big leap for them to steal from anyone else.

For the New Providence settlers or semi-permanent residents, this was something of a disaster. One of them, John Vickers, was a seaman on the sloop *Mary*, when Hornigold captured her the previous November. He had been kicking his heels around Nassau ever since. In the summer of 1716, he gave a deposition to Governor Spotswood of Virginia, which told of the volatile powder keg that was Nassau that spring. He stated that 'There are at Providence about fifty men who have deserted the sloops that were upon the wrecks, and committ great disorders in that Island, plundering the inhabitants, burning their houses, and ravishing their wives.' Clearly this represented a major change in the status quo. When Hornigold was firmly in charge, he was able to maintain some sort of control over his men. These newcomers, though, out to plunder Spanish treasure, had nobody to check their behaviour.[12]

One of these newcomers was Thomas Barrow, a British seaman who had recently served as the mate on a Jamaican trading vessel. Barrow claimed that he'd run away from his brig, after stealing 'a Spanish Marquiss's money and effects'. According to Vickers he rose to prominence among these incomers, who'd arrived in Nassau to 'fish' the Spanish treasure wrecks. Like many of them, Barrow didn't have a vessel of his own. This didn't stop him boasting. That spring, in the absence of Jennings, Barrow emerged as the self-elected leader of these wreckers. As Vickers put it, he 'is the chief of them and gives out that he only waits for a vessell to go out a pirating'.

Apparently, he also claimed 'that he is Governor of Providence, and will make it a second Madagascar'. This was a reference to the island of Madagascar in the Indian Ocean, or more accurately St Mary's Island off its north-eastern corner, which evolved into a major privateering haven during the late 17th century. Henry Every was one of these 'Red Sea Rounders' – pirates of that time who preyed on Arabic, Indian or Persian shipping in the Red Sea. For a brief time, he and others of his kind used St Mary's as a base. Now the shipless Barrow wanted to turn Nassau into a similar pirate haven. To be honest, Nassau was already well on its way to becoming this kind of lawless place.

According to Vickers, Barrow told anyone willing to listen that more men like him were coming and would help transform the Bahamian port. Barrow 'expects 5 or 600 men more from Jamaica sloops to join in the settling of Providence, and to make war on the French and Spaniards, but for the English, they don't intend to meddle with them, unless they are first attack'd by them.' This was a repeat of Benjamin Hornigold's old deception, that by acting like licensed privateersmen of the last war, they would escape prosecution. This was nonsense of course – if caught they would be tried as pirates. Barrow's actions also didn't bear this claim out. In Nassau harbour, Barrow and his followers boarded and plundered a brig from New England commanded by a Captain Butler. Then they rowed out and took a trading sloop from Bermuda and beat up its master. They then held him for a week or so, before leaving him and his vessel alone, because Barrow had decided they didn't suit his purpose.[13]

This was an extremely worrying development. Barrow's boasting suggested a feeling among this motley crowd of incomers that mere salvage wasn't enough, especially now that the Spanish had begun to properly guard their wrecks. It shows that these men were just as willing to turn to piracy if the opportunity presented itself. Barrow's actions underlined the point. The real problem was that while for the moment Henry Jennings' men were bound together by the long-established rules of privateering, where orders were followed, these incomers didn't abide by any such code. Even Hornigold's Flying Gang were better disciplined, as they'd learned to cooperate, as a string of successes had demonstrated. Barrow and his newcomers would be a law unto themselves, whether at sea or ashore. The whole situation was spiralling out of control.

This may have been part of the impetus behind Hornigold putting to sea again on a spring cruise. The *Benjamin* slipped out of Nassau in late March and headed west into the Bahama Channel. Hornigold then turned southward to transit the Florida Straits, and by the start of April he was off Mariel, on the north-west coast of Cuba, some 20 miles west of Havana. On 8 April, when he investigated the round bay that led to the Cuban port, he spotted a French sloop lying at anchor. She was the *Marianne*, on her way from Saint-Domingue to New Orleans, commanded by Captain Gardeur, an ensign in the French Navy. The *Marianne* had only about 20 men on board, as the rest of his crew were off in the ship's boat, on a social trip to the *St Marie* in the Bahía Honda. So, outnumbered ten to one, Gardeur wisely decided to surrender to the pirates.[14]

Hornigold secured the prize and discovered she carried a valuable cargo – in a deposition to Lord Hamilton it was valued at £11,500. Then, putting a prize crew aboard the French sloop, he headed back out to sea with his prize and turned west, keeping close to the Cuban coast. He'd learned from his prisoners that another French ship was in the Bahía Honda, but when he arrived off the bay, he saw that other pirates had already captured her. Then he recognized one of the pirate sloops. It was Henry Jennings' *Barsheba*. Hurriedly, Hornigold gave the order to turn away from the bay and head out into the Florida Straits. Inevitably, Jennings gave chase.[15]

As Hornigold watched, the *Barsheba* and a second sloop emerged from the bay's narrow mouth. Presumably the other ship he'd seen – the French prize – would follow them out. However, neither Jennings nor Hornigold expected another act of blatant piracy would change the situation dramatically. Both Samuel Bellamy and Paulsgrave Williams were aboard the *St Marie* as she recovered her anchor and raised sail. Calling their own men together, they waited until the French prize was heading towards the bay's entrance. Then, at Bellamy's signal their men rose up and attacked Jennings' small prize crew. Within moments the *St Marie* was in the hands of the two opportunists.[16]

Their remaining *piragua* was being towed astern of their prize, so they stopped the ship and brought the large canoe alongside. Then, after transferring the plunder from the *St Marie* and scrambling aboard, they cast off. By the time the *piragua* reached the entrance of the bay, Jennings was about six miles away to the north-west. So, Bellamy, Williams and their men headed east along the coast, into the wind, and slipped away. In all, their haul was valued at around 28,500 pieces-of-eight. It was a superbly timed double-cross by the Bellamy crew. Meanwhile, away to the north-west, Jennings decided to give up the chase. Hornigold in the *Benjamin* and his prize the *Marianne* had too great a head start. So, Jennings turned the *Barsheba* and *Mary* about, working their way slowly back to the Bahía Honda.

He was a little concerned the *St Marie* hadn't joined him, but at least he hadn't seen her leave the bay. When he finally reached the French prize, he learned what had happened – Bellamy's men had captured them, disarmed them and then stolen all of the plunder. Jennings was furious – he'd been made to look a fool in front of his own crew. When the hapless remaining *piragua* returned from its abortive raid on Mariel, Jennings cut the canoe to pieces and killed any of Bellamy's men who were unlucky enough to be aboard her. He also turned on Captain Young, whose only crime was to be kidnapped by Bellamy, along with his sloop. Young and his remaining crew were set ashore, while Jennings had the sloop burned to the waterline. Bellamy and Williams had got away with it – for now – but as far as Jennings was concerned, they were dead men walking.[17]

As darkness fell, the two pirates were delighted with the success of their audacious theft. At that point, their *piragua* was intercepted by Hornigold's *Benjamin*, somewhere off Mariel. After some discussion, Bellamy and Williams decided to join forces with Hornigold. Their *piragua* was secured to a towing line astern, her loot was stowed in the sloop, and the two groups spent the rest of evening swapping accounts of their brushes with Jennings. The next morning Hornigold gave Bellamy command of the sloop *Marianne*. He must have recognized the potential of a leader in the 27-year-old mariner. Then the two ships sailed together in consort, cruising off the western end of Cuba.[18]

Although the normally busy sea lane remained empty, they did come upon one sail, which turned out to be another pirate ship – the eight-gun sloop *Postillion*, commanded by Olivier Levasseur. Despite Hornigold's pretence of being a privateer, still waging war against Britain's old enemies, he and Levasseur got along and eventually decided to cruise together. In some sources Levasseur is nicknamed *La Buse* ('buzzard'), but in others this becomes *La Bouche* ('mouth'), which somehow seems more convincing. He had a reputation for his verbal skills, and he probably sweet-talked Hornigold into working with him. Like Hornigold, Levasseur had been a privateer who had turned pirate when the war ended. So they had that in common, although Levasseur had given up any remaining pretence of operating as a privateer. He and Hornigold would hunt together as pirates for another four months.[19]

The cruise itself proved unremarkable. Their first prize was a ship, intercepted in the 100-mile-wide Straits of Yucatán between Mexico's Yucatán Peninsula and the western end of Cuba. She turned out to be an English logwood ship, sailing from Campeche to the Netherlands. Hornigold wouldn't have made her a prize, but his men overruled him.

It seems Bellamy, Williams and Levasseur all agreed with Hornigold's men. So, the English ship was plundered, then ordered to join them, at least for a while. Three days later, off Cabo Corrientes, they came upon two Spanish brigs, laden with cocoa. These were both captured and plundered. This, at least, was an attack they could all support.[20]

By early May they found themselves off the Isla de los Piños (Isle of Pines), off the south-western coast of Cuba. In the sheltered anchorage there, off Siguanea, they found a group of English sloops at anchor. Their crews were taking on water and chopping firewood. Hornigold needed to careen the *Benjamin*. Without scraping the marine growth and barnacles off the underside of her hull, she would become slow and sluggish. His privateering illusion didn't stop him pressing the British seamen there to help do the work. Once the *Benjamin* was grounded and laid on her side, Hornigold had his first good look at her hull. It wasn't in good condition – in fact, without some major re-planking she would begin leaking, or even risk foundering. Still, without access to a shipyard there wasn't anything he could do about it. So, after careening and releasing the British seamen, the cruise continued.[21]

They moved east along the southern coast of Cuba. The plan was to base themselves in Hispaniola, where Levasseur knew of a good lair they could use for attacks on shipping in the busy Windward Passage. First, though, Hornigold needed to get rid of his cargo of plunder. The hold of the *Benjamin* was filled with goods taken from their prizes. So, before they began their hunt of the Windward Passage, Hornigold insisted on returning to New Providence. There he could sell his cargo, and either try to repair his great sloop or else sell her off. In any case, around the end of May Hornigold and Levasseur parted company, with promises to reunite after the visit to Nassau. Hornigold had no idea what to expect in Nassau if Jennings was there. It didn't help that he still had the *Marianne* with him. Jennings wouldn't like being reminded of that frustrating incident off the Bahía Honda.[22]

After Bahía Honda Jennings returned to Nassau in the *Barsheba*, accompanied by the *Mary* and the French prize *St Marie*, now stripped of its plunder. His men weren't particularly pleased she had been stripped of her valuables, but they were probably more sanguine about it than their captain. On 22 April they entered the harbour, making a fine sight. The large, ship-rigged *St Marie* was especially impressive, as Jennings had armed her with guns taken from other prizes, stowed in the holds of the sloops instead of ballast. Now she carried 32 guns of various sizes and so looked more like a powerful naval frigate than the French merchant ship she was. After dropping anchor, Jennings and his fellow captains went ashore, to enjoy the greatly improved delights of Nassau, which now boasted tented brothels as well as wood-shack and palm-frond taverns.[23]

The *St Marie* was left in charge of Jennings' quartermaster, Allen Bernard. A few days later he went ashore, searching for Jennings. Since they'd come in, most of the crew of the little flotilla were left on board their ships, and they'd grown restless. When he found his captain, Bernard reported that men from the *Barsheba* had gone aboard the *St Marie* and were ransacking her. When Bernard refused to return and deal with it, a drunken Jennings claimed ill health, and wouldn't face his mutinous crewmen. However, Leigh Ashworth and James Carnegie were more responsive, and returned with Bernard to quell the revolt. There they found men had been ferrying goods ashore and were stacking them in piles on the beach of nearby Hog Island. The three officers were helplessly outnumbered. All they could do was watch.[24]

The root of the problem was the division of the spoils. If the *St Marie* was taken back to Jamaica to be condemned as a legal prize by the Vice Admiralty court, the men feared they'd lose their share, as it would be discovered the ship had been taken illegally. So, they wanted their share of her cargo before she left Nassau. In the end they hired a small local sloop, the *Dolphin*, to transport the cargo to Jamaica for them. Ironically, its master was Neal Walker, the son of the former judge, privateer and vigilante. This move by the crew shows deep divisions opening in Jennings' band of salvors. Now that Jennings had crossed the line into piracy, a lot of his men wanted out.

When he sobered up, Jennings realized he couldn't stop this. So, he decided to make the best of a bad situation. He had his quartermasters Joseph Eels of the *Mary* and Allen Bernard draw up a false cargo manifest, while Jennings wrote letters for them to take to his business associates and government contacts in Jamaica. Then the *Dolphin* left for Jamaica. At this stage Jennings couldn't know how the arrival of the sloop would be received in Jamaica. He would either cover his tracks, and keep his status as a privateer, or he'd be branded a pirate. Depending on the political situation there, it could go either way.[25]

That done, Jennings had to regain control of his men. His best course, he felt, was to lead them on another raid on the Spanish salvage camps. Rumour had it that the Spanish had gone. This time, though, Jennings wouldn't be raiding them alone. No fewer than 24 vessels of various types accompanied him on the short voyage across the Bahama Channel. When they reached the Palmar de Ays they found the rumours were true – the salvage camps were deserted, and the soldiers had gone. A handful of patrol ships guarded the coast, but they withdrew when the Bahamian armada appeared. So, as soon as they landed, the Bahamians, along with several groups of treasure hunters from Jamaica, were free to 'fish' the wrecks.

The looting didn't go that well, as the Spanish had already cleared the beaches of specie. The poorly equipped British wreckers were reduced to wading in the shallows, or combing rock pools. Only Jennings had the ability to do more, as he still had his group of 14 former pearl divers with him. According to the *Barsheba*'s surgeon, John Cockrane, they were able to recover some coins from the water. Still, it wasn't the haul Jennings had hoped for. That done, Jennings then led his three ships to the south-west, heading towards the Windward Passage and then on to Jamaica. He still felt his association with Lord Hamilton would allow him to make a profit on the cargo sent ahead in the *Dolphin*, and on the sale of the *St Marie*. Unfortunately for Jennings, he was sailing into the middle of a major political storm.[26]

Governor Hamilton was fighting a rearguard action against the Jamaican Assembly, and by the time Jennings arrived the Bahamian sloop *Dolphin* had already reached Jamaica, adding fuel to the political fire. Her hold was filled with goods plundered from the French ship, which were viewed with suspicion by the Jamaican authorities. Neither Lord Hamilton's nor Jennings' Jamaican backers and contacts could protect the privateer from this legal irregularity, and so a swift condemnation of the prize in Jamaica's Vice Admiralty court was unlikely. This became an impossibility when the French intervened, sending a delegation to Lord Hamilton, demanding their stolen ships and cargoes back. It seemed Jennings was the scapegoat for both captures – his own *St Marie* and the *Marianne*, which Hornigold had taken. To make it worse, the French governor of Saint-Domingue even suggested the so-called privateer's Jamaican estates should be sold, by way of reparation.[27]

This, together with the complaints against Jennings from the Spanish governor of Cuba, amounted to a damning body of evidence against the privateer. The case was clear. Britain, France and Spain were at peace. His Letter of Marque allowed him to attack only pirates, not former national enemies. So, in looting the salvage camp at gunpoint the previous December, Jennings and his followers had acted like criminals rather than privateers. As this crime was essentially committed on a beach, the Admiralty Court in London viewed it as an act of piracy. Similarly, there was no excuse for his attack on the *St Marie*. She wasn't a pirate ship, or even a pirate prize. The only pirates there, according to the law, were Jennings and his crew.

Seeing the way things were developing, Jennings went into hiding, probably somewhere close to Bluefields, where the *Barsheba* and *Mary* were anchored. The *St Marie* had been taken to Port Royal for condemnation in the Vice Admiralty court, so that was now out of reach. It would, inevitably, be returned to its French owners, as would the cargo unloaded from the *Dolphin*. In late July, when Lord Hamilton was arrested by the members of the Jamaican Assembly, Jennings' pirate-hunting Letter of Marque was cancelled. In any case, by that point it had become worthless, as Jennings was viewed as a pirate himself. So, within a week or so of Hamilton's arrest, Jennings and his followers slipped out to sea to escape the inevitable wrath of the judiciary. The final blow came in mid-August 1716, when Henry Jennings was officially declared a pirate, along with his captains Leigh Ashworth, James Carnegie and John Wills. Jamaica, once a friendly base, was now closed to all pirates – especially Henry Jennings.[28]

In early June Hornigold's great sloop *Benjamin* arrived in Nassau. Hornigold had recently left his pirate colleagues Samuel Bellamy and Olivier Levasseur in Saint-Domingue after a joint cruise around Cuba which had lasted for several weeks. His own French prize, the *Marianne*, remained with Bellamy and the rest of Hornigold's Flying Gang, who were kept busy preying on shipping in the Windward Passage. For Hornigold, this trip to Nassau was all about the *Benjamin*. The poor state of her timbers below the waterline meant that, as he couldn't dock her – because all civilized ports were closed to him – he needed to get rid of her. The pirate soon learned of the trouble caused by Thomas Barrow and his wreckers, although many of them seem to have left for Florida, tagging along with Jennings' three ships when they left to 'fish' the wreck sites.

After a few days, Hornigold found a suitably gullible buyer for the *Benjamin* – Captain John Perrin of Gloucester, Virginia, a trading captain who was just as happy to buy Hornigold's stolen French and Spanish cargo she carried in her hold. Hornigold didn't sell her guns, though, and once the sale was made, he bought a much smaller sloop, the 30-ton *Adventure*, and set about turning her into a well-armed pirate vessel. She wasn't nearly as large and prestigious as the *Benjamin*, and after witnessing the transaction, Thomas Walker wrote of Hornigold that it had 'disabled him from doing such damages upon the high seas as he would have done if he had continued his command'. This, too, would have reduced Hornigold's stock within Nassau's pirate community. For him it was a necessary evil, as if he'd kept the *Benjamin*, then, without being able to repair her, he risked foundering in mid-ocean.[29]

Around the end of June, Hornigold and his crew left Nassau and headed back to Levasseur's hidden lair in Saint-Domingue. That meant that this revamped Flying Gang had around 200 men and three sloops at their disposal – the French prize *Marianne*, commanded by Bellamy, the *Postillion* under Levasseur, and Hornigold's new sloop, the *Adventure*. In Hornigold's absence, the others had preyed on shipping passing through the Windward Passage, and neither pirate crew had cared much about the nationality of their victims. Hornigold was annoyed to discover a handful of British ships had been stopped and ransacked. Despite everything, Hornigold was still keen to maintain his imaginary position as a privateer, while his colleagues – indeed most of his Flying Gang – wanted to attack whatever juicy vessels they could find. This would inevitably lead to a confrontation.

Sure enough, during a cruise that August the three captains came across another British ship. Hornigold refused to attack her, while Bellamy and Levasseur had no such qualms. They, after all, were true pirates. This refusal to take part in the attack proved too much for Hornigold's crew, and once back in Saint-Domingue they took a collective stand and demanded to hold a vote. There were roughly 120 men in the crew, and when the vote was called, over three-quarters of them voted to overrule Hornigold. From now on they'd attack whomever they liked. When Hornigold refused to accept their ruling, they discussed what to do next. After all, the sloop *Adventure* belonged to Hornigold – it wasn't a shared asset. In the end, most of them – all the men who voted to hunt any ship they wanted – elected to jump ship. They would leave Hornigold's *Adventure* and join the crew of the *Marianne* or *Postillion* instead.[30]

Hornigold was left with his sloop and just over two dozen crew – men who'd stayed loyal to him during the voting. He returned to Nassau, chastened and soured by this taste of betrayal. For his old crew, they could now serve under men who wouldn't hesitate to attack any prize they came across. This parting of the ways had also broken up a powerful pirate union. Earlier that summer, those three pirate sloops could have achieved a lot. Now, without Hornigold's drive, the others seemed to lack the motivation to push themselves. For the next few weeks Bellamy and Levasseur continued to prowl the waters of the Windward Passage, but they didn't come across much more than small trading craft. So, in September they decided to head east to the West Indies. From there they would continue down to the Spanish Main. These, they thought, were perfect pirate hunting grounds.[31]

Meanwhile, in late August Hornigold's *Adventure* arrived back in port in Nassau, with just 26 crew on board. Once there, Hornigold set about recruiting a new crew. Inevitably, he also encountered Henry Jennings – the first time the two rivals had met since the Bahía Honda affair. By that stage, though, although there was no trust and very little respect between them, Nassau had changed, and both pirate captains felt their old mantle had slipped a little. So, it made sense to co-exist, at least until they'd recovered their former status. The old rivalry was set aside – at least for the moment. Instead, they would 'rub along' – get along with each other because they had to. Together they had a chance of imposing some sort of order over the chaos that was Nassau, and of creating a pirate haven that suited them, rather than one that pandered to the needs of Thomas Barrow and his dissolute 'wreckers'.[32]

FIVE

Profile of a Pirate

B Y 1 7 1 7 I T W A S clear that there was a pirate problem in the Americas. The growing number of attacks attested to that, and merchants and shipowners began to feel the pinch as insurance premiums increased markedly for voyages in American waters. For most people, it was hard to gauge the scale of the problem, especially at first. What we know about pirate attacks comes mainly from the depositions of the merchant vessels' masters. Essentially, these are crime reports, describing who robbed them and exactly what happened. Another source is the letters from colonial governors or naval officers, writing to their masters in London, to describe the scale of the pirate problem in their own corner of the Americas. Finally, there are the newspapers, which from 1716 on became increasingly full of salacious snippets of information, describing pirate attacks and what happened to their victims.[1]

This all helps to work out the crime patterns – which pirates were at sea, where they were operating and how successful they were. Looking for information about the pirates themselves is a much harder business. For that we must turn to the reports of pirate trials and the recorded statements made by pirates facing the gallows. Most of those last-minute confessions were invented – the work of the likes of clergymen who wanted to demonstrate remorse and repentance on the steps of the gallows, or newspapermen eager to shock and titillate their readers.

We also have the work of Captain Charles Johnson, whose 1724 best-seller, *A General History of the Pyrates*, contains revealing snippets that tell us something about pirate crews, how they operated and what drove the pirates to a life of crime on the high seas. For more we have to dig a little deeper. Even in the early 18th century it was considered bad form to hang somebody without working out who they were. So, the records of Vice Admiralty courts are often a real treasure trove of information. If a pirate crew were caught, then the men would usually be examined. Their statements were written down, and many of these have survived. Not only does this help flesh out our understanding of what these pirates did before they were caught, but it also tells us a lot about age, nationality, maritime experience and the how and the why of their turning to piracy. Thanks to all that, we can build up something of a pirate profile.[2]

We can trace the rise of piracy in American waters to the aftermath of the War of the Spanish Succession. Although this increase didn't happen immediately after the Peace of Utrecht in early 1713, by the following year the number of pirate incidents were clearly on the rise. We can trace the activities of the pirate Benjamin Hornigold back to February 1714, when he was linked to 'several piracies'. Hornigold was only one pirate of several operating around that time. In that initial press report, he was linked to another pirate called West, 'and accomplices'. There were several others operating in the Caribbean around the same time, and this too is reflected in the newspapers. What set Hornigold apart was his association with Nassau. By turning the place into a secure pirate haven, Hornigold opened the door to what amounted to a growing stream of pirates.[3]

Many of these either joined Hornigold's crew or set up on their own, while basing themselves in the Bahamas. After all, it was an ideal spot: there was no legal authority there to stop them, and the archipelago was perfectly placed for cruises in the surrounding waters, including the Bahama Channel and the Windward Passage.

These early Bahamian pirates included men like Thomas Barrow, a former seaman and logwood cutter, who was desperate for his own craft, and John Cockram, who raided on his own account from August 1713 on, before joining forces with Hornigold. Cockram would go on to supervise the selling of Hornigold's stolen goods. Another of Hornigold's lieutenants was John West, who had commanded a large *piragua* while hunting with Hornigold in the Bahama Channel.[4]

Others would soon follow, the most notable of these being Henry Jennings. By 1716 at the latest, their number would include the likes of Edward Thatch (or 'Blackbeard'), Samuel Bellamy, Paulsgrave Williams and Olivier Levasseur. A report by privateering captain Mathew Musson, written in spring 1717 claimed that 'Five pirates made the harbour of New Providence as their Place of Rendezvous' and went on to name these 'commanders' as Benjamin Hornigold, Henry Jennings, Thomas Burgess, James White and Edward Thatch. In all, Musson claimed that these pirates had a combined strength of 360 men.[5]

By October 1717, an account claims this number had grown to around 800 men, while another from July places it at over 1,000. By that stage their ranks included pirate captains such as Nicholas Brown, Stede Bonnet, Josiah Burgess, Edward England, James (or Charles) Martel, Richard Richards, Charles Vane and Paulsgrave Williams. Many others would follow. In effect a whole spider's web of piracy was growing outwards from Nassau, to entangle much of the Caribbean and the Atlantic seaboard. Eventually it would spread to West Africa and even the Indian Ocean. At its centre was Hornigold, and to a lesser extent, Jennings.

As for the total number of pirates at sea, several figures have been proposed, but most historians agree that between 1714 and 1725 no more than 1,000–2,000 were active at any one time. This included those operating throughout the Americas, the West African coast and the Indian Ocean. Probably up to half of them were based in Nassau. In 1717 the Philadelphia merchant James Logan estimated that 1,500 were active in American waters. Of these, around 800 were based in the Bahamas. When the frigate HMS *Phoenix* put into Nassau in February 1718, to officially promulgate news about a royal pardon to the pirates, her captain estimated the number of pirates at 'about 500, all Subjects of Great Britain, and young, Resolute, Wicked fellows'.[6]

Writing in 2004, the historian Marcus Rediker examined the number of pirates operating during this period. After considering these same sources, he wrote 'These figures seem broadly accurate. From records that describe the activities of pirate ships and from reports or projections of crew sizes, it appears that 1,500 to 2,000 pirates sailed the seas between 1716 and 1718, 1,800 to 2,400 between 1719 and 1722, and 1,000 in 1723, declining rapidly to 500 in 1724, to fewer than 200 by 1725 and 1726. In all some 4,000 went, as they called it, upon the account.' So, if we consider this a fair assessment, we can place the total number of pirates at large around the globe in 1717–18 at around 2,000, with around 800 based in Nassau if we take James Logan's estimate as accurate.[7]

We know from the depositions, newspaper articles, official letters and trial transcripts that most of these pirates operated in sloops. These vessels could vary greatly in size, from a dozen tons up to 100 tons. Some were too small to carry guns, while some, like Benjamin Hornigold's great sloop *Benjamin*, could mount up to 12 guns. From the evidence of Captain Musson we also have an idea of the size of a typical crew – around 65–100 men per sloop. That meant that approximately eight to 12 sloops were operating out of Nassau at the peak of its piratical activities, from late 1716 until early 1718. So, the whole pirate menace of this period was created by no more than a dozen pirate crews and pirate captains. The tally of vessels they attacked was somewhere in the hundreds. Seldom, then, have so few pirates had such a major impact on history. It is little wonder that the authorities regarded them as such a menace to the established order.

In 1724, when Captain Charles Johnson published *The General History of the Pyrates*, it became an instant best-seller. His publishers were delighted that so many people were fascinated by these tales of fearsome pirates defying society and cruising through exotic tropical waters. Part of the titillation these tales offered was that the lives of the pirates Johnson luridly described were so very different from those of the readers. By reading the book, people could experience a little touch of escapism, both from the tight confines of 18th-century decency and social norms and from the drabness of their everyday lives. Perhaps the same fascination lies behind the popularity today of television shows about serial killers, mafia bosses and drug lords.[8]

Many people would have read Johnson to understand how these pirates first took to their criminal calling. After all, the likelihood was that the pirates would be caught at some point and would face trial and execution. Becoming a pirate meant that the seaman would immediately sever all ties with his former life. At that moment, when he stepped over the line of legality, he would never be able to see his family again, walk through the streets of a bustling port, or share yarns in harbour taverns. He was now an outcast, excluded from all contact with the so-called civilized world. Why then, during the early 18th century, did so many young seamen take such a drastic step? The simple answer was the combination of freedom, plunder and excitement that a pirate life offered them.

For those willing to come, the word spread throughout the ports of the Caribbean and the American seaboard that the Bahamas were a pirate haven. Some were drawn there by the chance of plunder, adventure or simply a chance to escape the banality of their lives. For a few this would have been temptation enough for them to sign up with a pirate crew, if they'd take them. Most of the men who made up the dozen or so pirate crews in Nassau would have been experienced and highly trained young seamen, in the prime of their lives. While most pirates would have been seamen, others came as well – logwood cutters, fishermen, or even untrained landsmen – if they had other redeeming qualities, such as strength, agility or handiness in a fight.[9]

While the initial wave of Nassau pirates tended to be seamen who were already known to each other, later far more were recruits, invited to join a pirate crew when the merchant ship they were on was captured. They would soon be amalgamated into the crew, and then the whole process was repeated when another prize was captured, and her crew were given the same option. Unwillingness to join the pirates was rarely met with hostility. The choice in almost all cases was a completely voluntary one. Many even begged the pirates to accept them into their crew. A few, though, such as the carpenters forced to join Samuel Bellamy's crew, had no option as the pirates decided they needed their set of skills.

The chain that volunteering created could stretch for some considerable length. For instance, in 1718 the small-time Nassau pirate Christopher Winter, a Bahamian pirate who had sailed with Benjamin Hornigold, captured a British sloop from Jamaica between the Bahamas and Cuba. The sloop's first mate, Edward England, promptly volunteered to join Winter's crew. Then, when Winter decided to leave the Bahamas for Cuba, England and a group of others split away from the original crew and went their own way. In late 1718 England captured a ship off the West African coast, and one of the volunteers from her crew was the Welsh seaman Howell Davis. Almost immediately afterwards, Davis and a few others broke away from England's crew but were captured and imprisoned in Barbados; they were spared a hanging on the promise that they'd accept a pardon. Davis, however, had no intention of ending his newfound piratical career.[10]

On his release Davis gathered a new crew – a group of seamen that included Thomas Anstis and Walter Kennedy. In early 1720 Davis captured a slave ship off the Guinea coast, and one of her crew, Bartholomew Roberts, volunteered to join Davis' crew. This was the next link in the chain. Kennedy later served with Roberts, while Anstis broke away to become a pirate captain in his own right. Another seaman, John Phillips, was captured by Anstis off Newfoundland, thereby creating another link in this chain of volunteers. This chain ended with Phillips, though, as he was captured and subsequently died in a prison revolt. The sequence this highlights is a striking one that helped perpetuate the existence of the pirate menace for years, often long after the original pirates in the chain were dead or had hauled down their black flag.[11]

This trend certainly worried the authorities. Several governors and other colonial officials wrote to London expressing their concern. For example, in 1718 Colonel Benjamin Bennett of Bermuda wrote, 'I fear they [the pirates] will soon multiply for so many are willing to joyn with them when taken.' If these volunteers were captured soon afterwards, they could claim with all sincerity they were pressed into service by the pirates. However, the judicial authorities who tried these men knew that pirate crews rarely recruited sailors against their will. So, most of the pirates who tried this defence were strung up with the rest of their shipmates.[12]

As the pirates operated farther afield from the Bahamas, they came across new groups of mariners willing to join them. One of these groups were fishermen, whose hard lives made work aboard a pirate ship seem preferable to eking out an existence in the cold, stormy seas of the Newfoundland fishing grounds. Johnson claimed that British ocean-going fishing vessels and whalers 'transport over a considerable Number of poor Fellows every Summer, whom they engage at Low Wages, and are by their Terms to pay for Passage back to England'. Given this, the arrival of a pirate ship in their fishing grounds offered a unique opportunity to escape from all that.[13]

Although most of the original group of Nassau pirates didn't turn to piracy through mutiny, many others did. Rediker estimated that 'At least thirty-one mutinies erupted on merchant ships during the 1710s and 1720s, many of them occurred on vessels involved in the African slave trade.' Once they'd taken that step, the mutineers were already facing justice at the end of a rope. So, piracy was probably the only option open to them. This was especially true if the mutiny had been a bloody affair. Johnson recounts one of the bloodiest in November 1724, aboard the merchantman *George Galley*: 'Ten that night was the time they fixed for their bloody execution, when all the persons to be sacrificed were asleep, except Captain Fernau who then had the watch on deck. Accordingly, Winter went down to Thomas Guy the surgeon, Peterson to the chief mate Bonadventure Jelph, and Daniel MacCawley to the poor scriven, and presently cut their throats.'[14]

This was a particularly brutal and premeditated mutiny, orchestrated by the second mate, the Orcadian John Gow – and it was only the start of the bloodshed. Johnson continued, 'In the meanwhile Melvin and Rawlisson seized the captain to throw him overboard, but in struggling he got away from them.' One of the pair slashed at his captain's throat with his knife but failed to kill him. Then the pair 'laid hold of him again, and endeavoured to throw him into the sea, but [was] still struggling with his murderers [when] Gow came up with a pistol and shot him through the body.' After that, the mutineers confined the rest of the crew in their hammocks until they'd secured the ship. Then, after declaring Gow to be their new captain, they all agreed to become pirates.

These mutineers were seamen, which made them prime candidates for a pirate crew. Less sought after were landsmen, but these too flocked to Nassau in search of a berth aboard a pirate ship. Many of the landsmen were indentured servants, forced to work off the cost of their passage by several years' worth of labour. Many people in early 18th-century Europe entered indentured servitude in the first place to avoid grinding poverty at home, seeing it as a chance to make a fresh start in the New World. It was soon found, however, that the chances of making it on your own without money were slim. These, though, were the lucky ones.[15]

At least they'd entered indentured servitude voluntarily. Others were forced into it, and were shipped to the American colonies or the West Indies in chains as a result of crimes committed back home. For example, Jacobite sympathizers caught up in the aftermath of the failed 1715 Jacobite rebellion found themselves shipped off across the Atlantic as indentured servants. For the authorities in Britain, this had the added bonus of removing people whom they deemed politically suspect. The same applied to agrarian agitators or those fighting for improved working conditions.

The average length of voluntary indenture was two or three years. For convicted felons or political prisoners, this could be significantly longer – often a decade or more. Given the climate of the West Indies or even the Carolinas, this usually amounted to a death sentence. It is easy to see why many indentured servants wanted to escape. For many this meant escaping one of the sugar islands by sea, taking passage in a vessel whose captain and crew didn't ask too many questions. Of course, it would help if the runaway was a sailor, but well-built landsmen could also be useful if they showed an aptitude to be trained in the skills of seamanship. Ultimately, many runaway servants headed to Nassau, which they saw as a place where they'd finally be free.[16]

To some extent the same principle also applied to West African slaves. On some occasions, sizeable proportions of pirate crews were made up of former African slaves who had either managed to run away, or who'd been captured while being transported in a slaver and been offered the chance to join a pirate crew. This, though, was rare. West African slaves were considered less useful to pirate crews than untrained landsmen, due to the cultural and linguistic barriers that existed between the two groups. If freed or runaway slaves showed skills as mariners, or the ability to fight, then they were usually recruited. At one stage in 1718, Blackbeard commanded a sloop where over half of his crew were of African descent. For most pirates, it seems that skin colour was no real barrier to membership of a pirate crew.

If they lacked any suitable skills, some of these runaways could be used as menial help on board pirate ships. In time, like other former slaves who had maritime experience, they would eventually become fully integrated members of the crew. In 1718 Governor Nicholas Lawes of Jamaica wrote to the Council of Trade to complain about the problem of slaves running away to sea: 'Those people have been so farr, from altering their evil courses and way of living and becoming an advantage to us, that the greatest part of them are gone and have induced others to go with them a pyrating, and have inveigled and encouraged severall negroes to desert from their masters.' This was concerning to the authorities as much because it undermined the social order of Britain's colonies as because it boosted the number of pirates at large in American waters.[17]

Several Caribbean islands had mixed-race communities, where groups of runaway slaves lived in the hills. These and other 'free' Africans found their way on board pirate ships. The only reason they often failed to appear in official records is because when they were captured, they were usually treated not as pirates, but as runaway slaves. They would be stripped, beaten and then returned to the auction block.[18]

In the 18th century, being a sailor was a young man's game. Most were in their mid to late 20s. This age range is borne out by the lists of pirates brought to justice. Some others were older, and probably more experienced. Because of this age gap, seamen in their 30s would probably exude an air of authority compared to their shipmates and would be the prime candidates for roles such as quartermaster, boatswain or gunner on board a pirate craft.[19]

As we've seen, in February 1718, when he visited Nassau, Captain Pearse of the frigate HMS *Phoenix* described the 500 pirates he encountered there as 'all Subjects of Great Britain, and young, Resolute, Wicked fellows'. This is interesting, as it suggests virtually all the pirates he encountered during his brief visit were British. However, court records often suggested a pirate crew was a little more diverse than that. From these records we can see that some pirates were French, Dutch, Danish, Portuguese, Spanish, Swedish or Portuguese, However, Pearse's term 'Subjects of Great Britain' was broader than the British Isles, as it embraced seamen from Britain's American colonies as well as Jamaica and the West Indies. Indeed, given the geographical and social links with New Providence, many of the pirates there – at least those who appear in the records – originally came from Jamaica.[20]

As for seamen from Great Britain itself, this seems to have followed the proportions of the populations that made up the United Kingdom. That meant the large majority were English, while a smaller number were Scottish or Welsh, and a sizeable portion came from Ireland. For the most part these seamen-turned-pirates hailed from Britain's port cities; the records show them coming from places like London, Bristol, Liverpool, Plymouth, Belfast, Cork, Dublin, Swansea, Leith and Aberdeen. Those coming from the American colonies tended to be from ports too, or island groups. As we have mentioned, Jamaicans predominated, followed by Barbadians, but a number also hailed from the colonies of Massachusetts, South Carolina, Rhode Island, Pennsylvania, Virginia and New York.[21]

In this respect a pirate crew would have reflected the make-up of most British-flagged ocean-going merchant ships of the day. While there may have been language differences, most of these seem to have been overcome. This was especially true for a predominantly French crew, such as that of Olivier Levasseur's sloop *Postillion*. When up to 50 pirates from Benjamin Hornigold's pirate sloop *Adventure* transferred into the French sloop, they seem to have melded easily into the predominantly French ship's company. It was almost as if they were agreeing with the English government official who in 1697 claimed that pirates 'acknowledge no countrymen, that they had sold their country and were sure to be hanged if taken, and that they would take no quarter, but do all the mischief they could'.[22]

From this we begin to form a useful profile of the typical Nassau pirate of this period. He would most likely be a British-born seaman in his mid to late 20s, and, wherever he was born, he probably first went to sea aboard a merchantman sailing from a major British seaport such as London, Bristol or Dublin. By the time he became a pirate he had several years of experience before the mast, and was considered fit, agile and a prime seaman. He might have been disillusioned by the harsh conditions and treatment he experienced as a seaman, and he had a hardened dislike of authority, either afloat or ashore. The likelihood was his ship was taken by pirates, and at that point he volunteered to join their crew. He was well aware of what that meant in terms of cutting himself off from his past life, and the high chance that he faced death if caught. Still, he thought this was well worth the newfound freedoms he enjoyed under the black flag.

Whatever the reason a man had for turning to piracy, he would have been well aware that there was now little chance of returning to his former life. Even if he accepted a pardon, he'd still be marked as a troublemaker by any merchant captain or shipowner who was taking on new hands. This helps explain why many of the pirates who did accept pardons often drifted back into their old ways. For many, though, this break with so-called civilization was a conscious decision. It also meant an end to a life of harsh service before the mast, and a submission to an authority seen as unjust and uncaring. For many, it was much more preferable to live as a free man and pirate for a few months or even years, before inevitably succumbing to death in battle, disease or the hangman's noose.

We know from the statements given by pirates before and during their trials that for many their main motivation was the rejection of authority. They chose, through their own free will, to become pirates. In the early 18th century, the captain of a merchant had complete power over his crew. Some sadistic captains made life a living hell for their crew. Some of them literally got away with murder by driving men to their deaths, forcing them into the masts in a storm, or starving or beating them when they felt that punishment was needed to make them do their duty. Even if the captain were just and fair, his crew often had to contend with brutal or venal officers and boatswains. Corrupt captains, quartermasters or shipowners could deny men the food they needed or feed them rations that weren't fit for the ship's rats. When the voyage ended, the owners often found reasons to withhold a seaman's hard-earned wages.[23]

In July 1726, William Fly was tried as a pirate in Boston and found guilty. He was sentenced to be hanged on Boston's waterfront as a warning to other mariners who might consider turning to piracy. Condemned men were usually given the opportunity to say a few last words beneath the gallows. The authorities expected this would involve a display of remorse, or at least a blubbering plea for mercy. Fly had other ideas. He showed courage and composure to the end. He also took this last opportunity to tell the assembled crowds exactly what he thought of the system that had driven him to piracy. He proclaimed that 'All Masters of Vessels might take Warning by the Fate of the Captain that he had murder'd, and to pay Sailors their Wages when due, and to treat them better; saying, that their Barbarity to them made so many turn Pyrates.' With that he was hanged, remaining defiant to the very end.[24]

In his gallows speech, the pirate William Fly summed up his demand with the phrase 'Bad Usage'. By this he meant the often-shocking maltreatment of sailors by their captains, and the appalling conditions sailors often had to endure for little reward. His dying words beneath the gallows were a plea for justice. He died as he'd lived – a man fighting an unjust system that treated common sailors little better than animals. It is small wonder that many sailors of the time saw pirates as men fighting for sailors' rights, by attacking the ship captains and shipowners who benefited from a tyrannical and uncaring system. Of course, those in authority didn't always see things that way. When the merchant ship captain William Snelgrave was held captive by pirates off West Africa, he said of them, 'they pretend one reason for their villainies is to do justice for sailors'; their real motive, he thought, was a combination of laziness and greed.[25]

Still, the pirates had a point. For merchant or naval seamen, serving under a tyrannical captain could turn any voyage into a living hell. The captain had every right under the law to do what he liked. For example, Captain Haskins of the *Laventon Galley* was infuriated by an upper yardsman, John Phillips, when he didn't report on deck for an evening watch. So, Haskins went below decks and set about the sailor with a marlin spike as he lay sleeping in his hammock. He then sent the bloodied man aloft to set the topgallant, dressed only in his shirt and breeches. Phillips braved the freezing rain and swaying mast to perform his task but began convulsing in shock as a result of the assault. When his shipmates went aloft to help him down, Haskins shouted that he'd shoot the first man to help Phillips. The sailor survived, but only just. This brutality was far from unique. Accounts of sailors being beaten or whipped half to death for minor errors, or forced to spend whole days aloft in a gale, are not uncommon. Several statements made by pirates facing the gallows tell the same story. Many of them, it seems, were driven to desert and became pirates thanks to the brutality of those in authority.[26]

Shipowners and captains should have paid attention to these last words of condemned men. However, most of the time when seamen cited cases of brutality, or even murder, the Vice Admiralty courts sided with the ship captains. So, the complaints never came to trial. Wage regulations for seamen came into effect only in 1726, and although it was never officially admitted, the recent upsurge of piracy might have played its part in this much-needed legislation. By limiting the worst excesses of shipowners and captains, the authorities acknowledged the validity of some of the pirates' most common grievances.[27]

Until then, though, seamen continued to face the dangerous, harsh conditions of regular mercantile work, the brutality of captains and officers, and often short rations and the lack of proper pay at the end of it all. It was common practice to sign on for one voyage at a time. If a sailor caused trouble, he was never hired again, especially if word got out that a particular sailor was a troublemaker. If employment couldn't be found, then these seamen could face destitution in a port, becoming beggars or pickpockets to survive. Faced with this, it was easy to see how, if the opportunity presented itself, a sailor would be tempted to make his way to Nassau to join a pirate crew or agree to join one if his ship was taken by pirates on the high seas. In either case, life could hardly be worse.

Life was a lot different on a pirate ship, which was run along far more democratic lines, where every man had a say in just about everything the ship and its crew did. The only exception was during the chase of a prize and any subsequent battle. In those circumstances the authority of the pirate captain was total, and only he had the right to decide how to carry out the attack. Afterwards, the normal democratic system resumed, and if the crew felt unhappy about their captain's actions, then they could tell him, chastise him, or even vote to have him removed. This was a world away from the way merchant or naval ships were run. For probably the first time in his life, a sailor felt that his opinion counted, and that he had a say in his own future.

Meetings were held to decide the division of food and drink, the election of officers, where to hunt for prey, whether to attack a particular target, and what to do with a prize and its cargo when it was captured. Members of a crew even had a say in which volunteers to admit into their own ranks, the fate of any prisoners and the way any plunder was divided.

While a pirate captain might have undisputed authority on board his ship once the shot started flying, the rest of the time he was simply another voice among the many in the crew. Of course, this wasn't strictly true. Pirate captains were elected by the crewmen, and were usually men of experience, charisma and authority. So, it was unusual for a captain to be deposed without his crew having good reason. Typically, this could include a lack of success, timidity in action, the refusal to attack certain ships or a run of bad luck.[28]

The notion of electing officers would have been anathema to shipowners or merchant or naval officers, but for the pirates it played a key part in maintaining their freedom of will. A pirate captain was answerable to his men, and one who went against the wishes of his crew could expect trouble. Electing a captain was a straightforward business. The pirate Walter Kennedy recorded how it was done:

> They chose a captain from amongst themselves, who in effect held little more than that title, excepting in an engagement, when he commanded absolutely, and without control. Most of them having suffered formerly from the ill-treatment of their officers, provided carefully against any such evil, now they had the choice in themselves. By their orders they provided especially against quarrels which might happen among themselves, and appointed certain punishments for anything that tended that way; for the due execution thereof they constituted other officers besides their captain, so very industrious were they to avoid putting too much power into the hands of one man.[29]

Pirate captains had no special privileges. They shared the same fare as their shipmates, they ate with them, and often they didn't even have their own cabin. Even if they did, there was no guarantee of privacy, as the rest of the crew had as much right to sleep in the captain's cabin as he did. The captain's one great strength was that he had been elected to the job by a majority of his peers. He was probably older and more experienced than they were, and, by necessity, he had the skills needed to navigate using the stars, to chart a course, and to know his job as a mariner. This usually meant he had to have a modicum of education, and at the very least he needed to be able to read and write. Most sailors of this era didn't have any of these skills, which greatly limited the pool of possible candidates for captaincy. This, too, is why skilled and educated mariners were in high demand in Nassau.

Above all, a pirate captain needed to keep most of his crew on his side. He did this through bringing them success and plunder, or if necessary, by creating loyal factions he could rely on. Without this support he was liable to be unceremoniously demoted by his crew or cast ashore. The crew of Charles Vane marooned him on a deserted island, while the crew of Benjamin Hornigold refused to accept his reluctance to attack British ships. Naturally some captains were harder to remove from office than others – like Edward Thatch, who relied on ferocity to ensure a lack of opposition among his men. That said, even Blackbeard was afraid of being ignominiously ousted by his crew if prizes dried up.

In fact, the captain wasn't even the most influential figure on board a pirate ship. It was the quartermaster who really controlled the ship. He was responsible for keeping the peace on board and mediating in the event of a dispute. Once a prize was taken it was the quartermaster who supervised the division of the loot, and the storing of plunder on behalf of the crew until it was divided out. Above all, he was there to prevent the captain from assuming too much power. Like the captain, the quartermaster was elected by his shipmates, and he could be removed just as easily. He could also be promoted. If the pirate force expanded, a quartermaster was a prime candidate for election to any new command. That was as close as the Nassau pirates got to creating their own hierarchy – and it was a system that collectively they had full control over. This truly was democracy in action.[30]

Essentially, pirates were building their own social order – one freed from the constraints of class, convention and tradition. As a result, they went to great lengths to enforce their democratic rights. This meant they ensured they would remain free from the tyrannies they'd experienced at sea before turning to piracy. In effect, they created a democratic utopia for the common sailor, which turned the established order of things upside down. This is what the authorities feared even more than the disruption of mercantile trade. The pirate democracy smacked of a revolt against what the establishment regarded as the natural order of things; it was a dangerously radical trend that had to be stopped before it spread. It was this fear that explained why the British authorities went to great pains to stamp out the pirate menace with such force and urgency.

SIX

A Commune of Pirates

T HE NASSAU OF THE summer of 1716 was very different from
the place that existed just a year before. The sinking of the
Spanish Treasure Fleet saw to that. In the space of a year the sleepy,
run-down port that had served as a base for Hornigold's low-key piracy
operation had given way to something very different. Now it was a
bustling hive of activity, with numerous vessels filling its once near-
empty harbour, and the blackened ruins of the port itself had given
way to a shanty town of wood and canvas. More permanent buildings
were being thrown up, or the ruins of old ones were being rebuilt.
Taverns, brothels and gaming houses had sprung up, and plundered
cargo sat in piles along the beach. In many ways it was a re-creation of
the long-lost buccaneering haven of Port Royal, only this time without
the thin veneer of legality and order that set Jamaica apart from New
Providence. For a few brief years, Nassau would be the biggest piratical
community in the world.

Before the Franco-Spanish raid of October 1703, the Bahamian island of New Providence was a backwater, but a reasonably self-sufficient one. It was the seat of government in the Bahamas, administered on behalf of the Lords Proprietors of Carolina. It was therefore an offshoot of what amounted to a private colony. Four decades earlier, in 1663, King Charles II had granted a charter to eight English noblemen to establish a colony in the Carolinas. These English grandees were absentee owners. Instead of managing the nascent colony themselves, they appointed a governor to do the job for them. Eventually a deputy governor was appointed to control the northern half of the colony, and in 1712 this was hived off to create two colonies – those of North and South Carolina.[1]

When the first group of Lords Proprietors died they passed on their position to their friends, heirs and relatives, or others they had business dealings with. What they didn't do was invest in their private colony or provide sufficient money for its defence or its economic development. They were happy enough, though, to benefit from the taxes and duties they gleaned from it. Inevitably there was a growing tide of resentment against these men, who acted like absentee landowners unwilling to maintain their property. Matters came to a head during Queen Anne's War (1702–13), when the colonists themselves had to repulse attacks by the French and Spanish with no help from the Lords Proprietors, and very little from the British government. At the same time, conflicts arose between the original settlers and plantation owners, who began altering the region's agrarian economy.

The Bahamas had already been colonized by the time Charles II issued his charter, with a struggling settlement established in Eleuthera. In 1666, three years after the Lords Proprietors' royal charter was signed, settlers arrived in New Providence and built a second fledgling colony there. Four years after that, in 1670, the English king extended the Lords Proprietors' charter to encompass the Bahamas. They decided to appoint a governor to administer the islands on their behalf, and one duly arrived in New Providence the following year. Most of these governors lasted just a short while before quitting their post. In 1694 the post was granted to Nicholas Trott, a tobacco trader from Bermuda, who had business links with the Lords Proprietors.[2]

This marked something of a boom time for the Bahamas. In New Providence, Trott encouraged new settlers by offering them parcels

of land, and, to reflect the royal coup of 1688, the Stuart-sounding
Charles Town was renamed Nassau in honour of the new Dutch-
born king, William III. However, Trott got little support from his
colony's absentee landlords; so, when Henry Every appeared, the
governor didn't feel he needed to be burdened by his duty to them
or to the English Crown. This brief association between pirate and
governor certainly boosted the Bahamian economy, but it also created
a precedent – an association with crime. The Bahamas already had a
name as being the refuge for those on the margins of colonial society.[3]

Governor William Beeston of Jamaica wrote a scathing description
of Trott and his successor, Nicholas Webb, saying that 'those [govern]
over a few barefoot people that get into those places to avoid their
debts, [and] take on them the title of Excellency and Captain General,
which to support, they squeeze and prejudice His Majesty's subjects
and authority. Whether they have any authority for those characters I
know not, but sure I am that it's a great diminution to those honourable
titles.' In other words, Beeston saw the Bahamian governors as little
more than pirates themselves, and any officials they appointed were
little more than charlatans compared to officeholders in properly
established crown colonies.[4]

The Franco-Spanish raid of October 1703 effectively finished off the
Bahamas as a viable colony. True to form, the Lords Proprietors had
done nothing to defend the place and, as the colony was a private one,
neither had the British government. Nassau was sacked and burned,
and the fort Governor Trott had painstakingly built out of local
stone was stripped of its guns. No effective rule was re-established
in the Bahamas, and the islands were left to fend for themselves. This
didn't mean that there wasn't a vestige of order and decency in the
place. Despite being private colonies, Vice-Admiralty courts had been
established, in both Charles Town in the South Carolina colony and
Nassau in the Bahamas. Although the Bahamian court's sessions ended
at the end of the war, the judge, Thomas Walker, still remained in New
Providence, and, as we've seen, he wasn't afraid to act as a law-and-
order vigilante if he saw it was necessary.

Over the previous half-century Bahamians had shown they weren't
averse to the 'fishing' of shipwrecks – it had formed a useful source of
income for the islanders for several decades. So too had smuggling,
and Harbour Island and Eleuthera were still benefiting from it. From

Governor Trott on, they'd also had a loose relationship with piracy. While honest men like Walker might not like it, the locals were no saints when it came to operating on the fringes of the law. The arrival of Jennings and his men in January 1716 marked a real turning point for Nassau and New Providence. Before that, Benjamin Hornigold's low-key version of piracy had benefited the economy of the islands, through his association with the smuggling communities of Eleuthera and Harbour Island. Walker had tried to stamp that out but had failed. Now, faced with this surge of unwanted humanity, he was powerless to stand up to them.

New Providence was no place for law, and certainly not one for order. It slid into chaos, one boatload of lawless incomers at a time. The men who pitched up in Nassau during this period were usually even more barefoot than the locals and had no desire to blend in with the islanders. Most had come to 'fish' the wrecks but were also willing to join up with any bands of pirates who offered them a berth. A line had been crossed when Jennings first arrived in Nassau. After that, the Bahamians were no longer in control of their own island. Instead, this burgeoning community of violent criminals, thieves, adventurers, profiteers, crooked merchants, prostitutes and the desperate represented little more than an anarchic mob, willing and able to tear everything down if it suited them.

Probably the worst of these incomers were the wreckers – a group of around 50 men who had turned up in Florida in late 1715 to 'fish' the wrecks, operating just out of reach of the Spanish salvors there. Then, in early 1716, they abandoned the shipwrecks and turned up in Nassau. Their back stories varied, but most were seamen who had jumped ship to hunt for treasure. They were the type of men Captain Balchen of the frigate HMS *Diamond* had warned about. In Colonial America 'fishing' wrecks was a common activity in the aftermath of a shipwreck, especially in the Outer Banks of the Carolinas or in the Bahamas. This could be done properly, with native divers or diving bells, or it could involve nothing more than bare hands, picks and crowbars. Most wrecked ships were merchantmen, with little of value on board. The Spanish treasure ships of the 1715 *flota* were the holy grail for these scavengers.

So, as treasure fever swept the Americas, seamen and settlers alike abandoned their usual work and headed to the Palmar de Ays. The legalities of wrecking were a grey area at best, and unless wrecks were closely guarded their salvage was a free-for-all. Normally, salvors would be unarmed, but in this case, with so much at stake, many would have armed themselves before heading to Florida by sailing vessel, canoe or longboat. Few, though, would have arrived on foot – neither the Spanish nor the indigenous Florida peoples took too kindly to interlopers. So, armed with weapons as well as tools, these wreckers flocked to the area. For the most part, all this took time to organize, and none reached the area before the Spanish had arrived to salvage the more accessible wrecks themselves and guard their possessions.

It was only Henry Jennings who was prepared to cut the Gordian knot. Unlike Thomas Barrow and these small-time wreckers, he simply attacked the salvage camps and took everything the Spanish had. In January 1716, when Jennings arrived in Nassau, there were very few independent wreckers there. They had headed directly to the Florida coast. Over the next few months, following the reinforcement of the salvage camps and the posting of guards, these wreckers drifted away. Most headed to Nassau. This, then, is the group of wreckers that Thomas Barrow rallied behind him. When both Jennings and Hornigold left Nassau, Barrow began putting on airs, and even proclaimed himself the governor of New Providence. It would have been a fatuous claim, were it not backed up with a policy of intimidating New Providence's settlers and threatening all those who opposed him.[5]

He terrorized the islanders, as, according to John Vickers, he caused 'great disorders', including robbery, assault, arson and rape. With a growing band of wreckers at his back he must have felt omnipotent, at least when there wasn't any more powerful figure there to challenge him. Interestingly, when either Hornigold or Jennings were in Nassau, Barrow backed off and didn't attempt to usurp their authority. So, Barrow knew his limits. This said, even Jennings and Hornigold couldn't completely control their crews. The looting of the St Marie's cargo by the crew of Jennings' Barsheba is a case in point. When ordered to stop the plundering by three of Jennings' captains, the rebellious crewmen ignored them and continued to divide the goods. They didn't do this according to the privateering regulations Jennings was supposedly abiding by, but by their own piratical code which was more favourable to the crew.[6]

It all seemed to indicate a move from established authority to something else entirely. Clearly, whatever Hornigold and Jennings might have thought, or whatever fictional claims they stuck to, their men knew better. They had been operating like pirates, and by now they were prepared to act like them too. From the buccaneering days, men like these abided by their own codes, where captains and quartermasters were elected by the crew, and where they all had a share in decision making. Some even mimicked the written codes first seen during the buccaneering era, where the way plunder was shared out was laid down, as were the allocation of portions to men who had been wounded.

As if the two groups of pirates and the wreckers weren't enough, there were other elements in the make-up of Nassau that summer. The largest of these groups were the logwood cutters. Logwood (*Haematoxylum campechianum*) was a type of flowering tree that proliferated in Central America and was richly prized for the purple dye it produced. Although it grew in areas controlled by the Spanish, during the late 17th century a logwood industry sprang up as cutters from English or French colonies headed to the largely uninhabited coast of the Bay of Campeche in what is now Mexico, or the Gulf of Honduras on the far side of the Yucatán Peninsula. There they harvested logwood trees, which were also valued by papermakers as well as for their medicinal properties.[7]

Despite occasional crackdowns by the Spanish, and the constant risk of being captured by Spanish naval patrols, the logwood industry thrived. By the early 18th century, some 2,000 logwood cutters were engaged in this harvest, and roughly a hundred ships a year visited these remote Caribbean shores. Many sailed there from either Jamaica or from Britain's colonies in North America. It was big business. It has been estimated that 12,000 tons of logwood were exported from the region each year and were sold in New England for £9 a ton. From ports like Philadelphia, New York or Boston, logwood was shipped to Europe.[8]

The Spanish obviously knew about this, but it was only occasionally that they tried to stop the trade. They called them *Los hombres de la Bahía* (The Bay Men), after the Bahía de Campeche where many of them operated. There were Spanish logwood cutters too, but their export prices were regulated and much higher than those of the interlopers.

So this illegal harvest continued. Finally, in late 1715, the Spanish decided to crack down on the Bay Men. The impetus for this was that some of the logwood cutters had expanded their business to incorporate piracy. That autumn it was reported that there were two pirate sloops based in the Bay of Honduras, and several *piraguas*, crewed by up to 250 men. They preyed on other logwood cutters, on Spanish coastal traders, and on larger ships passing through the Yucatán Channel.[9]

So, in early 1716 a Spanish naval squadron of four ships, led by Admiral Don Alonso Philippe de Andrade, appeared in the Bahía de Campeche and systematically rounded up most of the Bay Men and captured their vessels. These logwood cutters were taken to Vera Cruz and imprisoned, but a few of their companions avoided the Spanish sweep of the bay and escaped out to sea. Word was also sent to the logwood cutters in the Gulf of Honduras, who made themselves scarce. Many returned home, but a sizeable number headed to the Bahamas, including those who'd turned to piracy, and who had avoided capture by the Spanish. That meant that around the same time as the wreckers were beginning to arrive in New Providence, so too was a steady stream of refugee logwood cutters.[10]

These were tough men, most of them were experienced sailors, and, as already noted, some were pirates. Alexander Spotswood, the governor of the Virginia colony, described them as 'loose disorderly people from the Bay of Campeache, Jamaica, and other parts'. He may have had a point. In 1719, during the trial of the pirate Stede Bonnet in Charles Town, the colony's most senior lawyer Richard Allein said of the logwood cutters that 'nine parts in ten of them turned pirates'. While this may have been an exaggeration, they certainly provided a useful pool of suitable recruits for pirate crews. This may explain why, a little later, a number of pirates preyed on the logwood cutters who had returned to the Central American coast after the Spanish raid and had resumed their operations there. It made sense if some of these pirate crews were former Bay Men themselves and knew where to look for logwood vessels worth plundering.[11]

Another important group in New Providence – indeed in the Bahamas generally – were the colonists from Eleuthera and neighbouring Harbour Island, a little to the north-east of New Providence. Unlike New Providence, the settlers in Eleuthera had been left alone to farm peaceably on their colony, and its agriculture was far more developed.

It was estimated that around 600 people lived in the Bahamas at this time, and most of them were on Eleuthera. Approximately half were slaves, serving as agricultural labourers in the farms and small plantations of the island. Generally, the slaves kept themselves apart from the goings-on in Nassau, and so were not drawn into the excesses of the piratical community that developed there.

However, Eleuthera and Harbour Island were also the bases for traders, smugglers and occasional sellers of plundered goods, whose sloops provided a link between Nassau and the outside world. Richard Thompson from Harbour Island and his handful of small Bahamian sloops of up to 40 tons maintained a regular trading connection with Charles Town in the South Carolina colony. They also made voyages as far afield as St Thomas, Curaçao and even Boston. They returned with trade goods and supplies, and probably people too, including slaves, to serve as agricultural labourers on Eleuthera. This meant that, for a fee, Thompson was able to act as a go-between, allowing more respectable merchants in other colonies to benefit from the cut-price cargoes offered by the Nassau pirates.[12]

One of the reasons Thompson felt so secure was because Harbour Island was well defended. The island itself was only three miles long and less than half a mile wide, but it formed part of a lagoon on the north-eastern end of Eleuthera. The only navigable entrance was known as Harbour Mouth, off the southern end of the island, which ran between it and a spur of Eleuthera. Thompson had placed a gun battery there, which effectively sealed it off from unwanted visitors. Although the beach on the island's eastern side was undefended, landing there was deemed impractical, particularly if the islanders were forewarned, armed and were lining the wooded edge of the beach. Eleuthera, too, with its long, thin coast ending in two hammerhead-shaped patches of arable land, was also hard to attack due to a lack of suitable anchorages. In general, the islands were far enough away from the free-spirited chaos of Nassau to avoid being tainted by it. Still, despite being at a distance from Nassau, both islands maintained a close trading relationship with the Nassau pirates, and their vessels would have been regular visitors to the pirate haven.[13]

As for New Providence itself, by 1715–16 the island still hadn't recovered from the devastating Franco-Spanish raid of a dozen years before. Of those who weren't killed, most left the Bahamas and moved to the American mainland. Those who stayed probably didn't have the wherewithal to move. It is unclear how many settlers remained – some accounts place it at 30 families, and others at just 20 people. Before the 1703 raid there had been 300 houses there of various types and sizes, so this represents a major depopulation. Those who stayed were left to their own devices and had no help from either the Lords Proprietors or the government in London to rebuild their shattered community.

This may be in part because the Lords Proprietors didn't have a particularly good opinion of these colonists. As early as 1701, Governor Elias Haskett said of them that collectively they had an 'uneasy and a fractious temper'. He added that they 'neither believe that they ought to be subject to the power of God or the commands of the King'. Most damning of all, he finished by saying, these settlers are 'not scrupling to do all manner of villany to mankind, and will justifie and defend others which have done the like'. It was a pretty damning verdict, but just a few years before, these same settlers had formed an alliance with the pirate Henry Every.[14]

The islanders had no means to defend themselves. Fort Nassau had been rendered useless in 1703, when the French and Spanish took the best of the fort's guns, and spiked the rest, before throwing them onto the rocks below the fort. As a British captain noted after a visit there in the summer of 1710, there was no authority in New Providence, and every man simply did what he thought was best. This naval observer added that in the Bahamas 'the strongest man carries the day'. Just a few years later that 'strongest man' would be the likes of Hornigold, Jennings and Barrow.[15]

The arrival of the pirates, wreckers, logwood cutters and others transformed the struggling colony. In 1707, a visiting mariner reported that only three unburned houses remained in Nassau – one being that of Ellis Lockwood, the last governor to take up his post in the Bahamas. The roads in the town were overgrown with weeds, while elsewhere in the islands roads had almost ceased to exist. Although the settlers who remained had rebuilt their homes, these were usually crude, square, one-room log cabins, with any wattle walls made from mangrove branches. They were thatched with palmetto leaves and usually had only a single doorway. Cooking was normally done in a nearby shack or lean-to.[16]

Nassau in 1716 was little more than a collection of ruins – some of which were lived in – as well as tents, huts, lean-tos, shacks and huts. The influx of incomers eventually led to a demand for accommodation. At first, this would have meant more tents and shacks, but over time some men with greater resources or needs began to rebuild the ruined buildings of the town, or build modest ones of their own. This wasn't done by the pirates or wreckers themselves, but by those who moved to Nassau to support this growing lawless community: the tavern-keepers, brothel owners and cooks who established themselves to supply the needs of these men.

As was the case in Port Royal half a century before, the best way to make money from men like the Flying Gang was to provide for their most basic needs. This meant facilities for drinking, gambling and prostitution. Although a former judge, Thomas Walker had also been a privateersman, and it was unlikely he was especially prudish. He described how these pirates seemed keen to 'sell and dispose of their piraticall goods, and perfusely spend [plunder] they take from ye English French and mostly Spaniards.' Walker said that 'entertaining' these pirates was the standard way of distributing their plunder. The extremely high ratio of men to women in Nassau meant that these prostitutes could charge a premium rate for their services.[17]

Other less basic needs were provided by a range of other residents of the pirate haven. Carpenters, blacksmiths and small vessel shipwrights were needed, as were other trades which supported mariners – sailmakers, barrel-makers, coopers and caulkers as well as unskilled labourers, who would be hired to careen vessels, or to act as stevedores. Of course, not all the women in Nassau were prostitutes. Some were married and accompanied their spouses to the Bahamas, or established businesses that could cater for the men's needs, including washing and cooking. In the New Providence settlement women were well accustomed to hard work, tending crops and livestock, and so these extra duties would have been a useful addition to their income.[18]

What they would have fed the pirate community was almost certainly the same fare that was routinely eaten throughout the Bahamas. Fish was, of course, extremely plentiful, but the Bahamians also ate some types of non-migratory seabirds, as well as land crabs, lizards and iguanas, and sea turtles. The settlers in both New Providence and

Eleuthera raised cows, sheep, pigs and goats, which would undoubtedly have been sold in improvised marketplaces in Nassau. So too would locally produced vegetables, such as black-eyed peas, groundnut, cassava, corn, yams and pumpkins.

In the main, though, the pirates plundered food from the ships they captured, and this became their most common fare. The depositions written by victims of pirate attacks often contain lists of alcohol – mainly rum, but also port, brandy, Madeira and wine – while a ship's stock of food was almost always taken. For instance, in mid-December 1716, Hornigold and his new associate Teach captured the trading vessel *Lamb* in the Windward Passage. Among the items taken from it were 'Three barrills of Porke, one of Beef, two of Pease, three of Mackrill five barrills of Onions Several Dozen caggs of Oysters'. The pirates of Nassau, or those who were able to profit from them, were unlikely to starve.[19]

Other trades were needed too. Small-time merchants other than the Thompsons and Darvells established themselves to take advantage of the rock-bottom prices available from trading in stolen goods. Plunder could also be used to buy weapons and gunpowder, although for the most part these were simply taken from prizes. Ordnance was routinely taken from captured ships and stored in the hold instead of regular stone ballast. As a result, there was almost certainly a need for artisans skilled in maintaining or repairing weaponry, including gun carriages. All in all, Nassau during this period was a reasonably self-sufficient community, and what residents couldn't obtain on the island, there was a good chance they could plunder at sea.

The real problem was that it was a desperately volatile place. Men like Thomas Barrow saw to it that with their bullying and posturing. The New Providence settlers couldn't antagonize men like him for fear of violent retribution. It wasn't just Barrow of course – other lawless incomers or even pirates from well-established crews knew they could prey on the island's residents, and there was nothing anyone could do to stop them. Even Hornigold had threatened to burn down Thomas Walker's home and attack his family. Men like Barrow were much worse, and could burn, kill, rape and steal with relative impunity.

In 1716, Barrow demanded 20 shillings from a visiting mariner, Captain Stockdale, and threatened to whip him if he didn't pay. Stockdale paid Barrow and his wrecker follower Peter Parr, who gave

Stockdale 'a receipt on the publick account', as at the time Barrow was boasting he was the governor of New Providence.[20]

In the end there was only so much the local islanders could take. During the summer of 1716 many of the remaining islanders fled to other parts of the Bahamas or took passage to the American mainland, including Thomas Walker and his family. After a particularly heated confrontation with Benjamin Hornigold, Walker decided to quit New Providence. In July he abandoned his house – one of the largest and most pleasant on the island – and left. At first, he went to the Bahamian island of Great Abaco, 80 miles to the north, where he had friends among the island's handful of settlers. A month later, in August, he continued to Charles Town. There he told the authorities how Nassau was now in the hands of the pirates. Thomas Walker was the last Bahamian figure of any real standing and authority in New Providence. With him gone, any last semblance of government or restraint ceased to exist.[21]

So, the pirates of Nassau were left to rule themselves. Thomas Walker's departure and his report to the Lords Proprietors coincided with Governor Spotswood of Virginia's letter to London, which reported that pirates had taken over the Bahamas. This meant that by August at the latest, the authorities knew about the situation. The fact they did nothing about it for so long was a major factor in the rise of piracy in American waters. It has been claimed that the pirates established their own form of government in 1716 – one which continued to operate for almost two years. In his extremely well-researched book *The Republic of Pirates*, first published in 2007, journalist and historian Colin Woodard coined the term 'The Pirate Republic'. This is a term which has gained traction over the past decade. Catchy though it is, however, it doesn't really explain what Nassau was like in its piratical heyday.[22]

The word 'republic' suggests grand things. From the Latin *res publica* – literally, 'the public thing' – it suggests a form of government that involves rule by the citizenry. It harks back to the Roman Republic, established over two and a half millennia ago, where in theory power lay in the hands of Rome's wealthier citizens. The term had its roots in the Greek *politeia*, which can be translated in various ways, but generally refers to citizenship and the rights of the citizen. In the classic sense, a republic is a form of government in which the citizens govern the state for the public good. The English term 'commonwealth' can also be used to mean roughly the same thing.

In the original Roman and Greek, the notion of *res publica* and *politeia* was linked to a place, usually a city-state such as Rome or Athens, and this continued into the early modern period, with the creation of Italian city-states, most notably the Venetian Republic. By this time, the term had come to refer to states which weren't run by monarchs, such as the Dutch Republic or the English Republic (or Commonwealth) created in the aftermath of the English Civil War. By the later 18th century, the notion of these egalitarian states evolved into a more liberal form of republic, of the kind created in France and the United States of America. In all these cases, regardless of whether all citizens had a say in their election, the actual job of governing was done by an elected body, supervised by a head of state.

Clearly there are problems in applying the term 'republic' to the pirate community that sprang up in the Bahamas in the early 18th century. It suggests a far more formal type of government than the one that existed in Nassau. In fact, there's no real evidence that there was a government there at all – at least not one that anyone might recognize. The whole foundation of *res publica* was the enshrinements of rights – of having citizens of the state have their say in the way they were governed. Certainly, elements of most historical republics disenfranchised some of its community – women, people of colour, the poor and the young, for example. In New Providence, there is no evidence to suggest that anyone had any rights at all, enshrined or otherwise. There was no structure of government there, no administrative organization and no code of law – in fact, there was no law whatsoever.

So, 'republic' is probably the wrong word to use in regard to Nassau in the early 18th century. Another argument against giving this very *ad hoc* pirate community any kind of respectable status is that there was no legal or civic glue binding the place together. The speed with which this community collapsed from 1718 on proved just how unstable it was. In *The Republic of Pirates* Woodard proposes that this republic was a semi-organized confederacy of pirates who worked together to build a community. He argues that the governance of Nassau was dominated by a pirate code, and that the democratic structure that existed within the pirate community ensured that the republic would be run on fair and just lines.

The notion of a 'pirate code' takes the known egalitarianism that existed among pirate crews and projects it onto a much bigger canvas – the governance not of a ship, but of a whole pirate community. Certainly, there are examples where the pirates worked together for the good of their community. The re-arming of Nassau's fort in late 1716 using guns taken from captured ships is a case in point. However, this falls short of proving that a 'Pirate Republic' existed – a structure that was never mentioned by contemporaries such as Woodes Rogers, the British governor sent to the Bahamas in 1718 to stamp out piracy there once and for all.

An argument can be made that pirates were inherently democratic, and they were known to follow their own piratical rules of conduct. This is true, as far as it goes, but the rules really applied to the way shipboard life was managed, and primarily refer to the safeguards that established the rights of the crew to a share of the plunder. Not one word survives which suggests they were ever applied to state-building. It has also been claimed that the pirate community of Nassau was a social experiment – a brief egalitarian flourishing of democratic ideals in a world dominated by the restrictive mores of civilization and society. It is hard to see, though, where the actions of men like Thomas Barrow fitted into this libertarian utopia.

The idea of a pirate utopia is not a new one. In his *A General History of the Pyrates*, published in 1724, Captain Charles Johnson wrote a long and rambling chapter about the pirate colony of 'Libertalia', founded in the late 17th century by a French pirate, Captain James Misson. According to Johnson, Misson founded his pirate community as a place where all creeds, colours and beliefs could co-exist, and all oppressive institutions such as slavery, organized religion and monarchy were banned. On board Misson's pirate ship *Victoire*, all things were held in common, and all wealth was shared. According to Johnson, Libertalia was established in Madagascar in the Indian Ocean. This, however, was entirely a work of fiction – most probably a somewhat clumsy attempt to encapsulate the social views of a number of contemporary pirates.[23]

In theory, Libertalia was based on a real place, the Île Sainte-Marie off the north-east coast of Madagascar, which was a pirate haven during the time of Henry Every and remained in use until around 1720. This island, now called Nosy Boraha, was no utopian Libertalia.

Instead, it was a utilitarian base used by pirates to prey on shipping in the Red Sea and the Indian Ocean, but it gradually fell into disuse thanks to effective pirate-hunting in the area. By the 1720s, visitors to the island describe the remaining pirates there as starving, destitute and without any vessels. Interestingly, one of the last pirates to use the island as a base was Benjamin Hornigold's old partner, Olivier Levasseur, in 1721.[24]

Certainly, there is something to all this; the low-key radicalism of the pirates was noted by those who came into contact with them and was recorded in their last words before being executed. There is an easy slide from the notion of a self-governing pirate utopia to a self-governing pirate republic, but in both cases, there is no historical hook on which to hang the idea. Nassau was never established as anything other than a temporary haven for those living outside the law.

There is one more argument, though, for some form of community spirit and joint endeavour in pirate Nassau: the improvements to the port's defences. Today, Nassau's harbour looks narrow, jammed in between the town waterfront and Paradise Island, the landscape boxed in with luxury hotels, yacht marinas, commercial docks, bridges, a freight terminal, the towering buildings of downtown Nassau and a remorseless procession of gigantic cruise ships. In the early 18th century, it was a much more tranquil place, and the best natural harbour in the Bahamas. Back then, Paradise Island was known as Hog Island. Nassau harbour could accommodate numerous large ships – one near-contemporary author claimed it could accommodate the entire Royal Navy. It was protected by a sandbar, which was pierced by two channels, only one of which could accommodate large ships.[25]

This spot, in front of the channel, was where Governor Trott built Fort Nassau, roughly where the Hilton Nassau now stands, half a mile west of the cruise ship port. After the Franco-Spanish raid of 1703, the fort was abandoned, and Nassau remained unprotected as the islanders lacked the ability to replace the guns and repair the fort. This remained the situation until the summer of 1716, when Benjamin Hornigold returned to Nassau after his cruise around Cuba and the Windward Passage. He noted how the harbour was much busier than it had been when he'd left two months earlier, but he also realized that despite the guns on the small pirate ships, the island remained undefended. So, he decided to do something about it.[26]

He set about repairing and re-arming the fort. Between them the ships belonging to Hornigold and Jennings were reasonably well armed, while guns taken from the many mercantile prizes were also left rotting on Hog Island. He had his Flying Gang and possibly other pirate crews gather a number of suitable guns and, using sleds and pulleys, had them brought to the fort and emplaced there on newly built wooden carriages. Although it wasn't recorded, he also almost certainly had teams of masons, blacksmiths and carpenters working on repairing the fort itself, re-hanging its gates and clearing its approaches of undergrowth. Finally, he had the place stocked with supplies of food, water, powder and shot. A garrison was provided by men from the Flying Gang. Unfortunately, no records exist of how many guns were remounted there, and of what calibre.[27]

This re-arming of the fort was a major undertaking, and it would have taken a great deal of labour and commitment. It could – and has – been argued that this represented the community pulling together under the leadership of the island's governing body. There is no evidence of this though. It seems that it was all done on Hornigold's initiative, using his money and his followers. In early December he also took hold of a prize – a large 40-gun Spanish merchant ship – and anchored her covering the seaward side of the channel. This provided Nassau with a second battery, with the opportunity of raking any opponent should they try to force the harbour entrance. It was ingenious, practical and solved the problem of the harbour's defence.[28]

So, it was Hornigold who organized this one act of mutual protection – for that was exactly what it was. It certainly wasn't the work of the assembly of a republic, ordering construction or re-armament work to be carried out following a civic debate.

So, if Nassau was never a pirate republic, then what was it?

In fact, the nature of the pirate community of Nassau was much simpler than a grandly named republic. It never operated as a single political entity. Instead, factions existed there: the followers of Jennings and Hornigold, and, later, those of Hornigold and Vane. Nassau itself was divided between the pirates and those who supported them – the illegal merchants and smugglers, prostitutes and innkeepers – and the Bahamian colonists themselves, who still strived to make a living

133

from the land despite the influx of these volatile newcomers. It was no republic, either formal or informal.

A more accurate model is the one proposed by Peter Kropotkin (1842–1921), the anarchist philosopher and scientist. His ground-breaking anthropological study *Mutual Aid* (1902) explored the idea of mutually beneficial cooperation within both the animal kingdom and human communities. By all accounts pirate Nassau was an anarchic place, with its own way of doing things. This doesn't mean it lacked any communal structure. Instead, acts such as re-arming the fort, establishing links with merchants and overcoming internal factional divisions are all examples of mutual aid in tune with the Kropotkin model. When this spirit of reciprocity ended amid the division created by the offer of a pardon, the pirate community fell apart. So, pirate Nassau was almost exactly what Kropotkin was describing.[29]

Nassau, then, was a temporary and transient pirate community developed through mutually beneficial cooperation, and one which served its collective needs. There is no evidence of any striving for a grander motive. Nassau the cooperative pirate community most certainly existed. Nassau the so-called pirate republic never did. So, perhaps community might be a better word, or, if we take a leaf from Kropotkin, we might even call it a pirate commune. That certainly provides a better model for understanding the birthplace of the pirate menace than just about anything else.

SEVEN

Edward Thatch

W ITHOUT A DOUBT THE best-known pirate of this era was Blackbeard. His cognomen, adopted in 1717 at the height of his piratical career, is as recognizable a brand name today as it was then. His whole grizzled appearance was designed to intimidate, while his fearsome reputation helped guarantee both success and a notorious immortality. He was the defining pirate of the age and the most successful of the original band of Nassau pirates. However, we know all too little about him before he turned to piracy, save for a few scraps or pointers. Despite this, Blackbeard, or rather Edward Thatch, is a man whose actions were instrumental in creating the pirate menace that plagued the Americas, and whose career spans its rise and fall. Today, while the names of others are half forgotten, Blackbeard continues to be remembered as the archetypal pirate of this turbulent age.

At sunset on 17 December 1716, Captain Henry Timberlake was in the Windward Passage, some 25 miles to the west of Cape Tabran and nearby Cape Dona Maria, at the westernmost end of Saint-Domingue.

He took a quick look around. The coast of Hispaniola to the east was out of sight, but its presence was marked by low clouds. Over on his starboard bow, a little to the south-west, was the tiny island of Navassa, little more than a two-mile-long plug of rock sticking out of the sea. It was now 5.30pm, and he knew that in an hour it would be completely dark. Still, he was confident he was on course, and if the wind held fair, he would make landfall off Morant Point, the eastern end of Jamaica, the following morning.

Timberlake was the master of the 40-ton brig *Lamb*, a small British-flagged trading vessel on her way to Kingston, Jamaica. In her hold was a modest cargo of shingle and seasoned barrel staves, vital for Jamaica's rum distilleries. Once darkness fell, night lanterns were lit and the voyage continued, with only the watchkeepers remaining on deck. Then, a little before 8pm, Timberlake was roused from his tiny cabin by shouts from the deck above. When he reached the deck, there was enough moonlight to see what the fuss was about. A mile astern of them a large sloop was coming up fast, and clearly planned to intercept them. Timberlake was sure they were pirates, but he knew he had no real chance of outrunning them. Sure enough, when she drew to within hauling distance, the sloop fired a number of warning shots, and a shout ordered the *Lamb* to heave to.[1]

Timberlake did what he was told. A few minutes later the two vessels were lying close to each other, and the captain of the sloop ordered the *Lamb*'s master and two crewmen to row over to him. When Timberlake came aboard the sloop, Benjamin Hornigold was waiting for him. Timberlake discovered he and his men were now prisoners on board the pirate sloop *Delight*. While he was held there, Hornigold's men ransacked the *Lamb*. According to the deposition – essentially a crime report – that Timberlake later gave to the Jamaican Council, the pirates were after provisions – barrels of pork or beef, dried peas, fish, oysters, ship's biscuits and onions. It was a mundane enough haul, but Timberlake reported that the pirates also took most of his clothes and many of the ship's stores. To add insult to injury, they then threw Timberlake's cargo of barrel staves over the side.

The whole attack took around an hour. Timberlake and his men were still on board the *Delight* when a second pirate sloop appeared out of the darkness. Timberlake never knew her name but said she was armed with eight guns. This time her crew lowered a canoe, and several men joined Hornigold's boarding party. Only then, once they'd all ransacked the *Lamb*, were Timberlake and his two fellow prisoners allowed to return to their vessel. When Timberlake asked who was in command of this second vessel, he was told her captain was Edward Thach. Spelling was informal in the early 18th century, and there are several variants of the same name. Today this pirate captain is usually known as Edward Teach or Thatch – and better known as 'Blackbeard'. It was an unimpressive career start for a man who'd soon become the most notorious pirate of his age.[2]

For such an important figure we know surprisingly little about his origins. One of the problems with many pirates is that they appear on the historical radar only once they've started to break the law. So, were it not for Henry Timberlake's deposition, we wouldn't have an account like this – the earliest verifiable appearance of Blackbeard. Even his birthplace is open to debate. In his *A General History of the Pyrates*, Captain Charles Johnson begins his account of him by saying, 'Edward Teach was a Bristol man born, but had sailed some time out of Jamaica, in privateers, in the late French War.' This was the second edition of the book – the first one had a limited run and sold out within weeks. So, the second edition became the standard version and has been reprinted many times. In fact, fresh editions of the pirate bestseller are still being published today.[3]

What is particularly interesting is that Johnson changed details between the two editions. In the rare first edition, Johnson spelled the pirate's name as Edward Thatch. He also said that he came from Jamaica rather than Bristol. This first edition contained a number of easily detectable errors, such as Thatch working as a topmast hand aboard the pirate Stede Bonnet's sloop *Revenge*. The change may well be an attempt by the author to correct mistakes in his earlier edition. However, in the cases of the spelling of the pirate's name and his place of birth, there is still no definitive answer – only a near certainty. The search for Blackbeard's roots has led champions to propose a number of places, including North Carolina, the Caribbean and South-West England. Not all of them can be right.[4]

When researching a biography of the pirate, this author combed the records of Bristol to no avail. Around Gloucester, some 25 miles up the River Severn, the name 'Thatch' has been traced in local records. Nothing, though, ties these to the pirate himself. The notion that he was born in North Carolina is quickly dismissed for lack of evidence, although history has a way of surprising us with new discoveries which can turn things around. The most convincing solution to the birthplace question was provided by the genealogist Baylus C. Brooks, who reinforced the Jamaica link – the origin first suggested by Johnson. Today, this remains the most probable origin of the pirate, and helps fill in some questions about his life before he turned to piracy.[5]

If the Jamaican origin is correct, Edward Thache (the younger) was the son of Edward and Elizabeth Thache of Spanish Town. Brooks confirmed the Gloucester link, as Edward, a mercantile captain from Jamaica, was born in Stonehouse, a hamlet a few miles south of Gloucester, in 1656 during the last years of the English Protectorate. His wife, Elizabeth, was also from the same area. It is unclear when the couple moved to Jamaica, but the likelihood is that their son Edward the Younger was born around 1683, the second child of the couple, following the birth of a daughter, Elizabeth the Younger. By that time the father was described as a mariner, but he also owned a plantation. He died in 1706, seven years after the death of his wife Elizabeth. By then, their son Edward was also a mariner.[6]

At the time his father died in November 1706, Edward the Younger was serving in the Royal Navy, a volunteer aboard HMS *Windsor*, a fourth-rate ship-of-the-line of 40 guns. She had been built in Rotherhithe on the Thames in 1695 and had served in both the East and West Indies as well as home waters. In 1706, she returned to the Caribbean as part of a British squadron, and put into Port Royal in late July. This is probably when Thache joined her. As a volunteer he was probably given a special non-commissioned status, such as a writer or boatswain's mate, but details of his service are sparse. For the next year *Windsor* operated off the Spanish Main and Saint-Domingue but saw little in the way of action. The last record for Thache was in late August 1707, when he was discharged, listing the reason for his departure as 'preferment', which suggests he might have been rated as a midshipman – a junior officer without commission. His name, in this instance, is given as 'Thatch'.[7]

Then the trail goes cold. Johnson claims 'Teach' operated as a privateersman operating out of Jamaica. This is perfectly possible. As a prime seaman with naval experience and strong local connections, he would have been an ideal recruit for any privateering crew. Again, there is no record of him, as official documents usually list only the privateering captain. The likelihood is that from 1706 to 1713, Thatch remained a mariner, probably a privateer, and was based back in Jamaica. However, given his local connections, he was regarded as a gentleman, even though he hadn't inherited his father's land. He was almost certainly educated to a decent standard for the time, and thanks to his naval experience he was also well versed in seamanship, naval tactics and the art of gunnery. In other words, Edward Thatch's background and experience gave him the abilities he needed to become a first-class pirate.[8]

By December 1716 at the latest, Thatch had command of his own eight-gun sloop, crewed by around 90 men. He was also operating in consort with Benjamin Hornigold. Quite how he reached that point remains unclear, although there are hints, including references to him operating as a sloop captain out of Philadelphia. With luck, fresh research will bridge that gap. The next mention comes seven months later, in March 1717. A privateering captain, Mathew Musson, ran his sloop aground on Cat Island to the south-east of Eleuthera. While he was stranded there waiting for a spring high tide to free him, he chatted to local fishermen, who told him a little about the pirates who were operating in the Bahamas.

He wrote a letter to the deputy governor of the South Carolina colony, telling him what he'd discovered. The letter reported that 'Five pirates made ye harbour of Providence their place of rendevous, vizt. Horngold, a sloop with 10 guns and about 80 men; Jennings, a sloop with 10 guns and 100 men; Burgiss, a sloop with 8 guns and about 80 men; White, in a small vessel with 30 men and small arms; Thatch, a sloop 6 guns and about 70 men'. That was probably a mistake. It was more likely that Thatch had the same sloop as he had the previous December, with the same number of guns, and probably the same large crew of 90 men.[9]

Once more, though, Captain Johnson muddied the waters slightly. He said, 'In the spring of the year 1717, Teach and Hornigold sailed from Providence for the Main of America, and took in their way a billop [shallop – a small fishing vessel] from the Havana, with 120 barrels of flour, and also a sloop from Bermuda, Thurbar, master, from whom they took only some gallons of wine, and then let him go; and a ship from Madeira to South Carolina, out of which they got plunder to a considerable value.'[10]

Edward Thatch, although his name was spelled several ways.
He is best remembered as 'Blackbeard'.

The link between Benjamin Hornigold and Edward Thatch is a problematic one. Many see it as one between a gifted apprentice and his mentor. In fact, Thatch was every bit as gifted a mariner as Hornigold and a much more effective pirate. He didn't worry about pretending to be a privateer in case he was caught. Thatch simply grabbed what he wanted from whomever he wanted, and to the devil with the consequences. So, he is best seen as an equal associate of Hornigold, rather than an apprentice. This quote from Johnson, however, hides a growing tide of dissent among the Flying Gang. It is unknown whether Thatch supported the rebellion that took place that autumn, when Hornigold's crew voted to depose him as their captain. This is exactly what had happened to Hornigold the previous summer, off Saint-Domingue. Then his crew left him his sloop *Adventure* but deserted *en masse* to join Bellamy and Levasseur, who had fewer scruples. This time, though, they took the sloop too.[11]

After that incident on the Bahama Channel, Hornigold returned to New Providence, where he quickly formed an unlikely alliance with Henry Jennings. This coincided with copies of *A Royal Proclamation concerning Pyrates* reaching Nassau. The proclamation announced that Jennings was officially considered a pirate. There were hints, though, that the tightening of attitudes towards former privateers turned pirates might have a loophole. The suggestion was that a pardon was likely to be offered, so that men like Jennings and Hornigold could submit to the Crown and in return be absolved of their piratical sins. This caused yet more division in Nassau, as the pirate haven became divided between those welcoming the pardon, and those who'd have nothing to do with it.[12]

This was the moment when Edward Thatch struck out on his own. Freed of his association with Hornigold, he and his men could go where they liked. That summer, Thatch spent time in Nassau preparing his eight-gun sloop the *Revenge* and hand-picking his crew from those who opposed the idea of a pardon. It was around this time that Thatch adopted his nickname – Blackbeard. It fitted nicely with his appearance, and Thatch, already a tall, broad, imposing figure, went to great lengths to make himself look even more fearsome.

It was Johnson who described Blackbeard's emergence most vividly: 'So our hero, Captain Thatch, assumed the cognomen of Blackbeard, from that large quantity of hair, which covered his whole face, and frightn'd America, more than any comet that has appear'd there a long time.' He then added a lurid description about Thatch's beard: 'This beard was black, which he had suffered to grow of an extravagant length. As to breadth, it came up to his eyes. He was accustomed to twist it with ribbons, in small tails, after the manner of our Ramilles wigs, and turn them about his ears.'[13]

His whole appearance was designed to be terrifying, but Thatch didn't stop at his distinctive beard: 'In time of action, he wore a sling over his shoulders, with three brace of pistols hanging in holsters like bandoliers, and stuck lighted matches under his hat, which, appearing on each side of his face, his eyes naturally looking fierce and wild, made him altogether such a figure, that imagination cannot form an idea of a fury from hell to look more frightful.' It was a great act. It would take a brave merchant captain to stand up to a demonic figure the likes of Blackbeard.[14]

At some point in the early autumn, Thatch left the Bahamas on his first fully independent cruise. His newly acquired and re-armed 12-gun sloop *Revenge* was the perfect pirate-hunter, with a captain and crew who knew their business. By late September Thatch was cruising off Cape Charles in Virginia. It was there, on 29 September, that he came across the 40-ton sloop *Betty*, on the last leg of her voyage from Madeira to Williamsburg in Virginia. The pirates were delighted to find her cargo was wine from the island, and they promptly drank their fill. That done, Thatch ordered the prize to be set ablaze, and the sloop's crew put over the side into a longboat and told to row for the shore.[15]

This was only the start. In late October the *Boston News Letter* reported that a merchantman commanded by a Captain Codd was captured off the mouth of the Delaware River 'by a Pirate Sloop called *Revenge*, of 12 Guns, 150 Men, Commanded by one Teach, who Formerly Sail'd Mate out of this Port'. The article then reported three other pirate attacks in the same area, which were almost certainly carried out by Thatch, although they didn't mention him by name. He went on to capture three more prizes off the Virginia Capes, one of which was a sloop that he kept and crewed as his own sloop's consort. In every attack, he asked for volunteers to join him. This way he was able to reinforce his crew.[16]

The *Boston News Letter* added an intriguing line. It reported, 'On board the Pirate Sloop is Major Bennet but has no Command.' This was Major Stede Bonnet of Barbados, the original owner of the sloop *Revenge*. A gentleman, a plantation owner and a well-placed man of society on the island, Bonnet had the ultimate mid-life crisis and left wife and family and estate to become a pirate. Unusually, he hired his own crew and bought his own sloop. The Barbadian shipping records have her leaving the island in late April 1717 without clearing their departure with the authorities. Despite his lack of experience, Bonnet, a major in the Barbadian militia, was determined to prove his worth as both a mariner and a pirate.[17]

The two pirates had probably met in Nassau late that summer, and, according to Johnson, Thatch suggested that he should mentor the inexperienced Bonnet. In fact, it was probably Hornigold who proposed that Bonnet would benefit from having the far more experienced Thatch operate his sloop for him. The unfortunate Bonnet had no choice but to agree. So, Bonnet virtually became a prisoner on his own sloop, the *Revenge*, which Thatch effectively commandeered as his own. Johnson has the two pirates meeting off the Delaware Capes, but the Nassau rendezvous is by far the most likely location of this ill-matched pirate union.

By late October Blackbeard was still in the same waters, cruising off the New Jersey coast. It was late in the season, however, and most pirates tended to head south for winter to avoid the worst of the Atlantic storms. Farther south the hurricane season was now over, and the weather was considerably more pleasant than that of the Atlantic seaboard of North America; so, with Bonnet still on board as his guest, Thatch headed out around the Bahamas archipelago, to make landfall at the top of the Leeward Islands. He then continued south, keeping to seaward of the chain of islands. He planned a cruise around the islands, hoping to prey on the trading ships which served these sugar-rich island colonies. He didn't know it then, but this was where Blackbeard would really start making his mark.

On 17 November 1717 Thatch spotted a large merchant ship approaching them from the Atlantic. At that moment they were about 60 miles east of the French island of Martinique. Blackbeard was in the 12-gun *Revenge* and was accompanied by a second sloop. He gave the order to give chase, and they overhauled the ship after a brief pursuit. Captain Pierre Dossett surrendered after putting up a token face-saving resistance. Their prize turned out to be *La Concorde*, a three-masted and ship-rigged slave ship of 200 tons, outward bound from the French port of Nantes, having recently visited the West African coast. As a slaver, her cargo consisted of around 200 West Africans destined for the slave market of Martinique's Fort-de-France. After capturing his superb prize, Thatch took her to the secluded island of Bequia, to the south of Martinique. There he set about converting *La Concorde* into his new flagship.[18]

The slave ship mounted 16 guns, but Thatch had been collecting ordnance from his prizes, and these guns were installed in the new pirate flagship. At the same time, carpenters reduced the height of her forecastle and quarterdeck, and removed the slave decks in the hold and the barricades in the waist. Within two weeks the ship had been transformed from a slaver into a powerful warship, mounting no fewer than 40 guns. At this point Thatch renamed her the *Queen Anne's Revenge* – a sly dig at the Hanoverian monarch sitting on the British throne. Once he was done, he released his French prisoners and allowed them

A three-masted ship of the period, in this case a French merchant ship, not unlike the slaver La Concorde, *captured by Blackbeard off Martinique.*

to sail north to Martinique in one of his smaller prize sloops, but the slaves themselves were kept in fetters and left in a stockade on Bequia, where they would soon be reclaimed by the French crew.[19]

It was now late November 1717. He resumed his cruise, this time heading north through the Leeward Islands. At the start of December Thatch captured the large Boston merchantman *Great Allen*, on passage from Barbados to Jamaica. Her cargo turned out to be timber and silver plate, around £8,000 worth of it. This was Thatch's best haul yet. He kept the American ship with him for a day as his crew ransacked her within sight of the island of St Lucia. Thatch developed a dislike for her master, Captain Christopher Taylor, and had him whipped. He then cast him and his men into an open boat and set the *Great Allen* ablaze. The cruise continued. *Queen Anne's Revenge* and her two accompanying sloops captured three other local sloops as they headed north.[20]

Then, off Crab Island, a few miles from Antigua, they fell in with a third sloop, the *Margaret*.

Fortunately for posterity, her master, Captain Henry Blackstock, gave a detailed description of the pirate leader. He said that Thatch was 'a tall, spare man, with a very black beard, which he wore very long'. This was the first description of the pirate captain, and one that probably served as the inspiration for Johnson's much more exotic version. From that point, in the eyes of a horrified world, Edward Thatch had become the notorious and highly distinctive pirate known as Blackbeard.[21]

At this point, in his account of Thatch's life, Johnson also describes a fierce naval battle between the *Queen Anne's Revenge* and the British frigate HMS *Scarborough*, the West Indies guardship. The battle was entirely made up and was probably the result of Johnson confusing Thatch with another French pirate whose flagship was attacked and destroyed by the *Scarborough*. Still, the British frigate was prowling in those same waters, and she represented a real threat to Thatch and his crew. Despite carrying more guns than the *Scarborough*, they had no real chance of taking on the Royal Navy in a stand-up fight. Her presence may have been what encouraged Thatch to quit the West Indies. So, he headed west to Hispaniola. There, he put in to Samana Bay in Santo Domingo, on the island's eastern shore. The Spanish were much less of a threat, the bay was sparsely populated, and Thatch and his men could celebrate Christmas and New Year without looking over their shoulders.[22]

A few weeks after the start of the new year, Thatch headed back into the Caribbean with two vessels: the *Queen Anne's Revenge* and the sloop *Revenge*. This time he planned to travel over a thousand miles to the east, to the Gulf of Honduras, where he intended to prey on the logwood cutters who worked there, plundering their ships and ransacking their stores. This route, though, took Thatch dangerously close to Jamaica, where the Royal Navy had a presence. Presumably he kept out of sight of the island as he sailed by, as there is no record of him being spotted. According to Johnson, he first made an appearance at the Turneffe Islands, off what is now the coast of Belize: 'At Turniff, ten leagues short of the Bay of Honduras, the pirates took in fresh water. While they were at anchor they saw a sloop coming in, whereupon Richards in the sloop *Revenge* slipped his cable and ran out to meet her'. On seeing the black flag raised the sloop lowered her sails and was taken into the bay.[23]

She turned out to be the 80-ton sloop *Adventure* from Jamaica, commanded by David Herriot. She was a lovely vessel – roomy, fast and with enough space to mount up to a dozen guns. Inevitably, Thatch decided to add the *Adventure* to his little squadron. The pirates spent a week in the islands, before heading on into the gulf. This time the force split up, Richard Richards taking the sloop *Revenge* along one side of it, and Thatch cruising along the other shore in *Queen Anne's Revenge*, with the *Adventure* following her under the command of Israel Hands. It was now the middle of April. The sweep of the gulf proved a great success. The pirates captured three sloops and a large three-masted ship – the *Protestant Caesar* from Boston, which had fought off the *Revenge* and escaped before being cornered by Blackbeard's flagship. That kind of plucky resistance wasn't to be tolerated by Thatch.

Captain Weir and his men from the *Protestant Caesar* took to their boats and fled ashore when Thatch appeared. So, they had an excellent view of the pirates ransacking their ship, and then burning her to the waterline. That way, they couldn't claim they'd beaten the pirates. Another reason for setting the ship ablaze might have been the pirates' dislike of Boston, where the year before the six survivors of the pirate ship *Whydah* had been hanged. Of the logwood cutters' sloops, all were ransacked, but only one was burned.[24]

Once Thatch and his men had finished their sweep of the gulf, they headed back out to the open sea. This time, Thatch headed north followed by the two pirate sloops. They would have made slow progress, as the prevailing winds blew from the north-east. So, they headed east to Trujillo on the coast of Honduras then curved over towards the Cayman Islands, to pick up a more favourable wind. Around the end of April, they passed through the Yucatán Channel and continued towards the north-east, following the coastline of Cuba as it led towards the Bahía Honda and then Havana. They were now at the southern end of the Gulf of Mexico, with the Florida Straits ahead of them. Beyond that lay the Bahama Channel, and either a return in triumph to Nassau, or a cruise up the Atlantic coast of North America.

Off Havana they captured a small Spanish sloop, at which point Thatch decided to continue on to the north to take a look at the Spanish treasure wrecks on the Palmar de Ays. As Johnson put it, 'The rovers sailed to Turkill [Trujillo], and then to the Grand Caymans, a small island about thirty leagues to the westward of Jamaica, where they took a small turtler, and so to the Havana, and from thence to the Bahama wrecks.' They spent several days 'fishing' the wreck sites of the 1715 treasure fleet, but probably found very little there. What was left had been picked clean or was too deep to be recovered. It was probably there, though, that Thatch and his men agreed to their next bold move. They would try their hand at holding a major port to ransom.[25]

On the afternoon of 22 May 1718, Edward Thatch embarked on his most ambitious escapade yet. Arriving from the south, he appeared off Charles Town (now Charleston, South Carolina) with the *Queen Anne's Revenge* at the head of a powerful squadron of four smaller pirate vessels. The prosperous and thriving port was the largest city in the South Carolina colony, and one of the busiest ports in North America. It lay at the head of a small bay, whose narrow entrance was protected by a sandbar. By positioning himself off the main channel past the sandbar, Thatch was able to completely blockade the port. His 40-gun flagship, the *Queen Anne's Revenge*, was more than a match for any warship, and at that moment the nearest Royal Navy frigate was over 400 miles away, in Virginia's James River. So, Thatch was unassailable.[26]

His other four sloops were the *Adventure* and *Revenge*, commanded by Hands and Richards, and two newly captured vessels, the small Spanish sloop taken off Havana and a second sloop, one of three vessels he had

THE PIRATE MENACE

pillaged on his way up from Florida. His first victim was the pilot boat that came out to help these five approaching vessels through the bar and into the harbour. She was also escorting out a large merchant ship, the *Crowley*, bound for her home port of London. Unknowingly, Captain Robert Clark sailed the *Crowley* straight into Thatch's clutches. She was carrying passengers, who soon found their baggage rifled and their purses taken. She wasn't the only outbound ship the pirates captured, as the alarm still hadn't been raised. Even when the city realized what was happening the following morning, there was no way the Carolinians could warn other ships, unsuspectingly approaching the port from the open Atlantic.[27]

Over the next few days Thatch and his men captured several more prizes. Two outward-bound three-masted ships were captured the day after the pirates' arrival, commanded by Captains Craig and Hewes. The latter ship, the *William* of Weymouth, was the last one to be caught on her way out of the port. Everything else was captured when they tried to enter Charles Town. Two small 'pinks' – vessels with long overhanging sterns – and a brig slaver were taken, the latter, a Bristol vessel, having just made landfall there from the coast of Angola. A little later that afternoon this double capture was followed by another ship arriving from Boston. Thatch and his men plundered her too.[28]

Then, when the prizes eventually dried up, Blackbeard decided to be even more audacious. Johnson describes his next move:

> Teach detained all the ships and prisoners, and, being in want of medicines, resolved to demand a chest from the government of the province; accordingly Richards, the Captain of the *Revenge* sloop, with two or three more pirates, were sent up along with Mr. Marks, one of their prisoners, whom they had taken in Clark's ship, and very insolently made their demands, threatening that if they did not send immediately the chest of medicines and let the pirate ambassadors return without offering any violence to their persons, they would murder all their prisoners, send up their heads to the governor, and set the ships they had taken on fire.[29]

Effectively, the pirates were holding a major city to ransom – something that hadn't happened since the days of the buccaneers. When the news of this got out, it caused consternation throughout Colonial America.

Merchants clamoured for protection, colonial governors demanded a naval presence, and the inhabitants of coastal towns and cities feared that they would be next. Interestingly, Thatch's demand was amazingly modest. All he really wanted was a medicine chest. In Charles Town, Governor Robert Johnson sent riders to neighbouring colonies and to the commander of the British warships in the James River. It would take at least two weeks, though, before the warships could reach him. He'd already mustered his militia and was confident the city could defend itself if the pirates attacked. What he couldn't do was protect the port if the pirates decided to bombard it.[30]

In the end there was no question of refusing Thatch's demand. As Johnson recorded, 'The government were not long in deliberating upon the message, though 'twas the greatest affront that could have been put upon them; yet for saving so many men's lives they complied with the necessity and sent aboard a chest valued at between £300 and £400, and the pirates went back safe to their ships.' We still don't know what Thatch wanted with the medicine, but it could have been to counter the flux – yellow fever – an ever-present danger in the Caribbean. On the wreck site of the *Queen Anne's Revenge,* a venereal syringe was found, which may offer another explanation. In any case, this was enough for Thatch, and once the chest was aboard his flagship, he gave orders to lift the blockade.[31]

Of course, they didn't leave empty-handed. They had already plundered several vessels, and it was claimed that the passengers from the *Crowley* had been stripped of money, clothing and personal items valued at over £1,500 – the equivalent of around £300,000 today. So, Thatch sailed off and left the South Carolinians to recover from their week-long ordeal. Thatch and his ships headed north. By then the pirate captain had come to a realization. He knew that after so audacious an attack the Royal Navy would come looking for him. So, he needed to lie low somewhere. Thatch knew about the pardons on offer and had to consider his options. Applying for a pardon in either South Carolina or the Bahamas wasn't an option, as both governors would probably deny him one, in light of the Charles Town raid. Virginia was out of the question too. If he was to go through with this, Thatch was left with one remaining possibility. He would have to try his luck in North Carolina.[32]

The more Thatch thought about it the better North Carolina looked. The small, impoverished colony didn't have any significant mercantile trade like the neighbouring colonies of South Carolina and Virginia did. That meant there wasn't the same powerful mercantile lobby, which would challenge his request. The coast of North Carolina was also undeveloped, and the settlements fairly small. That made it a reasonably secure place to keep out of the limelight. Better still, if the rumours were true, the colony's governor Charles Eden was a man who could be persuaded, especially if money was offered. However, Thatch had two problems to deal with first. His force was now too large and powerful to be able to enter North Carolina's waters without causing alarm. He had to lose some of his four sloops. Even more significantly, prestigious though she was, he also needed to get rid of his flagship. Not only was she too large and powerful to be ignored by the Royal Navy, but she also drew too much water to pass into the colony's inland waterway. So, the *Queen Anne's Revenge* had to go.[33]

In early June 1718, either the 2nd or the 3rd of the month, Thatch's squadron approached Topsail Inlet, just beyond Cape Lookout, on the North Carolina coast. This little channel was the most southerly route through the Outer Banks. This 200-mile chain of sandbanks and low dune-grass–covered coastal islands acted like a barrier, with the Atlantic Ocean on one side and the calmer inner coastal waters of Pamlico Sound on the other. This was the gateway into North Carolina colony. Today the charming coastal town of Beaufort, North Carolina, marks the end of the inlet, which is now called Beaufort Inlet. In the summer of 1718, there was nothing there apart from a few fishermen's huts. Nobody, then, could see what happened next.

Topsail Inlet was less than half a mile wide, and it kept moving with every winter storm, which made it a notoriously tricky passage. The pirate squadron approached slowly, with the *Queen Anne's Revenge* in the lead. Halfway through it, Thatch's helmsman turned the *Queen Anne's Revenge* to starboard, and moments later the flagship ran hard aground. Thatch called out to Israel Hands, who was following in the sloop *Adventure*, and asked him to help tow the flagship off. While getting into position, the *Adventure* ran aground too. It is almost certain that Blackbeard and Hands had planned the whole thing. Although the *Adventure* could eventually be floated off and then repaired, the *Queen Anne's Revenge* was a total loss. This, of course, was exactly what Thatch wanted.[34]

Thatch's next task was to 'downsize' his crew and get rid of his guest, Stede Bonnet. So, Thatch asked Bonnet to go on ahead in a sloop to make an initial approach to the North Carolina governor. The colony's administrative seat was at Bath Town on the Pamlico River, some 70 miles away through Pamlico Sound. Bonnet agreed to approach Governor Eden, and to arrange the issue of a provisional pardon for everybody in Thatch's crew. He headed off in a small captured sloop, as Thatch insisted on keeping hold of the *Revenge* – Bonnet's own ship – to help in the attempted re-floating of the pirate flagship. Some 17 of Bonnet's original crew were still aboard her, and as many again left with Bonnet when he sailed off through the inland waterways. Thatch also had the small Spanish sloop with him that he'd captured off Havana.[35]

Once Bonnet left, Thatch made his move. His armed followers rounded up Bonnet's remaining crew members and ferried them out to a deserted island on the far side of the inlet. With her crew marooned, nobody could stop Thatch as he stripped the *Revenge* of all her sails and cordage, turning her into a useless hulk. Then he had his men salvage what they could from the *Queen Anne's Revenge* and the *Adventure*. All of their plunder was stowed in the hold of the Spanish sloop.

That wasn't the end of Thatch's double-dealing. He secretly gathered a small but loyal band of men around him. Then, in dead of night, they sailed off in the Spanish sloop. The rest of the pirate crew – nearly 200 of them – were furious. A few days later, when Bonnet returned, he found the beach where Beaufort now stands crawling with angry pirates. Bonnet's own sloop the *Revenge* had been stripped of her sails, and his loyal crew had been marooned on a nearby island. Worst of all, Blackbeard had absconded with all of their communal plunder. Bonnet was clutching the provisional pardon Governor Eden had offered, but by now the major realized he'd been duped into applying for it in the first place. He was as furious as Thatch's men, who were literally abandoned by their captain. Bonnet must have rued the day he'd willingly joined up with Thatch or trusted him.[36]

It took Bonnet a week to set the *Revenge* to rights, cannibalizing sails and rigging from the other vessels. Then he set off in pursuit of Thatch, whom he presumed had returned to sea, to resume his piratical cruise. He never caught up with him for the very good reason that Thatch wasn't at sea at all. Instead, he was in Bath Town, staying there as the guest of Governor Eden. In mid-June Thatch accepted Governor Eden's pardon for the pirate and his crew – or rather those who accompanied him to Bath Town. The others stranded farther down the coast were left to their own devices. So, officially, Blackbeard the notorious pirate had turned his back on piracy and was no longer a wanted man. Instead, he and his 30 closest followers were able to enjoy the fruits of their plunder and were freed from the risk of prosecution. It seemed that Edward Thatch and his men had truly turned over a new leaf.[37]

In secrecy the pirates divided their plunder between themselves. This, of course, was a better deal divided between 30 men rather than the 150 pirates that Thatch commanded off Charles Town. From that point on Thatch would seemingly live off his piratical earnings and entertain polite society in the colony with suitably salty yarns. He was also eager to build the facade that he planned to set himself up as a local mercantile trader. This justified him keeping hold of a small crew of reformed pirates. These same pirates must have really enjoyed their break from the sea, and the settlement's two makeshift taverns must have done a roaring business. It was almost as if Nassau had been revived in the Carolinas. This, though, was exactly the spectre of a fresh pirate haven that haunted a lot of people in the neighbouring colonies.

Not everyone was as convinced as Charles Eden that Thatch was a reformed character. Other governors would watch closely for any sign that the pirate had returned to his old ways. Meanwhile he rented a house on the outskirts of Bath Town, and, according to Johnson, he took a wife – a local girl who was just 16 years old. No marriage was verified, so the likelihood is that the teenager became the pirate's mistress rather than his wife. To keep his men occupied, he overhauled his Spanish-built sloop and renamed her the *Adventure*. He then started taking her out on small cruises into Pamlico Sound.[38]

He also established a remote base for the sloop on the western side of Ocracoke, one of the islands in the Outer Banks. This was all done under the cover of establishing a local trading operation. In the neighbouring colony of Virginia, Governor Spotswood was unconvinced. He watched Thatch's activities with interest, for any sign that he would return to piracy. If he did, and Governor Eden failed to act, then, with the help of the Royal Navy, Governor Spotswood would deal with the problem himself.[39]

EIGHT

Sam Bellamy

THE PIRATE MENACE THAT plagued the waters of the Americas and the Caribbean was created in one place. Nassau was 'ground zero' for the pirate scourge. Everything that followed, from Blackbeard's blockade of Charles Town to Bartholomew Roberts' attacks off the West African coast, can be traced back to that one spot. It was amazing that such a small group of pirates could spawn so many pirate groups, and then cause so much havoc. What began with Benjamin Hornigold and Henry Jennings quickly grew into something much bigger. While Edward Thatch is perhaps the most famous of Hornigold's successors, others, like Sam Bellamy or Olivier Levasseur, might have become less notorious, but they probably captured more prizes than Blackbeard ever did.

Once Bellamy rose to command his own pirate sloop he became, in effect, a working partner of Hornigold and Levasseur, and hunted in consort with them. Men like Bellamy, having proved their ability as pirate captains, would almost inevitably break away to hunt under their own flag.[1]

When we last heard of Sam Bellamy, he was cruising with the Frenchman Olivier Levasseur in the Windward Passage. Levasseur had the sloop the *Postillion*, and at first his crew included both Bellamy and Paulsgrave Williams. Soon Bellamy was given his own command, the French prize sloop *Marianne*. Her crew, it seems, anglicized her name to the *Mary Anne*. All told, Hornigold, Bellamy and Levasseur had around 200 pirates under their command – a powerful force, and a major threat to merchant shipping in this busy and important waterway. After all, the Windward Passage was a choke point on the main sea route between Jamaica, Saint-Domingue and the Spanish Main on one side, and the ports of Europe on the other.[2]

We have already seen how, when Hornigold rejoined them in the summer of 1716 after a brief visit to Nassau, he and the others had a falling out. The row was over Hornigold's insistence on not attacking British ships. The end result was that in August, the majority of Hornigold's crew refused to sail with him anymore. So, he and his new sloop the *Adventure* returned to Nassau, with just 26 men on board. One of them was Hornigold's gifted associate Edward Thatch. The remainder agreed to serve under Bellamy and Levasseur, and so they joined the crews of the *Marianne* and the *Postillion*. Each of the two sloops had a crew of around 80 to 90 pirates. What followed, at least for Bellamy, was a dramatic and meteoric rise from command of a canoe to a small pirate flotilla, led by a large and well-armed flagship, the *Whydah*.[3]

Thanks to the extensive research conducted by the team that found the wreck of the *Whydah* in 1984, and by the Whydah Pirate Museum in Cape Cod, Massachusetts, we know a fair bit about Bellamy's origins. He was born in the tiny Devon hamlet of Hittisleigh, some ten miles west of Exeter. It was a farming community, lying on the edge of the bleak, brooding expanse of Dartmoor. His mother died soon after his birth in early 1689, and the youngster and his five siblings were raised by their father, Stephen Bellamy. Sam spurned the rural life, and as a youngster he went to sea – the bustling port of Plymouth was half a day's walk away. What followed is unclear, as surviving records are sparse.[4]

By that time Queen Anne's War was at its height, and it has been suggested that Bellamy joined the Royal Navy. In fact, it would be hard not to if he set foot in Plymouth, as the press gangs there were busy sweeping up whomever they could find, even teenage landsmen like Bellamy. Work still needs to be done in tracing Bellamy's maritime career before the end of the war in 1713. Local New England legend places him in Cape Cod, Massachusetts, in 1715, where he supposedly had relatives in Eastham. His entry point to the colony was probably the bustling port of Boston. While in Cape Cod, it is claimed he met Goody (or Mary) Hallett from Wellfleet, but her parents rejected him as a potential suitor.

Whatever the real story was, his first appearance on the piratical radar came early the following year, when he was linked with the 'fishing' on the Spanish treasure wrecks on the Palmar de Ays. By then he had established an alliance with Paulsgrave Williams. And by the spring they had turned to piracy, hunting the Gulf of Honduras in small *piraguas*.[5] Once they captured a sloop, they were able to venture farther afield and hunt the lucrative sea lanes off the western end of Cuba. It was there that Bellamy and Williams ran into Henry Jennings, and double-crossed him before joining up with Benjamin Hornigold. All the time, Sam Bellamy was learning the piratical trade and proving his mettle as a pirate leader.[6]

In August 1717, after Hornigold left them, it was time for Bellamy, Williams and Levasseur to spread their wings. They stayed in their lair in Saint-Domingue until mid-September, at which point they set off on a cruise, heading clockwise around the Caribbean basin. That would take Bellamy and Levasseur to as far as the eastern end of the Spanish Main before the end of the year. The only problem was that it was late in the season, and bad weather was almost unavoidable. The first leg of the voyage along the southern coast of Saint-Domingue and Puerto Rico was uneventful. This, though, took them into waters where the European maritime powers all maintained a naval presence. However, the Leeward Islands were also rich in potential prizes.

Sure enough, in between the islands of Puerto Rico, St Thomas and St Cruze (St Croix), they spotted a large, heavily armed merchantman flying French colours. The two sloops split up, trying to approach her from two sides. As Bellamy drew close, the French captain turned his ship to starboard and fired a full broadside at the *Marianne*. Bellamy and Levasseur both tried to approach the ship, but the same thing happened every time. After an hour of this, Bellamy signalled the *Postillion* to disengage, and the two pirate sloops broke off the fight and continued to the east in search of easier prey. For the next few weeks, they combed the Virgin Islands for prizes before moving on to the Dutch colony of St Thomas. All they found, though, were small, largely worthless prizes, yielding little more than food and drink. So far, the cruise had been a disappointment.[7]

Then, on 9 November they came upon a British sloop in the wide channel between St Cruze and St Thomas. Bellamy fired a shot over the ship's bow, and she dutifully heaved to. She was the *Bonetta*, a British merchant sloop en route from Jamaica to Antigua commanded by Captain Abijah Savage. Bellamy and Levasseur ranged alongside and ordered Savage to come over to the *Marianne* in his boat. After he was taken prisoner, the two pirate ships sent over a prize crew, and the three vessels headed south, to drop anchor in a secluded bay on the north side of St Cruze. Nowadays the low-lying shore of Salt River Bay in St Croix is a tourist spot and a national park, close to the town of Christiansted, but in late 1717 it was uninhabited. The pirates spent two weeks there, careening their two sloops and using the crew of their prize to do the hard work. St Cruze would make an excellent temporary haven for a while.

When one of the prisoners escaped, the Swedish-born Peter Hoff was recaptured and beaten heavily for his temerity. Two of his shipmates, though, made it off the beach and hid in the island's undergrowth until the pirates sailed away. Before they left they thoroughly rifled the *Bonetta* and took whatever they fancied, from the clothes of some of the passengers, to people – an African slave and a young Native American servant. John King, the young son of one of the passengers, also ran off with them to become a pirate, leaving his horrified parents behind. The two pirate sloops then sailed off, leaving the *Bonetta* to fend for herself. She eventually reached Antigua, a hundred miles away, where Captain Savage warned the authorities that there were pirates on the loose.[8]

Bellamy and Levasseur sailed east and made landfall again off Saba, a small, rugged island owned by the Dutch, dominated by its volcanic peak which was hidden in cloud. To the south-west of the island they spotted a sail, and, on overhauling her, they fell in with another British merchantman, the *Sultana*, commanded by Captain John Richards. She was a three-masted ship-rigged galley, which meant she had ports for long oars, known as sweeps, allowing her to be propelled in a calm. She looked fast and sleek, and carried a decent armament of 26 guns.

Bellamy thought she was near-perfect. He'd been planning to upgrade from the *Marianne* to something larger, and here, in front of him, was the ideal ship. The *Sultana* heaved to, and Bellamy eagerly took her for himself. Then, they spotted another ship.[9]

This time it was Levasseur who gave chase, and in a short while his prey heaved to and surrendered. She was another British-flagged ship, a slow, bluff-bowed and unarmed merchantman, which like the *Sultana* was heading to the Bay of Campeche. Her master, Captain Tosor, watched as his ship was plundered, and several prime seamen were pressed into service with the pirates, whether they wanted to or not. One witness described them crying with grief as they were shipped over to the *Postillion*. The merchantman was then left to continue on its way, carrying the crew from the *Sultana* with her. With Bellamy taking over the *Sultana*, the pirates now had a sloop without a captain. So, Bellamy's friend Paulsgrave Williams was given command of the *Marianne*.[10]

Williams was from Boston in the Massachusetts colony, and he and Bellamy had become friends soon after the seaman's arrival in the port. Unlike the uneducated sailor, though, Williams was educated, a middle-aged family man, and some 11 years older than Bellamy. It was an unlikely friendship, and while it is unclear whether Williams had a nautical background, he decided to leave his family behind and run off to sea. So, he accompanied Bellamy in his venture to 'fish' the Spanish treasure wrecks, and turned pirate with him as they began their piratical career in the Gulf of Honduras. In fact, Williams proved a competent mariner and a reasonably successful pirate. Not only would he outlive Bellamy, but he would also know when to give up piracy and live to tell the tale.[11]

The cruise resumed, with Bellamy in the *Sultana*, Levasseur in the *Postillion* and Williams in the *Marianne*. They continued on to the east, towards the long chain of the Leeward Islands. This brought them close to the British-owned islands of St Nevis, St Kitts and Montserrat, with the island of Antigua behind them, which Bellamy knew was used as a base by the Royal Navy. This was a risky time for the pirates, as a British frigate – HMS *Scarborough*, guardship for the British Leeward Islands – might appear at any moment. Bellamy knew that by now word of their capture of the *Bonetta* would have got out, so he was wary. In the end, though, they sailed past the British islands without incident, or any prizes. It was now the start of December. Off the French island of Guadeloupe, they caught two small local trading craft and ransacked them for supplies. They then followed the island chain of the Windward Islands but kept to the west of them in case the *Scarborough* appeared.

After passing St Vincent, they headed south-west towards the small and deserted Isla La Blanquilla, where Bellamy hoped to careen the *Sultana* and modify her into a more effective pirate ship. Before they arrived there, though, on 19 December they came across a large three-masted, ship-rigged British merchant ship on her own in the open sea. The *St Michael* of Bristol had sailed from Cork two months before and had made her transatlantic landfall at Barbados. After taking on provisions, she was heading across the Caribbean to Jamaica. She was singularly unlucky to run into this three-vessel pirate flotilla some 120 miles west of St Vincent. Captain James Williams didn't have the speed to flee or the guns to fight, so he meekly heaved to and awaited his fate. She was carrying food, grain and casks of beef; so, rather than loot her, the pirates sent a prize crew over and took the merchantman with them.[12]

La Blanquilla was circular, low-lying, and ringed by white, sandy beaches – a perfect spot to careen a ship. Officially the island was owned by the Spanish and lay 60 miles north-west of the Isla de Margarita, which in turn lay off the coast of the Spanish Main. Unlike the pearl-producing island to the south, though, La Blanquilla was uninhabited. So, it suited Bellamy's needs perfectly. They spent two weeks there over Christmas and then celebrated the New Year with a banyan – a barbeque on the beach. While work continued on the *Sultana*, Bellamy, Levasseur and Williams decided where to go next. Olivier Levasseur decided to head off on his own in the *Postillion*, taking his crew's share of any plunder with him. Bellamy and Williams decided to head back up the chain of the West Indies and eventually return to Nassau.

In that time the *Sultana* was converted from a sailing vessel into a pirate ship. This was an extensive business. Ideally, the upper deck would be levelled from bow to stern, to make the ship a better fighting platform, and to allow boarding parties to move around quickly to where they were needed. So, any raised quarterdeck or forecastle tended to be removed. Then, extra gunports would be cut in the sides of the hull to accommodate more ordnance. Bellamy used a team from the *St Michael* to help him, including four ship's carpenters. He also transferred over the merchantman's four guns. When the job was done, the pirates prepared to sail off again and Levasseur and his men took their leave. Also leaving them was Captain Williams of the *St Michael*, whose thoroughly looted ship was allowed to continue her voyage to Jamaica. Bellamy, though, kept her four carpenters in case they came in useful.[13]

After the *Postillion* and *St Michael* parted company, Bellamy headed off to the north, keeping clear of the Windward Islands by cutting directly across the Caribbean towards the Virgin Islands. In late January 1717 the *Sultana* and *Marianne* made landfall at St Cruze, having put into their old anchorage there to avoid a tropical storm. When they arrived, Bellamy and Williams were surprised to see evidence of a sea battle. They saw the remains of a ship, burned to the waterline at the entrance to Salt River Bay, while another sloop was aground just inside the anchorage, her masts gone and her hull showing signs of heavy battle damage. On stepping ashore, they discovered the reason. These wrecks were all that remained of a two-ship pirate force and its gaggle of prizes.

A few weeks before these pirates had been careening in St Cruze when the *Scarborough* appeared under the command of Captain Francis Hume. It was 20 January 1717. The bay was too shallow for the frigate, but everything inside it was well within range of her guns. The frigate quickly destroyed the two vessels of the pirate squadron. The pirates tried to set up a four-gun battery on the Cabo de la Fleches, on the eastern side of the bay, but it was easily silenced by *Scarborough*'s heavier guns. With that the survivors fled into the island's rugged interior. They had been led by Captain Jean Martel, a French pirate who had recently based himself in Nassau. He had captured a three-masted ship-rigged slave galley, the *John and Martha*, and turned her into his 28-gun flagship. This, together with his eight-gun sloop *Revenge*, were what Bellamy and Williams had seen when they dropped anchor. Both vessels had been comprehensively destroyed.[14]

Of the three prize sloops which Martel had with him, one escaped with Martel in it and two were recaptured by Hume, who sailed them off to Antigua to be condemned as lawful prizes. The irony was that Hume had put into St Cruze looking for Bellamy. It was claimed that Martel, a former mariner and possible *flibustier* of Saint-Domingue, had accidentally run the *John and Martha* aground on the western entrance to Salt River Bay while attempting to evade the *Scarborough*, and set her on fire himself. In the process, 20 African slaves, still held in chains below decks, were burned alive. It seems Martel eventually made his way back to Nassau, where it is assumed he took the pardon offered to pirates in 1718, as from that point on his activities can no longer be traced.[15]

The survivors of Martel's crew appear to have joined Bellamy and Williams. So, with up to 100 new recruits, Bellamy's force was expanding dramatically. Their number now appears to have included several former African slaves who'd managed to escape both the British and Martel. Then, rather than linger in St Cruze, as the *Scarborough* might return, Bellamy led his two vessels north to Virgin Gorda, now part of the British Virgin Islands, a half-day's sail to the north. Although this was a British colony, its settlement of Spanish Town was undefended; so, for a while Bellamy made it his own. They spent a week there, and it was claimed several locals joined the pirate crews before Bellamy sailed off again. This time he decided to head west, to cruise in his old hunting ground, the Windward Passage.

This turned out to be an excellent decision. By the end of February, Bellamy and Williams were back in those familiar waters, cruising off the western shore of Saint-Domingue. There they spotted a large British-flagged merchant vessel, a three-masted ship-rigged galley, a little to the north of them. Bellamy ranged alongside the *Marianne* and suggested they both raise British naval ensigns to confuse their quarry. They split up and approached her steadily from astern, trying to give the impression they were British warships on patrol. Slowly they began overhauling their quarry, the 300-ton slave ship *Whydah* of London, which had left Port Royal a few days before, on the homeward leg of her triangular journey – Britain to West Africa, over to the Caribbean, and then back to Britain. She was a prize well worth taking.[16]

The *Whydah*'s master, Captain Lawrence Price, grew suspicious and increased sail. What followed was a chase northward that lasted for three long days. It took them through the Windward Passage, past Ragged Island and into the Bahamas itself. In the end, Price's attempt to flee proved a wasted effort. The two pursuers eventually drew within gun range, but Price warned them off with two shots at the sloop from a chase gun. It wasn't enough though. By now the crew

Jean Martel, a French pirate whose career ended at St Croix when he was ambushed by a British frigate.

of the *Sultana* and the *Marianne* were preparing to board their prey and were far more numerous and well-armed than Price's crew of slavers. So, he hauled up into the wind and waited for whatever would follow. They were within sight of the low snake-like coast of Long Island, some eight miles to the north, at the mouth of the Crooked Island Passage which led northwards past San Salvador and into the Atlantic. There, rolling gently in the swell, was Samuel Bellamy's greatest prize yet.[17]

He went on board to secure her, and then the pirate ships escorted the *Whydah* inshore, until the three dropped anchor off the south-western side of Long Island. Then, Bellamy was able to take a good look at his prize. The *Whydah* – or the *Whydah Galley* to give her official title – was similar to the *Sultana* in that both were three-masted ship-rigged galleys, but the new prize was roughly twice the size. She was brand new, having only been launched a few months before. She had fast, sleek lines, and she carried 18 6-pounder guns, although she had space and gunports for more. The *Whydah* was exactly what Bellamy wanted. So, he decided to keep her and make her his flagship. The *Whydah*, though, was a slave ship, and while she'd already deposited her human cargo in Port Royal, she still had the stench of a slaver about her.[18]

Still, Bellamy learned from the *Whydah*'s 50-strong crew that Captain Price was both fair and well respected. So, Bellamy decided to be generous. He told Price that he intended to keep the *Whydah*, but he would give him the *Sultana* in exchange, together with some of the plunder he'd accumulated on board her. As Bellamy's quartermaster, Richard Noland supervised the transfer of the plunder and stores from one ship to the other, along with ten of her guns. This brought the *Whydah*'s armament up to 28 guns – an impressive array for a man-of-war, let alone a pirate ship. That done, and after a handful of the slavers joined the pirate crew, Price parted company, sailing off with his remaining men aboard the *Sultana*. They must have considered themselves lucky to have been captured by pirates but released unharmed, to tell the tale.[19]

Before Bellamy did anything else, he and his men set about converting the *Whydah* to suit their needs. Much as they had with the *Sultana* at La Blanquilla, they cut down her hull, removing the roundhouse or pilothouse aft on her quarterdeck, reduced the height of her forecastle, and removed the slave barricades fore and aft of her waist. This was the barrier erected to protect the crew in the event of a slave rising on board. The *Whydah* was too large to careen, at least in those waters, but as she was newly built, marine growth on her lower hull wouldn't have been sufficient to reduce her speed. That, for Bellamy, was all-important. Slavers were built for speed, and Bellamy knew he now could outpace virtually any ship they encountered. That done, Bellamy was ready to put his new flagship through her paces.

It was the start of March, and Samuel Bellamy was determined to head north, to cruise up the Atlantic seaboard of Britain's North American colonies from South Carolina to Maine. After conferring with Paulsgrave Williams, he called together the crews of his two ships, and after some discussion they agreed to the plan. The *Whydah* and the *Marianne* would cruise independently once they reached the Carolinas, but the two vessels set a rendezvous, off Damariscove Island in the colony of Maine, some 25 miles north-east of the harbour of Portland. To reduce the risk, their plunder was divided between the two ships, and then, after taking on water, they set off, heading south and then west, keeping well clear of the reef-strewn waters of the Bahamas.

Within two days the *Whydah* had seized her first prize: the British three-masted merchant ship *Tanner*, intercepted off the north-western coast of Saint-Domingue. Her master, Captain John Stover, realized that resistance was hopeless, and so he surrendered his ship within sight of the old *flibustier* stronghold of Tortuga. Although British-flagged, the holds of the *Tanner* were filled with sugar cane, gathered in the plantations of Saint-Domingue, loaded on board in Petit Goave. Her destination was the French port of La Rochelle. This wasn't much use to the pirates, but they took some of her masts and spars to replace worn ones in the *Marianne*. Then, one of the *Tanner*'s crew, a young French sailor called Jean Shuan from Nantes, was so eager to join the pirate crew that he revealed where Captain Stover was hiding a pay chest, containing 5,000 French silver *livres*. As a result, Shuan was welcomed into the crew of the *Marianne*.[20]

The pirates then parted company with their prize and continued west, through the Old Bahama Channel and into the Florida Straits. They made landfall off the Florida Keys around Islamorada. From there they worked their way north through the Bahama Channel. At the back of his mind Bellamy was probably concerned about passing so close to New Providence. After all, his two vessels now carried a small fortune in plunder, and no pirate code of honour would have stopped the likes of Hornigold, Jennings or Thatch from trying to lay hands on it. So, Bellamy pressed on, despite the growing realization that the *Marianne* was in desperate need of an overhaul, especially to her masts and rigging.[21]

It was now late March. Having emerged safely through the Bermuda Channel, Bellamy planned to start his cruise off the New England Bay, which meant he avoided the inward curve of the coast and kept well out into the Atlantic, steering towards the north-north-east. On that heading he passed clear of Carolina's Outer Banks, intending to make a new landfall off Long Island around the middle of April. Despite being well clear of the usual shipping lanes, the *Whydah* still came across a prize – a small sloop, heading from Newport, Rhode Island, down to Charles Town, South Carolina. Her master, Captain Samuel Beer, was taken aboard the *Whydah* as the *Marianne*'s crew ransacked their prize. Afterwards, Beer wrote an account of the experience.[22]

What purports to be Samuel Beer's exchange with Samuel Bellamy is recorded by Captain Charles Johnson in his *A General History of the Pyrates*. It appears Bellamy had wanted to return Beer's sloop to him, but the crew of the *Whydah* refused this gesture of kindness. According to Johnson, Bellamy said, 'Damn my blood, I am sorry they won't let you have your sloop again, for I scorn to do anyone a mischief when it is not for my advantage.' He added, 'Damn the sloop – we must sink her, and she might have been use to you.' Bellamy might have been the pirate captain and had been in full command during the chase. Now, though, it was up to the collective wishes of the crew what to do with their prize.[23]

That anecdote rang true, but Johnson then added a small speech by Bellamy, to show how he justified hardening his heart: 'Damn ye – ye are a sneaking puppy, and so are all those who will submit to be governed by laws which rich men have made for their own security, for the cowardly whelps have not the courage otherwise to defend what they get by their knavery.' This, more than anything else, was a justification for piracy – an attack against a system stacked against the common seaman. Bellamy, though, wasn't finished. He added, 'But damn ye altogether. Damn them, a pack of crafty rascals! And you, who serve them: a parcel of hen-hearted numskulls!' He finished his rant with the lines 'They vilify us, the scoundrels do, when there is only this difference – they rob the poor under the cover of law, and we plunder the rich under the cover of our own courage!'

Whether this exchange ever happened is doubtful – we only have Johnson's word for it, and he appears to have added a lot of embellishments to his 1724 best-seller *A General History of the Pyrates* to titillate his readership. This exchange might well be apocryphal, but it also neatly sums up one of the main reasons seamen in this period turned to piracy. They felt that the system was stacked against them, and that only the shipowners and ship captains made money at the expense of the seamen's own labour. However, Bellamy's supposed flourish ended on a rousing note. He yelled, 'I am a free prince, and I have as much authority to make war on the whole world as he who has a hundred ships at sea, and an army of 1000,000 men in the field.'

After Captain Beer and his crew were transferred to the *Marianne*, and the small prize looted, Bellamy's men set Beer's sloop ablaze. The pirates then continued on their way. A few days later, the weather changed, and somewhere off the coast of Virginia they ran into thick fog. The *Whydah* and the *Marianne* lost sight of each other, and when the fog cleared Bellamy and his men saw no sign of their consort. So, Bellamy sailed inshore, until he came within sight of the Virginia Capes. Still, this wasn't a problem, as they now had two rendezvous points – Block Island off the Rhode Island coast, where they intended to maroon Beer and his men, and then Damariscove off the coast of Maine. So, after re-plotting his course, he headed north-east towards the first of these two islands.[24]

The next morning, Bellamy came across three ships struggling to move in the light airs off the Delaware coast. So, he captured them, one after the other. The *Agnes* of Glasgow was en route from Williamsburg in Virginia to Barbados, carrying sugar and rum. Captain Andrew Turbett watched as the pirates looted the rum, then let his ship go on her way. Next was the 100-ton snow-rigged *Ann Galley*, which was small and weatherly. Bellamy decided to keep her, and sent Richard Noland and a prize crew to take charge of her. Finally, the *Whydah* captured the small barque *Endeavour*, on her way from Brighton in Sussex to the Virginia colony. She too was looted, then left to complete her voyage with Captain Beer and his crew aboard as passengers. The last Beer saw of the *Whydah* she was heading away to the north-east, followed by the *Ann Galley*.[25]

A week later, on 26 April, the *Whydah* was off Nantucket, some 60 miles east of Block Island. Bellamy had decided to cruise off the fishing grounds there before heading to his first rendezvous. A few days before they were hit by a strong westerly gale, which cracked one of the ship's masts. Bellamy and his men repaired it as best they could, but they really needed to put in somewhere to make more permanent repairs. Block Island was a likely spot, but Bellamy wanted to spend a day or two cruising the fishing grounds before seeking out Williams' *Marianne* off the Rhode Island coast.

That morning he captured the small trader *Mary Anne* of Dublin, carrying a cargo of wine from Boston to New York. He decided to take her with him, and, summoning her master, Captain Andrew Crumpsley, aboard the *Whydah*, he pressed on towards Cape Cod. The *Mary Anne*, the *Ann* and the *Marianne* accompanied the *Whydah*. Then another fog descended – a commonplace thing in those waters – but in the middle of it they stumbled across another small trading sloop, the *Fisher* of Boston. Captain Robert Ingold revealed he was sailing to his home port from the Virginia colony with a mixed cargo. So, eager for a local guide, Bellamy added the *Fisher* to his small gaggle of prizes.[26]

They continued on towards the north, keeping well to seaward of Nantucket and then Cape Cod. The fog had thinned, but the sea became more restive as they sailed on. So too did Bellamy, as he noticed the *Mary Anne* was falling astern. He turned about and sought her out, but discovered that the Dublin sloop was leaking badly and the crew had been drinking. Still, John Brown, the pirate in charge of her small prize crew, swore he'd follow the *Whydah*. Instead, during the next few hours, she fell astern and was lost in the dark. By now, Bellamy had more serious things to worry about. The seas were becoming ferocious – a storm was brewing, and at around 10pm that night the conditions became desperate. The wind had strengthened to gale force and was blowing from the south-east, pushing them towards the Cape Cod shore.

Squalls of heavy rain lashed down, while lightning crashed overhead. The seas were becoming mountainous, with crests over 30ft high threatening to overwhelm the smaller ships. A little later, the crews of the *Ann* and the *Fisher* lost sight of the *Whydah*, but on all three craft the real danger was the looming lee shore, somewhere out there in the darkness to larboard (port). On board the *Ann*, Robert Noland heard the breakers and ordered his men to drop the anchor – praying it would hold. If it didn't, they would be smashed to pieces amid the surf. A short distance away the *Fisher* did the same. Miraculously, given the conditions, the anchors held – at least for the moment. The two small craft tossed on the end of their anchor cables, a few hundred yards from the beach, and less than two miles from the Cape Cod village of Eastham. Now it was up to Bellamy in the *Whydah*, somewhere out there in the darkness.[27]

She was a few miles farther north, battling through the same raging seas. Bellamy came to the same conclusion – he needed to try to anchor and ride out the storm. On his order the ship turned into the wind and dropped both of her great iron anchors. The crew must have prayed that they'd hold, but then, inexorably, the *Whydah* began sliding astern, drawing closer to the beach. The anchors were dragging. Bellamy only had one option left – to cut the anchor cables, turn his ship around, and try to run her aground onto the beach. That, at least, might give them all a fighting chance. The order was given, but the men at the wheel couldn't turn the ship. Instead, she was driven astern, propelled by the mountainous waves, until she was thrown stern first against the sloping shore. The masts snapped and fell overboard, and the dismasted hulk of the pirate ship was gradually and remorselessly pounded to pieces in the surf.

When dawn broke on 27 April the beach between Wellfleet and Eastham was littered with wreckage, and bodies. Several of the locals came in the shrieking wind and pelting rain to see if anyone had survived, and to search for valuables. They found no immediate sign of any survivors, so they set about picking through the detritus on the beach and searching the corpses.

Thomas Davis, a 22-year-old Welshman, was one of the carpenters press-ganged from the *St Michael* at La Blanquilla. He crawled ashore and knocked on the door of a farmhouse. The farmer, on hearing his story, took the dazed Welshman back to the beach, lying him across a horse. He had Davis show him the wreck and began plundering the wreckage, making several trips before the other locals arrived to join in. There they found a second survivor, John Julian, a Miskito Indian who'd joined Bellamy in the Gulf of Honduras and who'd served as his local pilot. Both survivors were turned over to the authorities but were acquitted of any charges of piracy. Julian was almost certainly sold as a slave, while Davis made his way to Boston, and obscurity.[28]

Everyone else aboard the pirate ship *Whydah* was now dead. In all, around 160 crewmen and captives lost their lives in the tempest. Over the next few days, the Eastham community buried 62 drowned corpses, all of which had been stripped of their valuables long before the local justice of the peace Joseph Doane arrived. Among them was 'Black Sam' Bellamy, their gifted captain and self-proclaimed 'free prince'. He drowned just a few miles from the home of Goody Hallett, the young woman he wanted to marry. For some, like the Reverend Cotton Mather, he had met his just deserts. Others were less guilty of moral turpitude, such as the crew of Bellamy's prizes, brought aboard the pirate flagship shortly before the disaster. Also lost in the wrecking was John King, the young boy who'd left his parents to run away with the pirates.[29]

Just down the coast, at daylight the exhausted men on board the *Ann* and the *Fisher* picked themselves up and looked around. Their anchors had held throughout the night, and although the seas were still rough and the rain was heavy, they noticed that by mid-morning the wind had veered. It was now blowing offshore. So, the two craft edged out to sea. A couple of hours later, Richard Noland abandoned the leaking *Fisher*, after moving everyone on board the *Ann*. He then set a course northward towards Maine. Two days later they reached Monhegan Island, some 12 miles from Damariscove Island, and hid there, waiting for the *Whydah*. Eventually, realizing what had happened to Bellamy, Noland quit the rendezvous and set off back towards the Caribbean, on his own pirate cruise.[30]

Back on Cape Cod, during the storm the *Mary Anne* had run aground on one of the larger sandbars just off the Cape Cod shore. The men aboard her could literally step ashore, and they did just that, waiting on the island for rescue. It came later in the morning, when two local men in a canoe appeared and agreed to ferry them ashore. As well as her own crew, the seven pirates aboard her survived and were duly arrested by Joseph Doane. They and the two survivors from the *Whydah* were taken to Boston where they were tried that October. Two were acquitted – Thomas Davis and his fellow *St Michael* carpenter Thomas South, who were able to prove they were coerced into joining

Bellamy's crew. John Julian was never tried – instead, he was quietly sold into slavery.

Six of the crew, though, were found guilty. They were all hanged in Charlestown, across Boston harbour from the city. They swung on the line of gibbets set up along the shore there and died under the stern gaze of the Puritanical Reverend Cotton Mather. Shortly before, they had all supposedly sought repentance of their sins. Even if they hadn't, it made a good moral story for Mather to publish. However, there was no room for repentance in the eyes of the law. On 15 November, a dull, grey, rainy day, those six pirates from the *Whydah* – Thomas Baker, John Brown, Peter Hoff, Hendrick Quintor, Jean Shuan and Simon von Horst – all died at the end of a rope, becoming some of the first pirates to die as a result of the official backlash against the pirate scourge that was sweeping the Americas.[31]

Unknown to the authorities in Boston, there were still a couple of strands to tie up. Before the storm hit, Paulsgrave Williams in the *Marianne* was off the coast of Rhode Island, where he had been brought up. He lingered there in Block Island Sound for several days and so missed the worst of the storm that hit Cape Cod, 80 miles away. Once the seas eased, on 28 April, he moved into Long Island Sound, where he captured a sloop from New Haven in the Connecticut colony, plundering her cargo of salt and recruiting three of her small crew. He then moved east to cruise the waters off Martha's Vineyard, where, on 3 May, he captured two more trading sloops. Best of all, he captured a pilot, who helped guide him past Cape Cod and on to Maine.[32]

They plundered another sloop on the way north and ventured ashore near Falmouth in Maine, for a spot of looting and to find another coastal pilot. In the end they found a friendly fisherman who guided them to Damariscove Island – the site of their rendezvous. They just missed Noland – he'd given up waiting a few days before and had already headed back out to sea. While they waited, Williams and his men set about repairing the *Marianne* using masts and spars they'd looted for the job. Finally, on 23 May, Williams gave up on Bellamy and the *Whydah*, and the *Marianne* set off southwards again towards the Bahamas. In fact, Noland's *Ann Galley* was heading there too. Both would continue to prey on any vessel they came across during their voyage. That was how they learned about the fate of Bellamy and his flagship.[33]

So, by the end of May, the two surviving pirate ships of Bellamy's squadron were back at sea, continuing their attacks and heading towards Nassau. By then, the final member of their original group, Olivier Levasseur, was over 6,000 miles away. After parting company with them off La Blanquilla that January, he'd headed for Brazil, Portugal's wealthy South American colony. He'd already upgraded from the *Postillion* to a 22-gun merchant frigate called *La Louise*. That May, while the remnants of Bellamy's flotilla were heading south to Nassau, Levasseur was cruising off Rio de Janeiro, preying on Portuguese slavers and merchantmen. During the summer of 1717 the *Marianne*, *Ann* and *La Louise* weren't the only pirate ships at sea. Instead, they were just a part of what was fast becoming a rising tide of piracy in American waters. Dozens of pirate groups just like them were at sea, and their tally of victims was growing steadily. Piracy was fast becoming a major problem, everywhere from the St Lawrence down to the River Plate.[34]

NINE

Stede Bonnet

EVERYONE LOVES A GOOD hanging. That certainly seemed to be the case on a brisk early December day in 1718. It seemed as if half the population of Charles Town had turned up to see the very public execution of a pirate captain. The hubbub swelled as the tumbrel approached the gallows, flanked by files of soldiers, The wealthier citizens watched from their balconies overlooking the waterfront, while the rest of the town jostled for a view over the heads of the immense crowd. Sailors even lined the masts of the vessels in the harbour, all eager to catch a glimpse of the pirate's final moments. This wasn't just any pirate captain though. This was the 'gentleman pirate', Major Stede Bonnet, one-time wealthy landowner on Barbados, a devoted family man, and an officer in the island's militia. His fall from grace had been spectacular. Now the expectant vultures of Charles Town had come in their hundreds to see him die.

A few months before, he had been on board a vessel of the master pirate Edward Thatch's squadron as they blockaded Charles Town harbour. This had sent shockwaves through colonial America, and even though Bonnet had no real say in the operation, his name was irrevocably linked with that of Blackbeard. Now, on the morning of 10 December 1718, Bonnet was about to pay the ultimate price for this association. The gentleman pirate could expect no mercy. A clergyman heard Bonnet's final words of repentance and offered a prayer for the lapsed man's soul. Then the crowd hushed and strained to hear Bonnet's own speech – his words of sorrow and repentance. After he spoke, he was handed a nosegay – a small posy of flowers – and he held this in front of him in his tightly bound hands. Then, at a signal from the magistrate, the cart was pulled away, and Stede Bonnet, the gentleman pirate, died jerking on the end of the hangman's rope.

It is hardly surprising that Captain Charles Johnson devoted a whole chapter of his *A General History of the Pyrates* to Stede Bonnet. After all, unlike almost every other pirate in Johnson's book, Bonnet was a bona fide gentleman – someone who should have spent his days upholding the established order rather than fighting against it. The whole story was so sensational that Johnson couldn't avoid including it in his book. Although Bonnet wasn't a very good pirate, or a particularly successful one, thanks to Johnson he ended up rubbing shoulders with the likes of Edward Thatch, Bartholomew Roberts, Sam Bellamy and Charles Vane. His capture and trial were the sensation of the age, covered by newspapers in both Britain and the Americas. It was little wonder that his execution was so well attended.

The real novelty of Bonnet was that he never needed to turn to piracy at all. He was a gentleman, a prominent member of Barbadian society, and a major in the local militia. Bonnet was really one of the last people anyone expected to be drawn into the sordid criminal world of piracy. Johnson said of him, 'the major was a gentleman of good reputation in the island of Barbados, [who] was master of a plentiful fortune, and had the advantage of a liberal education. He had the least temptation of any man to follow such a course of life, from the condition of his circumstances. It was very surprising to everyone, in the island where he lived, as he was greatly esteemed and honoured, before he broke out into open acts of piracy.'

At Bonnet's trial in Charles Town, the judge described him as 'a gentleman that has had the advantage of a liberal education and being generally esteemed as a Man of Letters'. That was perfectly true. Stede Bonnet was born in St Michael's Parish in the south of Barbados in 1688, the eldest son of a third-generation plantation owner. He inherited the family estate seven miles outside Bridgetown when he was six years old and was raised by his mother in the full expectation that he would take over the running of the family's extensive sugar plantation when he came of age. Almost 100 slaves worked on their 400-acre plantation, one of the largest on the island. A map of the estate even shows they had their own animal-powered mill to produce syrup from their sugar cane. He was groomed to become a leading member of the tight little clique of Barbadian society, and in 1709, when he was 21 years old, he married Mary Allamby, the daughter of another plantation owner. He also became a major in the Barbadian militia that was based in Bridgetown. Bonnet, then, was set fair for a comfortable but conventional future.[1]

However, the couple's first son died while still an infant. Bonnet seemed to fall into a depression, despite the successful birth of three more children – two boys and a girl. According to Johnson, the Barbadians thought he was suffering from 'a disorder of the mind, which had been visible in him some time before this wicked undertaking'. Johnson also alluded to an unhappy marriage and possibly even bouts of insanity. Then, in 1716, everything came to a head. The background was the anger in the island over the pirate attacks by Samuel Bellamy and Paulsgrave Williams in the Windward Islands, which were threatening to disrupt trade – and the flow of sugar to its markets in America and Europe. This may have been all it took to raise the possibility of piracy in Bonnet's mind. So, the 28-year-old wealthy Barbadian planter decided to throw everything away and become a pirate himself.[2]

His mind being made up, he set about it in an extremely unusual way. First, the inveterate landsman bought a 35-ton sloop and had it delivered to Barbados. Presumably he told others in his social circle that he planned to fit her out as a privateer, to send out to hunt pirates like Bellamy and Williams. She was the perfect pirate vessel, capable of mounting ten guns and holding a crew of up to 70 men. Once she was almost ready, Bonnet went around the waterfront taverns of Bridgetown, and first recruited an experienced sailing master and then a crew. He was probably the only pirate in history to go about the business this way – and offer a wage to his men. The owner of a potential privateer would

Stede Bonnet, the so-called 'gentleman pirate',
sailed for a time with Blackbeard.

usually offer his crew shares in the plunder rather than cash over the barrel. Bonnet, though, was clearly inexperienced in such things. Then, before they sailed, he stocked his sloop with all the supplies, weapons and equipment they'd need for a privateering cruise. As a final gesture of piratical rebellion, he christened his vessel the *Revenge*.[3]

Then, in April 1717, he put to sea. The event was recorded by Captain Bartholomew Chandler, who commanded the frigate HMS *Winchelsey*, the Royal Navy's guardship in those waters. He wrote, 'There ... has been lately, over on the coast, a pirate sloop from Barbados, commanded by one Major Bennet, who has an Estate on that Island, and the Sloop is his own.' Chandler added, 'This advice I had by letter from thence, that in April last He ran away out of Carlisle Bay at night ... he had aboard 126 men, 6 guns and arms and ammunition.' Sure enough, the Barbados shipping returns for that month record that the *Revenge* was 'gone without clearing'. By the end of April at the latest, Stede Bonnet, former Barbadian plantation owner, was at sea and about to embark on his own pirate cruise.[4]

He avoided cruising the waters of the West Indies, where he might be recognized or run into the *Winchelsey*. Instead, he headed for the Atlantic seaboard of the American colonies, which he reached sometime during the late spring. He then spent a month cruising off the Virginia Capes. There, according to Johnson, 'He took several ships, and plundered them of their provisions, clothes, money, ammunition etc.' The irony was that Bonnet could have bought these goods outright. Most pirates attacked merchant vessels to find plunder, and to find provisions or drink. Bonnet, though, was doing it as a hobby.[5]

Johnson went on to list his victims: 'The *Anne*, Capt. Montgomery, from Glasgow, the *Turbet* from Barbados, which for country sake, after they had taken out the principal part of the lading the pirate crew set her on fire, the *Endeavour*, Captain Scott, from Bristol, and the *Young*, from Leith.' It was interesting that Stede ordered the Barbadian vessel to be burned, presumably in a half-hearted attempt to hide the evidence of his crime from his fellow Barbadians. As a surety he even had his crew refer to him as Captain Edwards. Still, it was quite likely he'd been recognized. However, instead of killing the *Turbet*'s crew – the ultimate way of preventing disclosure – Bonnet set them ashore on the Virginia coast. He then headed north towards New York, where he captured a sloop off the eastern tip of Long

Island. Johnson claims that shortly afterwards, Bonnet put in at Gardner's Island, off the southern coast of Long Island, where 'he purchased provisions for his company's use, which they paid for, and so went off again without molestation.'[6]

After that, Johnson claims that Bonnet sailed the *Revenge* south again to the Carolinas, and in late August he appeared off the bar outside Charles Town. There he took two prizes – a sloop from Barbados and a brig from New England, both stopped while heading into the port. The Barbadian sloop was commanded by Captain Joseph Palmer and carried a cargo of rum, sugar and slaves. After ransacking the New England brig, Bonnet's men let her go. The Barbadian sloop was kept with them, and a few weeks later, when they put into a secluded inlet in North Carolina to careen the *Revenge*, they burned their prize. This was probably near Cape Fear; a year later, Bonnet would use the river as his base. The burning of the sloop was undoubtedly another attempt by Bonnet to cover his tracks. Once again, Palmer, his crew and his slaves were set free.[7]

At this point, Johnson's account and the evidence trail begin to tell different stories. According to Johnson, while they were in the Carolinas Bonnet didn't really know what to do next. Perhaps he was tiring of the pirate lifestyle. As he put it, 'After the sloop was cleaned, they put to sea, but came to no resolution what course to take. The crew were divided in their opinions, some being for one thing and some another, so that nothing but confusion seemed to attend their schemes.' He then suggested a lack of regard for their wage-paying captain, which in itself went against the usual principles of pirate life. Johnson continued, 'The major was no sailor, as was said before, and therefore had to be obliged to yield to many things that were imposed on him during their undertaking, for want of a competent knowledge in maritime affairs.' It seems clear that Bonnet was now losing control of his crew.[8]

Then, Johnson had him 'fall in company with another pirate, one Edward Teach … commonly called Blackbeard'. Johnson's account changed as new editions of his book were printed. In fact, they sailed south, as in October they were drawn into battle with a Spanish patrol vessel – probably a large sloop-of-war operating out of Havana. Somewhere in the Florida Strait the crew of the *Revenge* spotted a Spanish merchantman, close into the Cuban coast. They attempted to attack her but found out too late she was a warship. According to the news reports, before the pirates could escape their sloop was badly battered, and up to half her crew were killed or wounded. Bonnet himself was wounded in the brief fight. From subsequent events it seems that this encounter ended Bonnet's enthusiasm for his piratical adventure.[9]

After that close and deadly encounter, the battered *Revenge*, no doubt guided by the wishes of her crew, headed to Nassau so she could be repaired. In was now late autumn 1717. This may be where Edward Thatch and Stede Bonnet joined forces. No doubt Benjamin Hornigold encouraged this union. However, it's also possible that Thatch was off cruising when the *Revenge* put into Nassau, and the two joined forces at sea, most likely off the Delaware Capes. That Nassau was the location of the union between Thatch and Bonnet is more likely in the way suggested in the November edition of the *Boston News Letter*. When Bonnet left Nassau, most probably in early September, with Thatch by his side, his crew had been reinforced by men from Nassau, including William Howell, whose testimony would later help fill in some of the gaps in Bonnet's story. The *Revenge* also now boasted an impressive armament of 12 guns. From the start, there was little doubt who was in command.[10]

The November edition of the *Boston News Letter* carried an article which mentioned Bonnet by name from a report received a few weeks before. It spoke about the attacks by a pirate called Teach, who was in command of the pirate sloop *Revenge*. It then added the following snippet of information:

> On board the Pirate Sloop is Major Bennet, but has no Command, he walks about in his Morning Gown, and then to his Books, of which he has a good Library on Board, he was not well of his wounds that he received by attacking a Spanish Man of War, which kill'd and wounded thirty to forty men. After which putting into Providence, the place of Rendevouze for the Pirates, they put the afore said Capt. Teach on board for this Cruise.[11]

Although Johnson places the coming together of Thatch and Bonnet in early 1718 – a date all but impossible given Thatch's timeline of pirate attacks – he did capture the relationship between the two pirate captains which the newspaper article alluded to: 'To him [Thatch] Bonnet's crew joined in consortship, and Bonnet himself was laid aside, notwithstanding the sloop was his own; he went aboard Blackbeard's ship, not concerning himself with any of their affairs, where he continued till she was lost in Topsail Inlet, and one Richards was appointed captain in his room.' He added, 'The major now saw his folly, but could not help himself, which made him melancholy. He reflected upon his past course of life and was confounded with shame when he thought upon what he had done.' According to Johnson, he declared that 'he should be ashamed to see the face of any Englishman again', hinting that, if he survived, he would flee to Spain or Portugal.[12]

So, for the next eight months, Stede Bonnet was virtually a prisoner on his own vessel. It was effectively commanded by Thatch, and then, once the pirate captured *La Concorde* and turned her into his flagship *Queen Anne's Revenge*, he put Richard Richards in command of the *Revenge*. Reading between the lines, Johnson already alluded to Bonnet's tendency towards despondency or melancholy. It was likely, then, given his seemingly fragile mental health, that Bonnet slipped into a depression which lasted throughout his association with Edward Thatch. Before he left Barbados, he had an extensive library installed in his cabin. Perhaps he took solace among his books, while Thatch and Richards did what they pleased with his finely built sloop.

What helped Stede Bonnet get out of his all-consuming depression was the tantalizing thought of a royal pardon. After all, he hadn't done that much as a pirate, especially compared to others like Hornigold, Jennings, Bellamy or Thatch. He could also claim he'd been under virtual house arrest since the previous autumn when he'd first formed his one-sided partnership with Edward Thatch. So, when Thatch sent Bonnet off in a small sloop to obtain a provisional pardon for them all, Bonnet must have felt his spirits rise. He sailed from Topsail Inlet to Bath Town on the Pamlico River, where Governor Eden of the North Carolina colony maintained a residence. This was the answer to all his woes. With luck he could eventually face humanity again and rejoin polite society, with the added exciting label of 'reformed pirate' to his name.[13]

The terms of the royal pardon were generous. It was open to all pirates who 'Shall on or before the 5th of September, in the Year of our Lord 1718, surrender ... to any Governor or Deputy Governor of any of our Plantations beyond the Seas'. That meant Bonnet was well within the window of time stated in the offer. The only slight problem was that the immunity given in the pardon applied only to crimes committed before January 1718. So, it didn't cover the attacks made by Blackbeard in the Gulf of Honduras, or off Charles Town. However, provincial governors also had the right to waive this clause if they saw fit. Bonnet had the excuse that he didn't participate in these attacks, and it didn't apply to him. The interpretation, though, was up to the individual colonial governors. This was probably one of the reasons Thatch sent the polite and mild-mannered Bonnet to negotiate with Governor Eden rather than go himself.[14]

Furthermore, Bonnet felt more than willing to repent for his sins and to promise never to commit piratical acts again. The meeting between Stede Bonnet and Governor Charles Eden went well – the two men clearly got on with each other – and after a day or so, Bonnet left Bath Town with a provisional pardon, both for Thatch and his men, as well as for himself and his own original crewmen. For Bonnet it was a thoroughly satisfying outcome. He must have been in a greatly improved mood when he returned to Topsail Inlet. What he found there, however, ended that in a skipped heartbeat. Blackbeard had absconded with all the plunder – a cache of stolen goods that by their agreement should have been shared with Bonnet and his men. Instead, Thatch had marooned Bonnet's followers on a deserted sandy island nearby and set most of his own crew adrift on the North Carolina shore.

Bonnet's mood quickly turned to rage and a burning desire for revenge. He discovered that while Thatch had left him the *Revenge*, she had been thoroughly plundered and stripped of her sails and rigging. It would take weeks to get her ready for sea again. But that is exactly what a now-thoroughly motivated Bonnet planned to do. He would refit her, then set off in pursuit of Blackbeard. His priority, though, was to rescue his crew. It seems that on their barren island, they 'remained there two nights and one day, without subsistence, or the least prospect of any, expecting nothing else but a lingering death, when to their inexpressible comfort they saw redemption at hand'. It was, apparently, only by luck that 'Major Bonnet happened to get intelligence of their being there, by two of the pirates who had escaped Teach's cruelty'. They had found a boat among the fishermen's huts, in the 'poor little village at the upper end of the harbour'. Bonnet then used this vessel to recover his marooned crewmen.[15]

Bonnet also enlisted some of the other pirates Thatch had deserted on the beach, and together they worked furiously to make the *Revenge* ready for sea. The likelihood is that Bonnet also hired some of the local fishermen to help speed things up. Then, the now aptly named sloop was ready to set out after Blackbeard. If Bonnet had thought about it long enough, he'd have realized he was on a fool's errand. He had a chance to walk away from piracy once and for all. He might even have convinced himself he was genuinely pirate-hunting by pursuing Thatch. However, he should also have known that once the *Revenge* put to sea it was almost certain that his crew would take control over events, in that annoyingly democratic way that pirates did.

However, when news reached him that Thatch had been sighted just 40 miles away on Ocracoke Island, there was no holding him back. The desire for revenge overcame common sense. So, as soon as she was ready, the *Revenge* set off in pursuit. As Johnson put it, 'it happened too late, for he missed of him there, and after four days' cruise, hearing no farther news of him, they steered their course towards Virginia'. In fact, by the time the *Revenge* arrived off Ocracoke, Blackbeard was safely in Bath Town. For some reason Bonnet and his men presumed Thatch was out cruising for prey. They never expected him to be meekly seeking a pardon.[16]

The first ship they encountered off the Virginia Capes was a small coaster, and Bonnet traded with her rather than pillage her cargo. It seems he wasn't quite ready to return to piracy – at least not yet. Next the *Revenge* came upon a small sloop laden with rum. This time Bonnet couldn't hold back his men, who ransacked the vessel and drank her entire cargo. Bonnet and his men had now crossed the line. There would be no pardon for them. In the eyes of the world they were pirates again. After lapsing back into their old ways, neither Bonnet nor his crew could expect any mercy if they were caught. Still, Bonnet held on to a faint and foolhardy notion that by giving a false name he would somehow escape justice.

So, he had his men call him either Captain Edwards or Captain Thomas. He also decided to change the name of his sloop from the *Revenge* to the *Royal James* – in honour of the exiled Jacobean king. Bonnet had changed. He was no longer a gentleman of quality. He was recasting himself as a rebel, and was now willing to cock a snook at King George I. It was unlikely anyone was fooled by all this, as by now his reputation and unusual backstory was the talk of the Americas. Still, to maintain at least an illusion of legality, he didn't plunder ships *per se.* Instead, he offered his victims a token payment for the goods they plundered. The idea was, if caught, they could claim they were trading rather than stealing. Again, though, this didn't fool the authorities, who knew exactly what Bonnet and the *Royal James* were doing.[17]

Johnson provides a useful catalogue of his attacks, which resumed off the southernmost of the Virginia Capes: 'He took off Cape Henry two ships from Virginia, bound for Glasgow, out of which they had very little besides a hundredweight of tobacco. The next day they took a small sloop bound from Virginia to Bermuda, which supplied them with twenty barrels of pork, some bacon, and they gave her in return two barrels of rice and a hogshead of molasses.' Johnson added that two of the crewmen from this sloop volunteered to join the pirates and left aboard the *Royal James* with them. Johnson continues, 'The next they took was another Virginiaman bound for Glasgow, out of which they had nothing of value, save only a few combs, pins and needles, and gave her instead thereof, a barrel of port and two barrels of bread.' It was a pitifully miserable haul, and certainly not worth losing the right to a pardon over.[18]

Still, Bonnet was committed to his course, and he intended to carry on until things improved. His crew, though, were less impressed and grew restless. For the moment, they played along with Bonnet. Johnson continued his catalogue of attacks: 'From Virginia they sailed to Philadelphia, and in the latitude of 38° North they took a schooner coming from North Carolina, bound for Boston; they had out of her only two dozen of calfskins, to make covers for guns.' The only good news for Bonnet was that two of the schooner's crew joined his crew. By this stage Bonnet and his men felt they'd be better quitting the Atlantic seaboard and heading to the West Indies instead. First, Bonnet wanted to lay hands on more supplies. So, the attacks continued. Off the mouth of the Delaware River, they took two snows, both bound for Bristol, which yielded some money – presumably the vessels' pay chests – and the pirates also captured a 60-ton sloop, but she appeared to be sailing in ballast, so had nothing on board worth plundering. By now Bonnet's crew were utterly sick of all this. Either they'd lay hands on plunder, or they'd get rid of their captain.

Then, on 29 July, they came across a 50-ton sloop called the *Fortune*, on her way from Philadelphia to Barbados. This time the boarders were led by Robert Tucker, Bonnet's quartermaster, who confronted the sloop's commander, Captain Thomas Read, and hit him repeatedly with the flat of his cutlass. When others tried to intervene, Tucker sliced at them. This meant that Bonnet's web of pretence – paying for goods, false names – had now been dropped. This was no-holds-barred piracy, and to the devil with the consequences. Bonnet had all but lost control of his men. All that prevented the situation becoming worse was that a portion of the crew sided with Bonnet rather than Tucker and wanted no part of the quartermaster's increasingly violent methods.[19]

In fact, a week before seven of them deserted in the 60-ton sloop they'd captured, preferring to take their chances with the authorities than to stay aboard the increasingly anarchic *Royal James*. After that, things grew even more volatile. At the end of July, they took a sloop anchored off Lewes in Delaware, her hold full of drink. They stayed alongside her all night, as Tucker and his men caroused, singing and giving Jacobean toasts. At this point, they had a collective decision to make. Bonnet probably had little say in it, as Robert Tucker was the *de facto* pirate captain. They ruled out the planned move to the West Indies, at least until November and the end of the hurricane season. Instead, they'd return to their lair in North Carolina, careen the ship, and lie low until it was time to head south.

By now, after more than a year at sea, a voyage around the Caribbean and a sea battle, the *Royal James* was badly in need of repair. Her hull was covered in marine growth and some of her planks had sprung, which meant that she leaked badly. So, they put in to the Cape Fear River, taking two prizes with them, and found a spot where they could careen their sloop. They even captured a small local boat, so they could use her timbers for the repairs. This and the vital repairs that followed to seal her hull and re-rig her mast took several weeks. Johnson suggested that 'they stayed too long for their safety ... they were obliged to remain here almost two months, to refit and repair the vessel.' This was probably unfair. These repairs were necessary, and the pirates had no idea the authorities knew where they were and were out looking for them.[20]

In fact, word of their sojourn in Cape Fear had reached Charles Town. Unfortunately, the consistently unlucky Bonnet had lost out again – and once again it was thanks to the pirates of Nassau. Their attacks on shipping off the coast of the South Carolina colony had infuriated the Carolinians, who wanted vengeance on the pirates. So, Governor Robert Johnson ordered two well-armed sloops to be hired, the *Henry* and the

Sea Nymph, and these were then fitted out, provisioned and crewed. Then they were sent out on an anti-piracy patrol. Their commander was Colonel William Rhett, whose orders were to 'very much irritate the pirates who infest the coast in great numbers'.[21]

Despite his rank, the 50-year-old Rhett was a man of many parts. He was a plantation owner, a militia colonel, a merchant shipowner and captain, and a colonial politician and administrator. His townhouse in Charleston stills stands to this day – one of the oldest in the city. Eleven years before, Rhett had played a prominent part in repelling a Franco-Spanish attack on Charles Town. He was, essentially, the South Carolina colony's man of action. So, when the colony decided to become proactive and go pirate hunting, William Rhett was the obvious man to lead the expedition. Although his main target was Charles Vane, he was also on the lookout for Stede Bonnet, or even Edward Thatch, all of whom had been cruising in the colony's waters that summer.

On 26 September 1718, after cruising northwards for almost 140 miles, Rhett's small squadron arrived off the mouth of the Cape Fear River in the North Carolina colony. So far, the voyage had been uneventful – but that was about to change. As Johnson recounted, 'in the evening, the colonel with his small squadron, entered the river, and saw, over a point of land, three sloops at an anchor, which were Major Bonnet and his prize'. Rhett decided to attack the next morning, on the incoming tide. Bonnet and his rebellious crew saw the two sloops arrive off the river mouth. At first the pirates thought they were merchant sloops, coming in to anchor for the night. If so, then capturing them during the night would be simplicity itself. Gradually, it dawned on the pirates these were both armed sloops-of-war and they were there to fight them.[22]

After the initial panic this caused, the pirate crews settled down and prepared themselves for the fight that lay ahead – presumably at dawn the following day. In fact, it was Bonnet who moved first, long before the sun came out. The pirates quietly slipped their moorings, and the *Royal James* began creeping down the river in the pre-dawn darkness, with almost no sails spread, to reduce the chances of the enemy seeing her approach before it was too late. Instead, they were using the current to slip downstream. The sails were bent on, though, ready to raise when needed. All of the pirate sloops' guns were double-shotted, their crews standing by to fire when the order came. Bonnet – or rather Tucker, who was really the man in command that morning – planned to slip past the anchored sloops in the pre-dawn darkness, firing into them as he went. He'd then made a break for the open sea.[23]

That morning there were 45 men on board the *Royal James*, including Bonnet. If it came to a boarding action, they would be outnumbered about three to one, as the Carolinian sloops carried around 70 men apiece. The pirates' best hope was to take Rhett by surprise, slip past him, and make sure the enemy didn't get a chance to grapple and board. Unfortunately, as the *Royal James* came within musket range of the two South Carolina sloops, she ran hard aground on a hidden sandbank in the river mouth, not far from where the Civil War era Fort Fisher now stands. By that time the *Henry* and the *Sea Nymph* were under way and closed in on their seemingly helpless victim. Suddenly, they both ran aground too, one hitting a sandbar followed by the second a minute later. It really was a ludicrous situation, with all three sloops stranded, facing each other, with their guns unable to bear on the enemy. So, in the *Royal James*, the *Henry* and the *Sea Nymph* there was nothing they could do apart from wait for the incoming tide to lift them clear.

There was one other option. All three sloops were within musket range of their opponents, just a hundred yards or so away from them. The crews were all well-armed. So, even if their main guns couldn't bear, they could all shoot at each other. Rhett's sloops, however, were at a real disadvantage when it came to a gunfight. All three of the sloops were sitting on the pair of sandbanks on either side of the main channel. They had effectively beached, so their hulls were sloping the same way, to starboard for the pirate-hunters and to larboard – or port – for the pirates. The pirates were a hundred yards to the east of Rhett's two sloops, which meant that while the hull of the pirate ship protected her crew, the decks of the two pirate-hunters were fully exposed to musket shot from the *Royal James*.

The two sides kept up the musket exchange for five gruelling hours, by which time Rhett had lost 12 men dead and 18 more wounded, two of them gravely – almost a quarter of his force. The pirates were suffering too, but by the end of this they had only nine wounded, although they were all hit in the head and had little chance of surviving the day. By now the tide had turned, and it was coming in fast. The Carolinian sloops were a little closer to the sea and were smaller than the *Royal James*. So, the chances were that the incoming tide would free them first. Sure enough, it was the *Henry*, the smallest of the three sloops, that slowly righted herself and was lifted off the sandbar. With water under her keel at last, and with just her jib set, the *Henry's* commander Captain Masters steered his sloop into mid-channel.[24]

Then he turned her to larboard and let fly the jib, bringing the vessel to a gliding halt. By the end of the manoeuvre her starboard gun battery was aimed at the bows of the *Royal James*. Now, at point-blank range, her four-gun broadside could sweep the pirate deck with grapeshot. The pirates, with their sloop still aground and their guns pointing the wrong way, would be unable to fire back. By this time the *Sea Nymph*, with Rhett on board, was starting to free herself too, and she too would pull off the same manoeuvre. When Masters called on the pirates to surrender, Bonnet, Tucker and the rest were forced to bow to the inevitable. They meekly surrendered rather than be cut to pieces by the pirate-hunter's guns.

All in all, it was a very satisfactory day for the pirate-hunters. Rhett spent the rest of the day rounding up his prisoners, including the now infamous Stede Bonnet. Nine of them had died of their wounds, or would by the time the prisoners returned to Charles Town. Fourteen of Rhett's men had been killed too, making it a particularly costly little battle, as well as a singularly unusual one. The Carolinian wounded were tended, and prisoners of the pirates were taken aboard Rhett's sloops, and the two sloops the pirates had captured were prepared for sea. Then, Rhett led his little five-vessel squadron out past the river mouth and into the Atlantic. That done, he set a course for Charles Town, where Bonnet and his men would be handed over to the colony's magistrates, before standing trial – and undoubtedly face the hangman.

Colonel Rhett's pirate-hunting squadron reached Charles Town on 3 October, and crowds cheered their arrival as if they were conquering heroes. That is exactly what they were – the first colonial pirate-hunters to really fight back against the pirate menace. Stede Bonnet, a name familiar to anyone who read the newspapers, was now in custody and about to stand trial. There was little doubt that he would answer for his crimes. He was, in fact, the first prominent pirate captain to be arrested. This meant that his trial would be one of the most high-profile ones of its time. The same excited crowd jeered the prisoners as they were marched away to be locked up in the city's Court of Guard, near the Bay Street waterfront. At the time, Charles Town had no proper jail. Once there, though, they were guarded closely by a detachment of the South Carolina militia – Colonel Rhett's loyal men.

Despite his crimes, Bonnet was still regarded as a gentleman, and unlike the other prisoners he was lodged in the private house of Nathaniel Partridge, the city's provost marshal. A few days later he was joined by two of the *Royal James'* senior crew members – sailing master David Herriot, and the boatswain Ignatius Pell. The reason was, over the past few days both men had promised to give evidence against their fellow pirates, if they were treated with leniency at the trial. The house, though, was only lightly guarded. After all, Bonnet might have been a pirate, but he was also a gentleman, and he'd given his word.[25]

But his word wasn't enough. Late on the night of 24 October, Bonnet and Herriot slipped past the sentries posted outside the Partridge house, helped by a local supporter, the merchant Richard Tookerman, who had made his fortune trading in stolen pirate goods brought to him from the Bahamas. That night he was able to help return the favour, most probably with the connivance of Nathaniel Partridge. The two pirates escaped, making their way through the city's streets towards the banks of the Cooper River on the eastern side of the city. There they were ferried across in a canoe owned by Tookerman, paddled by his men. Then the two escapees were left to their own devices at the start of the open countryside on the river's eastern bank. A reward of £700 was offered for their re-capture, and after a quick investigation, Nathaniel Partridge was fired from his post as provost marshal as it was felt he'd helped in the escape. Tookerman was later arrested. In the city itself, an armed gang besieged the Court of Guard, demanding the release of the prisoners – a demonstration no doubt organized by profiteering merchants like Tookerman.

By that time the two fugitives had reached the coast a little to the north of Charles Town harbour, where they found a canoe used by a local fisherman. They promptly stole it and then tried to paddle to freedom. Then Bonnet's bad luck struck again. A strong wind blew in from the Atlantic and the seas became increasingly rough, rising to gale force. The canoe was driven back towards the coast, coming ashore on Sullivan's Island in the northern end of the Charles Town bar. Unfortunately for them Colonel Rhett had sent armed patrols to look for them, and during the evening of 8 November one of these stumbled across the two bedraggled and half-starved fugitives, accompanied by two slaves owned by Tookerman.[26]

In the exchange of fire that followed, Herriot and the two slaves were killed, at which point Bonnet surrendered. He was duly bound, and the next morning he was frogmarched back to Charles Town at gunpoint and unceremoniously thrown into the Court of Guard. He must have been surprised to find it empty. The reason was simple. After the demonstration outside the place two weeks before, the city's magistrates decided to bring the trial forward, to avoid further unrest. So, the massed trial of the 33 surviving members of the crew had begun on 28 October, four days after Bonnet absconded.[27]

Presiding over the Vice Admiralty court was Nicholas Trott, the colony's chief justice and a nephew and namesake of the Bahamian governor who once consorted with Henry Every. That, though, was long in the past. This Nicholas Trott was vehemently opposed to piracy and all its attendant evils. The result was hardly in doubt. The transcripts of the court session survive, and for the most part they contain a diatribe against the 'enemies of mankind' and the menace that these pirates pose to civilization, the rule of law, free commerce and the word of God. Given all that, the defendants didn't really stand a chance. To speed things up, Judge Trott concentrated on the taking of the two sloops *Fortune* and *Francis* back in early August, when Bonnet was operating off the mouth of the Delaware River.

Judge Trott had ample evidence of these attacks and signed depositions of the vessels' masters. All but two of the 33 men standing trial pleaded not guilty. The exceptions were John Levit of North Carolina and James Wilson of Dublin. The defenders' case rested on the argument that at the time of the attacks they intended to become law-abiding privateers but were short of provisions. So, they had simply borrowed what they needed from the two sloops. Trott and his jury were having none of it. The prosecutors had little trouble proving that they had plundered the ships and benefited by sharing out booty of about £10 a head.

That was enough to condemn all but four of the men, who had joined the pirate crew after the division of spoils from the two sloops. Consequently, on 7 November, of the 33 men accused, all of them were found guilty of piracy. All but the four who'd joined the crew later were condemned to death – the others, Jonathan Clark of Charles Town,

Like most pirate executions, the hanging of Stede Bonnet was carried out overlooking a harbour, as a warning to other mariners.

Thomas Gerard of Antigua, Thomas Nicholas of London and Rowland Sharp of Bath Town were given other lesser sentences. Three days later, at dawn on 8 October 1718, a total of 29 of the condemned men were hanged at White Point, at the boggy tip of the Charles Town peninsula. There, in full view of the men on board the ships in the harbour, they drew their last breath. Robert Tucker, the pirate who'd orchestrated Bonnet's return to piracy, was one of the men who died that morning.

Finally, on the day after his return to Charles Town, Captain Stede Bonnet was arraigned and tried on 10 October. His trial was swift and efficient. It was declared that he 'pyratically took and rifled no less than 13 vessels'. Again, Judge Trott was concentrating on the ones Bonnet had attacked after he left Thatch's company. The facts were already proven – this was just about dispensing justice. After a long diatribe, Trott declared that Bonnet had been 'corrupted, if not entirely defaced by the scepticism and infidelity of this wicked age'. He then lectured the white-faced Bonnet about the nature of sin, the nature of repentance and the need to answer for one's sins to God. After quoting biblical scripture at length, Judge Trott ended by declaring the lecture was merely the discharging of his duty as a Christian.

That done, he would do his office as a judge. Effectively, then, there was no trial. In Trott's view the trial had already been held – this was merely about passing on the sentence of the Vice Admiralty court. With that, Judge Trott announced the sentence: 'That you, the said Stede Bonnet, shall go from hence to the place from whence you came, and from thence to the place of execution, where you shall be hanged by the neck until you are dead.' Bonnet wailed and put up what onlookers described as a pathetic display. Some witnesses pleaded with the judge for clemency, or to send Bonnet to Britain for trial, but Trott was adamant. Others in the city – mainly the merchants – demanded an immediate execution. In the end, the judge left Bonnet to consider his fate for a month. Finally, on 19 December 1718, the 30-year-old Major Stede Bonnet was taken out to White Point and hanged.[28]

TEN

The Carrot and the Stick

T HE YEAR 1717 WAS a busy one for Admiralty clerks. They were the ones who worked in the offices of the Vice Admiralty courts and recorded the statements made by the victims of pirate attacks. There were six of these courts along the Atlantic seaboard of Britain's American colonies, plus four more in her island colonies of Antigua, Barbados, Bermuda and Jamaica. These depositions – statements made by the captains of plundered merchant ships – are a real treasure trove for modern-day historians, but they also tell a story of terror, violence and destruction, which often left these same captains penniless. Taken together, the depositions underline the story being told by colonial governors and the newspapers – the Americas were in the grip of a pirate menace.

Another group of clerks, the secretaries of British colonial governors, were also kept busy. These governors maintained a regular correspondence with the Council of Trade in London's Whitehall, other government departments and even the royal court. While the legal depositions build up a picture of the types of pirate attacks being carried out, it was the governors who truly showed just how serious the situation had become. One of the first of these was Alexander Spotswood, governor of the Virginia colony. As early as July 1716, he wrote a stiff letter to the Admiralty in London reporting on the growing menace in the Bahamas:

> I have receiv'd information upon Oath that a number of profligate fellows have possess'd themselves of the Island of Providence. That the Crews of several Vessells fitted out at Jamaica for fishing on ye Wrecks have committed divers piracys, both on ye French and ye Spaniards, in those Seas, and being afraid to return home, are preparing to settle at Providence, and to strengthen themselves there against any power that shall attack them; That they have now a French Ship of 32 gunns, which they took last March, and have now mann'd her out with an intention to make prize of all French and Spanish Ships that come in their way.

In essence, Governor Spotswood was highlighting the rise of both Benjamin Hornigold and Henry Jennings.[1]

There was more, though. Spotswood, the man who had played a part in starting the 'gold fever' that swept through Jamaica and other settlements, was now aware where this had all led. He continued, 'And tho' they give out that they will spare the English, yet that Gang at Providence have already taken and plundered some Vessels belonging to New England and Bermuda, and it is not to be doubted but whenever their Occasions require they will use all others in the same manner.' This was clearly a reference to Hornigold and his claim that he was still acting as a privateer rather than a pirate. It also showed that other pirates in Nassau – even Hornigold's own crew – were less fussy about whom they attacked.

Spotswood also realized that this wasn't good for the Bahamian colonists. He added:

> Sundry of the Inhabitants of Providence, terrifyed with the barbaritys already committed there, have left the Island, a more particular Acc't whereof I have sent to the Lords Commissioners for Trade. Your Lo'ships will be pleas'd to consider the dangerous Consequences of suffering such a Nest of Rogues to settle in the very mouth of the

Gulph of Florida, where the trade of Jamaica and of the South Sea Company must fall into their hands, and, indeed, the whole Trade of this Continent may be endangered if timely measures be not taken to suppress this growing evil.

Still, Spotswood had a solution. He wanted to send in the Navy: 'I hope your Lo'ps will, therefore, judge it necessary that another Ship of Force be speedily sent hither to Cruise on this Coast for ye protection of our Merchantmen; And if it shall be found practicable, in Conjunction with the Shoreham, to attack those pyrates in their Quarters before they grow too formidable.' This letter was a real wake-up call to the British government. The nest of pirates in Nassau – Spotswood's 'growing evil' – was threatening to harm the whole trade of the American continent if it continued unchecked. The trouble was, at the time his letter arrived in the Admiralty, the Royal Navy lacked the strength to launch a full-scale attack on Nassau.

At the end of the war in 1713 it had dramatically cut its strength, with ships placed in mothballs – 'in ordinary' – and their crews paid off. By 1716, it had only a small squadron on hand to guard American waters – two fourth-rate ships-of-the-line of 50 guns each, one in Boston and the other in Barbados, and six fifth-rate frigates of 28 to 42 guns apiece, scattered from Newfoundland to the Leeward Islands. Backing them up were a few small frigates carrying 20 or 24 guns, and a pair of 14-gun sloops. These were based in either Port Royal in Jamaica or Bridgetown in Barbados. This was enough to maintain a naval presence and no more. It was little enough to patrol over 3,000 miles of coastline, let alone to guard the sea lanes, protect the colonies and take on a nest of pirates.

Soon, though, other voices would add to Spotswood's lone appeal. The following spring, in April 1717, a group of concerned Virginia merchants also wrote to the Council of Trade in Whitehall, claiming, 'Our Coast in now infested with Pyrates. God knows what damage they'll do to Trade. Ships are dailey going out and coming in.' This last was a reference to the alarm caused by pirates like Hornigold, Thatch and Bellamy, whose cruises off the Virginia and Delaware Capes had effectively paralysed trade. Many shipowners and merchant captains preferred to duck back into port when sighting a suspicious ship than risk being taken by these pirates.[2]

The sun-kissed beaches of St Croix, now part of the US Virgin Islands.
It was here that the pirate Jean Martel was ambushed by the Royal Navy, and
Sam Bellamy and Paulsgrave Williams came to repair their battered pirate ships
on the then-uninhabited island. (Bill Ross/Getty Images)

Cape Coast Castle on the coast of modern-day Ghana was once the largest
British fortress on West Africa's Gold Coast, and the site of the largest pirate trial
of the era – that of the crew of Bartholomew Roberts. Over 50 of them were hanged
from its ramparts. (John Elk III/Getty Images)

Marconi Beach at Wellfleet, Cape Cod, Massachusetts. It was here in April 1717 that the pirate ship *Whydah* was wrecked, and Sam Bellamy and almost all of his crew were drowned. Both the wreckage and the bodies were scattered along the beach for about two miles in each direction. There were only two survivors. (Jeffrey Coolidge/Getty Images)

Havana in Cuba was the island's Spanish colonial capital, and the port of departure for the Spanish Treasure Fleet of 1715, as it began its voyage across the Atlantic to Seville in Spain. It was here that the salvage efforts were orchestrated, and expeditions planned to extirpate the pirate threat in the neighbouring Bahamas. (Bruce Yuanyue Bi/Getty Images)

Today, Nassau is a hugely popular tourist destination, its harbour visited by numerous cruise ships. In the early 18th century, it was a thriving pirate haven. This spot, Junkoo Beach, was where Governor Rogers hanged pirates in 1718, in front of Nassau fort. No trace of the fort remains today, and a luxury hotel was built on its remains. (SkyHighStudios/Getty Images)

Ocracoke Island in North Carolina's Outer Banks was once the lair of Edward Thatch, or 'Blackbeard'. It was here that he and Charles Vane held their infamous banyan, or beach party, which raised the spectre of the island becoming a new pirate haven along the lines of Nassau. (written/Getty Images)

Harbour Island, off Eleuthera in the Bahamas, was a smuggling haven and an entrepôt of pirate plunder. It was well defended and generally left alone by pirates and government officials alike. (SkyHighStudios/Getty Images)

Edward Thatch acquired his cognomen 'Blackbeard' thanks to his unusually dark and wild-looking beard. Thatch cultivated and even augmented it using ribbons and match cord, to enhance the intimidating aspect of his savage appearance.

Sebastian Inlet on Florida's east coast was where some of the Spanish Treasure Fleet of 1715 was wrecked, and where the Spanish then established their salvage camps. It was here, too, that Henry Jennings came, to take whatever salvaged treasure he and his men could carry. (Getty Images)

Governor Woodes Rogers tried to bring law and order to the Bahamas, but many pirates soon returned to their old piratical ways. Rogers also struggled to make the Bahamas commercially viable – a real problem as he had personally staked his own wealth on the success of the colony.

A French slave ship of around 1720. These vessels were built for speed, which made them well suited to the needs of pirates. *La Concorde* of Nantes, captured by Edward thatch off Martinique in November 1717, probably looked very similar. Thatch then put in to Bequia, where he converted her into his pirate flagship, the *Queen Anne's Revenge*.

Governor Alexander Spotswood of the Virginia colony was no friend of pirates, as they hindered the development of his colony's trade. So, when Edward Thatch established himself in the neighbouring colony of North Carolina, Spotswood orchestrated the pirate-hunting operation that would lead to Blackbeard's death.

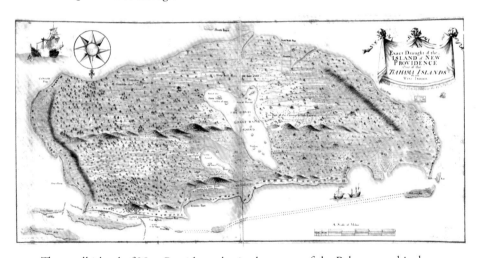

The small island of New Providence lay in the centre of the Bahamas archipelago, and its harbour, Nassau, boasted a commodious protected anchorage. By 1716 it became a thriving pirate haven and the epicentre of the pirate menace. In this map, north is at the bottom.

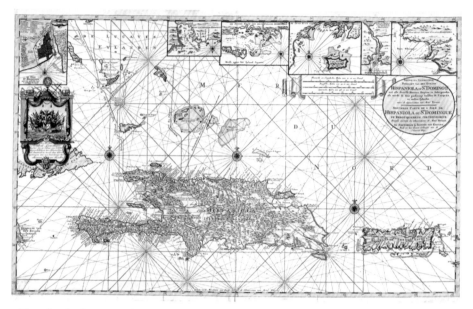

The island of Hispaniola in the Caribbean, shown here in this 18th-century map, is now divided into Haiti and Santo Domingo. This was where the buccaneering movement started. By the early 18th century, its western portion had evolved into the thriving French colony of Saint-Domingue.

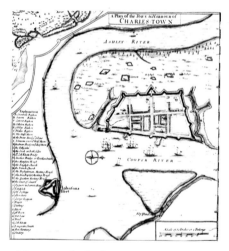

The port of Charles Town in the South Carolina colony was one of the principal mercantile centres in North America, which made its blockade by Edward Thatch in 1718 such a shocking event in Britain's American colonies.

Edward Thatch, or Blackbeard, was aware that intimidation was a powerful tool for a pirate captain. By developing a menacing appearance and an equally fearsome reputation, he sought to encourage his victims into surrendering instead of putting up a fight.

The following month, in May 1717, Spotswood tried again. In another, more urgent letter to the Admiralty, he reported that things had got much worse:

Y'or Lord'ps will perceive, by the Information I now send, how just my fears were, and how much the Trade of this Colony has already suffered. The number of Pyrates is greatly increased since, and 'tis now no inconsiderable force that will serve to reduce them if they once come to furnish themselves with Ships of force, w'ch they cannot be long unprovided among those w'ch use the Trade of the West Indies and of this Country, and seems to be their principal aim on this Coast.

In other words, the pirate nest at Nassau was now a formidable place, and it would need a major operation to deal with it.[3]

His one local guardship in Virginia waters, the 32-gun frigate HMS *Shoreham*, was due to return home for an urgent refit. Spotswood pleaded with her commander, Captain Thomas Howard, to stay until a suitable replacement arrived, but Howard's hands were tied. He was under orders to take his frigate to Woolwich Dockyard, where she would be rebuilt from the keel up. Still, he agreed to delay the departure for as long as he could. That way he could convoy trade off the Virginia and Maryland coasts until a relief guardship arrived. It was up to Spotswood, though, to clear the arrangement with the Admiralty. So, he explained the arrangement to the Admiralty, adding, 'This, I hope, will be judged a necessary service, and such as will excuse the Capt's delaying the execution of his orders for his immediate return home, which would leave a great part of the Trade of those two Plantations at the Mercy of the Pyrates, and even give them an easy access into our Bay and Rivers to plunder the Inhabitants.'

Spotswood felt the situation was so desperate that he was prepared to challenge the Admiralty in order to protect his colony's merchantmen. What he really wanted, though, was not just a replacement for *Shoreham*, but a powerful squadron:

I doubt not yo'r Lo'ps will use y'r Interest that a sufficient force be speedily dispatched to those Coasts for securing the Trade, and particularly to the Bahamas, to dislodge the Pyrates from thence where they have settled their Generall Rendevouze, and seem to look upon these Islands as their own, and it is high time some measures were taken to reduce them, either by force or by an offer of pardon upon their Submission; the first is that w'ch will undoubtedly Fortify others from falling into the like wicked Courses.

Governor Spotswood of Virginia wasn't the only voice clamouring for help. By late 1716, Peter Heywood, President of the Jamaican Assembly, had become the island's acting governor after he toppled Lord Hamilton. That September, he wrote to the Admiralty effectively penning an addendum to Spotswood's letter sent five months before. Heywood wrote: 'Shou'd the pirates, or any foreigners make a settlement there, it wou'd cost much more to dislodge them, then to secure those Islands in time, which seems absolutely necessary to be done, for that they are by their situation the key to the whole Gulph of Florida, so that whoever is master of them, may if they please be master of all the Spanish and most of the French trade in those parts.'

The clamour to do something was growing. Still, both the Admiralty and the Council of Trade continued to prevaricate. As late as April 1717, the Council of Trade wrote to the Admiralty, enclosing a copy of Heywood's latest report of 'the increase of pirates and the mischief they have done in these parts'. They added that in their opinion 'some speedy care shou'd be taken therein, lest our Trade in those seas continue to be interrupted by them, and they become too powerfull to be reduc'd without an extraordinary force and expence, which you will please to lay before H.M. for His pleasure thereupon'. Heywood had claimed that the pirates were taking up to half of the vessels sailing between the British, French and Spanish islands in the Caribbean, and so represented a monumental disruption to trade.[4]

Of course, it was difficult for the Admiralty to work out the scale of the pirate menace. They had no real idea just how many pirates were based in the Bahamas, or whether these attacks along the Atlantic seaboard and in the Caribbean were being carried out by them. The claim that there was major disruption to trade in American waters, however, couldn't be ignored. This was especially true if Heywood's claim was accurate, that half of his colony's vessels had been plundered, and that shipping was refusing to sail from American ports, for fear of attack. Something obviously had to be done. The trouble was, nobody in either the Admiralty or the Board of Trade really knew what that something was. Fortunately for them, a well-connected former privateering captain had the solution.

On 3 September 1717 it was announced that a new governor was to be appointed for the Bahamas. It was a position for which the successful applicant had lobbied hard. The man charged with cleaning up the islands was Woodes Rogers, former shipowner, slave trader and privateer. He was now a man on a mission. For the past two years he had worked hard to get to this moment, lobbying politicians, courting men of influence and campaigning to have his scheme considered by London's powerbrokers. His aim was to deal with the rise of piracy by appealing to these pirates' better nature – tempting them back into the caring arms of their king and country. It was a bold idea – some might even say a naive one. Still, it might just work. Thanks to the growing clamour by governors, merchants, shipowners and sea captains, Rogers was a man who was in the right place at the right time.

Rogers was the son of a shipowner, with interests in the Newfoundland fishing business. He was born in Poole in Dorset around 1679, but his family moved to Bristol when he was 11, where he was sent to school. His formal education ended when the teenager was apprenticed to a Bristol mariner, who made regular fishing trips to Newfoundland. So began Rogers' long association with the sea. He did well, and in 1705 Woodes Rogers married Sarah Whetstone, the eldest daughter of a rear admiral and a friend of the Rogers family. When his father died the following year, Woodes inherited the family shipping business. Over the next few years Woodes ran this and established himself firmly in Bristol society. His wife Sarah gave birth to three children.

Then, in 1707, Woodes Rogers' life changed dramatically following a visit from William Dampier, the celebrated buccaneer explorer, naturalist and author. A friend of Rogers' late father, Dampier suggested that the son back a privateering expedition he was planning to the Spanish Americas. Rogers agreed, and the two men set about financing the venture. By the following summer everything was ready, and in early August the two privateers *Duke* and *Duchess* left Bristol bound for the Spanish Main. The voyage would take three years and saw mutiny and attempted piracy by some of the crew, sickness and death, the rounding of Cape Horn, and the rescue of a shipwrecked Scottish mariner, Alexander Selkirk from Juan Fernández Island in the

Pacific Ocean. Selkirk would later become the inspiration for Daniel Defoe's *Robinson Crusoe*. There was also plenty of plundering.

In February 1709 Rogers plundered Guayaquil in modern-day Ecuador, and the following December he captured the richly laden Manila treasure galleon *Nuestra Señora de la Encarnatió y Desengaño* off the Mexican port of Acapulco. With this ship and a second prize in tow, Rogers decided to return home by circumnavigation. They crossed the Pacific without major incident and reached the Dutch colonial port of Batavia in the East Indies. There Rogers was operated on to remove a musket ball in his face, lodged there during his fight for the galleon. He bore a slight scar for the rest of his life. Still, in October 1711 the expedition returned safely to London, where Rogers was the toast of the town.[5]

He had earned a fortune, but his stop in Batavia caused problems, as he faced a lawsuit from the East India Company for breaking its trade monopoly in eastern waters. This was settled, but it ate into the voyage's substantial profits. To make up for that, Rogers wrote a book about his adventure, *A Cruising Voyage Around the World*, published in 1712, which became a best-seller. It also made Rogers a household name. However, family debts incurred during his absence meant that the money didn't last. In the end he was declared bankrupt, and he and Sarah separated. Still, his reputation was sound; in 1713, Rogers organized a new expedition, this time a slave-trading one to the East Indies. While in Madagascar, Rogers encountered the remnants of the pirate haven on nearby St Mary's Island and formed a plan to reform them through the clemency of the British Crown.

On his return in 1715, the whole scheme was confounded by the opposition of the East India Company, which was suspicious of any outside interference in a region it regarded as its own preserve. However, by then Queen Anne had been succeeded by the Hanoverian King George I, whose advisers saw another use for Rogers' scheme. This coincided with the rise of piracy in the Americas, and so Rogers was invited to redraft his proposals. Instead of dealing with the pirates of the Indian Ocean, he would counter the spread of piracy in the Bahamas. So, Rogers set to work. He toured London, speaking to anyone of influence willing to hear him. Bit by bit, Rogers gained the ear of government.

He was helped by people like Governor Spotswood, whose letters highlighted the growing problem on the far side of the Atlantic.

The wrecking of the Spanish Treasure Fleet saw many hundreds of wreckers flocking to the Bahamas, and these incomers aligned themselves with the pirates already operating there. If this growing crisis was to be dealt with, the government needed a plan. Its only truly effective option was a large-scale invasion of the archipelago to bring it firmly back into line. This approach, though, wasn't favoured by the Admiralty. Fortunately for everybody, Woodes Rogers had a plan that was both cost effective and ready to put into motion.

Woodes Rogers' proposal had two strands. First, he would offer a pardon to the pirates of Nassau, much as he'd tried to arrange for the much smaller group in Madagascar. Rogers would then attempt to employ the former pirates in British mercantile ventures, although this strand of the scheme was never fully developed. The offering of a pardon was similar to the idea proposed by Governor Spotswood back in his letter to the Admiralty in May 1717. At the time, he'd suggested reducing the number of pirates in Nassau by force, or 'by an offer of pardon, upon their submission'. It was a ploy used with some success before, most notably in 1688, during the last days of the reign of King James II of England and James VII of Scotland. His *Proclamation for the more effectual reducing and supressing of pirates and privateers in America* set the tone for what followed. Three decades later, George I's own proclamation of 1717 followed this same familiar course of offering a carrot, while waving around a very big stick.

Still, Rogers needed political support if this scheme was to be applied to the pirates of Nassau. He found it in Joseph Addison MP, the newly appointed Secretary of State for the Southern Department. Essentially, he was responsible for Britain's American colonies, as well as its relations with southern Europe and Ireland. It was an extensive brief, but Addison, a true polymath, was up to the task. As a politician he was a Whig and so formed part of the ruling party in government, which held more liberal views than their reactionary Tory opponents.

Addison was close friends with the Anglo-Irish literary figure Sir Richard Steele – a fellow Whig Member of Parliament. Together they founded both the Kit Kat Club, a Whig gentlemen's club, and the *Spectator Magazine*. Addison was also an author and a playwright, best known for his biography of the Roman senator Cato, staunch political defender of the Roman Republic. By 1717, although the 46-year-old Addison was in poor health, he was still astute enough to recognize a crisis when he saw one. As the Secretary of State, he had already been trying to judge the scale of the pirate menace facing the American colonies. Copies of the letters of colonial administrators, honest law-abiding men like Thomas Walker of New Providence, and the captains of Royal Navy warships had all crossed his desk. It helped him build up a picture – an increasingly alarming one.

These well-respected men were talking about 1,000 or more pirates in American waters, and possibly twice that. Addison knew that merchant ship losses were mounting, as were insurance prices, thanks to an increase in claims. He had already decided to take action but had no clear idea what that might be. It was only when he met Rogers in late 1716 that the notion of a royal proclamation began to germinate. So, from early 1717 on, Addison, Rogers and Steele met repeatedly and thrashed out the bare bones of this new pirate proclamation. The two politicians stalked the corridors of power and knew whom to convince that their idea was a sound one. Just as importantly, despite his mildly republican sentiments, Addison also had the ear of the King.

This had been tried before. James II's proclamation of 1688 was only the first of several piracy proclamations. In 1698 'An Act for the more effectual Suppression of Piracy' was passed by Parliament and approved by King William and Queen Mary. This lengthy document laid out the expansion of the Vice Admiralty court system, to deal with the rise in pirate attacks following the end of the War of the Grand Alliance the year before. It also offered to reward informants who reported on piratical activities, as well as penalized anyone who either traded with pirates or offered them aid. It harked back to the anti-piracy laws first laid down two centuries before during the reign of Henry VIII. The Tudor king threatened death to those convicted, along with the loss of lands and possessions. The laws did little, though, to encourage pirates to surrender to the authorities. Why would they when all they'd get was the noose?

This lack of motivation, though, was dealt with in 1701, when 'An Act for the Apprehension of Pirates' was passed into law. Interestingly, it named a specific pirate – Henry Every, the man who'd visited Nassau after his successes in the Indian Ocean. He hadn't been caught, and the East India Company was less than happy. This act, signed by Queen Anne, called for governors or Vice Admiralty courts to pardon any pirates who reported on their fellows and brought in stolen ships and plunder. It laid out a compensation scheme whereby a quarter of the value of the ship and cargo would be paid over, and a full pardon issued for previous crimes. Bounties were also offered for those who brought pirates to the authorities, which of course made bounty hunting an appealing prospect. This, though, wasn't quite what Rogers had in mind.

Rogers was a sailor and knew the code of privateersmen and sailors. He thought it unlikely any pirate crews would betray their shipmates or surrender any stolen ships or plunder to the authorities. So, Rogers and his newfound political colleagues came up with an altogether more liberal solution. The aim was not just to wait around for individual pirates to turn themselves in; what Rogers envisaged – something he'd first tried off Madagascar – was the offering of a mass pardon to a whole pirate community. This was real groundbreaking stuff. Ultimately, he not only wanted to deal with the growing pirate crisis, but to re-establish British rule in the Bahamas. The situation in Nassau had been allowed to fester for too long, and so to deal with the pirates there would probably take a major military and naval effort. Rogers' solution was to achieve his aims without a shot being fired. All he needed was a suitably enticing proclamation.

There were other elements to negotiate too. For a start, officially the Bahamas didn't belong to the British Crown but to a private group, the Lords Proprietors of the Carolinas. Although they'd done little or nothing to help the archipelago for the past decade or more, they still owned it and therefore had to be involved. So, guided by Addison, Rogers approached them and negotiated the relinquishing of their rights to the islands. The most persuasive argument in Rogers' armoury was that the pirates of Nassau were threatening the economy of the Carolinas with their attacks on shipping. They also provided a safe haven for runaway slaves and indentured servants – people the South Carolina colony's plantations needed to guarantee a profit. In the end, the Lords Proprietors agreed to release the Bahamas to Rogers and his partners for 21 years in return for a token fee.

So, Rogers had his colony. It would be run on behalf of the British Crown but would in effect be another private colony run by Rogers and his backers. Still, the Crown seemed willing to appoint Woodes Rogers as the Bahamas' official governor and support his endeavour with whatever resources they could spare. In effect, Rogers would be both the Bahamas' governor and proprietor. Given these terms, the government then declared that Rogers couldn't be paid a salary. Any profit he made from the colony would have to come from his own taxes, raised from the labours of the islands' settlers and seafarers. This meant that Rogers really had to turn the Bahamas into a viable colony, or he'd go bust.

The big day came on 5 September 1717. That was when King George I officially signed his piracy proclamation, formally entitled 'An Act for Suppressing Pirates in the West Indies'. Essentially, it was what Rogers and his political friends had been advocating. It began by stating that, since 24 June 1715, 'Piracies and Robberies on the High Seas' had caused damage to British merchants and traders, and that the King had 'Appointed such a Force as we judge sufficient for supressing the said piracies.' That was the threat of the stick. In fact, at the time this was just an illusion. The only Royal Naval force with the power to intervene in the Bahamas was the Jamaica Squadron, with four frigates and several smaller warships, backed up by a sizeable military garrison. However, when the proclamation was made law, nobody had officially asked the Admiralty for its support.[6]

Then came the carrot. The act said that while the suppression of piracy by force was imminent, it was more effective to achieve this another way. It then laid out the alternative to violence. If the pirates should surrender themselves to an official representative before 5 September 1718, then they 'Shall have our Gracious Pardon' for piratical crimes committed before 5 January. In other words, everything revolved around making sure copies of the act reached the Nassau pirates, and that they stopped their attacks by 5 January 1718. If they kept attacking, then they would be dealt with by force. If they didn't, and surrendered quietly, then they would receive a full pardon for all of their crimes.

It was a simple enough arrangement, and one Rogers felt could work. The aim was to reduce the pool of pirates in Nassau from 1,000 or 2,000 to – it was hoped – just a few hundred. Then, the British authorities would send in the Navy, to root out these last intransigent pirates. When they were caught, they could expect no mercy under the law. The act even laid down a scale of reward for anyone apprehending a pirate or helping bring them to justice. If it was a pirate captain, the reward was set at £100. Lesser officers, such as the master, boatswain or gunner, garnered £40, lower ranks £30, and ordinary members of the pirate crew £20.

Finally, from 6 September 1717 – the day after the proclamation was signed – there was another incentive on offer, a Judas clause. Essentially, it encouraged a pirate crew to turn on itself. It laid down that any member of a pirate crew who 'caused to be seized or delivered any commander or commanders of such pirate-ship or vessel, so that he or they be brought to justice, and convicted of the said offence' would earn a £200 reward. This, frankly, was a stroke of genius and had Rogers' fingerprints on it. He had concocted a similar clause when drawing up a provisional pardon for the Madagascar pirates. Now, he would offer a small fortune to any potential turncoat among those pirate crews who refused to surrender.

Two days before the proclamation was enacted, Rogers was told that King George had approved his scheme and that he would be appointed as the governor of the Bahamas and its military commander. Two months later, Rogers was granted an audience with the King at St James' Palace, and the whole venture was given the King's formal sanction. Still, it took another two months until Woodes Rogers was formally commissioned as 'Our Captain General and Governor in Chief' on 6 January 1718. This warrant blamed the neglect of the Lords Proprietors for allowing the islands to be in danger of being lost to the Crown, after being 'plundered and ravaged by pirates and others'. So, after more than a year of planning and campaigning, no end of political manoeuvring and meetings in London's clubs, the whole venture was formally approved. The Bahamas had a new governor.

It was all very well signing a proclamation. For it to have any effect, though, word of it had to reach the pirates. First, a verbatim copy of it was published in *The London Gazette* on Saturday 14 September 1717. The government knew that copies of key British newspapers were eagerly awaited in the American colonies, and so the news would cross the Atlantic by way of that week's batch of outbound merchant ships. Copies of the proclamation were also sent to all the colonial governors and to the various Vice Admiralty courts. Finally, several hundred copies were printed out, and these accompanied the packages to the governors. Their job, then, was to distribute these wherever sailors might frequent.[7]

The fastest route across the Atlantic ran from Britain down to the Canary Islands, or even the Cape Verde Islands, and from there westward to the Windward Islands. A fast dispatch boat could make the

4,000-mile voyage in three to four weeks if the winds were favourable. Most merchant ships, though, took longer. On average, this meant a voyage of six to eight weeks. So, the earliest the news could reach the West Indies was the middle of October, but more likely it would be November or even early December before word arrived in ports like Philadelphia, New York or Boston. Then, those printed copies had to be distributed, and then, somehow, they had to reach the pirates of Nassau. It was a long, convoluted and somewhat random process.

It was essential that the news reach Nassau, as well as any pirates at sea. It was 5 December 1717 when Edward Thatch and his crew first learned of the proclamation. His new flagship, *Queen Anne's Revenge*, was cruising off the large Spanish-owned island of Puerto Rico when the pirates intercepted the British sloop *Margaret* sailing from St Kitts. Her master, Captain Henry Bostock, was ordered aboard Blackbeard's ship, where he and five men were held prisoner for several hours. During that time Thatch questioned Bostock about merchant shipping in the area. While he refused to help, some of Bostock's seamen were more than happy to oblige. Later, one of them volunteered to join the pirates, while three more were forced to sail with them.[8]

During their exchange, Captain Bostock passed on some vital news to Thatch. He hadn't seen the copy of the *London Gazette* that contained a copy of the royal proclamation of 5 September, but he'd spoken to others who had. Official word still hadn't reached St Kitts when Bostock sailed from the island a few days before. He also thought that in Antigua, Walter Hamilton – the Governor of the Leeward Islands – hadn't received copies of the proclamation. That meant that copies of the newspaper had brought word of the proclamation to the West Indies long before the official channels had done the same.

This ties in with the evidence from other colonies. The *Boston News Letter* first carried a report of the proclamation in its edition of 9–16 December. It would be expected that Governor Samuel Shute of the Massachusetts Bay and New Hampshire colonies received official word at the same time. From Boston copies of the newspaper and most probably the printed copies of the proclamation were carried on outbound trading ships, and so the word radiated out from the Massachusetts port relatively quickly. So, we can be fairly sure that by the end of December 1717 at the latest, the official announcement of the proclamation had reached other key colonial figures along the

American seaboard – Acting Proprietor Hannah Penn of Pennsylvania, and governors Alexander Spotswood of Virginia, Charles Eden of North Carolina and Robert Johnson of South Carolina.[9]

Even more significantly, towards the end of the month a copy of both the *Boston News Letter* and the official announcement of the royal proclamation reached Governor Benjamin Bennett in Bermuda. Bennett had been warning the Council of Trade and the Admiralty about the pirate menace for the best part of a year. Now, finally, something was being done about it. On his own initiative, Bennett had several hundred copies of the proclamation printed in Bermuda, and then asked his son Captain Bennett to take a fast Bermudian sloop to Nassau to distribute the copies among the pirates. In late December, thanks to the courageous Bennett the Younger, copies of the royal proclamation were in the hands of the likes of Benjamin Hornigold, Henry Jennings and the rest.[10]

The proclamation created an uproar in New Providence. Until that moment, every pirate in Nassau had accepted the fact that they'd crossed the line and there was now no way of going back. Once they'd taken to piracy, they had cut themselves off from their old life and from friends, family and home. If they were caught, they'd face a trial and then almost certainly a very public execution. Now, with no warning whatsoever, the British king was throwing them a lifeline. If the Nassau pirates were indeed a cross section of seamen of the period, then very few of them could read. So, they'd rely on the few who could – usually pirate captains and quartermasters – to tell them about the pardon. They were left with a real dilemma. Should they accept the pardon and return to their old life without any penalty, or should they continue their pirate career and to the devil with the consequences?

Inevitably, opinions were divided. Over the next few weeks, the pirate commune became split into two rival political parties. Those who were eager for a second chance were probably in the majority, but many refused to countenance what amounted to a meek surrender to the very authority they were rebelling against. The pro-pardon faction coalesced around Henry Jennings. After all, he'd never really wanted to become a pirate in the first place. He saw himself as a treasure hunter who had been forced to align himself with the pirates of Nassau when the authorities in Jamaica had turned their back on him. When Captain Bennett arrived, Benjamin Hornigold was at sea in the *Benjamin*, but he'd always seen himself as a law-abiding privateer. So, undoubtedly, he'd be keen to accept a pardon and would urge others to do the same.

Then there were the others – the pirates who refused to surrender to authority. Some of them were out-and-out pirates who revelled in the freedom such a life gave them. Some bore grudges against the establishment, or against shipowners and merchant captains – or indeed everyone who'd ever lorded it over them. A few would have political reasons too; for instance, there is some evidence that the Nassau pirates included those with Jacobite sympathies who didn't recognize the legitimacy of the Hanoverian king and his ministers. Many, though, felt that their piratical careers were on the rise, and they didn't intend to stop now when there were so many rich pickings to be had. Over the next few weeks, the pirate Charles Vane emerged as the unofficial leader and spokesman of these 'die-hard' pirates.

When Captain Bennett returned to Bermuda, he told his father that there were only about 400 pirates in Nassau when he visited the place, although others were out at sea. Of these, he said that as many as 300 were eager to accept the pardon. He added that he was fired on as he entered the harbour, but Bennett the Younger put this down to a token act of defiance by a handful of men. In his letter to London, Governor Bennett reported that 'Capt. Henry Jennings one of them (who left off that way of living some months since) has arrived here, who with seven others have surrendered themselves'. At that stage Bennett had no authority to formally accept Jennings' surrender in Bermuda, but he did so anyway, and issued him and his men with a provisional pardon.[11]

By the time Jennings returned to Nassau, he found that Charles Vane had been busy rallying men to his die-hard cause. The tense situation continued into January. When someone raised a British Union flag above the recently renovated Fort Nassau, Vane's die-hards stormed the fort, beat up its occupants, ripped down the flag and hoisted their own piratical black flag. It was a miracle this rift among so many heavily armed pirates didn't end in bloodshed. Meanwhile, many of the die-hards were still sailing off to attack shipping, and their prizes were brought back to Nassau to the dismay of Jennings and his supporters. Then, Benjamin Hornigold arrived with two large Dutch merchant ships in tow, captured by him in the Gulf of Campeche. Both had been well armed, and Hornigold had planned to mount these guns in the fort. Now, though, he found himself in the middle of a full-on crisis.[12]

As Jennings had hoped, Hornigold's instinct was to accept the pardon. According to Captain Johnson's *General History*, Hornigold and Jennings were instrumental in calling a meeting, or general council, of the pirates in an attempt to clear the air. The die-hards, though, weren't prepared to compromise. As Johnson put it:

[T]here was so much noise and clamour, that nothing could be agreed on. Some were for fortifying the island, to stand upon their own terms, and treating with the government upon a foot of a commonwealth. Others were also for strengthening the island for their own security, but were not strenuous for these punctillios, so that they might have a general pardon without being obliged to make any restitution, and to retire with all their effects to the neighbouring British plantations.

In other words, many of the die-hards wanted to defend New Providence and hold it against anything the British could throw at them. Others were keen to accept the pardon and head off to somewhere like Harbour Island, out of reach of British officialdom. As neither of the two factions could agree, nothing was done, apart from the moving of Hornigold's newly acquired guns into the fort. However, it seems some of the die-hards had another plan. Some of the Jacobite sympathizers among the pirates contacted a renegade naval officer, George Cammocke, with the notion of declaring the Bahamas a Jacobite colony. They told him they planned to reject the pardon and instead to declare themselves the subjects of James III, the Jacobite king in exile. Cammocke, then in Spain, thought this was a marvellous idea, and eagerly supported the die-hards' fanciful scheme.

The 52-year-old Cammocke was an Irishman who'd joined the Royal Navy as a teenager and rose to the rank of captain. He was clearly an enterprising and courageous officer, but his naval career ground to a halt in 1713 when he disobeyed orders in the Mediterranean. He was dismissed from the service but was eventually employed by the Spanish and attained flag rank. He was a Jacobite, and when the pirates' proposal reached him he was enthusiastic. He proposed to purchase a 50-gun ship-of-the-line from the Spanish, crew her with Jacobites, and then sail to the Bahamas as a Jacobite admiral. The islands could then become a privateering base for the Jacobite cause. In the end, the scheme came to naught, as the British established control of the archipelago before Cammocke's expedition could be organized.[13]

Meanwhile, during the opening weeks of 1718, the two groups of pirates co-existed and prepared for the moment when the British would arrive to enforce their carrot and stick policy. As nobody could agree to fortify the island, several of the die-hards bowed to the inevitable and quit the place. Charles Vane took a sloop, the *Lark*, and hid her in a secluded anchorage on the south side of New Providence, ready to make his escape if he had to. The pirate Edmund Condent and almost a hundred others planned to head off to West Africa in the sloop *Dragon*, while Christopher Winter took his sloop and crew off to Cuba and based himself there until the volatile situation resolved itself. Others drifted away or, like Paulsgrave Williams, Edward England and 'Calico Jack' Rackam, planned to make their departure when the time came. It didn't help that nobody really knew what was going to happen next.[14]

Among the pro-pardoners, Hornigold, like Jennings before him, considered sailing to Bermuda to surrender to Governor Bennett, in return for a provisional pardon. Instead, he sent a well-armed sloop to Port Royal, where she could act as a pirate-hunting privateer if the need arose. He also wrote a letter to the naval commander there, explaining what was going on in Nassau and requesting that a Royal Naval warship be sent there to protect the pirates who were willing to accept a pardon, or who already held a provisional one. In the end, this scheme was overtaken by events. In Nassau, Hornigold and Jennings reluctantly joined forces to strengthen their position, persuading their crews to support their pro-pardon stance, securing control of the fort, and preparing for the day when the British finally arrived to take control of the island.[15]

Shortly after dawn on 23 February, a small British frigate was seen approaching the harbour entrance. She was HMS *Phoenix*, a sixth-rate frigate of 24 guns under the command of Captain Vincent Pearse. An intelligent and active man in his late 30s, Pearse had volunteered to take the news of the pardon directly to the Nassau pirates, with the aim of persuading as many pirates as possible to accept it. His scheme was duly approved by Governor Robert Hunter of the New York colony. So, on 5 February, the *Phoenix* slipped past Sandy Hook into the Atlantic and shaped a course south towards the Bahamas. This was a somewhat bold move by Pearse, as he didn't have Admiralty approval for this enterprise. He realized his 24-year-old ship and her crew were sailing into danger. Still, he hoped his initiative, if everything went well, would meet with their Lordships' approval.[16]

Captain Pearse was expecting trouble when he entered the harbour, but the fort remained silent as the frigate glided in. The tension eased somewhat, but still Pearse wasn't taking any chances, and he kept half his crew at their guns as he dropped anchor. He noted that the harbour itself was full, with some 14 vessels at anchor flying a range of flags – British, French, Spanish, Dutch – and black or red pirate ones. Five of them were large vessels of various kinds, while the rest were sloops. Once safely at anchor Pearse ordered the ship's longboat to be lowered, and his deputy, Lieutenant Symonds, was sent ashore at the head of an armed landing party and a file of marines, to distribute copies of the royal proclamation.[17]

The landing party didn't know what to expect when it reached the beach and faced the crowd of men waiting there for them. Lieutenant Symonds carried a white flag, meaning he came in peace, but his marines remained vigilant. They needn't have worried. The pirates proved to be civil, and, when the proclamation was read out, according to Pearse it was met with 'a great deal of joy'. Of course, it helped that these were the pro-pardon pirates. Vane and his die-hards were nowhere to be seen. Hornigold was happy to give Symonds a detailed account of the situation. Inevitably, this involved Vane. Hornigold reported that the pirate had left New Providence in the *Lark*, accompanied by 16 of his supporters, and was hiding off a nearby island until the frigate sailed away. He hadn't reckoned with Pearse though.

Fully briefed by his First Lieutenant, Captain Pearse decided to track down the pirate, to make his point that the Bahamas were now under British control. Vane was hiding behind one of the tiny barren islets that formed a chain to the south-east of New Providence, between it and Great Exuma. When he came upon the *Lark*, Pearse ordered his gunners to fire a series of warning shots. Vane was trapped and outgunned – he had no option but to surrender. Once on board the *Phoenix*, Vane claimed he and his men planned to accept the pardon and were on their way to Nassau. Pearse didn't believe a word of it. He kept Vane aboard the frigate, took the *Lark* as a prize and returned to Nassau.[18]

The pro-pardon faction was delighted, but when he met Pearse, Hornigold counselled caution. Pearse recalled the conversation with

Hornigold, who 'informed me that my taking the sloop had very much alarm[ed] all, the pyrates believing that [the] men taken in her would be executed'. Hornigold advised that leniency would convince many of Vane's faction to join the pro-pardoners. So, Pearse let Vane and his men go but kept the *Lark* as a prize. That done, and with Hornigold's help, Pearse arranged to offer any pirate who submitted to him a provisional pardon. So, three days after arriving in Nassau, amid a teeming tropical downpour, Pearse had groups of pirates brought aboard the *Phoenix*. Then, in his cabin, he accepted their surrender and handed over his signed pardons.[19]

The whole process took several days, but by its end Pearse had 209 names on his list – all men who'd agreed to submit to British rule in exchange for a pardon. These included a number of the former die-hards. Even Charles Vane agreed to the deal, although it seems certain nobody expected him to honour the arrangement. In fact, the die-hards were hard-pressed to hide their true feelings. On 1 March, when the *Phoenix* was dressed overall in celebration of George, the Prince of Wales's birthday, the die-hards set a captured merchant ship ablaze in the harbour as a symbol of defiance. Two weeks later, on the evening of 16 March, Vane and 16 of his followers slipped past the anchored *Phoenix* in a small longboat and made for the open sea. They'd had enough of playing games.

Vane was no ordinary pirate. He knew that the tide was against him – the flocking of over 200 pirates to accept a provisional pardon was proof of that. So, if he wanted to save the pirate haven, he needed to convince the bulk of his fellow pirates that they were backing the wrong horse. After making his escape from Nassau, Vane probably established himself on the eastern tip of New Providence, somewhere beyond East Point. Then he waited. The next evening Vane's band was joined by 24 more die-hards in a second longboat. That gave Vane a decent-sized force of 40 men – enough to man a sloop. The waiting continued. Finally, on 21 March, Vane's chance came.

There was only a light breeze that morning, and, out to sea, approaching the island from the east, was a small trading sloop. She'd come from Jamaica and was heading into Nassau. Instead, her crew found themselves attacked and overpowered by Vane and his men. Very sensibly, they surrendered without a fight. This, though, was only the first part of Vane's grand scheme. He now planned to flaunt his prize in front of Captain Pearse. The main entrance into Nassau harbour was on its western side, where the channel was deep enough to take large ships. However, on its eastern end there was another channel, between the eastern end of Hog Island and the shore of New Providence. The water was shallow there and filled with sandbars. However, for those who knew, there was a narrow, shallow channel just deep enough for a small sloop to pass through.

The pirates were aware of it – the eastern channel was a possible escape route if the harbour was attacked. Beyond it lay a wide, shallow bay – now known as Montagu Bay. That's where Vane brought his prize and dropped anchor, in full view of Captain Pearse, the crew of the *Phoenix* and the pirates of Nassau. He was deliberately taunting Pearse and cocking a snook at the Royal Navy. On board the *Phoenix*, Pearse must have raged impotently. He knew from his chart that a sandbar called Potter's Key lay between him and Vane's prize, and that his frigate had too deep a draught to pass through the eastern channel. Anyway, Vane's anchorage was too shallow for the frigate to get close to the pirates. So, after Pearse moved the *Phoenix* closer to the eastern channel, where her guns could cover any approach to Nassau, he considered what to do next.[20]

The obvious solution was a cutting-out expedition. Using his ship's boats, a few dozen well-armed sailors and marines might be able to sneak up on the pirates under cover of darkness and put them to the sword. So, Pearse gave the orders, and he and his men spent the rest of the day preparing for the attack. Sunset that evening came at around 7.20pm, and an hour later it was sufficiently dark to hide the British approach. The sound of jollity floated over the water from Vane's prize, but still Pearse stayed his hand. Finally, just before 1am on 22 March, he made his move. The frigate's 32-foot-long pinnace was used in the attack, which was led by Lieutenant Symonds accompanied by around 36 sailors and marines. All went well as they passed through the channel and rowed with muffled oars past Potter's Key. Everything depended on surprise.

Then, when they were just a hundred yards from the sloop, the darkness was pierced by musket flashes – dozens of them. It seems that despite the revelry on board, Vane had been keeping watch on the harbour, and his lookouts had seen the British boats make their approach through the channel. The men from the *Phoenix* fired back, but it was clear the assault was thwarted. They were outnumbered, and to go ahead with the attack would be suicide. So, reluctantly, Symonds gave the signal to withdraw. Jeers and shouts followed them across the water as they rowed back to the *Phoenix* and their hugely disappointed captain. Fortunately, there were no casualties.[21]

The following morning, Captain Pearse realized he had a problem. When he asked the pirates whom he'd just pardoned to help him deal with Vane, they appeared singularly reluctant to help. As Pearse put it, 'I summon'd the inhabitants to assist me in surprizing these pirates ... but by their actions they seem'd more inclinable to assist [rather than] to reduce them.' He added that the pardoned pirates assisted Vane by providing him with supplies, while rejecting any requests from Pearse to help him deal with the die-hards. Pearse also noted that many of the pirates, 'on all occasions showed no small hatred to government'. Perhaps the pirates of Nassau weren't quite as ready to accept British rule as Pearse had supposed.[22]

For the next two days there were no further incidents, and both sides watched each other warily. However, Pearse was busy organizing a small convoy of four trading sloops, which he planned to escort as far as the open waters of the Atlantic. Once there, the convoy would disperse, and the vessels would continue on their own to their destinations in Rhode Island, South Carolina and Florida. The convoy sailed from Nassau on 23 March, accompanied by the *Phoenix*, and everything went according to plan. Pearse parted company with the convoy two days later off the coast of Abaco, then headed south to patrol the Providence Channel. There he helped to protect a pair of trading sloops heading towards Nassau. Finally, on 30 March, as he was running short of water, he followed them into the harbour.[23]

On Pearse's arrival, he found that Vane had been busy. On the night after the convoy sailed, Vane and his men had rowed into the main harbour and set fire to one of Hornigold's Dutch prizes. The second one was run aground and wrecked on Hog Island. A third prize ship, the *Mary Galley* of Bristol, was also burned to the waterline. This was a deliberate attack against Hornigold and Jennings, whose prize ships these had been. The message was clear: without the Navy there to defend them, the pardon signers couldn't protect themselves. Vane and his prize weren't there when the *Phoenix* returned on 30 March. It appeared Vane had sailed the day after the convoy had left port, just hours after his dramatic raid on Nassau harbour.

Once he was at sea, Vane followed the convoy and sidestepped the *Phoenix* once she'd left the four sloops to continue to their destinations. However, his first victim wasn't from the convoy at all. On 29 March Vane overhauled the sloop *John & Elizabeth* a few miles off the coast of Abaco Island. She was on her way to Nassau from St Augustine in Florida, carrying a cargo of mixed goods and merchandise. Her master, Benjamin Bell, surrendered his ship without a fight, but Vane still seemed angry, and afterwards Bell claimed that he and his men felt themselves lucky to escape with their lives. The pirates plundered the sloop's cargo, equipment and clothing worth £1,000 pounds, as well as several hundred pieces-of-eight. This, though, wasn't the prize Vane was after, and Vane let her go.[24]

On 31 March, the day after Pearse's return, Vane returned to Nassau. Once again, the die-hards anchored to the east of the main harbour, behind Potter's Key, where the British couldn't reach them. To Pearse's horror, he saw that the pirates had a new prize – a familiar-looking sloop. She was the *Lark*, the vessel Pearse had confiscated from Vane just over a month before. After claiming her as a prize, Pearse had turned the *Lark* into a trading sloop out of his own pocket, and she sailed with the convoy a week before, with three sailors from *Phoenix* to watch over the hired hands – all of whom were former pirates. Vane had captured her off Harbour Island three days before, while the *Phoenix* was patrolling the Providence Channel. Once again, the pirate had outsmarted the naval captain. While this was bad enough, it soon turned out that the three British sailors in the *Lark* had deserted and volunteered to join Vane's crew.[25]

Over the next few days Vane's men made daylight sorties into the main harbour in small boats as the pirates tested the British defences. This, though, was really for the benefit of the pardoned pirates of Nassau, watching all this from the beach. When they drew close enough, Pearse's crew opened fire on them with small arms and even 6-pounders, forcing the pirates to keep their distance. While all this was going on, Vane's men had landed in Nassau to recruit more pirates and intimidate those who refused to join them. Vane also used his boats to take two more coastal traders, both of which were captured to the east of New Providence, then whisked into the shallow waters beyond Potter's Key. Pearse was unable to save the sloops, despite trying to warn them. As a result of all this, Vane's gang almost doubled in strength. He could now boast almost 80 men under his command.

Finally, on 4 April, Vane slipped out to sea in the *Lark*. The small, fast, six-gun sloop was now well-manned, making Vane a real threat to merchant shipping anywhere within range of the Bahamas. Once he left, some sort of order returned to Nassau, but it was clear to Captain Pearse that much of the enthusiasm for British rule had now waned. The demoralizing effect of Vane's antics had seen to that. In his report to the Admiralty, Pearse argued that 'If another Ship of Warr had been with me, I should have been able to have prevented ... the rest from going out againe.' He meant Vane's men, but frankly the loyalty of the other pardon signers was equally questionable. Before he left, Pearse claimed that they had threatened him and his men if they didn't leave soon.[26]

Pearse thought this was a problem that could be overcome when Governor Rogers arrived with a powerful force of ships and men. Before he left, the commander of *Phoenix* told Hornigold, Jennings and the other ringleaders of the pardoned pirates that he expected Rogers to arrive at some point during the summer. Then things would be very different. He asked them to keep faith, and to make sure that Rogers was well received. Above all, he wanted to make sure that they would remain steadfast in the face of more threats by Vane and his die-hards. For the moment they had gone off on a pirate cruise – goodness knows where – but no doubt would return to Nassau soon enough and cause more trouble.

On 8 April, the *Phoenix* weighed anchor and left Nassau, accompanied by another small convoy. She grounded briefly at the harbour entrance, but the rising tide lifted her free, and the frigate then shaped a course for New York. In his cabin, Captain Vincent Pearse began drafting his report to the Admiralty, and he would repeat the need for small warships that could root out the pirates when they hid in the shallow waters that made up so much of the Bahamian archipelago. Above all, it was abundantly clear that as long as Vane was at large the threat posed by the Nassau pirates would never go away. He and his die-hards held too much sway with them and would continue to cause trouble until they were brought to justice. This was no longer Pearse's problem. That would be the job of the new Bahamian governor, Woodes Rogers.[27]

ELEVEN

Woodes Rogers and Charles Vane

I N HIS *A GENERAL History of the Pirates,* Captain Johnson didn't even try to explain Charles Vane's origins. Instead, it seems he emerged fully formed in the summer of 1715. As Johnson put it, 'Charles Vane was one of those who stole away the silver which the Spaniards had fished up from the wrecks of the galleons, in the Gulf of Florida.' We know he was described as a subject of the British king by the authorities, so that's a start. As for the rest of the story, all we have is a puzzle with a few random jigsaw pieces held together by supposition, hearsay and scraps of circumstantial evidence. This, though, is largely irrelevant to our tale. What mattered were his actions, and his dramatic stand against the authorities determined to make an example of him.[1]

Beyond his nationality – Charles Vane was almost certainly an Englishman – we have little to go on. In the early 18th century, there were two main groups of Vanes in England – the main one in Kent and another up north in County Durham. In the 17th century the northern

Vanes were stout Parliamentarians, and on the orders of Charles II one was beheaded in 1662, an unrepentant republican to the last. It has been suggested that Charles Vane the pirate was the grandson of Henry Vane the republican politician, but this is merely supposition. It might, though, help explain the pirate's anti-establishment bent. But it is more likely that Vane came from less exalted stock. Records show a number living in Sussex and Kent. From descriptions of Vane in 1718–21, we can place him in his late 30s, and he was probably about 40 years old when he died. This suggests he was born around 1680 during the last years of the reign of Charles II. Given the way things worked at the time, the likelihood is that Vane first went to sea as a teenager, say around 1695. It is estimated that over a third of the known pirates of this period first sailed from London, the busiest port in the country, which makes it likely that if Vane came from somewhere like Kent, then he would have done the same.[2]

It has been suggested that Vane spent some years in Port Royal, but this would have been after both its buccaneering heyday and the devastating earthquake of 1692. It remained a relatively busy port, despite being overshadowed by the rise of nearby Kingston. Vane's activities there are unknown, but he probably served aboard merchant ships – either local traders or transatlantic ones. He might also have served aboard slave ships, plying the triangular trade route between Britain, West Africa and the West Indies. By the time Vane was in his early 20s, around the early 1700s, he would most probably have been regarded as a prime seaman, with the skills needed to carry out just about any task of seamanship that was asked of him. However, like so many other hundreds of seamen of this time, his name hasn't yet been found in any official documents.[3]

So, until some compelling evidence about the young Charles Vane emerges, everything about him is mere supposition. Around this time, England – or Britain from 1707 on – found itself at war with both France and Spain, and an ally of the Dutch. This raised the prospect of privateering, and from the records we know that Port Royal became a reasonably busy privateering haven during Queen Anne's War. There is a good possibility that Vane served aboard one of these privateering vessels. After all, it would help explain how, shortly after the war ended, he emerged as such a skilled pirate. Again, we have nothing much to base anything on until 1715 and the loss of the Spanish Treasure Fleet off the Florida coast.

*Charles Vane, the leader of the die-hard pirates of
Nassau who refused to accept a pardon.*

The one exception to all this vagueness is found in the trial of Charles Vane for piracy, held in Jamaica in late March 1720. In the court articles the prisoner is described as 'Charles Vane, late of the Town and Parish of Port Royal' and his profession described as 'Mariner'. As the trial was held in Spanish Town (or Saint Jago de la Vega), less than eight miles as the crow flies from Port Royal on the far side of Kingston Bay, it was more than likely that the court recognized Charles Vane as a local mariner. If we assume that Captain Johnson was correct, and that Vane volunteered to join the salvors who ventured from Jamaica to pillage the Spanish treasure wrecks, then that meant he probably left Port Royal to join this venture in either December 1715 or January 1716 as part of Jennings' second wave.

If we assume that, from then on, and for the rest of 1716, Vane attached himself to Jennings' star, then he would have crewed one of Jennings' sloops, like the *Barsheba*, or possibly Leigh Ashworth's ten-gun Jamaican sloop *Mary*. That means Vane was most probably involved in Jennings' cruise off the coast of Cuba that April, and the attack on the French merchantman *St Marie* of La Rochelle in Cuba's Bahía Honda. The likelihood is that Vane then returned to Nassau with Jennings on 22 April 1716, when the pirates brought the *St Marie* into the harbour, escorted by Jennings' *Barsheba* and Ashworth's *Mary*.[4]

If indeed Charles Vane had taken part in the capture of the *St Marie*, then in the eyes of the law he'd crossed the line. He was now officially a pirate. It would be a while, though, before his name became known to the British authorities. Then, thanks to his leadership of the die-hards, his activities would become more notorious than those of Jennings, Hornigold or even Thatch. It has been suggested that Vane was a ringleader during the plundering of the *St Marie* in Nassau harbour in May 1716, but again he never appeared in any official account of the pirates of Nassau, even in the report sent to the Lords Proprietors by Thomas Walker of New Providence. So, Vane's activities still elude us.[5]

The likelihood is that Vane remained in Nassau for much of 1716 and early 1717. Although he was associated with Henry Jennings, and most probably formed part of his crew, nothing ties him to any pirate activities during this period. However, by the way he quickly rose to prominence as the *de facto* leader of the die-hards, we can safely assume that by the spring of 1718 he was a pirate of some considerable influence. There is some evidence to suggest Vane had become the captain of a pirate sloop by the summer of 1717, possibly called the *Ranger*. However, no trail of depositions has yet been found to link him to any pirate attacks. It is probable that he remained attached to Jennings' star until the unexpected offer of a royal pardon tipped the whole pirate commune on its head.[6]

When news of the pardon first reached New Providence from Bermuda, the pirate commune was split into two factions – those who were eager to accept the pardon, and those who refused to surrender to the authorities. As the weeks went on, Vane emerged as one of the principal leaders of the second faction, and harangued his fellow pirates, trying to convince others that his stance was the right one. Others in his camp included Paulsgrave Williams, the old sidekick of Sam Bellamy; Christopher Winter, a captain who'd developed a reputation for ruthlessness; Winter's colleagues, Nicholas Brown and Edward England; and 'Calico Jack' Rackam and Edmund Condent. All of them would go on to command their own pirate crews as part of the die-hard group who'd rejected the pardon or reneged on it.

It has been suggested that, like some of his fellow pirates, Vane had Jacobite sympathies. This, though, appears to have been much less important than his general rejection of authority. While he might have entertained becoming a semi-legitimate Jacobite privateer, his actions showed that any official government was anathema to him. During his encounters with Captain Pearse of HMS *Phoenix* in February and March 1718, it was clear that he rejected royal authority, less on the grounds that the King was Hanoverian than because he refused to be considered a subject of the Crown – any crown.[7]

Vane only signed his name ('Charles Veine') to the list of pirates who'd surrendered to Captain Pearse under duress. After all, he'd been captured by the British captain a few days before. On being pardoned, he immediately returned to piracy and then deliberately taunted Pearse. The way he did this suggested his main motive was to undermine Pearse's temporary authority in Nassau, and to discourage the pirates who'd signed the document of surrender from supporting the pro-pardon faction. In the process, he was deliberately showing his opposition to Captain Pearse, the Royal Navy and the authority of the British Crown. From that point on, Vane would be a marked man.[8]

Charles Vane left New Providence on 4 April in his six-gun sloop the *Lark*. She was well manned with up to 70 pirates in her – all die-hards who'd rejected Britain's authority. It seems Vane wasn't prepared to go on a long cruise. Instead, he'd spend just over a month operating in Bahamian waters. Really, he wanted to make himself scarce until the *Phoenix* had left the area. He also had a grudge against Bermuda. After all, it was the son of the island's governor who'd brought copies of the royal proclamation to Nassau. Vane therefore wanted to punish the Bermudians for this. Some victims suggested that Vane intended to punish the islanders for capturing a pirate, Thomas Brown.[9]

By then, Brown had been released, either due to a lack of evidence or because he had signed the provisional pardon. So, the real reason for Vane's vendetta with the Bermudians was revenge for the distribution of the royal proclamation. To him, Bermuda was the source of the problems currently afflicting his free-spirited pirate commune. So, Vane turned south towards the south-eastern corner of the Bahamas. This was a favourite destination for Bermudian vessels, who collected cargoes of dried-out sea salt from Crooked Island, Mayaguana, and the Turks and Caicos. If Vane wanted to annoy Governor Bennett of Bermuda, this was a great place to start. There were well-used watering places for passing ships at Crooked Island and Mayaguana, and just as importantly this hunting ground lay astride the quickest sea route between Jamaica and America's Atlantic seaboard.

What followed was a pretty spectacular rampage that was almost certainly done to make a point. The Royal Navy might be able to send frigates to the Bahamas, but they couldn't control its waters, which were the preserve of pirates like Vane who knew where to hide and where to strike. One of the first of his victims was a Bahamian trading sloop, the *Betty*, sailing from New Providence to Jamaica. On 17 April, her master, Benjamin Lee, decided to put in to Crooked Island to take on water and found four sloops at anchor there, off the watering hole. He stood in and was almost ready to drop anchor himself when the largest of them 'fired a shot at him and hoisted a bloody pendant'. It was Vane's *Lark*, now renamed the *Ranger*, accompanied by three prizes.[10]

Lee hauled down his colours and was ushered aboard the *Ranger* while the pirates ransacked his sloop. They then took the *Betty* to the western end of the island and stripped her of gear and tackle which Lee claimed was worth £200. That done, they handed Lee his sloop back and allowed him to take on water. With that Vane took the *Ranger* out to sea, accompanied by a captured sloop acting as his consort. He was off hunting again. The haul from the *Betty* was hardly worth the effort of taking it, but Vane had more luck two days later. This time it was the turn of a three-masted ship, which Lee spotted as he sailed past, lying heaved-to in the company of Vane's two sloops. She had been on her way from Jamaica to Boston when she was captured, and again Captain Richards surrendered without a fight.[11]

On 22 April, the sloop *Fortune* of Port Royal was taken by Vane eight miles off Crooked Island, and this time her master, George Guy, tried to run. The pirates overhauled his sloop and fired on her, forcing Guy to heave to. As a punishment Captain Guy was brutally assaulted by the pirates. Afterwards the crew were set ashore, and Vane made off with the *Fortune* as his prize. Afterwards, one of Guy's men left a detailed account of Vane's ferocity. This showed that Vane and his men were becoming increasingly violent, particularly if their victims offered any kind of resistance. It was almost as if Vane was determined to show that he and his die-hards would brook no nonsense in waters they considered their own.[12]

Other attacks followed, including the Bermudian sloop *William & Mary* captured off Rum Cay, just north of the Crooked Island Passage. The haul was pitiful – little more than a few ounces of ambergris and some pistols. According to her master, Captain Edward North, Vane had a sailor lashed to the bowsprit, a loaded musket barrel shoved in his mouth, and burning slowmatch waved in front of his eyes, to find any hidden money aboard the sloop. Eventually, Vane and his men left the sloop's crew alone, although they took an unwilling African crewman with them when they left.[13]

That same day, within a mile of the *William & Mary*, Vane also captured the Bermudian sloop *Diamond*, which they brought alongside their other prize. This time Vane's crew assaulted the master, John Tibby, and randomly picked one of his crew to hang from the sloop's yardarm. The unfortunate seaman was unconscious when they cut him down. As if that wasn't enough, one pirate then hacked at the prisoner with his cutlass, until his shipmates stopped him from actually killing his victim. In the end, all they took was 300 pieces-of-eight and another black slave. That done, they moved the *Diamond*'s crew onto the *Ranger*, and then set the Bermudian sloop ablaze. They also dismasted the *William & Mary*, before bundling all their prisoners aboard her and sailing off in the *Ranger*.[14]

By the time Vane returned to Nassau on 28 April, he'd plundered upwards of a dozen vessels, seven of which were from Bermuda. He had effectively brought trade in those waters to a standstill. His victims reported him threatening that he and his fellow die-hard pirates would attack and capture Bermuda and turn it 'into the new Madagascar' – in other words, a new pirate haven. They had been heard toasting damnation to the King 'and all the higher powers', and some came out with Jacobite toasts. Fortunately for both Charles Vane and probably Captain Pearse, the *Phoenix* had sailed by the time the *Ranger* returned to Nassau. Vane would continue to use the island as his base during the weeks that followed, and he would take more prizes. His main aim, though, was to show that the Nassau pirates, rather than the British authorities, were in charge in the Bahamas.[15]

Of course, there was a danger in all this. Before the *Phoenix* left, Captain Pearse had told Hornigold and the others that an expedition was being sent out from Britain, and it would bring out the new British governor for the islands. While Hornigold and the majority of the other pro-pardon pirates bided their time, waiting for that expedition to arrive, others decided to make themselves scarce. Several important pirates were away from Nassau that summer, including Edward Thatch and Edmund Condent. If Vane was caught in port when the expedition arrived, then as soon as the British stepped ashore and spoke to Hornigold's faction, he'd be marked out as the ringleader of the die-hards and taken prisoner. Vane, though, had no intention of going quietly.

So, after just a few weeks in port, he put to sea again. By now the *Ranger* mounted eight guns and carried a crew of around 90 men. Once again, he returned to his old hunting ground in the Crooked Island Passage. On 23 May, he came upon the small 14-ton trading sloop *Richard & John* off Crooked Island. She was commanded by Joseph Cockram, the younger brother of Hornigold's old shipmate John Cockram, who now worked for Richard Thompson of Harbour Island. The Cockrams were often in Nassau and were usually seen as allies of the pirate commune as they sold their plundered goods for them. This made no difference to Vane. Cockram and Thompson were in business with Hornigold, not Vane, and he had no plans to help the friends of his pro-pardon rival.

By stopping and ransacking the *Richard & John*, Vane was deliberately biting the hand that fed him – or rather supplied the

Nassau pirates with their main link to the outside world. Earlier, by burning the prizes of the pro-pardon pirates in Nassau harbour, Vane had effectively declared war against Hornigold and the others. Now, by capturing Joseph Cockram's sloop, putting him ashore and then making off with the vessel, Vane was escalating the conflict. So, if the British governor didn't arrive soon, the signs were that the two pirate factions in Nassau were on a collision course and would most likely begin fighting among themselves.

Vane's cruise continued, as he headed south across the Old Bahama Channel to the Windward Passage. On 14 June he captured a two-masted Bermuda-rigged schooner and turned the vessel over to his quartermaster, Edward England. Following a vote by the *Ranger*'s crew, his old post as quartermaster was filled by John Rackam, commonly known as 'Calico Jack'. Next, they came upon a French three-masted ship which had just left Port-au-Prince. This time Vane decided to keep the 200-ton ship for himself, making her his flagship. In return he bundled the French captain and crew into the *Ranger* and sent them back to Saint-Domingue.[16]

They then captured another French ship in the Gulf of Gonâve, a brig called the *St Martin* of Bordeaux, which was heading towards Port-au-Prince carrying a cargo of brandy, white wine and claret. The pirates promptly drank their fill and deposited the captain and some of his passengers and crew on the shore near Léogâne. Some 13 of them, either voluntarily or not, remained with the pirates. Then, fearing French retaliation, they quit the gulf and set a course back to Nassau. Vane now had an impressive squadron under his command – his new French-built flagship, England's Bermudian schooner, the Bahamian sloop *Richard & John*, and the newly captured brig *St Martin*. He would certainly make an impression when he returned home.[17]

Vane returned to New Providence by way of the Crooked Island Passage, and then northwards to the north-east end of the Providence Channel between Abaco and Eleuthera. It was there, at dawn on 4 July, that they came upon a cluster of vessels off Harbour Island. This was a bonus. That morning the pirates took three trading sloops: the *Drake* and *Eagle*, both of Rhode Island, and the *Ulster* of New York. They weren't carrying much of value, save for the wine and spirits in Captain John Draper's *Drake*. The *Eagle* yielded nothing but local timber, while the *Ulster* carried bread and sugar. Still, once the crews were dropped ashore, the pirates kept the three prizes. These all added to the size of the flotilla, making the return to Nassau even more spectacular. The spirits, too, would help fuel the welcome home party.[18]

That wasn't all. As they approached Nassau, this veritable pirate armada captured two more trading sloops, the *Dove* and the *Lancaster*. The former was a local Bahamian vessel, but the *Lancaster* was from Charles Town in the South Carolina colony. Ironically, she was commanded by Neal Walker, the son of Thomas Walker of New Providence, the former pirate-hunting judge of the Bahamian Vice Admiralty court. When his father had fled from New Providence in late 1716 he moved to Charles Town, where his son became the master of a sloop. He was on his way from Charles Town to Jamaica when he was captured. The two sloops were duly added to Vane's fleet for his dramatic entrance into Nassau harbour on the evening of 4 July.[19]

With a harbour filled with his prizes, Vane was now a major player in Nassau. His arrival encouraged waverers to join his ranks, and when the die-hards landed, they came to settle scores. Vane quickly established control over Nassau at the point of a cutlass and ruled the pirate port as a *de facto* governor. Benjamin Hornigold and the other leading pro-pardon pirates either kept quiet or withdrew into the island's interior in an attempt to ride out the storm. According to Johnson, 'He reigned there as governor twenty days, stopped all vessels which came in, and would suffer none to go out.' Johnson added that in Nassau, 'he would suffer no other governor than himself.' Effectively, it was piratical martial law. Over those 20 days, Vane let it be known that he planned to sail for Brazil with his die-hards, hoping to join forces with other pirates there. In the end, he left it all too late.[20]

Charles Vane, the self-styled governor of Nassau, knew that the British would be coming in force. That's why he planned to quit the Bahamas and sail off with his supporters to South America. However, Woodes Rogers' expedition was already nearing the archipelago. The armed merchantman *Delicia*, carrying the future governor of the islands, was accompanied by the small armed sloops *Buck* and *Samuel*, the transport ship *Willing Mind*, and three warships – the 32-gun frigate HMS *Milford*, the 20-gun frigate HMS *Rose* and the ten-gun sloop-of-war *Shark*. This meant that Rogers had the firepower to force his way into the harbour if he had to, but he hoped that Captain Pearse of *Phoenix* had been right – that the pirates of Nassau were, for the most part, eager to surrender, and many of them had already accepted provisional pardons. Still, Rogers was prepared for anything.

His squadron contained everything he needed to help him establish his colony – an independent company of newly raised British regular soldiers, many of them discharged veterans, as well as over 200 colonists, including wives and children. The holds of his ships were filled with the tools and seed they'd need to reclaim the largely abandoned arable land in New Providence. There were also building materials, provisions, medical supplies and weapons. The governor's small staff included secretaries, government clerks and even gentlemen volunteers, eager to take on the challenges of colonial administration in the islands. First, though, he had to deal with the pirates.

What happened on Woodes Rogers' arrival in Nassau on 24 July has already been recounted in the Prologue. In short, half of his squadron entered Nassau harbour without being fired on by the fort, but a single roundshot – a token of defiance – was fired at them from what turned out to be Charles Vane's new French-built flagship. She was now a powerful three-masted ship-rigged pirate ship of about 22 guns, which Vane had just renamed the *Revenge*. While she was no match for the British frigates, she was still powerful enough to put up a real fight. Then, to add insult to injury, when an officer from HMS *Rose* was sent over to the pirate ship to discover why he'd been fired on, Vane had a letter handed to him, addressed to Governor Rogers.[21]

Rogers was still on board the *Delicia*, which together with the powerful *Milford* had anchored just outside the harbour entrance. The smaller armed sloop *Samuel* was sent off to block the exit from the harbour's smaller eastern entrance – the one used by Vane during his encounter with the frigate *Phoenix* a few months before. So, Captain Whitney of the frigate *Rose* had the letter rowed out to the governor. It was quite an amazing document. It stated that the remaining pirates would be willing to accept the royal pardon, if offered to them, but only on certain terms. These were 'That you will suffer us to dispose of all our goods now in our possession. Likewise, to act as we think with everything belonging to us'.[22]

For Vane and his men, this meant their collection of recently captured prizes. If Rogers didn't accept those terms, Vane warned him that 'we are obliged to stand to our own defence.' He signed it 'Charles Vane and Company'. Vane couldn't have expected much.

After all, he'd already accepted a pardon, and then reneged on it. The prizes in the harbour had all been recent captures, and so the evidence of his wrongdoings was laid bare. Effectively, he was only biding time as he prepared his hurried, improvised escape.

Unfortunately, Vane's plan involved the sacrificing of his new three-masted 24-gun flagship. He had his men unload her and fill her decks with pitch, tar and anything else that would burn. The guns were all double-shotted and run out, and powder barrels were stacked nearby. Shortly before 2am on 25 July, Vane boarded a fast sloop, the *Katherine*, and with the help of England's schooner, he turned his fireship the *Revenge* until her bows pointed towards the four British ships anchored just inside the main harbour entrance, several hundred yards to the west of them. There was a light breeze from the south-east, which was perfect for his plans. Vane then gave the order to set fire to his makeshift fireship. A small team at the helm held her on course as she headed straight for the British ships at the harbour entrance. On board them, the alarm was raised, orders were shouted, and the crew tumbled on deck. In half a dozen ships they were set to work, unfurling and loosing sails, cutting anchor cables and standing ready with water pumps, boathooks and buckets of sea water. All the while the raging inferno bore down on them.[23]

That night Woodes Rogers was a lucky man. For a few horrific minutes it looked like the fireship would collide with the frigate *Rose* and the sloop *Shark*. Both captains cut their anchor cables and loosened sail, trying to bear off, but they could all feel the heat from the raging flames now. Guns fired off at random, as the priming charges in the double-shotted guns ignited and the guns erupted. Slowly, very slowly, Captain Whitney of the *Rose* felt his ship turn towards the harbour entrance, and then she began moving. With yards to spare they crept out of the way, and the burning fireship lumbered past them, sparks jumping from her onto the wooden decks of the frigate. The *Revenge* then continued on towards the harbour's southern shore and ran aground directly in front of the silent fort.[24]

Captain Whitney ordered the other British ships in the harbour – the *Willing Mind* and the armed sloop *Buck* – to drop anchor again where they were. Both were useless in a fight, as their decks were crammed with soldiers, civilians and other forms of landsmen. Then, shouting through his speaking trumpet, he told the commander of the ten-gun sloop-of-war *Shark* to use his remaining bower anchor to take up position astern of the frigate. Both warships anchored, broadside on to the pirate ships to the east of them, blocking the anchorage with their formidable batteries of guns. Whitney kept his men at their posts until dawn, in case the pirates tried anything else. However, the rest of the night was quiet, and shortly before 6am the first signs of dawn were seen in the east. If the night was anything to go by, then this was going to be another eventful day.[25]

At around 7am, the *Delicia*, *Milford* and *Samuel* all entered Nassau harbour. Then, just after they passed Hog Island, first the *Delicia* and then the frigate *Milford* ran aground on either side of the unbuoyed channel. Only the *Samuel* made it through. She was due to be relieved off the eastern entrance to the harbour by the *Buck*, but now both sloops had to stay with the stranded ships, in case they were needed. High tide came at around 10am that morning, and both ships were eventually floated free. It was a somewhat embarrassing start to the governor's official entrance into his capital. On the shore in Nassau, the remaining pro-pardon pirates watched, all the while glancing over at Vane to see what he would do next. Woodes Rogers had assembled a formidable force in the harbour, and any attack by the die-hard pirates would be a suicidal venture.[26]

By then, the *Katherine* had withdrawn into the eastern harbour on the far side of Potter's Key. During the early hours of the morning, in the aftermath of the fireship attack, Vane's men had gone ashore in Nassau and looted supplies, weapons and whatever else they fancied, and took them aboard the schooner. Vane's sloop seemed relatively safe beyond the shallow channel between Hog Island and Potter's Key, but in the late morning he saw activity among the British ships. The armed sloop *Buck* was heading down the harbour, followed by the *Samuel*, which was filled with Rogers' troops. It looked like they planned to force their way through the channel.

It was time to go. Vane headed towards the open sea, making it out through the channel between Hog Island and Long Island just as the *Buck* entered the eastern harbour. The offshore wind worked in his favour, and the *Katherine* raced off to the east, in the general direction of the southern tip of Eleuthera. The *Buck* gave chase, followed at a distance by the *Samuel*. One feels for the soldiers in the *Samuel* as the sloop entered the open sea, but the race went on regardless. The *Buck* was gaining on the pirate sloop until Vane passed the lee of Long Island and New Providence. Then she surged ahead, and by mid-afternoon the pursuers were forced to give up the race. Vane had defied Governor Rogers much as he had Captain Pearse, and both times he'd escaped to carry on his attacks. The difference now was that thanks to Woodes Rogers, New Providence was no longer a friendly pirate haven.[27]

Rogers remained on board the *Delicia* that day but called over Commodore Chamberlaine from the *Milford* to help plan the official landing the following morning. A landing party was sent ashore to contact the pro-pardon pirates remaining in Nassau. The British party was met on the beach by a group of pirates led by Benjamin Hornigold. He assured the Royal Naval officers in the landing party that the die-hard pirates had left, and those who remained were all loyal to King George, and to the new governor. Hornigold and his followers assured them that the former pirates who'd signed the provisional surrender documents on board HMS *Phoenix* were still eager to confirm the arrangement and to have their provisional pardons ratified.

In other words, they wouldn't cause any trouble, and would do just about anything to keep the peace. A more convincing spokesman was Thomas Walker, the former judge, who had returned to his home in New Providence in the wake of Captain Pearse's visit. He confirmed that the pirates were telling the truth. So, at 11am on Wednesday 27 August 1718, Woodes Rogers stepped onto the sands of the Bahamas for the first time. At that moment an 11-gun salute was fired off by both *Rose* and *Shark*, which were anchored in front of the fort, their guns ready just in case. The soldiers of Captain Robert Beauchamp's Independent Company presented arms as smartly as they could, as their standard flapped above them, to add a touch of martial colour to the proceedings.

On the Nassau waterfront Rogers was met by former justice Thomas Walker, and the two men greeted each other with great enthusiasm. Each had the measure of the other and liked what they saw. Next, Rogers was introduced to Benjamin Hornigold, followed by a brief conversation with the other leading pirates in the crowd. Then, once his soldiers had formed themselves up into an honour guard, Rogers walked to the fort accompanied by both Walker and Hornigold and flanked by Captain Beauchamp's soldiers. The place was dilapidated, with the gates rotten and hanging open, and vegetation creeping up its walls.

Once inside, Rogers was shocked to discover there was only one 9-pounder gun left on the firing platform, and it didn't have the tools needed to fire it. Still, needs must, and after a naval colour party struggled with the flagpole, preparing it for what followed, Rogers chatted to the judge and the pirate as his own staff joined him, and the crowd of around 300 former pirates and colonists filled the fort's small, weed-strewn parade ground. Rogers' secretary passed him a copy of the royal warrant appointing him to the post. With that in hand, the new governor 'read himself in' to the assembled crowd. At that moment, on reading the King's words, Woodes Rogers officially became the new governor of the Bahamas.[28]

At that point the colour party raised the Union flag on the fort's flagpole, and the warships in the harbour fired another salute. It seemed to Rogers that Hornigold and his pirates were genuinely pleased to see British rule restored and soldiers to protect them against both Vane and his men and a possible attack by the Spanish. This, though, was only the start. Now that Governor Rogers was officially in charge, he and his staff set about re-establishing British control of the island. This began with the occupation of the fort by the soldiers, who set about cleaning it of detritus and debris, and building temporary lodgings for themselves made from tree trunks and palmetto fronds. The colonists were ferried ashore and furnished with sailcloth tents while they prepared to venture inland to claim plots of land for themselves.[29]

Meanwhile Commodore Chamberlaine was busy too. He and his officers examined the vessels at anchor in the harbour and worked out which had been stolen recently – since the cut-off date of 5 January 1718. In most cases this was all but impossible, but at least they were able to return Vane's recent prizes to their owners – the five sloops taken by the pirates off Harbour Island and in the Providence Channel. Chamberlaine also organized the landing of guns and carriages for the fort, taken from abandoned ships in the harbour. So, within a week of Rogers' arrival, Fort Nassau, despite her crumbling facade, was able to offer some form of defence if the harbour was attacked. Another battery was also set up on a point a mile to the east of Nassau, which covered the small eastern entrance to the harbour. With the island securely in his hands and reasonably defensible, Rogers was able to turn his attention to forming some kind of government.

On 1 August, just five days after landing in Nassau, Rogers announced the formation of a provisional council to help him govern the archipelago. It included Thomas Walker, as well as several of Rogers' own officers and entourage, including Sir William Fairfax from his staff who was appointed the new judge for the Bahamas. Rogers was keen to re-establish a Vice Admiralty court as soon as he could, so he could legally begin dealing with any of the die-hard pirates who fell into his hands. A surprise member of the governing council was Richard Thompson of Harbour Island, who had made himself a small fortune acting as the middle man, selling on pirate plunder. Still, he was a well-respected figure in the Bahamas, and a well-connected one too. Rogers needed men like Thompson if his colony's economy was going to prosper.[30]

Governor Rogers had three other pressing problems. The first was what to do with the 209 pirates who held provisional pardons. Some of them had returned to piracy and sailed off with Charles Vane. The remainder, though, were officially pardoned having sworn an oath of loyalty to the British Crown. There were more pirates beside these two groups, though – probably around 500 or so. Some of them had been pardoned elsewhere, and had since arrived in Nassau, while others were to join their pardoned brethren. Rogers' council patiently sorted all this out, basing itself either on board the *Delicia* or in the old governor's house, which Chamberlaine's carpenters had hurriedly restored. While this was going on, Rogers set the former pirates to work, clearing Nassau of the weeds and vegetation which had crept into it. He also had them help repair the fort, establish the eastern battery, and clear the tracks leading into the island's interior.[31]

Rogers' other two problems were both about security. Vane was still at large and had plundered two trading sloops while still in Bahamian waters. One of his victims reported that he'd heard the pirate boast that he planned to join forces with Edward Thatch and would then return to Nassau to exact revenge on Rogers. Even more ominously, in early August he learned that Spanish pirates had been operating in the Crooked Island Passage, claiming that they were legitimate pirate-hunting privateers carrying Letters of Marque signed by the governor of Cuba. Vane's victims told him that the Spanish intended to invade the Bahamas, to destroy the pirate commune there. That meant that

Rogers and his counterpart in Havana were potentially on a collision course that could lead to a new European war.[32]

This couldn't have come at a worse time. Commodore Chamberlaine had orders to depart Nassau as soon as the governor was installed and the island made defensible. That meant that Rogers was about to lose the protection of the Royal Navy. So, on 16 August, Chamberlaine put to sea in his frigate, *Milford*, and set a course for New York accompanied by the sloop-of-war *Shark*. The smaller frigate *Rose* would remain in Nassau until mid-September, when she too would follow Chamberlaine to New York. So, to defuse the Spanish threat, Rogers wrote to the new governor and captain general of Cuba, Gregorio Guazo y Calderón de la Vega. He assured him that the islands were cleared of pirates and were now officially held by the British Crown.

He decided to send the message in the sloop *Buck*, which had pursued Vane as he fled from Nassau. The 75-ton, six-gun sloop slipped out of Nassau on 10 September, laden with trade goods destined for the markets of Havana. She was accompanied by a second trading sloop, the *Mumvil Trader*. The *Buck*'s original crew had been depleted by yellow fever, and so these were augmented by a handful of former pirates. The trouble was, both groups seemed eager to throw off the traces of authority as soon as the chance arose. Sure enough, off the coast of Hispaniola the crew mutinied and killed the ship's master, Jonathan Bass. Then, after transferring their loyal shipmates to the *Mumvil Trader*, they hauled up the black flag and set off on their own pirate cruise. It was reported that their ringleader was Walter Kennedy, a Londoner and one of the *Buck*'s original crew.[33]

Eventually, Governor Gregorio y Calderón learned of the new government in the Bahamas and the crisis passed. In truth, the stories of a Spanish invasion of the Bahamas were just that. The Spanish governor had his own problems. He was facing a revolt on the island led by the leading plantation owners, and so the news that the pirates had been driven from the neighbouring archipelago came as something of a relief. Still, it demonstrated just how vulnerable Rogers was. The mutiny of the *Buck*'s crew deprived him of a useful armed sloop, but the departure of the *Rose* in mid-September effectively left him without any real protection in the Bahamas beyond the range of Fort Nassau's guns. If British rule in the Bahamas was to continue, Rogers needed more help from Britain.[34]

The pirate problem had not gone away. In mid-September a report reached Nassau that Charles Vane had been sighted in the Bahamas, operating off Green Turtle Key, on the north-eastern end of Abaco. This news came from a group of Vane's men who had become separated from the rest of the crew and ended up heading to Nassau. The pirates were duly arrested while Rogers pondered what to do next. In the end he called for Benjamin Hornigold. Hornigold agreed to accept a commission from the governor as a pirate-hunter – essentially a privateer with a pirate-hunting Letter of Marque. He and John Cockram would gather a reliable crew, man a sloop – presumably Hornigold's own *Benjamin* – and set off after Vane. On 18 September they left Nassau and headed north.[35]

This, then, was the real start of Rogers' fight back against the pirates. Hornigold, with Cockram acting as his deputy, crept around Abaco and anchored behind Green Turtle Key where they could see Vane's brig, accompanied by two other vessels – either prizes or other pirate ships. The two turned out to be vessels he'd recently captured off Charles Town. Hornigold watched and waited, hoping for a chance to get Vane on his own. After three weeks Vane returned one of his two prizes to her crew, and the captives sailed off towards South Carolina. Then another sloop appeared from the south. She was the *Wolf* from Nassau, whose crew were ostensibly out hunting for the turtles that gave the key its name. As Hornigold watched, they sailed right up to Vane and were welcomed with open arms.[36]

That meant that the crew of the *Wolf* were in league with the pirates. The sloop's master, the supposedly reformed pirate Nicholas Woodall, was no doubt giving Vane an up-to-date report of Governor Rogers' activities in Nassau and the general feeling there towards British rule. The news must have angered Vane, who took out his ire on his remaining large prize, the 300-ton ship-rigged three-masted *Neptune*. He ordered his men to hack down her masts and rigging, and then fired a shot into her hold, possibly in a failed attempt to sink her. Vane then left the anchorage in his brig, and, together with the *Wolf*, he made off to the west.[37]

Once Vane was out of sight, Hornigold brought his sloop alongside the damaged ship and helped prevent her from sinking. He gave Captain John King of the *Neptune* and his crew water and provisions and told them he'd bring help. Then he set off after the pirates. He came upon the *Wolf* off Grand Bahama Island, but there was no sign of Vane. Hornigold captured the *Wolf*, arrested Woodall and his men, and with his own crew installed sailed back to Nassau with the *Wolf* as his prize. By rights, the sloop was now a legitimate prize as her crew had consorted with the pirates. So, they were deemed pirates themselves. Governor Rogers, of course, was delighted. This was his chance to make a very important point.[38]

Rogers would have loved to try Woodall and his crew in Nassau. However, the Vice Admiralty court there had still not been formally re-established, and so it had no real legal authority. So, Rogers had the *Wolf*'s crew put in irons and shipped off to London, where they would be handed over to the Admiralty court. He sent a letter, which told the Board of Trade that the capture of Woodall and his men greatly strengthened his position in New Providence as it gave heart to the pardoned pirates. It was a strange situation in Nassau. Hornigold's re-invention as a pirate-hunter had gone down well in Nassau, but there was still bad feeling, and some of the pirates who'd accepted a pardon were almost certainly biding their time before they could resume their old ways. Only the threat of legal punishment and Hornigold's men kept them in check.

By this stage Henry Jennings had left the island and returned to his native Bermuda. As a former pirate holding a full pardon, he could resume his place on the island. Besides, his plundering of the Spanish Treasure Fleet had made him a wealthy man. He was wise enough to know when to back out of the game. Others followed suit and joined the crews of trading sloops or larger ocean-going merchantmen and were – at least for the moment – reformed characters. Rogers, though, was aware that many of the former pirates still couldn't be trusted. On 4 November, Rogers learned that the crews of all four trading sloops he'd just sent to Cuba had returned to piracy. It seemed they planned to head to Abaco and join Vane. So, Hornigold was sent off to sea again to round them up.

Sure enough, he found some of them off Vane's old stomping ground of Green Turtle Key, off the north-eastern side of Abaco. They put up a brief resistance, but after a rapidly accomplished boarding action they were overwhelmed and the survivors captured. Hornigold returned with ten prisoners and three dead pirates. Rogers was again delighted. As he put it in a letter to the Council of Trade, 'I am glad of this new proof Captain Hornigold has given the world, to wipe off the infamous name he has hereto been known by.' Again, though, Rogers had no legal way to try his prisoners, or even a suitable jail in which to hold them. So, after having them put in irons aboard the *Delicia*, Rogers called a meeting of his governing council on 28 November, to see if they had any suggestions.[39]

Their main worry was that if they delayed, or showed any hesitation, Vane's supporters in Nassau might try to rescue them. So, they advised Rogers to bring them to trial anyway and worry about the legal position later. This was a gamble too, as it might spark a revolt among the prisoners' old pirate shipmates. Still, on 9 December, after almost two weeks aboard the *Delicia*, the ten prisoners were taken to Fort Nassau and held there by Captain Beauchamp's soldiers. Then, Rogers assembled his court. It was presided over by Chief Justice William Fairfax, while Governor Rogers himself sat in, to supervise the proceedings. Also present were six hastily sworn-in justices. One of them was Thomas Walker, who now, at last, had the chance to hold the pirates of Nassau to account.[40]

He was joined on the bench by Captain Robert Beauchamp, commander of the Independent Company, Captain Wingate Gale of the *Delicia*, Nathaniel Taylor from Harbour Island, merchant captain Peter Courant, and, surprisingly, Josiah Burgess, a former pirate and now captain of the New Providence militia. The trial was held in the grandly labelled 'His Majesty's Guard Room in the City of Nassau'. In truth, it was little more than a large wooden shed built on one side of the fort's courtyard. Rogers knew he was on shaky legal ground. As the council minutes put it, he had 'no direct Commission for tryal of Pirates'. Still, he saw it as his duty in line with his official position as Vice Admiral of the Bahamas, and in line with similar pirate trials held in other colonies.

He also made sure that all his justices were willing to stand in judgment, regardless of any legal quibbles. That done, the trial began on the morning of Tuesday 9 December. The ten defendants were charged with 'mutiny, felony and piracy'. If found guilty, there was no question – the condemned men would hang. The ten manacled defendants were brought into the 'Guardroom' escorted by an armed guard. Their ringleader was John Augur, former master of the trading sloop *Mary* of New Providence. Six of the others were from the trading schooner *Batchelor's Delight*, and three from the trading sloop *Lancaster*. These were the trading vessels Rogers had sent to Cuba that November. The accusation was that on 6 October, off Green Key near San Salvador Island, they 'piratically and felonously' took the three vessels, put their loyal crew ashore then sailed off towards Exuma.

The pirate ringleader, John Augur, and another defendant, Dennis McCarthy, surrendered to Captain Pearse of the *Phoenix* and so had been granted a pardon. Having gone back on their word, they could expect no mercy. Seven of the others don't seem to have been pirates previously, but they too, if found guilty, needed to be made an example of to discourage others from doing the same. The trial began, and a string of witnesses from the loyal crew were able to attest to the guilt of nine of the prisoners. The exception was John Hipps, boatswain of the sloop *Lancaster*, who the court learned had been pressed by the pirates against his will. He was acquitted. The evidence against the other nine defendants was damning, and the trial was adjourned in the late afternoon, with Judge Fairfax declaring it would reconvene the next day.

At 10am the following morning the court resumed, and, after a final batch of evidence, the prisoners were removed while the court deliberated. They were ushered in again for the verdict. First, a mightily relieved John Hipps was acquitted, although for the moment he was still sent back to the *Delicia* in irons. The others were all found guilty. Judge Fairfax then intoned the sentence that the condemned men 'be carried to the Prison from whence you came, & from thence to the place of Execution where You are to be hang'd by the Necks till You be dead, dead, dead, And God have mercy on Your Souls.' The court announced that the execution would take place at 10am on the morning of Friday 12 December. Some of the prisoners begged for clemency, or a stay of execution to prepare for their end, but Rogers was adamant. The execution would go ahead as planned.

Following Admiralty custom, this would usually take place on the shoreline, which was deemed ground within the jurisdiction of the Admiralty. So, Rogers decided to hang the men on a hurriedly erected scaffold, built just below the ramparts on the seaward side of the fort. At 10am on 12 December, watched by a crowd of about 300 former pirates and a handful of local settlers, the nine condemned men were bound and then led up to the ramparts by the acting provost marshal, Thomas Robinson. On the ramparts and outside the fort's gate by the gallows, Captain Beauchamp's men had their muskets loaded just in case. Others manned the battery on the ramparts, where, as a precaution, the guns had been loaded with grapeshot. Woodes Rogers was taking no chances of a riot, a rising or a rescue attempt.[41]

It was a dangerous moment for Rogers, as nobody really knew how the crowd would react. After all, some of them were friends of the condemned men and had sailed with them.

As the prisoners appeared on the ramparts some of the crowd cheered them, while others remained sullen. Prayers were intoned and psalms sung, before the prisoners were ushered down a ladder onto the beach, then up another onto the scaffold. Each of the condemned men had a noose fastened around his neck. Then more psalms were sung, those who wanted it were given a last drink, and the pirates were given a chance to speak their last words. The crowd craned forward to hear, but the line of soldiers stood between them and the scaffold. This was another dangerous moment as their words might well incite a riot.[42]

Some, like the Irishman William Dowling and former prizefighter William Lewis, were befuddled with drink while the teenage George Bendall protested his innocence to the last. By contrast Dennis McCarthy was defiant, having dressed for the occasion with blue ribbons around his wrists, knees and in his cap. He declared that there was a time when the former pirates in the crowd in front of him wouldn't have let him die like a dog. Thomas Morris was similarly dressed, only in red ribbons, and he declared that he wished he'd been a greater plague to the Bahamas than he had been. William Dowling took the opportunity to confess to the murder of his own mother before he fled from Ireland. The final words spoken, Governor Rogers ordered the provost marshal to prepare for the hanging. Then, at the eleventh hour, he intervened. Rogers ordered George Rounsivell to be spared, and he was untied and led away, amazed at his good fortune. Like Rogers he was from Dorset, of good parents, and the governor took pity on him.

With that, on the provost marshal's signal, the barrels holding up the stage were pulled aside, the stage collapsed, and the eight pirates 'swang off'. For the most part the watching crowd remained silent, although some cheered and others jeered. Nobody raised a hand in opposition to Governor Rogers and his men. It was all a dramatic piece of theatre, but at that instant, as the eight pirates jerked and choked, an important piece of history was made. That moment, 11am on 12 December 1718, marked the official end of pirate Nassau. The once-thriving pirate commune had been replaced by the rule of government and law and order. The mass hanging sent out a clear signal that the Bahamas were now closed to pirates, marking a major sea change in the fight against the pirate menace.

TWELVE

The Pirate-hunter

A T THE SAME TIME as Governor Woodes Rogers was battling
Charles Vane in the Bahamas, Edward Thatch was living a life
of leisure in Bath Town in the North Carolina colony. In mid-June
he was pardoned for his crimes by Governor Charles Eden, and he
then settled down in the small waterfront township. He kept his small
Spanish-built sloop the *Adventure* and a handful of his former crew –
all men who'd also been pardoned. He let people know that he planned
to become a maritime trader, based there in Bath Town, and would
rebuild his life as an honest, law-abiding sea captain. He took the sloop
out into Pamlico Sound, and after a few weeks he established what he
claimed was a trading outpost on Ocracoke Island, on the Outer Banks.
This was, one presumes, passed off to reduce the length of his trading
voyages and to make his business more profitable. It also kept him well
away from any prying eyes.

While Governor Eden seemed quite content that Thatch was a
reformed character, others were less convinced by the charade. In the

neighbouring colony of Virginia, Governor Alexander Spotswood, a staunch opponent of piracy, was sure that Thatch was still a pirate and had hoodwinked Eden into believing he had turned his back on his old calling. So, after making sure his contacts in North Carolina would keep him well informed about Thatch and his activities, he watched and waited. Back in Bath Town, Thatch might have guessed that Spotswood was suspicious, but for the moment he was quite safe as, thanks to his association with Governor Eden, he enjoyed whatever protection the North Carolina colony could provide.[1]

This quiet retirement didn't last long. Most probably it was late July when Thatch and his men resumed their pirate careers. There were signs of trouble even before that. In Bath Town there were complaints of rowdiness and disorder, while the masters of local trading vessels accused Thatch's men of stealing provisions and liquor from them. These complaints reached the ears of Governor Eden, whose response was most probably to encourage the former pirates to return to sea and act like the mercantile traders Thatch claimed they intended to be. At least that would stop the thefts and the local disturbances for a while. To help things along, Eden approved Thatch's claim to ownership of the *Adventure*, the Spanish sloop he'd captured off Havana back in May.[2]

So, Thatch took the sloop *Adventure* to sea. Ostensibly, this was the start of a trading voyage to the Danish colony of St Thomas in the Virgin Islands. Instead, though, once he passed through Ocracoke Inlet into the Atlantic, Thatch took the *Adventure* north or east rather than south. One account of his activities claims he sailed up the Delaware River to Philadelphia, where he supposedly sold some of his piratical plunder. This, despite the presence of some local lore, has never been verified in the historical sources. He might well have reached the Delaware Capes but didn't prey on any shipping there as he had done the year before. Instead, Thatch headed out into the Atlantic, sailing east in the general direction of Bermuda.[3]

Once at sea, Thatch was in his element. According to Captain Johnson, he stopped and plundered two or three British merchant ships on the high seas, possibly somewhere to the east of the Delaware Capes. Having plundered them, he let them continue on their way. If this were true, then his brief foray into legality was short-lived – probably less than eight weeks. He was now, officially, a pirate once more and therefore was fair game for anyone who could bring him to justice.[4]

On 22 August he came upon a pair of French ocean-going merchant ships sailing in company with each other, passing almost within sight of Bermuda. They had come from the Caribbean and were on their way home, planning to pick up the Gulf Stream a little north of the island. Instead they found Thatch. The Frenchmen tried to ward off the pirates, and fired on the *Adventure* as she approached. Thatch, though, was determined and fired at his quarries until they yielded. It turned out that one of the two of them was empty, her hold filled with nothing but ballast. The second, though, carried a valuable cargo of cocoa and sugar. Once his two prizes had heaved to, Thatch transferred the crew from the laden ship onto the unladen one, then let her continue back to France.[5]

That left him with one French ship as a prize. According to an article in the *Boston News Letter*, mariners, possibly from Rhode Island, had seen Thatch's sloop in company with the French ship but had been warned off. However, he allowed a ship's doctor to come aboard the *Adventure*, to treat some wounded men – possibly pirates who'd been injured during the capture of the two French prizes. To avoid further prying eyes, Thatch took his prize with him back to Ocracoke. There he supposedly spent a couple of weeks lying off the western side of the island, unloading her cargo and shipping it in stages into a hired storage building in Bath Town.[6]

It was obvious this had been an act of piracy, but Thatch was counting on Governor Eden's willingness to turn a blind eye in return for a share of the profits. Johnson even suggested that 'the governor and the pirates shared the plunder'. However, it was a little more complicated than that. Thatch had counted on the French ship returning to France, and so word of his attack wouldn't reach the ears of Governor Eden – or any other British colonial governor for that matter. This would give him a chance to spin a story that would allow him to say he had a legitimate claim to the French ship and her cargo.[7]

So, on or around 24 September, Thatch met Governor Eden in Bath Town and tried to convince him that he had 'found the French ship at sea, without a soul on board her'. If true, then under Admiralty law she had been abandoned on the high seas and was legal salvage. Of course, this was nonsense – her French crew would eventually vouch for that. However, Eden summoned his Vice Admiralty court to decide the matter, based on the evidence Thatch had supplied and the testimony of four hand-picked members of his crew. A speedy verdict benefited the Carolinians too. By rights the court could claim a fifth of the value of the cargo for themselves to offset their own costs. So, to encourage them, Thatch delivered the requisite quota of cocoa and sugar into the storehouses of Eden and his deputy governor and chief justice, Tobias Knight.[8]

This worked splendidly. A few days later, at a meeting of the colony's Vice Admiralty court, the salvage rights were duly granted to Thatch and his men for their French ship and her cargo. With that document in his pocket, Thatch was able to sell the remainder of his cargo in Bath Town. Then, after sharing out the plunder, Thatch decided to hold a celebratory party. At some point in late September, the men Thatch had stationed on Ocracoke Island spotted an armed sloop approaching the island. It turned out to be Charles Vane's *Ranger*. This could have been a threat, but it soon turned out that Vane came in peace. This, then, called for a banyan.[9]

Sure enough, this is exactly what happened – a celebratory meeting of two pirate crews, and a week of merry-making on the beach at Ocracoke. According to Johnson, the two pirates saluted each other with their sloops' guns, and 'civilities passed for some days, when, about the beginning of October, Vane took leave and sailed further to the northward'. After Vane departed, Thatch was left with the problem of his French prize. After all, it was still evidence of a crime. Fortunately, he was able to persuade Eden and Knight that she presented a hazard to navigation in the shallow waters of Pamlico Sound. So, he was granted permission to dispose of her. The French prize was duly taken out into deep water, presumably outside the barrier islands in the Atlantic, and then set ablaze.[10]

That left Thatch and his men free of any last traces of their crime. So, as winter approached, Thatch and his men settled down to enjoy the fruits of their voyage. They now had two secure bases, one in Bath Town and the other 45 miles to the east at Ocracoke Island on the very edge of the open Atlantic. Best of all, they appeared to have the full support of the governor and his senior advisers, who were willing to give them legal protection. It seemed that everything was set fair for a comfortable winter in North Carolina, with every prospect for another proper piratical cruise in the spring. Thatch and his men must have been delighted that North Carolina was shaping up to be a pirate haven which outstripped the Bahamas in terms of its legal and civic amenities. Unfortunately for the pirates, they hadn't reckoned with Alexander Spotswood of Virginia, a colonial governor who wasn't nearly as forgiving as Charles Eden.

When Governor Alexander Spotswood of Virginia learned of the plundering of British merchantmen off his Atlantic coast, and then the case of the so-called abandoned French ship, he decided to take action. North Carolina might be another colony, but he still vowed to deal with Thatch, and 'expurgate the nest of vipers' there. Fortunately, he had the tools he needed. That November, two Royal Naval fifth-rate frigates were in Virginia waters, anchored off Kecoughtan (now Hampton) in the James River. HMS *Pearl* of 42 guns and HMS *Lyme* with 32 were a powerful force, and, while under Admiralty orders, he might be able to convince their commanders to help him out. So, he summoned them to Williamsburg, where they met in the governor's new but still half-finished mansion.[11]

While Captain Ellis Brand of *Pearl* and Captain George Gordon of *Lyme* were technically not answerable to Spotswood, they had both been sent to the American waters to counter the pirate threat, and this venture promised to achieve exactly that. Both unreservedly offered their support. After all, since their arrival they had done little but escort merchant ships and act as a deterrent. This scheme offered them a real chance to do something far more effective. As the senior, Captain Brand was placed in charge of the operation. Spotswood's sources placed Thatch at Bath Town, but there remained the possibility that he might be at his second base on Ocracoke Island. Both frigates drew too much water to pass through the Outer Banks into the coastal waters of Pamlico Sound. So, they needed to find another way to get at the pirates.

Fortunately, Spotswood had the solution. He would charter two civilian vessels of a suitably shallow draught – something less than eight feet. These would then be crewed by volunteers from the two frigates and sent south to strike the pirates in their lair at Ocracoke. Sure enough, on 15 November Spotswood negotiated the hire of two Virginia trading sloops, the *Jane* and the *Ranger*. As there was no conventional way of doing this, he paid for them out of his own pocket. These were both single-masted, carrying a simple fore-and-aft rig, and displaced somewhere between 60 and 100 tons. More importantly, they were both shallow-draughted, drawing about six feet of water. The only real drawback is that they were both unarmed. Brand considered transferring some naval 6-pounders into them, but to save weight, and therefore keep their shallow draught, he decided to leave them as they were.[12]

That done, Spotswood, Ellis and Gordon set about coming up with a detailed plan. In the end it was decided that Brand would lead the main force of the expedition, which would march cross-country to Bath Town. In the process it would cross from Spotswood's jurisdiction into the North Carolina colony, where he had no legal authority. For this raid, though, Spotswood didn't really care. He would rely on speed and surprise to avoid any interference from the North Carolina governor and his legislature. Brand would avoid marching through any major towns as he headed south, to reduce the risk of Eden or Thatch being warned about this armed incursion. Brand would command about 200 well-armed men – a mixture of sailors and Virginia militia.[13]

The second prong of the attack involved the two sloops, which had been sent down the James River to Kecoughtan. Brand's First Lieutenant on board *Pearl* – his second-in-command – was Lieutenant Robert Maynard. The 34-year-old Kentishman was given the job of leading the naval side of the expedition. His orders were to take the two sloops, manned by naval volunteers, and pass through Ocracoke Inlet. Then, after rounding up any pirates at Ocracoke, he would sail to Bath Town and blockade the town from the sea. The pirates would be trapped between the two pincers. Captain Gordon of the *Lyme* would stay behind, but he would stand ready to put to sea in case the pirates managed to escape. It was a bold scheme, and a politically controversial one. However, if everything went to plan, then it could deal with the threat posed by Blackbeard once and for all.[14]

On Sunday 17 November, Maynard took charge of the two sloops and set about preparing them for the venture. He had 57 men to crew them – 33 from the *Pearl* and 24 from the *Lyme*. The *Jane* was the larger of the two sloops, so Maynard used her as his flagship, crewed by the *Pearl* detachment. The men from the *Lyme* crewed the *Ranger* under the command of Mister Hyde, a midshipman from the *Lyme*. Maynard was given two pilots who knew the Outer Banks and Pamlico

Sound, and one was sent to each sloop, bringing Maynard's force up to 60 men, including Maynard himself. In fact, he had more – both sloops still retained their civilian masters and three of their seamen in the *Jane*, and two in the *Ranger*. They, however, weren't expected to fight. The sloops were then loaded with provisions, weaponry and ammunition.[15]

That done, as Maynard wrote in his report, 'This day Weigh'd & Sail'd hence with ye Sloops under my Command, having on board Proviso of all species with Arms, & Ammunition Suitable for ye occasion.' The great expedition had begun. As an incentive to Maynard's men, Governor Spotswood told Captain Gordon that the colony would pay a bounty for any pirate they brought back, dead or alive. Spotswood proclaimed that it would be 'For Edward Teach, commonly called Captain Teach, or Black Beard, one hundred pounds. For every other commander of a Pyrate Ship, Sloop, or Vessel, forty pounds. For every Lieutenant, Master or Quartermaster Boatswain, or Carpenter, twenty pounds. For every other inferior Officer, fifteen pounds, and for every private Man taken on Board such Ship, Sloop, or Vessel, ten pounds.' Maynard's men would now be eager to earn their bounty.[16]

As he headed out to sea, Maynard calculated what lay ahead. He was an experienced officer who had earned his lieutenant's epaulette in early 1707, more than a decade before, and he'd seen action, including a sea battle off Dunkirk in 1708. He had to pace his approach so he arrived off Ocracoke at dawn. He also had to coordinate his side of the operation with Captain Brand's overland attack. So, he had a lot to ponder. At nightfall on 17 November Maynard heaved to near Cape Henry and resumed his voyage at dawn. The two sloops passed out into the Atlantic and headed south. Maynard planned to stop any passing vessels he encountered, to ask for news. His real worry was that Thatch might escape the net closing in around him.[17]

The voyage south took the best part of four days, hampered by lumpy seas and a contrary wind. From passing coastal traders Maynard learned that Thatch wasn't at Bath Town at all, but was aboard his sloop *Adventure*, which was anchored off the western side of Ocracoke Island. Maynard timed his arrival so he reached Ocracoke Inlet soon after dark on Thursday 21 November. The tide was ebbing, so he decided to wait until dawn to launch his attack. His lookouts could see the topmast of Thatch's sloop looming above the southern side of the island. Maynard waited off the island through the night, with his lookouts ordered to report any movement of the pirate sloop. It seemed that Thatch hadn't bothered to post his own lookouts on the island, so he had no idea his nemesis was there, preparing for battle. Maynard's attack would come as a complete surprise.[18]

That night, Thatch was entertaining guests. A local trading sloop had anchored off the island, and Johnson claims Thatch entertained the sloop's master and three of her crew aboard the *Adventure*. Two of them were still aboard the pirate sloop the following morning. Thatch had only a skeleton crew aboard the *Adventure* made up of 25 men – half of his force. The rest were still in Bath Town.[19]

Dawn on Friday 22 November revealed a grey, leaden and overcast sky, which suggested rain was in the offing. Still, the sea around Ocracoke Island was calm and there was very little wind – a light breeze from the south-west. That suited Maynard. He and his men were already up, had eaten, and were busily preparing for what lay ahead. It had been a cold breakfast, as Maynard didn't want galley smoke to betray their presence. The lieutenant spent the time talking with William Butler, the local pilot, who was telling him the secrets of Ocracoke Inlet and the dangers of the sandbars that lay beyond. These shifted every winter, making precise navigation all but impossible. So, Maynard decided to send his longboat ahead to lead the way, sounding the depth with a lead line as it went. It set off at 7am, half an hour after dawn. They were finally going into action.[20]

The nine men in the 18-foot longboat gingerly worked their way through the channel and approached the southern tip of Ocracoke Island. Once past the sandbar stretching between Ocracoke and Beacon Island (now Portsmouth Island) to the south, the twisting channel snaked between a maze of sandbars, before finally opening up into the deeper waters of Pamlico Sound. The *Adventure* lay in the island's main anchorage, just over two miles to the north, near where Ocracoke town stands today. In late 1718, though, there was nothing there but a few crude fishing huts. It was around 7.30am when the longboat rounded the southern side of the island. The crew could see the pirate ship clearly and could make out figures on her deck.[21]

On board the *Adventure* the crew were slow in spotting the threat. Then, someone noticed the longboat and saw the masts of two vessels behind it, working their way through Ocracoke Inlet. They had visitors – and the chances were they wouldn't be friendly. According to Captain Johnson's account, the *Adventure* fired a gun at the longboat – a warning shot across her bows if you like. It was unlikely that they'd fire one of their eight 6-pounders – that would take too long. However, they carried a bow chaser and that was ready to go. Philip Morton, Thatch's gunner, fired it, and the 4-pound ball slammed into the water well short of the approaching longboat, skipping a little before it sank. Still, the warning had been heeded – the longboat backed off. Moments later, a sloop appeared, followed by a second. Thatch was roused from his cabin, and the pirates began preparing for battle.[22]

Maynard recovered the longboat and her crew as the *Jane* reached them. Then, with the boat towed astern, the sloop rounded the island's tip and began threading her way between the sandbars, heading towards the pirates. Neither side had raised any colours, so neither Maynard nor Thatch knew exactly whom they were dealing with. With this breeze and the incoming tide, it would take roughly 20 to 30 minutes for Maynard to reach the pirates' anchorage. All this time his two sloops lay exposed to the guns of the *Adventure*. On board the pirate ship, Thatch ordered the anchor cable to be buoyed and let slip – he could recover it later. Then, with light sails set, he waited for the two mystery sloops to draw closer.

Meanwhile, he made sure his guns would bear. Although we don't know for sure, it's likely that the *Adventure* carried 4-pounders, four on each beam, plus another 4-pounder chase gun in the bow. Their maximum range was little more than 1,400 yards, but their effective range was more likely 500 yards or less. So, after that warning shot, Thatch watched the two sloops creep closer and bided his time. Anyway, Thatch probably had his eight broadside-mounted guns loaded already; what followed suggests that they carried grapeshot – bags of scrap metal, nails and musket shot designed to scythe the enemy decks, cutting men down before they could board. This meant holding fire until the enemy came within musket shot – something less than a hundred yards.[23]

Mister Hyde's *Ranger* was now on the port side of the *Jane*, the two sloops advancing side by side, some 50 yards apart. As they approached the pirates, Maynard ordered most of his men to stay below decks, to reduce the risk of casualties. He had already thought this through, and had ordered the *Jane's* hatch covers to be removed, and extra ladders mounted, to speed the movement of men onto the upper deck. The helmsman, though, was fully exposed at the whipstaff – the forerunner of a ship's wheel – and others were standing by the sweeps, the sloop's long oars, in case they were needed if the light wind dropped away, or if the flood tide threatened to put them onto a sandbank. Maynard and his pilot would also have remained exposed, standing near the helmsman. It must have been an extremely nerve-wracking time, as they drew ever closer to the pirates' guns.[24]

So, to bolster his men's morale, when they were about 500 yards away from the enemy Maynard ordered both sloops to hoist their colours. The Union flag broke out atop the mast of the two sloops. Now Thatch would be in no doubt what these mystery sloops were. They belonged to the Royal Navy. Some newspapers claimed that at that point the pirates 'accordingly hoisted their black Ensign with a Death's Head.' In fact, there is no record of Blackbeard flying a flag during the battle. Then, when the range between the *Jane* and the *Adventure* had dropped to less than 300 yards, Maynard noticed the pirate sloop had turned and was now heading directly towards the beach at Ocracoke. Thatch was using his local knowledge. There was a sandbar that lay parallel to the beach, and he was trying to lure the British sloops onto it.[25]

When the range between them dropped to around a hundred yards, Blackbeard and Maynard hailed each other. Maynard recorded that the dialogue was brief and to the point: 'At our first salutation he drank Damnation to me and my Men, whom he styl'd Cowardly Puppies, saying, He would neither give nor take Quarter.' The newspapers, of course, printed a more expansive version of the exchange. The *Boston News Letter* claimed Thatch called out, 'Damn you for Villains, who are you? And from whence do you come?' Maynard replied, 'You may see from our Colours we are no Pyrates.' More followed, with Blackbeard finishing by raising a glass and toasting the British, then shouting 'Damnation seize my Soul if I give you Quarters, or take any from you.' Maynard replied that he expected no quarter, and nor would he give any.[26]

It made a dramatic story, but the likelihood of the exchange between Maynard and Thatch is minimal. After all, they had more to do than hurl insults. Still, drinking damnation to the enemy and calling them cowardly puppies was vivid enough. That exchange over, Thatch gave the order to open fire. His first target was the smaller British sloop

Ranger. Afterwards, Maynard recalled, 'Immediately we engaged, and Mr. Hyde was unfortunately kill'd, and five of his men wounded in the little Sloop, which, having no-body to command her, fell a-stern, and did not come up to assist me till the Action was almost over.' Effectively, a volley of musketry and a broadside of larger guns charged with grapeshot had knocked the *Ranger* out of the fight. She slewed away and touched on a sandbank. That meant it was only Maynard with his *Jane* who was still able to take on Thatch and his pirates.[27]

What happened next isn't clear – there are different accounts of it, from Maynard's own matter-of-fact report to the more colourful versions published in the press, or in Johnson's *A General History of the Pyrates*. Whatever the sequence, Thatch turned his guns on the *Jane*. At that range all four charges of grapeshot would have struck the British sloop. The *Boston News Letter* reported, 'Teach begun and fired some small Guns, loaded with Swan shot [grapeshot], spike Nails, and pieces of old Iron, in upon Maynard, which killed six of his Men and wounded ten.' It was a telling blow. After the battle, Captain Gordon listed Maynard's losses as 'the *Pearl* sloop [*Jane*] had killed and died of their wounds nine, my sloop [*Ranger*] had two killed. In both sloops there were upwards of twenty wounded.'[28]

It was a telling blow – or it would be if, at that point, Blackbeard hadn't run aground. He was in shallow water anyway, and it was suggested that the recoil of his guns was enough to press the *Adventure* up against a sandbar on her larboard (port) side. Maynard then moved out of her arc of fire and began lightening his ship to let his slightly deeper-draughted sloop move closer to the pirates. Still, boarding the enemy was unthinkable. The pirate broadside had cut down several of his men and he was now hard pressed to keep the *Jane* in the battle without calling up the men hidden below decks. That, though, would mean throwing away his trump card.

So, there was a lull in the fighting as Thatch also threw provisions over the side to help free his sloop in the rising tide. He managed it, and once back in the deeper water Thatch ordered his helmsman to shape a course directly towards the *Jane*. With her decks all but empty of men she must have looked like a prize ripe for the plucking. The *Ranger* was still out of the fight, a few hundred yards away. As the *Adventure* approached the *Jane*, Thatch could be seen in her bows as if ready to lead the boarding attack himself.

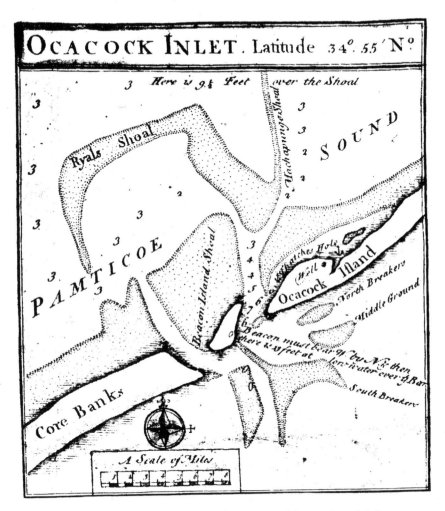

Ocracoke Island in the Outer Banks was turned into a pirate lair by Blackbeard and was the scene of his final battle.

The *Jane* was pointing roughly towards the *Adventure* when she approached, so the two vessels were bow on to each other. Thatch veered over at the last minute, his helmsman neatly placing the pirate sloop alongside the larboard side of the *Jane*. Thatch was in the bows, and even grabbed on to the *Jane*'s jibsheets to help steady the two ships as they bumped together. Then, on Thatch's orders, the pirates threw *grenadoes* onto the deck of the British sloop. These handheld fused cast-iron grenades exploded on the *Jane*'s open deck, throwing scraps of metal across it. Fortunately for the defenders, the handful of men left there – Maynard, the pilot William Butler, the helmsman Abe Demelt and another seaman – all escaped the lethal shards. None of them seem to have been lobbed through the sloop's open hatch.[29]

Then, Thatch gave the order to board the British sloop. Blackbeard led the way at the head of roughly half of his 25 men. The rest stayed aboard the *Adventure*. At that moment, Maynard signalled for his men in the hold to rush up on deck. Seconds before, the pirates thought they'd be facing a one-sided fight – a dozen of them against four or so defenders, with several others lying dead or wounded on the sloop's blood-splattered deck. Then, in a moment, a stream of well-armed British sailors swarmed up from below. Later, in a letter by the lieutenant published in the *British Gazetteer*, Maynard wrote, 'He enter'd me with 10 Men; but 12 stout Men I [had] left there fought like Heroes, Sword in Hand.'[30]

The numbers might have been a little off – before the action, Maynard had 34 men under his command, not counting the civilians. With nine or ten casualties, that still left him two dozen – roughly twice Thatch's boarding party. In any case, whatever the number, a bitter hand-to-hand fight began on the deck of the *Jane*, with no quarter offered or taken on either side. Captain Johnson published a dramatic account of the fight, with Maynard and Thatch seeking each other out amid the brutal mêlée for a duel to the death. Blackbeard often carried several pistols as well as his cutlass, and, undoubtedly, he fired these off as he fought his way aft along the *Jane*'s crowded deck. Some of the defenders may have fired back, and Johnson claims it was Maynard who first wounded the pirate captain with a pistol shot.

The *Boston News Letter* carried a dramatic account of this duel: 'Maynard and Teach themselves begun the fight with their swords, Maynard making a thrust, the point of his sword went against

Thatch's cartridge box, and bended it to the hilt. Teach broke the guard of it, and wounded Maynard's fingers but did not disable him, whereupon he jumped back and threw away his sword and fired his pistol, which wounded Teach.' By this stage it looked as if the British sailors had halted the pirates, and were now driving them back towards the *Jane*'s bows. At that point two crucial things happened. One was a British seaman cutting the grappling ropes that held the two vessels together. Then, as the sloops began to drift apart, one or two sailors worked their way around the back of Thatch, cutting him off from the rest of his crew.[31]

Maynard had almost certainly been wounded by this stage, and Thatch must have thought he could finish him off. Then, as the *Boston News Letter* described it, as Thatch fought Maynard, one of the British sailors struck the pirate captain: 'Demelt struck in between them with his sword and cut Thatch's face pretty much.' Blood must have sprayed from the horrible wound, but Thatch remained standing, swinging his cutlass like a cornered wild animal. As Johnson put it, 'he stood his ground and fought with great fury, 'till he received five-and-twenty wounds, five of them by shot.' Maynard and his men then moved in for the kill.[32]

The newspaper had the killing blow given by a Scottish highlander in Maynard's crew. It claimed, 'one of Maynard's men being a Highlander, engaged Teach with his broadsword, who gave Teach a cut in the neck, Teach saying well done lad; The Highlander replied, If it be not well done, I'll do it better. With that he gave him a second stroke, which cut off his head, laying it flat on his shoulder.' Edward Thatch fell to the deck, and in a moment the fight went out of the remaining pirates. However many men boarded the *Jane* that morning – anything from ten to 14 pirates – eight of them now lay dead or seriously wounded. The survivors either threw down their weapons or jumped overboard and tried to make it to the *Adventure*, or struck out for the nearby shore. The first round of the bloody fight was over.[33]

The blood-soaked Maynard now had a chance to pause and glance around him. He was delighted to see that the *Adventure*, lying several yards off his larboard side, was being engaged by the *Ranger*. During the boarding of the *Jane* she had worked herself free, and her crew took her alongside the starboard side of the pirate sloop. The sailors from the *Lyme* then boarded the *Adventure* and quickly subdued the pirates who'd been left aboard her. However, there was a final moment of high drama. One of the pirate crew was a black seaman – a former slave – known as Black Caesar. According to Johnson, he had been posted in the sloop's powder room with orders to blow the vessel up if she was taken. However, he was wrestled to the ground by two civilians – the men from the local trading sloop who'd spent the night there – and the lives of everyone on board were spared.

It was over. The surviving pirates who'd begged for quarter were taken prisoner, while the longboat was sent out again and more were dragged out of the water. Later, Maynard would comb the island for other pirates who'd made it ashore. The decks of the three sloops were still covered in blood, and dozens of men from either side were wounded – some of them grievously. Lieutenant Maynard himself had his hand bandaged, while he worked out the human cost of his victory. Afterwards, he put the losses on board the *Jane* as eight men killed and 18 wounded – a total of 26 of the 34 sailors under his command. One more of the wounded would die before he returned to the *Pearl.* Losses on board the *Ranger* were two killed, including the midshipman in charge of her, and about ten more wounded. The numbers varied, depending on whose report you read, but Maynard's tally was probably the most accurate.[34]

As for the pirates, a total of 13 of them were killed, and almost all of the rest wounded. The dead included Thomas Miller, the quartermaster of the *Adventure*; her gunner, Philip Morton; the boatswain Garret Gibbons; and her carpenter, Owen Roberts. Then there was Edward Thatch – also known as Blackbeard. He had been cut down, and, despite legends that his headless body then swam around the sloop, he had most assuredly been killed during the final moments of the battle aboard the *Jane.* Of the remainder of the pirates, they were all taken prisoner and would be shipped back to Virginia to stand trial. Maynard spent the next two days off Ocracoke, burying the dead and hunting for escaped pirates. One was found in the island's reed beds, his presence betrayed by the wildfowl he'd disturbed there.[35]

Then, Maynard prepared to sail for Bath Town. Before he left, though, he found his services were no longer needed. On Saturday 23 November, the day after the battle off Ocracoke, Captain Brand's column of men came within sight of Bath Town. He marched into the town, accompanied by a couple of prominent North Carolinians,

Colonel Moore and Captain Vial, who were there to help overcome any legal difficulties in what amounted to an invasion of the colony. Brand marched straight to Governor Eden's house to tell him what he was doing while his men threw a cordon around the town. Then, on Brand's order, they moved in. The citizens of Bath Town were taken by surprise, but while some protested, it seemed that the majority welcomed the arrival of the pirate-hunters. They pointed out where they could find their quarry.[36]

Several of the pirates might have escaped as the net closed in, but it seems the majority were elsewhere. In the end only six pirates were rounded up, including Thatch's first mate, Israel Hands. They were all duly placed in irons. After all the anticipation, it was something of an anti-climax. What worried Brand the most was that there was no sign of Edward Thatch. On questioning the townspeople, though, he learned that the pirate captain was in Ocracoke, aboard his sloop *Adventure*. So, everything depended on Lieutenant Maynard's naval part of the operation. Brand sent two canoes to Ocracoke – some 50 miles away – in an attempt to warn Maynard. Two days later they returned with the news that Maynard was victorious and Blackbeard was dead. The victory over the pirates was complete.[37]

In Ocracoke, the canoes reached Maynard just as he was preparing to sail to Bath Town. As he wasn't needed there, he decided to return to the James River. He sent the canoeists home in the trading sloop which had anchored next to Thatch the night before the battle. It arrived in Bath Town on 25 November with a letter for Captain Brand aboard, explaining what had happened. Once she was safely on her way, Maynard returned to sea in his two sloops, accompanied by a third – his prize, the pirate sloop *Adventure*. Like most of the dead pirates, Edward Thatch's body had been unceremoniously dumped over the side of the *Jane*. However, his head, which had been half severed in the battle, was hacked off as proof that the infamous pirate captain was dead. As the battered but victorious *Jane* made her way towards Virginia, Thatch's grizzly head hung from the sloop's bowsprit as the ultimate trophy in the war against the pirates.[38]

This, of course, wasn't quite the end of the story. For Governor Spotswood it was all highly satisfactory. Blackbeard was dead, as were several of his crew, while the rest were being shipped back to Williamsburg to stand trial. What he saw as a growing pirate threat

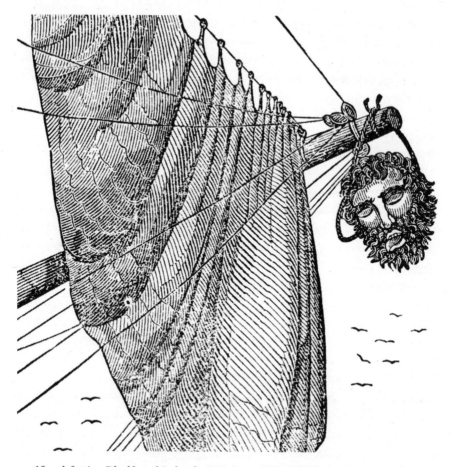

*After defeating Blackbeard in battle, Lieutenant Maynard hung the pirate's severed
head from his bowsprit as a trophy.*

in the neighbouring colony had been comprehensively crushed. Of
course, Governor Eden didn't see things that way. Before he left,
Captain Brand took the cocoa, sugar and other goods which had been
taken by the governor and his deputy as their share of the cargo from
the French ship Thatch had captured. Officially this was the property
of the Vice Admiralty court in North Carolina, and its seizure by the
Virginians sparked a legal wrangle which would drag on for years.[39]

For his part, Eden denied any cosy relationship with Thatch and
worked hard to clear his name and convince his superiors in London of
his innocence. But it was all somewhat unconvincing, and the scandal
continued to cast a shadow over Eden until his death in 1722. Governor

Spotswood found little joy in Eden's demise, as he too had spent years embroiled in a fight with his colony's own Assembly, the House of Burgesses. That autumn the Virginians managed to have Spotswood replaced as their colony's governor. At least that brought an end to the legal action surrounding Spotswood's invasion of North Carolina, and his part in the seizure of North Carolina's share of a pirate's plunder. As for the captured pirates themselves, justice would be far swifter – and considerably more draconian.[40]

The whole operation against Blackbeard had centred around Governor Spotswood's determination to strike a blow against the pirate threat. He wanted it made clear that he for one wouldn't be prepared to offer pardons to criminals, or let them off their crimes. He wanted the attack against Blackbeard to serve as a signal to the world that the fight back against the pirate menace had begun. This meant that the surviving members of Blackbeard's crew could expect little in the way of mercy. It was 1 December when Lieutenant Maynard's two sloops arrived off Kecoughtan, with Blackbeard's head still swinging from the *Jane*'s bowsprit. The crews of the *Pearl* and *Lyme* lined the yards to cheer them home.[41]

Then, after reporting to Captain Gordon and offloading his many wounded, Maynard was sent upriver with his prisoners who were duly landed at Jamestown and handed over to the Virginia militia. Locals crowded the waterfront there, eager to see the victors – and of course Blackbeard's severed head. That done, the prisoners were taken the eight miles to Williamsburg, where they were deposited in the town jail. Meanwhile, Captain Brand's column marched back overland, taking its prisoners and plunder along with them. On 18 December, Brand arrived in Williamsburg, and his prisoners joined their shipmates in the jail.[42]

The 16 prisoners languished there for three long months. Among them was Samuel Odel, one of the two sailors from the trading sloop which had been caught on board the *Adventure* when Maynard attacked her. Despite having helped save the ship from being blown up, he was swept up with all the rest. Five of the pirates, though, offered to testify against their former shipmates, in return for leniency. Four or these were former slaves, who could expect a return to slavery if they were spared the noose. The fifth was Israel Hands, and his testimony would prove crucial in the trial that followed.[43]

A large, well-armed British colonial sloop pictured off Boston Lighthouse in the 1720s.

The trial began on 12 March 1719. It was held in Williamsburg's Capitol building and was presided over by Spotswood himself in his role as head of the Vice Admiralty court for the colony. The crux of the prosecution was that Thatch and his men had all received a pardon from Governor Eden but had continued to carry out piratical attacks afterwards. In legal terms that meant the two French ships had been taken illegally. That in turn meant that a guilty verdict based upon proof would undermine Governor Eden's lawsuit against Spotswood. Proving that these men had committed piratical acts was fairly simple given the testimony offered by Israel Hands. The court then came to a speedy verdict. All but one of the condemned men were found guilty. The exception was Odel, who was given a warning and sent on his way.[44]

The mass execution of 13 pirates took place two days later, using trees lining the road between Williamsburg and Jamestown. One by one the pirates were strung up, then pushed off the back of a cart, to die at the end of a rope thrown over the tree, their bodies left to rot, as an example to other mariners. One of the other prisoners had died in custody – the result of his wounds. That left Israel Hands. After the trial, he seems to have disappeared from the historical record. He was almost certainly set free after giving his testimony, but no proof of that arrangement has ever come to light. Captain Johnson claims he died as a beggar in London, but his fate still remains something of a mystery. So too is the fate of Thatch's head, which was, supposedly, made into a drinking cup.[45]

This mass hanging was exactly what Spotswood had wanted all along. His clear message had been sent. This was a real telling blow to the pirate menace plaguing the Americas, but it was one which still had a few loose ends. One of these was the shabby treatment of the crews of the *Ranger* and *Jane*. In the end Spotswood tried to renege on his promise to pay them a bounty. After four years of wrangling, it was finally paid but divided among the entire crew of the *Lyme* and *Pearl*, rather than given to the men who'd actually taken part in the venture. As for Maynard, he got into trouble for dividing plunder found in the *Adventure* between his men. He resigned his commission in 1721 but returned to the colours a few years later and eventually rose to command his own ship. He died in his native Kent in 1751. Today, Robert Maynard is generally regarded as history's most celebrated pirate-hunter.[46]

THIRTEEN

Pursuing the Die-hards

IT HAD BEEN QUITE a remarkable year. In December 1717, the pirates of Nassau were thriving, with prizes filling the harbour and recruits flocking to the Bahamas to join them. Then, word of the royal pardon for pirates reached the island and everything changed. The pirate commune became divided, with the majority eager for a second chance – something the pardon would give them. The others were dead set against the idea and refused to give up the freedom piracy had given them. In February 1718, this fondness for liberty was put to the test when Captain Pearse arrived in HMS *Phoenix*. The pro-pardon pirates eagerly offered to surrender to the naval captain, in return for a provisional pardon. Others led by Charles Vane deliberately antagonized Pearse in a bid to demonstrate their opposition to any kind of officialdom and authority.

The ultimate test came in late July, when Woodes Rogers arrived with his expeditionary force, leading to both a challenge and a confrontation between him and Vane's group of die-hard pirates. As a result, Vane was forced to flee Nassau with one sloop and a band of his most determined followers. That effectively closed Nassau to the pirates. With the establishment of British authority in the shape of Governor Rogers, the days of Nassau as a pirate commune were over. From that point on, the carrot was replaced by the stick. Those pirates who remained at large – men like Charles Vane and Edward Thatch – became public enemies to be hunted down and brought to justice.

Elsewhere, British and colonial merchants lobbied the authorities, which in turn played a part in the stepping up of Royal Naval patrols in American and Caribbean waters. Now, the stick part of the policy was about to swing into action. There was a growing feeling, though, that the carrot and stick policy wasn't as effective as had first been hoped. It was aimed at former pirates, or seamen who might consider turning to piracy. This was why pirate trials and executions were seen as such an effective deterrent. However, several high-profile pirates were still at large, and despite the success of the Blackbeard manhunt, it seemed that seamen still were willing to embrace the pirate life if the opportunity to join a pirate crew presented itself. Governor Rogers noted that a number of pirates who had first surrendered to Captain Pearse of the HMS *Phoenix* had subsequently reverted to their old ways. The mutiny on the sloop *Buck* was proof enough of that.[1]

One of the problems was the time period covered in the 'Act for Supressing Pirates in the West Indies' (1717). Officially, pardons were offered only to pirates who had surrendered by 6 September 1718. If any pirate committed a crime after 5 January 1718, they were excluded from the pardon offer. The trouble was, by the time word of the act reached the Bahamas, or the various scattered groups of pirates who were at sea, this January deadline had already passed. In the Bahamas, many continued to carry out piratical attacks until the arrival of HMS *Phoenix* in Nassau a month after the deadline. So, it made sense to extend both of these deadlines – the one for pirate attacks and the other for surrendering to the authorities.[2]

Essentially, the various colonial governors who had to enforce the act needed a little more flexibility so they could avoid driving off pirates who genuinely wanted to embrace the offer but were ineligible. So, in December 1718, a second act was signed by King George I. It stated that as some pirates were ineligible due to 'not having had timely notice of our said Proclamation', the deadline to surrender to the authorities was extended until 1 July 1719. As before, the act also offered a reward for anyone who helped bring any of the die-hard pirates to justice after that date. The deadline for pardoning the committing of piratical acts was now 5 January 1719. As a result, when word of this reached the Americas in the spring of 1719, hundreds of pirates suddenly found themselves eligible for a pardon. This encouraged the steady trickle of pirates who gave themselves up, and it included some who had lapsed and could now return to the fold.[3]

Even without this extra time, during the last few months of 1718 there were signs that the whole carrot and stick policy might be starting to bear fruit. The execution of Stede Bonnet, the death of Blackbeard and the trials in Nassau were all highly visible deterrents.

Still, Governor Rogers and his handful of advisers were well aware that the temptation to join the die-hards would remain until Charles Vane was brought to justice. Since he left Nassau in July 1718, Vane had provided charismatic leadership to the die-hards and served as an inspiration to others who thought of reverting to piracy. In short, Vane had to be hunted down and executed. Only then could the Bahamas be deemed properly cleared of the pirate menace. Everything, then, depended on catching Vane.

After his dramatic exit from Nassau, Vane had continued to blaze his own piratical trail. He'd made his escape in the sloop *Katherine*, which was actually commanded by another die-hard pirate captain, Charles Yeats. After quitting New Providence, he headed south, to cruise the Old Bahama Channel, between the Bahamas and the northern coast of Cuba. It was there on 26 July, two days after leaving Nassau, that they captured a small Barbadian sloop. It was duly handed over to Yeats with orders to sail in consort with his own *Katherine*, which Vane continued to command. In his *A General History of the Pyrates*, Johnson claims they then captured a sloop, the *John & Elizabeth*. However, he appears to be confusing the dates, as this was the vessel Vane captured on 29 March, bound from St Augustine to Nassau. However, it seems he also captured a 12-gun brig during this period, and used it rather than the *Katherine*, which he probably returned to Yeats.[4]

Then, it seems that a few days later, according to the *British Gazette* newspaper from London, two ship-rigged vessels bound from Nassau to London were captured by pirates while still in Bahamian waters.

The pirates were almost certainly Vane and Yeats. According to the newspaper, the pirate captain threatened to destroy both of the vessels, but his crew refused to countenance 'such an inhuman piece of barbarity'. Instead, he held the men prisoner for five days before releasing them. On learning that two more ships were due to arrive in Nassau from London, the pirate captain threatened to chop them to pieces. This bravado, though, came to naught, as Vane released the men and their ships after thoroughly plundering them.[5]

After putting in to a secluded Bahamian anchorage to careen their vessels – most probably Green Turtle Key off Abaco – they were met by a sloop from Nassau crewed by men loyal to Vane. They brought supplies and news, providing Vane with details of the goings-on in New Providence, and the activities of Rogers' warships. This, no doubt, included word that the powerful frigate HMS *Milford* was due to leave for New York in mid-August, accompanied by the smaller frigate HMS *Rose*. Vane, apparently, responded by bragging that 'If there came two men-of-war to attack him, he would fight them.' He added that if he couldn't defeat them or escape, he would 'Blow up his ship, and send them on board and himself to Hell together.' This was sheer bravado – he had no real chance of taking on a Royal Naval frigate, let alone two of them.[6]

Then, in mid-August he decided to head towards the American seaboard, to hunt shipping off the port of Charles Town. Vane and Yeats arrived there on 30 August. In a repeat of Edward Thatch's actions three months before, they stationed their two vessels on the outer side of the sandbar which spanned the harbour's entrance, effectively blockading Charles Town with fewer than 120 men. This meant that no ships could leave port to warn any approaching merchantmen. As a result, over the next two days Vane captured several prizes. These included the three-masted merchant ship *Neptune* of London, the slaving brig *Dorothy*, also from London, and a small Barbadian sloop, the *Dove*.

As Governor Jonson put it, 'Lately two pirate vessels, commanded by one Vane, lay off the barr of this harbour, as they have often done, and took a ship from Guiney with negros, and two sloops bound in, and the next day attack't four ships outward bound, but what success he had with them wee could not be inform'd.' Vane was no fool though, and he suspected that after Blackbeard's attack in May the South Carolinians would probably have taken steps to defend themselves. So, he decided to move on.[7]

Unfortunately for Vane, so did Yeats. While they were off Charles Town, Yeats abandoned Vane and made off in his sloop. Vane chased Yeats in his brig, and even fired a broadside at his former consort, but Yeats managed to give him the slip. After escaping, Yeats took his thinly manned sloop south to the Edisto River, some 30 miles down the coast, and hid there until Vane disappeared. Then, Yeats sent a message to Governor Robert Johnson of South Carolina, offering to surrender to him in return for a pardon. Johnson agreed, and the pirates duly received their pardon. It was a pragmatic solution, which meant there was now one less problem for the authorities to worry about.[8]

Vane was never an easy man to deal with – he seems to have been prone to violent outbursts, and no doubt he was furious at what he saw as Yeats' betrayal. Still, after giving up the search he headed back out to sea and crossed over to the Bahamas. It was there, while anchored off Green Turtle Key near Abaco, that he was spotted by Benjamin Hornigold.[9]

Vane was actually very lucky. He abandoned the blockade of Charles Town in the nick of time. It was then that Governor Johnson sent out Colonel William Rhett and his two well-armed pirate-hunting sloops *Henry* and *Sea Nymph*, who scoured the coast for the pirate. The search lasted throughout September. However, instead of encountering Charles Vane, the pirate-hunters came across Stede Bonnet. On 27 September Rhett came across Bonnet and his sloop *Revenge* – now the *Royal James*, hiding in the Cape Fear River. As we have seen, the battle the following day ended with the capture of Bonnet and his men, who were duly shipped back to Charles Town to stand trial. It was ironic that at the time Charles Vane was still in the Bahamas, being watched by another pirate-hunter, Benjamin Hornigold.[10]

After leaving the Bahamas in late September, Vane headed north in his captured brig. Two weeks later, in mid-October, he appeared off Ocracoke Inlet. Edward Thatch was in Bath Town at the time, 50 miles to the west, but word of Vane's arrival off his Outer Banks sanctuary was taken to him. Blackbeard sailed out to Ocracoke to meet Vane, and the two crews fraternized on the island for the best part of a week. When Thatch appeared, the two pirate vessels even exchanged salutes, in a parody of Royal Navy protocol. Then the two crews had a banyan on Ocracoke. It ended amicably, although according to Johnson, Vane wanted to recruit Thatch to help him assault the Bahamas. Thatch sensibly declined, and after exchanging vows of friendship, the two pirate crews went their separate ways.[11]

It was mid-October when Charles Vane and his men sailed from Ocracoke. Neither of the pirate crews would have suspected that within a little over a month, Edward Thatch would be dead and Vane stripped of his command. After Ocracoke, Vane returned to the Bahamas. If Thatch wasn't prepared to join him, he would strike a blow against Woodes Rogers himself. He sensibly decided that Nassau would be too strong to attack. So, too, was Harbour Island, to the north-east of Eleuthera – the well-defended island fiefdom of Richard Thompson, the smuggler-turned-governor's adviser. So, he decided to strike at Eleuthera instead. It was, after all, the second most populous island in the Bahamas, and its settlers had supported Rogers. Besides, it was practically undefended.

It was around 20 October when the pirates struck. They landed on the relatively populous southern side of the island, probably around modern-day Winding Bay. Vane and his 90 hard-bitten pirates fanned out across the long thin island, looting and plundering with impunity. The following day the pirates sailed off, the decks of their brig resembling a farmyard thanks to all the stolen livestock on board. In the brig's hold was stolen rum and other spirits, dried provisions and some money, weapons and clothing. All in all, it was a productive little day trip for Vane and his men. They also made their getaway before Rogers, Hornigold or even Thompson could react.[12]

After his Eleuthera raid Vane headed south, bypassing New Providence through Exuma Sound to reach the Crooked Island Passage. This was a favoured pirate hunting ground as the channel was used by merchantmen heading home from Jamaica by way of the Windward Passage. Sure enough, on 23 October they spotted a sail. After chasing her down they discovered their prize was the 40-ton brig *Endeavour* of Salem, heading home with her holds filled with gunpowder and salt. Her master, John Shattock, later described how Vane had borne down on him, hoisted a black flag, and fired a gun to demand his surrender. Shattock did as he was told.[13]

It didn't do him much good though – the pirates held Shattock and his crew for two days while they plundered his ship, and Shattock was beaten. When he complained to the pirates' first mate, Robert Deal yelled back 'Damn you, old dog – then tell where your money is!'

The beatings and threats continued until Shattock revealed where he'd hidden the *Endeavour*'s small pay chest. Then, on 25 October, Shattock and his men were released. With that, Vane headed south towards Hispaniola – a place the Salem sailors had heard the pirates talking about – claiming they were planning to establish a base there.[14]

A month later, they still hadn't achieved anything. They'd lived off the livestock they'd plundered on Eleuthera and put in to secluded anchorages to eat and drink their fill. This was all very well, but it led to discontent among the crew. Then, while they were off the north-west coast of Saint-Domingue everything came to a head. On 23 November they spotted a sail to leeward of them. They closed in, and it was only when they were within a mile or so they realized that the large ship-rigged vessel in front of them wasn't an armed merchantman at all. When Vane broke out the black flag, their prey hoisted the ensign of a French man-of-war. They could see now she was a French frigate.[15]

They were outgunned. The frigate carried 24 guns, while the pirate brig carried a dozen, and these were of a smaller calibre. They had a small sloop sailing with them – a prize captured on the same day they took the *Endeavour* off Long Island in the Bahamas. Vane ordered them to turn away, at which point the Frenchman gave chase. At that point the pirates started quarrelling among themselves. Some, including the quartermaster John Rackam, wanted to turn and fight. Vane, though, declared that it 'was too rash and desperate an enterprise', as the French warship was twice their size. As the pirate captain he made the decision to avoid battle. In action, pirate democracy was overruled by the decision of the captain. The crew had no choice but to acquiesce.

The next day, when they were safely out of danger, it was a different matter. The crew demanded to hold a meeting, and Rackam demanded a vote of confidence in the captain. In effect, it was a challenge to Vane's rule. In the end, Deal and 15 others stood by Vane. Rackam and the remainder of the crew – some 75 of them – voted to depose their captain. As Johnson put it, 'A resolution passed ... branding him with the name of coward, deposing him from command, and turning him out of the company.' Vane was bundled into the small prize sloop, along with Deal and his 15 supporters. Then Rackam and the others sailed off through the Windward Passage in the general direction of Jamaica. Charles Vane, once the terror of the Bahamas, had been abandoned by his followers.[16]

After Rackam disappeared, Vane, Read and their remaining men pondered what to do next. After all, they had one small sloop, and probably an unarmed one at that. They had a tiny crew – too small to achieve very much – and they were short of provisions. Essentially, their only real option was to try to rebuild what they had. They decided to head to the Gulf of Honduras where the logwood cutters there would be relatively easy prey. They might also find a number of them willing to join them. The most direct route was through the Windward Passage, and then west, between Cuba and Jamaica. So, Vane set off and put their little sloop into as decent a condition as they could, to suit their needs.[17]

As they passed to the north of Jamaica they spent a couple of days cruising off the island's north-western side, around Montego Bay. There they captured two coastal *piraguas* and looted them of their supplies. Then they captured another small coastal sloop, much like their own vessel. Even better, most of the sloop's crew agreed to join the pirates. Planning for even more expansion among the logwood cutters, Vane decided to keep her, and he gave her to Robert Deal to command. On 16 December they arrived in the main logwood-cutting part of the Gulf of Honduras. There they captured a couple of prizes, falling to them as easily as they could wish. One of them was the New England sloop *Pearl*. Later, her master, Charles Rowling, complained that they were put in fear of their lives by their captors.[18]

Then, when the pirates decided to careen their two sloops, they made their captives do all the hard work before they were released. Two days later it was the turn of the sloop *Prince* from Maine. Again, her master, Thomas Walden, reported that the pirates were threatening. Unfortunately for Vane, it seems that very few of the 'Baymen' opted to join them. Still, with their sloops careened, their provisions replenished and a few guns added to their armament, Vane's two sloops headed towards the north-east side of the bay. Vane's plan was to base himself amid the Bay Islands, the small archipelago centred around the Isla de Roatán which lay some 40 miles north of the Honduran coast.[19]

It was around Christmas time of 1718 when they dropped anchor off the Isla de Guanaja to the east of Roatán. They established a camp on the southern side of the island and spent several weeks there, amid plentiful fish, game and fresh water. Pleasant though this interlude was, it wasn't pirating. So, in early February 1719 the two sloops put

to sea again, intending to head south to cruise the shipping lanes off
the Spanish Main between Panama and Curaçao. Their prizes were left
behind. Surely there would be some lucrative Spanish prizes to be had
there, which would help restore their fortunes.[20]

Instead, they had barely lost sight of the island when they were
caught in a storm. It quickly developed into a full-blown hurricane,
slamming into them from the west. The two sloops lost sight of each
other in the lashing rain and darkness. Eventually, Vane's sloop was
thrown against a reef off a small island they didn't recognize. The
sloop quickly began breaking apart in the pounding seas. They tried
to make it to shore as best they could, but only a handful made it. One
of the survivors was Vane. The castaways had been unable to rescue
anything from the wreck, apart from a few scraps of food that had been
washed ashore. The hurricane passed, but the misery continued. The
survivors had very little in the way of provisions, and the island itself
was almost devoid of anything edible. They only survived thanks to
the charity of some visiting Honduran turtle fishermen.[21]

Finally, in the early spring of 1720 a sail was sighted. The vessel
turned out to be a British one, from Jamaica, which was coming in for
water. When the seamen rowed ashore, they were surprised to meet a
group of ragged castaways waiting for them on the beach. Vane was
taken to meet the ship's master, a Captain Holford. Johnson described
him as an 'old buccaneer', but he almost certainly meant privateer. In
any event, the two men recognized each other. Holford was extremely
wary of Vane because he knew what kind of man he was. Johnson
described the conversation. In essence, Holford told Vane he couldn't
trust him, for fear of Vane inciting the crew to piracy. So, he gave Vane
and his men provisions then left them where they were.[22]

Then, it seemed that Vane's luck had finally changed. A few weeks
later another British ship approached the island, and again men rowed
ashore to refill their water casks. This time, nobody knew him. So,
Vane spun the tale that he and the others were castaways and would
work as crewmen if rescued. So, Vane signed on under an assumed
name. Then, a few weeks later, Vane's luck finally ran out. While
they were lying at anchor in the Gulf of Honduras, they were joined
by another British ship. It was Holford's. He was invited to dine
aboard, and while there, just by chance, he caught a glimpse of Vane.
Holford quickly told the captain just what kind of dangerous man

he was harbouring. So, Vane was placed in irons, and transferred to Holford's ship, which was returning to Jamaica. In March 1720, Vane was landed at Kingston, and held in prison until the Admiralty court could assemble.[23]

Vane's trial was held on 22 March 1720 in Spanish Town, the island's capital, formerly known as St Jago de la Vega. It lay a few miles west of Kingston, and across the bay from Port Royal. None other than His Excellency Sir Nicholas Lawes presided over the trial. He was the Governor of Jamaica, as well as the island's former Chief Justice, and was determined to eradicate piracy from his colony's waters. So, Vane could expect little in the way of mercy.[24]

As this was a Vice Admiralty court, six commissioners were appointed, all prominent landowners, shipowners or members of the Jamaican Assembly. All these trials followed a set pattern, with the authority of the court being established first, followed by a list of charges – almost all of which were based on the depositions of Vane's victims. The first of these dated from late March 1718, when Vane was cruising in the Bahamas, before the arrival of Woodes Rogers. The last of them was dated 16 December – the capture of the sloop *Pearl* in the Gulf of Honduras. It was all damning stuff, and it soon became clear that there could be only one verdict. Still, when asked, Vane pleaded not guilty. This of course, made no difference, as the court was ready for that.

A series of depositions were given, starting with three crewmen from HMS *Phoenix*, who verified that the prisoner was definitely Charles Vane. They were followed by other captains who'd been Vane's victims, finishing with Joseph Cockram. It all built up a picture of a violent criminal. Once all this was gone through, Justice Lawes asked if the prisoner had anything to say. Charles Vane remained sullen and silent. After a brief conference the commissioners all found Vane guilty. So, as Vane stood in the dock, Sir Nicholas Lawes read out the death sentence to be carried out on 29 March the following year, 1721. In between Vane remained in his jail cell, and all but forgotten about. The reason Vane languished in jail for almost a year before he was hanged was due to two things. First, the Jamaican authorities had a lot to deal with that year, including the quashing of a local insurrection by runaway slaves, or Jamaican maroons, and the speedy trial and execution of another group of pirates. Vane was so important that the authorities wanted to save his very public execution for the right moment.

The whole idea of executing pirates was designed as a lesson. It had to be done solemnly, and in full accordance with the law – justice had to be seen to be done. However, it was also a spectacle – a very clear warning to other mariners not to follow the pirate path. So it was that on the morning of Wednesday 29 March 1721, Charles Vane, one-time leader of the die-hard pirates of Nassau, was hanged at Gallows Point at Port Royal. He was joined there, on adjacent gallows, by his two surviving pirate crewmen, John Hanson and Robert Hudson.

Then, Vane's body was lowered to the ground, the noose removed, and his still-warm corpse placed on a cart. It was trundled to the shore, and the body transferred to a waiting longboat. Then it was taken out to Gun Key, in Kingston Harbour, wrapped in chains and iron bands, and suspended again, this time from a gibbet overlooking the harbour. There Vane's body would remain until the Caribbean sun bleached his bones. Had he been still alive, he might have recognized another pirate's remains in a nearby gibbet. They were those of his old coxswain and nemesis, 'Calico Jack' Rackam.

We last heard of Charles Vane's old crew when they abandoned him off the coast of Saint-Domingue on 24 November 1718. The pirate brig, renamed the *Revenge*, then sailed off down the Windward Passage. By a sizeable margin, the crew had elected their quartermaster John 'Calico Jack' Rackam as their new captain. We know little about him before he turned to piracy, except that he was English, 36 years old, with an education of sorts, and had been associated with Vane since he first rose to prominence as leader of the die-hards. For once, Captain Johnson, who wasn't averse to creating an imaginary backstory for his pirates, never came up with one for Rackam. Perhaps his nickname and his choice of crew made him memorable enough.

Rackam's nickname stemmed from his fondness for wearing calico, a textile made from heavy unbleached cotton, which was much finer than the canvas usually used to clothe sailors. It was also cheaper than treated cotton. The name 'calico' was derived from the southern Indian port of Calicut (now Kozhicode) on the Indian Ocean, where the fabric was produced. It was then usually dyed in bright colours and overprinted with chintz patterns – something that was becoming increasingly popular in Europe. So, in favouring calico, John Rackam was something of a fashionista.

*John Rackam, known as 'Calico Jack', was the pirate quartermaster
of Charles Vane, before taking over his ship and crew.*

After abandoning Vane, Rackam and his crew of die-hards passed through the Windward Passage and spent a week cruising off the eastern side of Jamaica. Finding nothing, they pressed on along the southern coast as far as Port Royal. This was foolhardy in the extreme as the port was used as a Royal Naval base. Still, Rackam's luck held, and instead of a patrolling frigate, on 11 December they came upon a large sloop. She gave them a good run for their money and almost reached the safety of Port Royal harbour before being overtaken. In fact, the attack took place within sight of the old buccaneering haven.[25]

Their prize turned out to be the *Kingston* of Jamaica on her way home from London. She contained manufactured goods, but the real prize for the pirates was a large consignment of gold pocket watches, which were, at least in theory, worth a small fortune. Plundering a vessel within sight of Port Royal was bordering on lunacy, but Rackam got away with it. His brig and her prize headed off to the east and then slipped away towards the relative safety of Cuba. It was just as well. The *Kingston's* Jamaican owners fitted out two armed privateering sloops and hired crews. Each master was provided with a pirate-hunting Letter of Marque signed by Governor Lawes. They then set off in pursuit of the pirates. Although they did not catch up with them that year, they kept looking.[26]

Johnson claimed that Rackam also captured a 'Madeiraman' – a vessel carrying wine from the island of Madeira – off the eastern or windward side of Jamaica. According to Johnson, they 'made hay out of her' – which essentially meant drinking her cargo. Then they let her go. Christmas that year was spent on a small deserted island, probably off the south-eastern coast of Cuba, where they finished the last of the wine. Johnson suggests the next few weeks were unproductive, as they captured nothing but a vessel carrying convicts from London's Newgate Prison bound for a new life in Jamaica's plantations. This claim, though, doesn't appear to be supported in any records.[27]

What can be verified is that by early February 1719 they'd reached the Isla de los Piños (Isle of Pines), the popular watering hole off the south-west coast of Cuba which was visited by Hornigold, Bellamy and Williams in 1716. They careened the brig *Ranger*, anchored the *Kingston*, then set up a camp ashore, most probably near the fishing village of Siguanea, a known watering spot. It was there that the Jamaican pirate-hunters caught up with them. With the brig back in the water, the pirate-hunters recaptured the *Kingston*, took the brig in tow and left, stranding Rackam and his men on the beach. At least, though, they still had the crate of pocket watches, which someone had taken ashore.[28]

The pirates were left without a ship. All they had to hand were a couple of local *piraguas*. They were really down on their luck, but by then they'd heard that the pardon had been extended, so there was still a chance they'd be allowed to surrender and then claim its protection. The pirate crew voted on it, but most weren't impressed by the idea of throwing themselves on the mercy of Governor Rogers. So, some decided to remain on the island, while others decided to try their luck elsewhere. Rackam, with six others, took one of the *piraguas*, filled her with provisions and put to sea. After rounding Cabo San Antonio, the westernmost tip of Cuba, they headed off towards New Providence, plundering Spanish fishing boats as they went.[29]

They finally reached Nassau in the middle of May. Somehow, Rackam managed to convince Governor Rogers that he and his men were wholly reformed characters. Despite being members of Vane's old crew, they had seen the error of their ways, and threw themselves upon the governor's mercy. Amazingly, it worked. Rackam and his six fellow pirates were all pardoned. It seems that during the months that followed, Rackam lived off his small stash of plunder, biding his time until something came along. Presumably he still had his share of the pocket watch haul to see him through. It was there, in Nassau, that he met the vivacious Anne Bonny. Thus began a friendship which to this day remains one of the best-remembered three-cornered partnerships in pirate history.[30]

When she first met Rackam, Anne Bonny was most probably working the port's remaining taverns and brothels, eking out a living as best she could. She had a husband, James Bonny, who had been a member of a pirate crew, arriving in Nassau just when the whole pirate business there was being wrapped up. So, he accepted a pardon, and he might well have acted as an informant for the island's authorities, warning them of anyone who might be planning to revert to their old ways. The backstory provided by Captain Johnson claims that Anne was Irish, from the port of Kinsale in County Cork, and the illegitimate daughter of William McCormac, a local lawyer. She was raised by a serving woman, Mary Brennan, but McCormac took Anne with him when he moved to London. It was there, thanks to him, that she supposedly took to dressing as a boy in a doomed attempt to retain an allowance.[31]

In 1710, though, McCormac took passage to Charles Town in the South Carolina colony, taking his ten-year-old daughter with him. As a child, Anne was described as having 'a fiery and courageous temper'. McCormac, who had now dropped the Irish prefix to become 'Cormack', had hopes that his daughter would marry well. Instead, it seems, she fell for a young sailor, James Bonny, and the couple eloped and married. The pair pitched up in Nassau sometime in mid-1718, and he joined a pirate crew, just weeks before the establishment of British rule. Bonny didn't sail with Vane and his die-hards but remained in Nassau with his young and troublesome wife.[32]

It seems that romance blossomed between Anne Bonny and 'Calico Jack'. A year later, in the early summer of 1720, Anne and James Bonny sought to annul their marriage but were refused permission. It was around then that Rackam decided to return to sea. This time he would take Anne with him. They recruited some other former pirates or other desperate people, and hatched a plan. One of their little band was another young woman called Mary Read.

Again, we have to turn to *A General History of the Pyrates* for any background on her, real or imagined. According to Johnson she was English, the daughter of a single parent. As a child she was dressed as a boy, so her mother could claim an allowance from the father's family. As a teenager Mary – known as 'Mark' – ran away to sea, then joined the army, fell in love with a Flemish cavalryman and became his mistress, and then common-law wife. On the soldier's death, she took passage to the West Indies. When the ship was captured by pirates, Mary – still disguised as a man – joined them, but eventually the crew sought a pardon, and Mary landed up in Nassau.[33]

The real story was probably very different and much less exotic. Working back, we can place Mary Read in Nassau around 1720. By then she would probably have been in her late 30s. Like Anne Bonny, she was described by pirate victims as having dressed as a man, but they were both definitely women. They were noted for being extremely profligate – cursing and swearing like common sailors. This in itself was an indication that Read might have spent time at sea, in her cross-dressing guise, or in military service – or both. What wasn't provided was any form of corroboration for Johnson's backstory.[34]

*Anne Bonny, the hard-fighting pirate shipmate of 'Calico Jack'
Rackam and Mary Read.*

In any case, this is largely immaterial. In the summer of 1720, as a friend of Anne Bonny and her lover, Mary Read was invited to join their venture – a return to piracy. Johnson claimed that 'Her sex was not so much as suspected by any on board until Anne Bonny ... took a particular liking to her.' Johnson went on to say that on hearing the news, 'Captain Rackam ... kept the thing a secret from all the ship's company'. This is plain nonsense. When Rackam and his followers escaped from Nassau, Governor Rogers posted a description of the pirate band, where he described Bonny and Read as women.[35]

On the evening of Thursday 22 August, Rackam, accompanied by eight accomplices, stole a canoe and rowed out to the unattended sloop *William*, riding at anchor in the harbour. This fast 12-ton, four-gun sloop was owned by a local trading captain known as John Ham – who apparently went by the marvellous nickname of 'Catch him if you can' Ham. They crewed her, raised her anchor and hoisted her jib. The sloop crept out of the harbour, but before they reached the open sea they had to pass Rogers' guardship, which that night was the *Delicia*. When challenged, the thieves replied that their anchor cable had parted, and so they planned to ride out the night outside the harbour, then return to sort it out in the morning. This was strange but plausible, and they were allowed to proceed.[36]

On 5 September, Governor Rogers issued a proclamation in Nassau, which was later published in the *Boston Gazette*. It named 'John Rackum' as the leader of the pirates, who was accompanied by two women, 'Anne Fulford alias Bonny, & Mary Read', as well as a group of men. Five of them were named (John Davis, George Fetherston, John Howell, Andrew Gibson and Noah Patrick). The sloop they stole was described as 'a Certain Sloop call'd the *William*, Burthen about 12 Tons, armed with 4 Great Guns and 2 Swivel ones'. It also listed the stolen canoe. Once clear of the harbour they shaped a course towards the east, then rounded New Providence to lie off its southern coast. There they plundered local fishing vessels and sent word to Nassau, to allow others to swell their ranks.[37]

A newspaper account claimed, 'Several Pirates are on the Coast of the Bahamas, among which is one Rackum, who Run away with a Sloop of 6 Guns, and took with him 12 men and two women.... The Pirates swear Destruction of all those who belong to this Island.' If this is correct, then about six men joined them from Nassau as they lay off the island,

Mary Read, who, like Anne Bonny, dressed in seamen's clothes, to avoid drawing undue attention to her gender.

and the identity of the two cross-dressing women was already widely known, both to Rogers and the rest of Nassau. Rogers' proclamation then described what happened next: 'The said Sloop did proceed to commit Robery and Piracy upon the Boat and Effects of James Gohier Esq, on the South side of this Island, also upon Capt. Isaac's Master of a Sloop riding at Berry-Islands in his Way from South-Carolina to this Port.' Rackam and his band were no longer just thieves. They were now officially pirates, and so could expect no mercy.[38]

Other small-scale attacks followed among the Bahamas' southern islands. During this time, according to those who encountered them, the two women wore men's clothes when carrying out attacks. This probably meant they wore seamen's canvas trousers or long shorts rather than more impractical dresses. This was scandalous in the eyes of early Georgian society. Women simply didn't do that kind of thing. The women's clothing, more than anything, accounts for the subsequent notoriety of Rackam, Bonny and Read. Captain Johnson, at any rate, cashed in on this by providing descriptions of the two women who dressed as pirates, and according to him outfought their male shipmates.

A Jamaican fisherwoman, Dorothy Thomas, described their appearance when the pirates came upon her off the north coast of Jamaica. According to her testimony the women 'wore men's jackets and long trousers, and hankerchiefs wrapped round their heads'. They were well-armed too, with 'a machette and pistol in their hands'. She added that the only reason she knew they were women was by the size of their breasts. Another claim was that the women were telling their male crew members to kill her, to prevent her from testifying against them all in court. Rackam, though, let the fisherwoman go.[39]

It seems Rackam spent the next few weeks in the Bahamas and according to Johnson, 'In the beginning of September, they took seven or eight fishing boats in Harbour Island, stole their nets and other tackle, and then went off to the French part of Hispaniola ... They afterwards plundered two sloops, and returned to Jamaica.' Sure enough, in Rackam's trial it was stated that seven fishing boats were captured, some two leagues (six miles) off Harbour Island. Similarly, on 1 October, according to the evidence, they captured and plundered two British-flagged sloops, some three leagues (nine miles) off the coast of Hispaniola. This places Rackam in what was most probably the Saint-Domingue side of the Windward Passage by the start of October.[40]

Their next victim was a schooner, taken some 15 miles off Port Maria on the north-east coast of Jamaica on 19 October. According to the testimony of a seaman, the pirates fired small arms at his schooner, forcing him to surrender. The pirates kept the crew prisoner for two days while they looted the cargo of 50 bales of tobacco and nine sacks of pimiento peppers. The next day it was the turn of the trading sloop *Mary*, taken off Dry Harbour Bay (now Discovery Bay) in the centre of Jamaica's northern coast. Her master, Thomas Dillon, reported that the pirates fired their main guns at him to force him to stop. They plundered his cargo and took the equivalent of £300 from the ship's chest.[41]

This was all very dangerous for the pirates, as not only was there a Royal Naval force based in Port Royal, but the Jamaicans had a number of pirate-hunting privateers at sea. Rackam was playing with fire. To anyone willing to look, his attacks revealed the course of the *William*, working her way down through the Windward Passage before making landfall in Jamaica. The pirates were then clearly heading westwards along her northern coast, taking advantage of the prevailing wind. That meant that if any privateer chose to, she could easily intercept the *William* off the western tip of the island. Sure enough, the authorities sent two privateering sloops to hunt him down, commanded by Captains Jean Bonnevie (or Bondevais) and Captain John Barnet. Meanwhile an oblivious Rackam continued his cruise to the west, passing Montego Bay to reach Jamaica's western coast.[42]

Late in the afternoon of Thursday 31 October Rackam and his crew came upon a *piragua* off Negril Point. That was the true westernmost tip of Jamaica. The *piragua* was crewed by nine turtle hunters, who offered to share their catch with the pirates in exchange for some drink. An evening drinking session followed as the sloop lay at anchor in the lee of the point, near the southern end of what is now Seven Mile Beach. Unknown to Rackam, though, they were being hunted. Captain Barnet's 12-gun privateering sloop *Eagle* and Captain Bonnevie's sloop were in the area, having sailed together from Port Royal. However, Bonnevie wasn't just on a privateering mission – he was making a trading run to the southern side of Jamaica. That afternoon as he rounded Negril Point he was a few miles ahead of his consort. It was then that he spied the *William*, which fired a shot at him. Bonnevie decided to pull back out of sight, to wait for Barnet.[43]

When the *Eagle* came up, Bonnevie told Barnet of the sighting. They were lying just to the south of the bulbous Negril Point, with the suspected pirate sloop a few miles to the north of them. Sunset was at around 5.35pm, with full darkness coming an hour later. Barnet decided to attack once it was evening. At around 10pm the *Eagle* came upon the *William*, lying at anchor close in to the shore. He hailed her, asking what she was. The reply came across the water that she belonged to John Rackam of Cuba. That was enough for Barnet. He hoisted his British colours, then yelled a demand that the pirate sloop strike hers. Instead, the pirates cut their cable and tried to escape. With that, Barnet's demand was met with the cry 'We will strike no strikes'. This was backed up by a shot fired from one of the *William*'s swivel guns. The battle had been joined.[44]

Barnet responded by spinning the *Eagle* about and delivering a six-gun broadside at close range, backed up by musket fire. One of the shots carried away the *William*'s boom, which meant she was virtually immobile. With that there were cries from the *William*, as some of her crew begged for quarter. According to Johnson, most of Rackam's crew hid in the ship's hold, but the two women pirates stood their ground and cursed the timidity of their weak-willed shipmates. Still, this was no real contest – the *Eagle* could just lie off where the *William*'s guns couldn't fire back, and pound the pirate ship into submission.[45]

John Barnet had the manpower to finish things off right away. So, he brought his sloop alongside the enemy and gave the order 'boarders away'. His men swarmed over the side of the pirate sloop and watched as the remaining pirates – including the two women – were forced to throw down their weapons. Rackam himself, it seems, had taken no part in the fight. After securing his prize, Barnet sailed on to the north-east, followed by the *William*, with her crew back in the hold, only this time they were wearing irons. Also accompanying her was Thomas Dillon's sloop *Mary*, which was still being held by the pirates, and was lying at anchor close to the *William*.[46]

The prisoners still represented a risk to Barnet, so he landed them at Davis Cove, some 12 miles up the coast on the north-western side of Jamaica. There they were handed over into the custody of Captain Richard James of the Jamaican militia. He would transport them the 90 miles to the jail in Spanish Town, where they would be held until their trial. That left Barnet free to sail anti-clockwise around Jamaica, tacking into the face of the prevailing wind, to reach Port Royal and a hero's welcome. It took the best part of two weeks for Captain James to escort his dozen prisoners to Spanish Town. By then Barnet had been in port for a week, word had spread, and everything had been prepared for the trial. Already incarcerated there was Charles Vane, sentenced eight months before and now awaiting his much-delayed execution. If the violent-tempered Vane had been allowed to meet his double-crossing quartermaster, the Jamaican Assembly might well have been spared the expense of a gallows.[47]

Rackam's trial began in Spanish Town on 16 November 1720. Standing accused beside him were nine other prisoners, a mixture of pirates and the unfortunate turtle hunters caught up in the action. The two women pirates were not tried with the others. Their time would come. Presiding over the court was Governor Sir Nicholas Lawes, assisted by William Needham, the island's chief justice, and 12 other commissioners, including Captain Vernon of the third-rate 64-gun ship-of-the-line HMS *Mary*, flagship of the Jamaica squadron. Another was Captain Davers of the 40-gun frigate HMS *Adventure*. As usual, this was a Vice Admiralty court, so there was no jury – Sir Nicholas and his commissioners would be judge, jury and executioner.[48]

In the end the evidence was utterly damning. By concentrating on crimes committed in Jamaican waters, and against any Bahamian vessels which were in port, the depositions the prosecutors needed were readily at hand. Still, the court's officials, particularly Lawes' court secretary Robert Baillie, had worked long hours to pull everything together. Inevitably, the pirates all pleaded 'not guilty', but there was no real doubt about the outcome. Instead, they listened as a string of depositions were read out and the evidence piled up. It was already known that they had been pardoned by Governor Rogers and had reneged on the deal. They had then deliberately returned to piracy, stealing a sloop from under the very nose of the Bahamian governor. So, they could expect absolutely no mercy.

Sure enough, the guilty verdict was passed, with the first five, including John Rackam, due to hang the following morning. It was claimed that on the night before his execution, Anne Bonny got a chance to see her old lover, and she cut him to shreds with her tongue: 'I'm sorry to see you here. But, if you'd fought like a man, you needn't have been hanged

THE
TRYALS
OF
Captain John Rackam,
AND OTHER
PIRATES, *Viz.*

Geroge Fetherſton,	Noah Harwood,
Richard Corner,	James Dobbins,
John Davies,	Patrick Carty,
John Howell,	Thomas Earl,
Tho. Bourn, *alias* Brown,	John Fenwick, *al'* Fenis

Who were all Condemn'd for PIRACY, *at the Town of* St. Jago de la Vega, *in the Iſland of* JAMAICA, *on* Wedneſday *and* Thurſday *the Sixteenth and Seventeenth Days of* November 1720.

AS ALSO, THE

TRYALS *of* Mary Read *and* Anne Bonny, *alias* Bonn, *on Monday the* 28th *Day of the ſaid Month of* November, *at* St. *Jago de la Vega aforeſaid.*

And of ſeveral Others, who were alſo condemn'd for PIRACY.

ALSO,

A True Copy of the Act of Parliament made for the more effectual ſuppreſſion of Piracy.

Jamaica: Printed by *Robert Baldwin,* in the Year 1721.

The frontispiece of the published transcript of the trial of 'Calico Jack' Rackam, held in Jamaica in 1720.

like a dog.' So, at dawn the following morning, 18 November 1720, John Rackam was hanged at Gallows Point in Port Royal, overlooking Kingston Harbour. Swinging at the end of gibbets next to him were four of his former crewmen: the *William*'s master George Fetherston, her quartermaster Richard Corner, and two others. Afterwards they were cut down, and Rackam's, Fetherston's and Corner's bodies were wrapped in chains and re-displayed from gibbets erected on three small islets in the harbour. Inevitably, the islet where the pirate captain was displayed became known as Rackam's Key. A few months later the body of Charles Vane would be wrapped in iron and strung up nearby.[49]

The next day (19 November) four more pirates were hanged, this time in Kingston, and two more were convicted – men whose wounds had led them to miss the previous day's trial. These two would follow their shipmates to the gallows on the following Monday morning, 21 November. Rather unfairly the court condemned the poor turtle hunters, whose only real crime was being in the wrong place at the wrong time. As for the two women pirates, their arrest had sparked a storm of public interest. This was, after all, an utterly scandalous business. Their trial began on 28 November. Once again Sir Nicholas Lawes sat in judgment, assisted by Needham and ten commissioners, including Captain Vernon. The course of this Vice Admiralty court followed the usual pattern, and both Anne Bonny and Mary Read pleaded 'not guilty'. As usual, the evidence was damning, and in the end Sir Nicholas' verdict was unavoidable. They were found guilty.[50]

Both women were forced to stand as they were asked if they had anything to say. They both remained silent. Then, the death sentence was read out: 'You, Mary Read and Anne Bonny, alias Bonn ... shall be severally hang'd by the neck, till you are severally dead.' In the end, the death sentence was never carried out. After the judgment was read out, as the court records put it, 'both the Prisoners inform'd the Court, that they were both quick with Child, and prayed that execution of the Sentence might be Stayed.' A doctor was sent for, who vouched that their claims were true. Both women were pregnant. The sentence was therefore 'respited'.[51]

It was just as well. Public opinion was all for hanging pirates, but not for the hanging of pregnant mothers. Besides, there was no law permitting the killing of an unborn child. The two women were returned to their cells, where they were expected to see through their labour.

Then the courts could decide their fate. As it happened Mary Read died in prison from a fever, in April 1721, just three months before her due date. She and her unborn baby were buried in nearby St Catherine's Church on 28 April 1721. As for Anne Bonny, she slipped out of the tale. She wasn't hanged, and no death records for her survive. Rumour had it that her father William Cormack quietly secured her release along with her newborn child. The real story might never be known, but this didn't stop Captain Johnson, writing half a decade later. For him, female pirates were literary gold dust, and he made the most of it.[52]

Back in the summer of 1718 the die-hard pirates of Nassau quit their former pirate haven full of passion and vigour. What followed, though, wasn't the reclaiming of old glories, or the creation of a new pirate commune, but a tale of steady decline, mixed with betrayal, tragedy and death. The execution of Charles Vane was a real coup for the British authorities, and it would serve as a stern and effective warning to other would-be pirates. As Captain Edward Vernon put it, 'He has been tried, condemned and executed, and is now lying in chains ... These punishments have made a wonderful reformation here.' However, Vane was really nothing more than a figurehead, the titular leader of the pirates who refused to recognize British authority. Even after his death, most of the die-hard pirates who had left Nassau with him had never been caught. While many would simply retire quietly, others still caused problems for some time to come. The pirate menace had been dealt a real blow, but it still hadn't gone away.[53]

FOURTEEN

The *Buck* Legacy

I F PIRACY WAS A weed, then its roots in the Bahamas had finally been cleared save for the occasional little shoot, which was quickly plucked out. However, it continued to thrive around the edges, threatening to grow and spread, and ultimately return to its old soil. While a lot of attention had been devoted to dealing with the main outbreaks, a few smaller incidents were left alone. Some of these proved particularly virulent. When it came to the spread of the pirate menace, the worst of these fresh outbreaks was the one that spread after the mutiny of one of Governor Rogers' sloops, the *Buck*.

The sloop *Buck* was part of Woodes Rogers' fleet which arrived off Nassau in late July 1718. She was a large sloop, of 35 tons, but she carried only six guns and a minimal crew of 12 men. Despite this she was rated as a private sloop-of-war. She sailed from Spithead with the rest of Rogers' fleet on 1 May 1716, laden with supplies and settlers. She was one of the first of the British vessels to enter Nassau harbour, and she led the pursuit of Charles Vane and his die-hards when they fled from Nassau. Afterwards, she combined two roles – an armed patrol vessel charged with protecting New Providence, and a trading sloop. The newly installed governor was keen to make his colony pay, and this meant establishing trading links with other colonies, including the Spanish in Cuba.[1]

One of the problems, though, was that the Spanish didn't realize that the British had re-established their control of the Bahamas. To them, especially in the eyes of the new governor of Cuba, Gregorio Guazo y Calderón Fernández, this neighbouring archipelago was still a nest of pirates. This was brought home to Governor Rogers on 8 September 1718, when Philip Cockram came to see him. The brother of John Cockram, Hornigold's former shipmate turned smuggler, Philip had just been released by the Spanish. He had been captured several weeks before while on a trading voyage to Cuba, and had been forced to act as a pilot for the Spanish as they surveyed the southern and western approaches to New Providence. This suggested that an invasion might well be in the offing.[2]

Rogers solution was to write a letter to the Cuban governor, telling him the Bahamas were under new management and that the pirate threat had been dealt with. He decided to send the sloop *Buck* to Havana with the letter, her hold filled with a cargo of trade goods. Her master, Jonathan Bass, had strict instructions to be as appeasing as he could to the Spanish. For the voyage she would be accompanied by the small trading sloop *Mumvil Trader*. To make up numbers, the crew of the *Buck* were bolstered by up to a dozen former pirates. This proved something of a mistake, as after taking on salt in the south-eastern Bahamas the two sloops headed into the Old Bahama Channel and made landfall on the coast of Hispaniola a few days later. They were probably somewhere near the Bahía de Môle in the north-eastern corner of Saint-Domingue. It was there that the crew of the *Buck* rose in mutiny and killed their captain.[3]

According to the *Buck*'s young Scottish surgeon, Archibald Murray, the first thing he knew of the rising was when he was woken up by someone hitting him with the flat of a cutlass. He saw a couple of well-armed crewmen standing there, looking threatening. He jumped up and dodged them, then ran to the captain's cabin. Inside he spotted a pair of pistols and, having woken the captain, urged him to take one to defend himself. Jonathan Bass had to tell him they weren't actually loaded. Moments later the mutineers forced their way into the cabin, and Bass and Murray had no choice but to surrender.

Soon, both sloops were in the hands of the pirates. Not all of their few-dozen crew wanted to join the mutineers, especially in the *Mumvil Trader*. However, the mutineers had the firepower to enforce their will. So, after transferring the loyal crewmen into the smaller sloop and calling for volunteers from among her crew, the mutineers hoisted the black flag and sailed off. The *Buck* mutineers had now become pirates. The 21-year-old surgeon was taken captive by the pirates just in case the newly created pirates needed his services. Apparently, the acting pirate captain, Walter Kennedy, shot Captain Bass before sailing off in his sloop.[4]

When the *Mumvil Trader* arrived in Nassau with the news, they placed the number of mutineers at just seven men: Thomas Anstis, John Clerk, Howell Davis, Roger Hughes, Richard Jones, Dennis Topping and Walter Kennedy. All seven mutineers had 'conspired to go off Pyrating with the Vessel'. Anstis, Davis and Kennedy would go on to become pirate captains in their own right. Even more worryingly, as historian Marcus Rediker put it, 'This core of conspirators would evolve into the most successful gang of pirates in the entire golden age.'[5]

Initially, the Londoner Walter Kennedy was made temporary captain until the pirates had made their escape. They anchored safely in Coxon's Hole, a secluded bay on the eastern coast of Cuba. This was probably the small mouth of the Rio Yumurí, now called the Boca de Yumurí, a few miles to the west of the northern end of the Windward Passage. Once there they held a proper vote. Johnson described what happened:

> After this a counsel of war was called over a large bowl of punch, at which it was proposed to choose a commander. The election was soon over, for it fell upon Davis by a great majority of legal pollers. There was no scrutiny demanded, for all acquiesced in the choice. As soon as he was possessed of his command, he drew up articles, which were signed and sworn to by himself and the rest. Then he made a short speech, the fun of which, was a declaration of war against the whole world.[6]

Most of what we know about Howell Davis comes from Captain Johnson, although once his piratical career began in earnest following the *Buck* mutiny, we can follow his trail through the reports of his victims. According to Johnson, he was born in Milford Haven in Pembrokeshire, one of the busiest ports in South Wales. As a result, as Johnson claims, he was 'from a boy brought up to the sea'. Most probably he was born around 1690, making him in his late 20s at the time of the *Buck* mutiny. It seems he made a few voyages from Welsh or English ports before the summer of 1718, when he first crossed the line into piracy. He was the first mate aboard a slave ship called the *Cadogan* from Bristol. She was a snow, a sizeable two-masted merchantman with a distinctive rig, combining conventional square sails with a small mast mounted aft, carrying a triangular trysail.[7]

On 11 June the *Cadogan* was on her way to the West African slave coast when she was captured off Sierra Leone by the pirate Edward England, a former shipmate of first Henry Jennings and then Charles Vane. England had taken part in Jennings' raid on the Spanish salvage camps in Florida and then served as Vane's quartermaster for a time on board the *Lark*. Unlike Vane, England never applied for a pardon, but was released nevertheless as an act of good faith. It didn't really pay off. He shipped out in a trading sloop, but according to Johnson the vessel was captured by the small-time Bahamian pirate Christopher Winter. England duly volunteered to join Winter's crew, but his timing was poor, as Woodes Rodgers was expected to arrive in the Bahamas at any moment. So, this was Winter's last pirate cruise, and he was already planning to find another way of making a living. Winter duly headed for Cuba, where he and another pirate, Nicholas Brown, took service with the Spanish *guarda costa*.[8]

For his part England and some others sought that opportunity to begin their own piratical cruise, using a small armed sloop which Winter had captured. England and his crew then headed out across the Atlantic towards the West African coast. It was felt, presumably, that there were rich pickings to be had there among the European slavers who visited to pick up their human cargo. At the same time, another small-time Nassau pirate, Edmund Condent, who was a vocal member of the die-hard faction, also left for the African coast in the great sloop *Dragon*, which carried a crew of 96 men. Between Winter, Condent, England and their followers, a sizeable portion of the die-hard faction had decided to quit Nassau in the weeks before Woodes Rogers' arrival. This meant that with the exception of Vane and his men, most of the anti-pardon faction of the Nassau pirates left the place during the early

Despite his name, Edward England was an Irishman,
who began his long career in Nassau.

summer of 1718. Others, like Paulsgrave Williams, opted to stay put and bide their time, waiting to see how events unfolded.[9]

Captain Skinner of the *Cadogan* was unfortunate to put in to Sierra Leone just as Edward England appeared off the small African port. On capturing the *Cadogan*, some of England's crew then brutally murdered Skinner. Johnson hints that this was the result of a longstanding grudge between some of the pirates and a former captain of theirs who'd treated them badly. Howell Davis, though, and some others, were released by England and sent on their way. Davis proposed that they turn pirate, but he was outvoted, and when the *Cadogan* reached Barbados the crew reported Davis to the authorities, who imprisoned him. There was no proof though – after all he hadn't actually committed piracy – and so he was released. So, out of a job, Davis made his way to Nassau. It was there that he was given another chance and a berth in the *Buck*.[10]

So, shortly after the mutiny of the *Buck*, Howell Davis found himself in command of a six-gun sloop with a small band of fellow pirates. They decided to use Coxon's Hole as a base and then cruise in the Windward Passage for a spell. They concentrated on the waters off Saint-Domingue and soon caught and captured a French trading sloop, armed with 12 guns. Then, they spied an even bigger prize in the offing, a French merchantman. She was extremely well armed, mounting 24 guns. Her crew was probably around 60 men, which was roughly twice that of the *Buck*. So, rather than take her head on, Davis used a *ruse de guerre*. Under the watchful eye of his prize crew, he had the French sailors from his prize dress in white shirts to make her look well manned. He also had them hoist a grubby tarpaulin as a makeshift black flag. Then, Davis approached the French merchantman in the *Buck*, which flew her own black flag.[11]

The Frenchman had her guns run out, and her captain yelled over, demanding that the impudent but puny pirate sloop surrender. Davis was expecting this, and yelled back a counter-demand – that the Frenchman surrender. He warned him that he was just waiting for his well-armed consort to come up, and together they would offer the merchantman no quarter. This threat was backed up when the prize sloop fired a gun at the merchantman, as if to test the range. This was enough for the French captain, who promptly hauled down his colours. Davis ordered him to come over to the *Buck*, with 20 of his men.

Once on board the sloop he took them prisoner, then ranged alongside the French ship and took possession of her.

It was a masterly stroke of deception – a six-gun sloop capturing a 24-gun ship – and it demonstrated that Howell Davis was as ingenious a pirate captain as he was a brave one. He kept the two prizes with him for two days, before sending his prisoners onto the large merchantman, then making off, leaving his two French prizes behind. He had, of course, stripped them of anything useful, including weapons, powder and shot, and spiked any guns he couldn't take with him. Other prizes followed, a couple of local French and Spanish trading sloops. However, Davis knew that word would have got out by now, and either the British or the French would soon be looking for him. Rather than go elsewhere in the Caribbean, he and his crew elected to cross the Atlantic and try their luck in the waters off West Africa.[12]

As England had known before him, there were rich pickings to be had there. During this period this was the region where most European slave ships picked up their human cargo, either through established trading posts or by dealing directly with local African rulers in towns such as Whydah (also called Ouidah) or Calabar. For the most part, the European trading posts were either run by the British Royal African Company, which held a monopoly on sanctioned British trade along the coast, or by the Portuguese. The Portuguese maintained several slave trading post on the West African coast, or in the islands they controlled in the Gulf of Guinea.

After crossing the Atlantic Davis made landfall in the Cape Verde Islands. There he decided to put into the small Portuguese island of São Nicolau, anchoring off the port of Tarrafal de São Nicolau on its south-western coast. Somehow, he managed to convince the local authorities that he was a legitimate English pirate-hunting privateer. It helped, of course, that he avoided the administrative heart of the archipelago, the port of Prai on the nearby island of Santiago, where there might have been people who'd ask more questions. The pirate crew even walked inland to visit the island's main settlement, Ribeira Brava, where they enjoyed the hospitality the island could offer. According to Johnson, when the pirates sailed off, five of Davis' crew decided to stay behind, as they liked the place so much, having met local women.[13]

They then looked into the harbour of Bona Vista, another of the Cape Verde archipelago a day's sail to the east. Finding nothing worth

Howell Davis, the Welsh pirate who led the Buck *mutiny before carving out a name for himself off the West African coast.*

plundering in the fishing haven of Sai Rei, they continued on to Maio, another island to the south. There they dropped their cover, and in the island's undefended harbour of Porto Inglês, Davis captured a British merchant vessel, the *Loyal Merchant* of Liverpool, which had just arrived there. She was a much better craft than the now leaking *Buck*, so Davis abandoned his old vessel to his British captives and claimed the 26-gun *Loyal Merchant* as his own. Before hoisting the black flag and leaving, he renamed her the *Royal James* – a reference to the Jacobite rivals to British royal authority.

According to Johnson, they were now short of water and Davis rashly decided to press on to the next island, Santiago, within sight to the west, to see if he could water there. He supposedly stepped ashore at Prai, but the Portuguese governor of the Cape Verde Islands, Serafim Sarmento de Sá, was suspicious of the Welsh merchant ship captain. Johnson then told a fantastic tale, saying how Davis and his men took offence at this, and attacked the governor's mansion and fort by stealth but were forced to withdraw. This colourful tale isn't backed up by any historical evidence. Davis was too intelligent to risk putting in to the Portuguese capital of the archipelago in a stolen ship, as she would probably have been recognized by shipping agents there. Instead, from Maio he shaped a course for the African coast, some 320 miles away beyond the eastern horizon.[14]

On 23 February 1719, the *Royal James* made landfall off the mouth of the Gambia River. During this period the Senegal and Gambia rivers were used extensively as watering and provisioning places by European slavers. Some 20 miles past the mouth of the Gambia River was the tiny James Island (now Kuntah Kinteh Island), which had been fortified by the Dutch, but by 1719 it was firmly under British control. Fort James in the middle of the Gambia River was an outpost of the Royal African Company, but it had fallen into disrepair after being fought over during Queen Anne's War. When Davis arrived off the river mouth, Fort James was in the process of being rebuilt. Instead, the commander of the half-built fort lived aboard a company ship, the *Royal Ann*, which was anchored nearby off the local trading port of Gallassee (or Jillifrey, now part of Albadarr, on the north side of the river).[15]

It was late afternoon when he arrived, and for the moment Davis successfully passed the *Royal James* off as a British merchant ship, claiming he planned to take on water and provisions. So, he anchored off Gallassee, where he and his crew appeared to settle down for the night. In fact, Davis was preparing a bold stroke. That evening, night fell at around 8pm. Once it was completely dark, three boats were lowered from the *Royal James* and, with muffled oars, they rowed silently over to the *Royal Ann*, anchored half a mile away off James Island. The pirates weren't noticed until they swarmed over the side of the British ship. It was a complete surprise, and while the officers and crew put up a brief fight, within about 20 minutes Howell Davis was master of the ship.

In Johnson's account, the fort's commander invited Davis to dine with him and the attack happened then. In any case, the result was the same – that night the pirate captain gained control of the Royal African Company ship, as well as the half-repaired fort, which was manned by only a small watch party. As a result, Davis became the master of the whole Gambia River. Effectively, the Gambia River had become a pirate haven. Almost as if on cue, the next morning a 14-gun pirate brig sallied into the mouth of the river, flying the black flag. She dropped anchor close to Fort James. It turned out to be a pirate sloop commanded by none other than Olivier Levasseur, the old pirate partner of both Sam Bellamy and Benjamin Hornigold. The pirate crews celebrated their unexpected union in Gallassee, as the two captains planned their next move.

When Olivier Levasseur had parted company with Sam Bellamy off Isla La Blanquilla off the Venezuelan coast in January 1717, he headed south towards Brazil. He had a lively time there, plundering local trading craft off the Portuguese colony and even the occasional ocean-going vessel. He even managed to add a 22-gun French merchant brig, *La Louise*, to his force, which became his new flagship. The *Postillion* sailed with him as consort. One of these larger prizes, a slave ship bound for Rio de Janeiro from Luanda in Angola, fought back, forcing Levasseur to batter her into submission. Then, after ransacking her, he left her to sink, with her Portuguese crew still aboard.[16]

He took off the slaver's cargo of 240 African slaves, but found these were a burden on board his sloop *Postillion*. So, he landed them on the Ilha de Santana, opposite the small Brazilian port of Macaé, some hundred miles up the coast from Rio. However, he was spotted by a small Portuguese warship, and a running battle to the south followed; Levasseur lost ten men before he shook off his pursuer. He put in to the Brazilian port of Cananéia, some 300 miles south of Rio de Janeiro, where he repaired his two vessels. It was there, in March 1718, that he learned that a French merchantman was at Paranaguá, just down the coast, but when he headed there he was caught in a storm, and his brig was driven ashore and wrecked on Cotinga Island, with the loss of most of her crew. Levasseur survived, and he was rescued by the crew of the sloop *Postillion*, who had weathered the storm. Incidentally, the wreck of *La Louise* was rediscovered in 2021.[17]

So, after probing a little farther south, Levasseur and his men turned northwards again, and by June 1718 he was back in the Caribbean. He encountered another pirate, the Londoner William Moody, who had recently turned to piracy and had captured a British merchantman, the *Resolution*, which Moody and his men renamed the *Rising Sun*. Walter Hamilton, governor of the Leeward Islands, reported that 'three pirate vessells that are cruising amongst these Islands, to wit, a ship of 24 guns, commanded by one Captain William Moody, a brig of eight guns, commanded by one Captain Frowd, and a sloop of six or eight guns.' The third unnamed pirate was Levasseur in the now-ageing *Postillion*.[18]

The pirates then made a foray northward towards the Carolinas, but by December 1718 Levasseur had returned to the West Indies and took part in the capture of the merchant frigate *Wade* near Antigua. This large merchantman was on her way to Jamaica, and one of her victims reported that they were attacked by the French pirate ship *Mary Anne* with a sloop, the *Postillion*, operating in consort. The pirates then took a Spanish trader, and according to a captive from the *Wade*, they abandoned and sank the *Mary Anne*, which was apparently in poor condition.[19]

Richard Frowd, Moody's deputy, was also operating in the area, capturing the merchant ship *Upton* of Belfast off Antigua a few days later. His vessel was a four-gun brig by this stage, working in consort with Moody's *Rising Sun*. It was a busy time, as Edward England was also operating in the West Indies in late 1718, as he captured the snow *Eagle* of New York in the Leeward Islands on 15 February 1719. However, the Royal Navy was patrolling in the area, and Governor Hamilton on Antigua was petitioning the Council of Trade in London to request that the Admiralty send more warships. Sure enough, that winter the Admiralty reinforced its American squadrons, as part of a renewed pirate-hunting operation.[20]

This was what encouraged Levasseur, Moody and eventually England to quit the West Indies and head to West Africa instead. Others would go too. In fact, there seems to have been a general consensus among the scattered pirate crews in American waters that it was much safer on the far side of the Atlantic. Now, Olivier Levasseur and Howell Davis had joined forces, and it seemed that the Nassau pirates were about to reinvent themselves some 3,600 miles away from their old haven. After a period of celebrating, the two pirate vessels put to sea. They headed south to Bunce Island, in the mouth of the Sierra Leone River. This was another popular slaving harbour, and the island was another fortified outpost of the Royal African Company, which traded in slaves, ivory and local hardwood.

The pirates gave the well-armed fort a wide berth and headed up the river, to the harbour where Freetown now stands. It was there that they spied the masts of another sizeable vessel. They came within range of her, and according to Johnson, the mystery ship then 'fired a whole broadside upon Davis'. It seems to have caused little or no damage. At the same time, she hoisted a black flag. Davis did the same, and the tension eased as the two sides realized they were both fellow pirates. It turned out the newcomer was a 24-gun pirate brig commanded by Thomas Cocklyn. He had been one of William Moody's crew, when Moody had quit the Caribbean for West Africa.

A few weeks before, the crew of Moody's *Rising Sun* had risen against their captain and tried to depose him. Moody prevailed and narrowly won the vote. As punishment, he marooned Cocklyn and the other rebels on the African shore, somewhere near Cape Verde. This harsh treatment infuriated his remaining crew, who rose in revolt and cast Moody and his supporters adrift in one of the ship's boats. Then, after recovering the castaways, the crew elected Cocklyn to be their new captain. What happened to William Moody afterwards is unclear. Johnson claimed that he returned to Nassau to accept a pardon, but there is no record of this. Instead, he appears to have vanished from the historical records. His fate might well have been a lingering death on the West African coast, or in the open Atlantic.[21]

The two pirate ships had become three. Between them, Thomas Cocklyn, Howell Davis and Olivier Levasseur made up a powerful pirate force of three well-armed vessels and around 200 men. That meant that only a Royal Naval frigate could sensibly oppose them, or possibly a Royal African Company warship, as they maintained their own guardships in the region. However, all of these men had some degree of shared history, or knew of their association with others they either disliked or distrusted. Some, especially Cocklyn, had a reputation for violence, and so the other two captains made sure to keep a close eye on him. That made any prolonged joint venture unlikely, as nobody trusted anyone else. Still, after some debate they decided their first target would be the fort at Bunce Island. On their way in they'd spotted half a dozen slave ships sheltering under its guns. Now they had the strength they needed to have a go at capturing them.

Using stealth, the pirates landed on the southern shore of the tiny island and assaulted the fort, taking its small garrison by surprise. Johnson described what happened: 'Those who defended the fort ... had not the courage to stand it any longer, but abandoning the fort, left it to the mercy of the pirates.' This was probably an exaggeration – the Royal African Company claims that the post held until the defenders had exhausted all their gunpowder. That was probably nearer the mark. Still, with the fort in their hands the six slave ships were easily captured, and then plundered. All in all, it was a highly successful little venture, and in theory it boded well for the pirate alliance. However, the distrust between the three captains and their crews had never gone away. So, after a period of celebrating and merriment, and with 'the strong liquor stirring up a spirit of discord among them', they decided to go their own separate ways.

As they parted, the three pirate ships riding on the swell at the mouth of the Sierra Leone River, Johnson claimed that Davis chided his two fellow captains, saying 'Hark ye, Cocklyn and La Bouse, I find by strengthening you, I have put a rod in your hands to whip myself, but I'm still able to deal with you both. But, since we met in love, let us part in love, for I find that three of a trade can never agree.' Leaving the others, Davis took the *Royal James* south towards the Gold Coast. He captured and plundered two British ships along the way. According to Johnson, he had a fight with a 30-gun Dutch frigate off the Ivory Coast, which he captured after a long-running fight. In fact, she was almost certainly a large, well-armed Dutch slave ship, which he captured off Little Cestos. Howell Davis renamed her the *Royal Rover* and claimed her as his flagship, after putting her Dutch crew ashore near Cape Palmas. The *Royal James* was given to Walter Kennedy to command,

and the two powerful pirate ships continued eastwards towards the Bight of Benin, where they hoped to find rich pickings.

They wisely kept out of sight of the powerful Cape Coast Castle, but late in the morning of 6 June 1719 they put in to the slave trading anchorage of Anamabu (now Annamaboe), eight miles farther down the coast. Three British slave ships lay at anchor there, theoretically protected by the guns of another Royal African Company fort. However, it had been badly neglected, and neither the guns nor the tiny garrison were up to the task of taking on a pirate mob. All three slavers were there to fill their holds with their human cargo, a job that was only half-finished when Davis arrived.

Shortly after noon, the two pirate ships came in sight of Anamabu from the direction of Cape Coast Castle. Then, as the leading ship came within gunshot of them, a black flag appeared at its masthead, and a warning shot rang out. Off the beach the local canoes fled for the palm-fringed shore, while in the small fort there was confusion and panic as the officer yelled at his men, who struggled to find the powder, shot and gun tools they needed to defend the anchorage. When they did fire, their shot fell far short of the pirates as they swept in and captured the three slavers, one after the other. There was virtually no resistance. It was as neat an operation as Howell Davis could have wished for. He now had three prizes: the three-masted ship-rigged 140-ton *Princess* of London, the similar *Royal Hind*, also from London, and the Barbadian slaving sloop *Maurice*. Soon all five vessels were anchored well out of range of the fort, as its garrison looked on.

The pirates then examined their lucrative haul of trade goods, bags of gold dust, their pay chests – and a nearly full cargo of bewildered African slaves. The slaves were put ashore, and after ransacking the ships the pirates asked for volunteers from among the slave ship crews. Many of them were keen to volunteer. On the *Princess*, for instance, there was nothing Captain Plumb could do to stop them. One of the volunteers from the *Princess* was the slave ship's second mate, an experienced 37-year-old Welsh seaman by the name of Bartholomew Roberts. He would soon make his mark as the most successful pirate of the age.

The two pirate ships continued on to the east, but by now the *Royal James* was leaking badly, and her pumps could barely keep her afloat. So, they beached her near Calabar to get a good look at the underside of her hull. It was a grim sight. After scraping off months of marine growth, they found that much of her lower planking was rotten and peppered with holes caused by teredo worms. The simplest course was simply to abandon her where she lay. So, after shifting over her stores and crew, the crowded *Royal Rover* continued out to sea on her own. At this point Davis decided to head for the Portuguese island of Príncipe, 250 miles due south of the slave coast.

When they arrived in the island's harbour, San António, it was early July. When challenged by an official sloop as he approached the harbour, Davis claimed that they were a Royal Naval vessel on a pirate-hunting patrol. He even fired a salute to the port's fort as he entered the harbour – and the honour was reciprocated. So, the deception worked, and the Portuguese governor of the small island, António Carneiro de Sousa, welcomed them. The trouble was, Davis couldn't keep control of his men. Later, the merchant captain William Snelgrave reported that 'The people ... discovered who they were by their lavishness.' They were chasing local women, drinking and being bawdy. Snelgrave claimed that Governor Carneiro had guessed who the incomers were, but 'winked at it, on account of the great gains'. In other words, the pirates were bringing money into the island.[22]

Still, for two weeks the pirates remained at anchor in the small harbour, repaired their ship and caused no real trouble. Then, disaster struck. One night a former slave slipped ashore, and, as he could speak Portuguese, told the islanders that the pirates had plotted to capture the governor and his leading advisers and hold them all to ransom. It seemed likely, as Davis had only just invited the governor and other important locals on board his ship for 'an entertainment'. So, Governor Carneiro laid a trap. The next morning Davis went ashore as usual, accompanied by ten of his leading officers – pirates who'd come to call themselves the 'lords'. An invitation reached Davis, inviting them all to the governor's house for drinks. On the path, the Portuguese militiamen sprang an ambush and fired at the group of pirates. Davis was grievously wounded by a musket ball to the groin. He tried to drag himself away into the undergrowth, but he died before he could make it. As Johnson tells it, 'just as he fell, he perceived he was followed, and drawing out his pistols, fired them at his pursuers; thus like a game cock, giving a dying blow that he might not fall unrevenged.'

Only Walter Kennedy and one other pirate escaped the ambush and were picked up by one of the *Royal Rover*'s boats. There was now something of an impasse, with the *Royal James* in the harbour where the two batteries of the Forta de Ponta da Mina couldn't bear on them.

Once back on board, Kennedy and the other pirates held a meeting to decide what to do next. First, they needed a captain. Kennedy seemed the natural choice, but there were other candidates too. Another of the 'lords', Thomas Anstis, also put himself forward, as did three others – a Scotsman from North Berwick in East Lothian, a Cockney from East London, and the newcomer, Bartholomew Roberts. Amazingly, after just six weeks among them, it was Roberts who was voted in as their new pirate captain.

Later, Kennedy claimed that Roberts had been elected largely because he came across as cunning and was a prime seaman, with an excellent knowledge of the seas. That probably meant that, unlike many, he had mastered the black art of navigation. His first task was to get them safely out to sea. So, Roberts took the *Royal Rover* down the anchorage a little, then dropped anchors bow and stern, so her guns bore on the fort. The small Portuguese garrison quickly abandoned their guns and fled up the wooded hill behind them. To make sure it was silenced, Kennedy and a landing party rowed ashore, entered the abandoned defences, and overturned the guns and carriages. They then set the fort ablaze before returning to the ship. No doubt some of the crew wanted to seek revenge on the islanders, but Roberts limited this to a boat raid on the harbour, where two Portuguese trading vessels were set ablaze. That done, the pirates headed out to sea under their new and highly promising captain.

John Roberts had been born to Welsh parents in the tiny hamlet of Little Newcastle, five miles south of Fishguard in the South Wales county of Pembrokeshire. His surname appears in local records suggesting his was a farming family. He took to the sea as a teenager, and by the time he'd arrived in West Africa aboard the *Princess* he was a skilled mariner, tall, strong, reasonably good looking and of a swarthy complexion. It was only after he joined Howell Davis' crew that he changed his name to Bartholomew Roberts. His nickname 'Black Bart' probably stemmed from his dark complexion rather than any particularly sinister characteristics – although he certainly had those too. Now, the farm boy from South Wales was a pirate captain.

On 26 July he was rewarded with a prize – a Dutch slave ship intercepted between Príncipe and Cape Lopez. She would be his first

Bartholomew Roberts, known as 'The Great Pyrate' –
and the most successful of them all.

capture of many. Off the cape it was the turn of the slaver *Experiment* of London, whose crew were pressed into service to fill the depleted complement of the *Royal Rover*. Her master, Thomas Grant, also claimed that the pirates took 50 pounds of gold dust before setting him ashore and burning his ship. Johnson wrote that Roberts wanted to return to the Gold Coast, but his crew weren't convinced. So, they voted on a choice between two other options – heading to Madagascar in the Indian Ocean, or crossing the Atlantic to Brazil. They opted for South America, and so the *Royal Rover* took on water and headed west. Just under a month later they made landfall at Fernando de Noronha, an uninhabited island well to the east of Brazil. There they careened the ship, took on water, and set off on the final leg of their transatlantic crossing. The cruise off the easternmost coast of Brazil was a disappointment, with only a tiny fishing vessel to show for their efforts. So, in mid-November, Roberts decided to take the fight to the Portuguese.

He sailed down to Bahía (now Salvador), which was a known assembly point for Lisbon's treasure fleet. Sure enough, the fleet was in the commodious harbour, preparing to sail. The merchantmen and treasure galleons were guarded by two powerful ships-of-the-line – powerful enough to reduce the *Royal Rover* to matchwood. Undeterred, though, Roberts conned his ship into the harbour, flying French colours. Once safely inside, he headed through the cluster of anchored ships and singled out one of the smallest merchantman. The pirates took her without the alarm being raised. When he asked her master which was the richest ship in the fleet, he pointed out a nearby galleon, the 40-gun *Sagrada Familia*. Taking his prisoners with him, he cast off and crept towards this fresh target. When Roberts had his Portuguese prisoner hail her, the galleon's captain became suspicious and ordered the alarm to be sounded. Throwing caution to the wind, Roberts headed straight for her.

Ranging alongside, he fired a full broadside at point-blank range, before the Portuguese gunners were ready. He then came alongside the galleon, and the pirates swarmed aboard her. The fight was brisk, violent and decisive. Within minutes the *Sagrada Familia* was in Roberts' hands as the defenders were wholly unprepared for such a ferocious assault. Only two of the pirates were killed in the action – a testimony to the speed and surprise of Roberts' attack. His next problem was to get his prize out of the harbour, past the guns on Fort San Antonio and San Pedro, and more importantly the two Portuguese ships-of-the-line. He took his prize under tow, and slowly – painfully slowly – they edged their way through the crowded anchorage, as alarm bells sounded all around them.

Once clear he found the two warships were closing in, although one was well ahead of the other. Roberts turned as if to fight her broadside to broadside, and she veered away, as if to bide time for her consort to come up. Instead, Roberts turned again, this time heading for the open sea. Amazingly, the gun batteries above them didn't open fire. Once in the open Atlantic, Roberts cast off the tow, and with his *Royal Rover* beside him, he raised sail and headed out, steering his prize northwards away from his pursuers. Gradually the two ships-of-the-line dropped astern, and they were clear. It was an amazingly cool-headed enterprise, and a total triumph. Bartholomew Roberts had pulled off the impossible.

Once they had a chance to count their haul, they found it came to an amazing 40,000 Portuguese gold moidores – the equivalent of around $20 million today. That didn't even take into account the sacks of jewels and precious stones they found on board. Against the odds, Roberts had pulled off a piratical achievement to rival Henry Every's capture of the fabulously rich Mughal treasure ship *Ganj-i-sawai* in the Indian Ocean quarter of a century before. That made it one of the most successful pirate heists of all time. One of these jewels was a diamond-studded cross which was made as a gift to Portugal's King João V. Roberts used it to bribe the French governor of Guiana, Claude Guillouet d'Orvilliers, when the pirates reached the backwater French colony around the middle of November. That paid for the freedom his men needed to celebrate their victory in fine style.

To cap the success, on 19 November Roberts even captured a sloop, the *Princess* of Rhode Island, which had chosen precisely the wrong moment to appear off the French colony's ramshackle capital, Cayenne, where Roberts had anchored his two ships. For Roberts it really was a moment to cherish. Despite all this, though, all wasn't well among his crew. It seems that a mutiny was brewing, as a group of 40 men planned to steal the *Royal Rover* and sail off in her. When Roberts learned of the plot, he had the men seized and sailed off to the deserted Îles de Salut (Salvation Islands), six miles from Cayenne. One of these three islands became known as the Île du Diable (Devil's Island), the site of the notorious French penal colony. Once there Roberts had the mutineers punished and marooned until they'd learned the meaning of loyalty. The pirate captain must have thought he'd dealt with the problem.

'Riches beyond avarice', it seems, is only a phrase. A few days later, while the pirates were lying off Cayenne, they spotted an American brig approaching. It was undoubtedly the well-laden one Captain Cane of the *Princess* had told him was due to arrive soon. So, Roberts boarded his captured sloop, now renamed the *Good Fortune*, and gave chase. The pursuit was long and fruitless, and it was followed by a tropical storm. When it eased, Roberts returned to the anchorage, only to find the anchorage empty. Roberts had taken about 40 men with him aboard the sloop. He left Walter Kennedy in charge of the two larger ships, with the rest of his crew. While Roberts was away, Kennedy had taken the two ships and their cargo of treasure and sailed off in them. It was a bitter betrayal, and Roberts and his men swore a bloody revenge.

Bartholomew Roberts learned the hard way never to trust a pirate. So, he had a pact drawn up – a pirate code – which governed the way everything was done aboard the now inappropriately named *Good Fortune*. A copy of this remarkable document survives, printed in Captain Johnson's *A General History of the Pyrates*. Unlike much of Johnson's information, this is one that smacks of being the unembellished genuine article. It governed the division of prize money, the settling of disputes and the consequences of mutiny or dissent. In all it was a very fair code, but it was laid down after a spectacular double-cross and a monumental betrayal of trust. Roberts wasn't going to let that happen again. Now he distrusted everyone unless they'd signed their name on his dotted line.[23]

FIFTEEN

The Great Pyrate

B Y THE END OF 1719 it was a full year since the death of Edward
Thatch and the hanging of Stede Bonnet. It was also a year and a
half since law and order were restored to the Bahamas, and almost two
years since the first copies of the anti-piracy act of 1717 were circulated
around the ports of the Americas. For the authorities charged with
countering the pirate menace, the signs seemed to suggest they were
winning the fight. Two years before, in December 1717, the captain
in charge of the Royal Navy's squadron based in Jamaica wrote, 'I
think the pirates daily increase, taking and plundering most ships that
are bound to this island.' Now, thanks largely to the dispersal of the
Nassau pirates, and those high-profile victories over their remnants,
colonial governors and shipowners alike were beginning to feel the
corner had been turned.[1]

Bartholomew Roberts, though, and men like Thomas Anstis,
Edward England, Olivier Levasseur, Walter Kennedy and several
others were about to prove them all wrong. The pirate menace was

far from over. Instead, it had entered a new and far more dangerous phase. Denied the safe haven of Nassau, the remaining pirates tended to venture farther afield in search of prey. Soon, although the heart of the problem remained the North American seaboard and the Caribbean, these pirates were operating in several parts of the world, from Maine to Madagascar. Worse, the whole business of piracy was becoming meaner. Before, its victims were usually allowed to escape with nothing more than a bruised ego to show for it. Now it was becoming increasingly common for ship captains to be assaulted, and sometimes killed. Then, there was Bartholomew Roberts, who was about to redefine what it meant to be a successful pirate.

After Kennedy's betrayal, Bartholomew Roberts was left with his eight-gun sloop *Good Fortune* and a crew of around 40 men. It wasn't much to set about reclaiming what he'd lost. At first, though, his disgruntled crew didn't give him a chance. They held another meeting, much like the one that had seen Roberts elected as their captain following the death of Howell Davis. This time, the men blamed Roberts for the loss of their fortune in plunder and elected Thomas Anstis as their new captain. That done, they had to start somewhere. Anstis captured his first prize – a flyboat intercepted off the neighbouring Dutch colony of Surinam. This small Dutch trading vessel carried the provisions they needed to head farther afield.[2]

The crew decided to head towards the West Indies. It was about 650 miles to Barbados, a voyage of around three to four days in these favourable winds. Although the island was the base of the Royal Navy's Windward Islands squadron, the chances of being intercepted were slim. Beyond Barbados lay the beautiful crescent of verdant tropical islands, and seas filled with prizes. Their first victim fell into their hands on Christmas Day – a two-masted New England schooner called the *Essex* of Salem. She was laden with provisions for Barbados, which the pirates plundered, and two of her New England crew even volunteered to join them. It was the perfect pirate Christmas.

Then Anstis dropped down to Tobago, where they captured a small French sloop belonging to turtle hunters. On 10 January 1720, it was the turn of the Barbadian sloop *Philippa*, which yielded a pair of guns as well as rum and supplies. Nine more men joined them, voluntarily or otherwise. That brought the crew up to just over 50 men, and the *Good Fortune* now carried a respectable 12 guns. Taking advantage of the wind, they returned to the waters off Barbados, where in mid-February they enjoyed something of a spree, capturing two British vessels in two days, the *Benjamin* and the *Joseph*. All these attacks were attracting attention, though, and following the loss of the *Benjamin*, fresh out from Liverpool, Governor Robert Lowther commissioned two pirate-hunting vessels to hunt down the pirates.

One of these was Captain Graves' six-gun Barbadian sloop *Philippa*, which had been plundered by the *Good Fortune* off Tobago the previous month. She was joined by Captain Rogers' 16-gun *Somerset Galley* of Bristol. They carried a total crew of 120 men – more than double the men under Anstis' command. The pirate-hunters left Bridgetown on 21 February, but by then the *Good Fortune* had left the area, and headed to the north-west, in the direction of the Leeward Islands. Captain Rogers, in charge of the expedition, picked up their trail thanks to an encounter with a French trader whose vessel had been ransacked by Anstis. This was one of two prizes Anstis captured between Martinique and Guadeloupe as he sailed north. One of them, a Virginian sloop, was kept by Anstis as a consort for the *Good Fortune*.

On 26 February, the two pirate sloops were approaching Antigua when they sighted what they thought were two juicy merchantmen to the west of them. They gave chase, and it was only when they were within musket range that the pirates recognized their quarry were actually hunting them. The prize sloop was the first to recognize the danger and turned away, fleeing as fast as she could towards the south. Anstis, though, was too close to pull that off, and so the *Good Fortune* and the *Somerset Galley* exchanged full broadsides. For some reason the *Philippa* hung back, but Captain Rogers was made of sterner stuff, and closed in to board the pirate sloop. That was enough for Anstis, who turned and fled.

The chase ran on, with the *Good Fortune* even throwing her stores overboard to lighten the ship and increase her speed. Eventually, the pirates pulled away from their pursuers, and as darkness fell Captain Rogers gave up the chase and turned back to Barbados. The pirate sloop had been quite badly damaged, and holed below the waterline. Seven of her crew had also been lost, and the total now was about 60, thanks to new volunteers, plus another 20 more men aboard the prize sloop. Later, Rogers claimed he'd killed 35 pirates in the battle. He was furious with the gun-shy captain of the *Philippa*. But Captain Graves probably had no appetite for the fight, having encountered these same hardened pirates a few weeks before.

There is a slight question in all this about the presence of a second pirate crew, this time a French one. It has been claimed that on 19 February the *Good Fortune* was joined by a pirate sloop called the *Le Roi de Mers* (*Sea King*), commanded by Montigny la Palisse, from Saint-Malo. He, it was claimed, took part in the battle but fled before the two sides came within gun range. This is probably a case of mistaken identity. The second pirate vessel in the sea battle was more likely to be the prize sloop, which lacked the manpower to take on the pirate-hunters and so veered away as soon as they realized whom they were facing. La Palisse, though, might well have been hunting in the area and would cross the path of the British pirates again.[3]

So, neither of the pirate-hunting captains covered themselves in glory in the sea battle, although Captain Rogers at least did his duty and tried his best. The pirates, though, having lost shipmates and with several of them wounded and their sloop battered, had no hesitation in blaming Anstis for their situation. He should have recognized the danger sooner, and turned away to safety. So, somewhere in a secluded cove in the Leeward Islands the crew of the *Good Fortune* held another council and voted to depose Thomas Anstis as their captain. Inevitably, Bartholomew Roberts was invited to lead them again. It was a decision made over a bowl of rum punch which would have amazingly far-reaching consequences.

Captain Johnson claims that after the battle Roberts 'could never endure a Barbados man afterwards, and when any ships belonging to that island fell in his way, he was more particularly severe to them than others'. After taking over command, Roberts put in to what was probably Grand Margot Bay on the eastern side of Dominica to careen the *Good Fortune*. They were immediately given a sign of better luck to come. They were met on the beach by a group of 13 British sailors, who had been abandoned there by a French captain. They all volunteered to join the pirates, which more than made up for their losses in the recent sea battle. While careening they sighted French patrol vessels passing by them to seaward – pirate-hunters sent out from neighbouring Martinique by François de Pas de Mazencourt, governor general of the French Antilles. It seems that they weren't spotted, but it was clear that moving on might be a good idea.[4]

Afterwards, Roberts had his crew design a new black flag, featuring an image of himself, a cutlass in one hand and an hourglass in the other – a symbol of death. He was standing astride two skulls. One was marked ABH, standing for 'a Barbadian's head', and the other AMH, for 'a Martiniquan's head'. It seems Roberts was someone who bore a grudge. The careening complete, they put to sea again and wisely headed away from the West Indies. Instead, Roberts decided to head somewhere he would never be expected – Newfoundland. This bleak, remote corner of North America was home to large fishing and whaling fleets that plied the bountiful waters of the Newfoundland Banks. If he had to lie low, at least he'd have a plentiful haul of victims.

After sailing north, keeping well clear of the shipping off the main ports in Britain's American colonies, the *Good Fortune* made landfall off Newfoundland's southern coast in mid-June 1720. Once there, Roberts decided to attack the major fishing station of Trepassey, in the southernmost corner of the huge island. So, on the morning of 21 June, the *Good Fortune* sailed into the crowded harbour 'with their black colours flying, drums beating, and trumpets sounding'. In theory there was an armed guardship there, the *Bideford Merchant*, but her master, Captain Babidge, and his crew fled ashore as soon as the pirates put in an appearance. That left the crowded harbour utterly at the pirates' mercy. Roberts and his men were like foxes in a hen coop.

Captain Johnson described what happened next: 'It is impossible particularly to recount the destruction and havoc they made here, burning and sinking all the shipping, except a Bristol galley, and destroying the fisheries, and [landing] stages of the poor planters, without remorse or compunction.' In all the total haul was something that would break every pirate record. The three-masted *Bideford Merchant* was taken by a boarding party led by Anstis, along with a galley from Bristol, the sloop *Sudbury* from Dartmouth, and 19 ocean-going fishing vessels. As well as that singularly impressive total were anything between 150 and 250 small fishing shallops – local fishing boats. All of this had been achieved without a single shot being fired at them. It was a tribute to Roberts' audacity – the same he'd shown in the capture of the *Sagrada Familia*. Once again, Roberts was a pirate captain at the top of his game.[5]

Roberts was particularly pleased about the merchant galley – a name often used for any type of sailing vessel that had oarports, allowing them to be powered by long oars if there was no suitable wind. The *Good Fortune* was leaking badly and had never really recovered from her battering in the sea battle off Antigua four months before. So, Roberts swapped the old worn-out sloop for this fine-looking two-master. While his crew celebrated ashore, and found half a dozen or more recruits from among the fishermen, Roberts forced carpenters to convert the galley into a fighting pirate vessel and armed her with 16 to 19 guns. He then pondered his next move.

He began by taking his new ship out for a cruise, with his old sloop *Good Fortune* acting as a scout and consort. In the process they came upon a French fishing fleet off the Grand Banks and captured several more large fishing vessels. One of these was a French three-masted square-rigged merchant ship of 220 tons, which was even more impressive than his previous captures. Roberts decided to keep her for himself. Her French captain and his crew were transferred into the galley, and the pirates set about transferring their guns and stores. When she was ready, she mounted an impressive 26 guns. This made her powerful enough to take on any potential prize she came across – only a sizeable man-of-war could outgun her. He decided to rename her the *Royal Fortune*, after the ship which Kennedy stole from him. That done, he gave his galley to the French captives and let them sail off to safety in her.

Then, over the next few days and farther to the south-east of the Grand Banks, Roberts found himself astride the busy shipping lane which followed the Gulf Stream as it curved eastwards across the Atlantic. Around 11 July they came upon *Le Roi de Mers* and Montigny la Palisse again. The pirate captains decided to continue the cruise together. There, in the shipping lane, they chased and captured one vessel after another. The haul included the *Richard* of Bideford, the *Willing Mind* of Poole, the *Expectation* of Topsham, the *Samuel* of London, the *Little York* of Virginia, the *Love* of Lancaster, the *Phoenix* of Bristol, the *Blessing* of Lymington, the *Essex* of Salem, and a couple of others whose names went unrecorded. It was a hugely successful spree. Between 13 and 18 July, Roberts captured ten vessels, many of them large ocean-going merchant ships, whalers or large transatlantic fishing vessels.

Later, the *Boston News Letter* printed a vivid description of the capture of the *Samuel*, provided by her master, Captain Samuel Cary: 'The first thing the pirates did was to strip both passengers and seamen of all their money and clothes ... with a loaded pistol to everyone's breast ... the next thing they did was, with madness and rage, to tear up the hatches, enter the hold like a parcel of furies, where with axes, cutlasses etc. they cut, tore and broke open all the trunks, boxes, cases and bales.' They took what they wanted and tossed the rest overboard. In all they took 40 barrels of powder from the *Samuel*, two large guns, and goods valued at around £10,000. Cary added, 'there was nothing heard among the pirates all the while, but cursing, swearing, damning and blaspheming to the highest degree imaginable.' Then, if they ever faced being captured, the pirates told Cary that they would 'immediately put fire with one of their pistols to the powder and go merrily to hell together.'[6]

All in all, Roberts' Newfoundland cruise was arguably the most successful hunt in the history of piracy. He'd captured about 40 ships of various sizes, not counting the hundreds of small fishing shallops they'd taken. This was a level of devastation which would grab the news headlines on both sides of the Atlantic. It was clear that the pirate menace was not only still there, but its threat was becoming more wide ranging, and far more destructive. So, the Admiralty responded by sending out more warships to patrol the Newfoundland fishing grounds, and diverting the frigates HMS *Phoenix* and HMS *Squirrel* from New York and Boston to the area. This didn't achieve anything though, as by then Bartholomew Roberts was long gone.

Knowing they would come looking for him, on 19 July Roberts set a course for Africa. La Palisse came with him, renaming his French-built sloop the *Good Fortune*, as Roberts abandoned his old worn-out sloop of the same name. As Howell Davis had before him, the *Royal Fortune* and the new *Good Fortune* headed for the Cape Verde Islands, the mariners' gateway to the West African coast. A navigational error meant that they missed their landfall and instead went too far south and were caught in the westward trade winds that carried them back out into the Atlantic. Their only consolation was a couple of prizes – a Portuguese slave ship and a French merchant brig. The pirates let both vessels go after ransacking them, but they took the surgeon from the French ship with them when they sailed off. So, bowing to the inevitable, Roberts headed back towards the Caribbean.[7]

They soon ran low on food and water. As Johnson put it, 'They had but one hogs head of water left to supply 124 souls for that passage.'

He added somewhat gleefully, 'without the miraculous intervention of providence there appeared only this miserable choice – a present death by their own hands, or a lingering one by famine.' However, providence seemed to intervene. In late August they finally made landfall on the coast of French Guinea, not far from their old haunt of Cayenne. They slaked their thirst, then headed over towards Grenada. They made landfall off the small island of Carriacou on 4 September, 20 miles north of Grenada, and anchored there in what is now Tyrell Bay, close to the modern town of Argyle.[8]

To their delight they found the place full of sea turtles. They also came across a Bermudian turtle hunters' sloop, *Relief*, which they pillaged of everything worth having, including its catch. The pirates remained at Carriacou for two weeks, recovering from their six-week voyage and careening their two ships. Later, Captain Richard Dunne of the *Relief* provided a description of Roberts' *Royal Fortune*, reporting, 'It carried 28 guns on its upper and quarter deck, and six swivel guns on its gunwale.' The accompanying sloop *Good Fortune* (formerly *Le Roi de Mers*) carried only six guns, and Dunne estimated that the combined crews numbered around 130 men. Now, though, Roberts was ready to strike again. This time, his hunting ground would be the West Indies.[9]

What followed was a cruise that secured Roberts' reputation as one of the most successful pirates of the age. From mid-September on he worked his way northwards through the sparklingly beautiful emerald and turquoise chain of the Windward Islands, taking whatever he wanted. Off Dominica they captured a French sloop and a New England snow. The French trader was 'laded with claret, white wine and brandy'. Although Roberts himself didn't drink, the haul would have delighted his crews. What did intrigue him was the discovery that the master of the New England sloop was Captain Cane, former captain of the *Princess* of Rhode Island – the sloop the pirates renamed the *Good Fortune*, and then abandoned off Newfoundland. Roberts had last seen her old captain off Cayenne, just before Kennedy's betrayal. While his men were hostile to their prisoner, Roberts merely grilled him, trying to learn exactly what had happened off Cayenne ten months before.[10]

Before they moved off, a bizarre trial for mutiny was held aboard the *Royal Fortune*. While in Carriacou, ten pirates had deserted, taking some of the communal plunder with them. Three of them were recaptured, and off Dominica they were held to account. In a mockery of a real trial, Roberts appointed himself judge and selected a dozen men to be the jury. All the prisoners were quickly condemned to death, but one of the pirates intervened, forcing them to spare the life of the most senior of the deserters, Henry Gatsby, the *Royal Fortune*'s sailing master. The plea from the pirate Valentine Ashplant ended with the words, 'Damn me, if he must die, I will die along with him!' In the end Gatsby was spared, but the other two were tied to the mast of the French prize and shot dead by a four-man firing squad – one the prisoners were allowed to choose from among their old shipmates.[11]

After that bizarre incident the pirates kept heading north. After passing Guadeloupe they reached the Leeward Islands, and on 27 September they arrived off St Christopher – now St Kitts. As he'd done in Newfoundland, Roberts decided on attempting a bold stroke. He sailed straight into the island's main harbour of Basseterre with black flags flying. The local garrison was slow to react, or unwilling to, and only began a desultory fire from the port's gun battery as the pirates had almost finished. They pillaged and then set ablaze two vessels in the harbour, one being the *Mary and Martha* of Bristol laden with sugar cane. The other one was eventually saved by the militia, who put out the fire.[12]

In a final insult to authority, Roberts wrote a letter to the island's administrators before he left. His captive from Carriacou, Captain Dunn, had been let go, but on reaching St Kitts he'd been arrested, on suspicion of aiding the pirates. In his letter, Roberts demanded his release: 'That poor fellow you now have in prison at Sandy Point is entirely ignorant,' he wrote, adding 'let me beg you, and use that man as an honest man ... If we hear any otherwise you may expect not to have quarters in any of your island.' He signed it 'Yours, Bartholomew Roberts'. It was an amazing letter – one of the few we know written by a pirate of the period – and it was brimful of Roberts' sense of justice, backed by more than a hint of threat.[13]

The pirates left St Christopher that evening, the fires from the ships still lighting up the waterfront of Basseterre. They then weaved through the scattered Leeward Islands, capturing several more trading ships there, before putting in to the French island of Saint-Barthélemey. Surprisingly, they were treated well by the islanders, including the colony's deputy governor. They spent two weeks there, anchored in Great Beach Bay, enjoying the delights of the small settlement of Philipsburg. Then, in mid-October, Roberts began a foray into the Atlantic, trying to intercept ships heading towards the American colonies. This proved reasonably successful – they pillaged three small sloops and a larger French brig, which Roberts decided to turn into his new *Royal Fortune*, exchanging her for the old one.

They sailed off in their newfound flagship but soon discovered the ship leaked badly. So, she too would have to be replaced. Their last prize, the sloop *Thomas* of Newton Abbot, was captured just south of Barbados on 30 October. A few days later they turned southwards again, this time avoiding the line of the West Indies, to reach Dutch Surinam just to the west of French Guiana. They then moved on to Tobago, where they took on water and provisions. They also careened both vessels in an attempt to patch up their leaks. They spent Christmas there, and by early January 1721 they were ready to resume their cruise. This time, Roberts decided to prey off the French islands of Martinique and Guadeloupe, in revenge for their hunting of him a year before. Revenge seems to have been a strong motivation for shoulder-chipped Bartholomew Roberts and his men.[14]

So, in January the pirates appeared without warning off St Lucia, just south of Martinique, and came across six sloops anchored in the lee of Pigeon Island, in the north-western corner of St Lucia. They burned three French sloops from Martinique, along with a Barbadian one, but they gave her crew the remaining French prize to sail off in. The last vessel, a brig from Rhode Island, was kept, and they transferred everything from La Palisse's French-built sloop *Good Fortune* (the old *Le Roi de Mers*), which was now leaking badly. La Palisse then scuttled her, and claimed the new American brig as her replacement.Inevitably, she was renamed the *Good Fortune* too – the third of them in a year. That done, on 16 January 1721 the two pirate brigs *Royal Fortune* and the newly renamed *Good Fortune* headed towards Martinique, just within sight of them to the north.[15]

By way of a ruse, Roberts' men flew Dutch flags as they passed the island to windward – a sensible precaution as the French Navy had ships based at Fort de France on the island's leeward or western side. On 18 January they reached Dominica, a little to the north, where they came across the three-masted Dutch slave ship *Puerto del Principe* of Flushing. She actually tried to fight off her attackers, but Roberts' two brigs soon forced her to surrender. On boarding her, according to the Governor of Bermuda, 'What men the pirates found alive on board they put to death after several cruel methods.' This, though, may be an invention, or at least an exaggeration. In a letter by the French governor of Martinique written shortly afterwards, there is no mention of a massacre of this kind. Even Captain Johnson, who thrived on salacious details, didn't mention it.[16]

The same day, they captured over two dozen sloops and smaller vessels off Dominica, most of which were French. So, it seems unlikely the pirates had the time to do much else apart from ransack their many prizes. None of these yielded anything particularly valuable. They were plundered more for any pay chest or money on board, as well as clothes and provisions, than any cargo. More importantly though, when word of these attacks spread, it all but paralysed maritime trade in the West Indies. The governors and naval commanders in the area were plagued by demands for action, and cargoes rotted on the quayside rather than risk losing them and their carrying vessel on the high seas. So, warships were sent to hunt down Roberts and stop his depredations once and for all.

Meanwhile, Roberts continued northwards, taking the Dutch slaver and two captured French sloops with him. Off Guadeloupe he lingered for several days, capturing two more French vessels. In late January he was spotted in the Leeward Islands. Then he seemed to disappear. In fact, he'd headed west and was holed up in Samana Bay on the eastern side of Hispaniola. It was to the north-east of Santo Domingo, the Spanish capital there. It was a wise move, as the Leeward Islands were now crawling with British warships. A few months later, the *British Gazette* reported that 'They write from St. Christophers that Captain Roberts, who is now the most desperate pirate of all that range upon those seas, calls himself Admiral of the Leeward Islands.' As a self-styled title, it wasn't really that far off the mark, at least when the Navy wasn't around.[17]

The pirates spent their time careening their ships and relaxing on the beach in what was, after all, a very sparsely populated corner of the Spanish colony. For the moment they were safe from attack, and it gave Roberts and his men a chance to consider what to do next. The West Indies was in ferment, and so it made no sense to return there. It would be pushing their luck a little too far. Meanwhile Robert Norton, captured off Pigeon Island in late January, was given the *Puerto del Principe*, along with much of her human cargo, and she was laden with other plunder.

Other slaves were freed if they joined the pirates. Norton was a former smuggler, and he and Roberts had arranged to sell the slaver's cargo and split the profit. On 7 March, Norton sailed off and never returned.[18]

There was also dissent among the crew. This had been bubbling up ever since the Kennedy betrayal and the desertion and execution off Carriacou the previous September. Some pressed men used the sojourn in Hispaniola to escape, while other pirates deserted, including Henry Gatsby who had run on Carriacou. He was recaptured by Roberts and kept prisoner on board. It's likely that Roberts and his men still needed Gatsby for the veteran sailing master's expertise in seamanship and navigation. Johnson claims that Roberts was becoming more authoritarian, as were his deputies, his self-styled lords – the surviving members of the *Buck*'s mutinous crew. Montigny la Palisse also decided to part company with them in Hispaniola. He left behind the brig *Good Fortune*, and set off in one of the captured sloops, with a crew of predominately French volunteers. That left the 18-gun brig *Good Fortune* without a commander. So, a vote was held, and surprisingly, Thomas Anstis was elected as her new pirate captain. Bartholomew Roberts though, still captain of the *Royal Fortune*, remained the commander of their little pirate squadron.

It was mid-March when they finally left Samana Bay and headed back to their old hunting grounds. Off Guadeloupe on 26 March, they captured the large three-masted merchantman *Lloyd* of London, on her way to Jamaica. By coincidence her captain was Andrew Hingston, whose ship had been burned in Basseterre the previous autumn. The pirates took her into nearby Barbuda and picked her clean, or threw everything they didn't want over the side. They also looted the crew's possessions, and when they found that the first mate – the captain's brother – had tried to hide two gold rings from them, they tied him to the ratlines and 'whipped him within an inch of his life'. Eventually, on 1 April, they let the *Lloyd* and her crew go.[19]

It was surprising the Navy hadn't found Roberts, Anstis and their two pirate brigs. HMS *Rose* was in the area, but Captain Whitney and his crew never sighted the pirates. They did find the *Lloyd*, though only after she'd been ransacked again, this time by an unidentified French pirate. In Antigua, the merchants were so alarmed at the apparent lack of naval protection that they petitioned London for help, saying that because of the pirates 'all intercourse is broke off betwixt these islands, to their very great damage.' There seems to have been widespread panic throughout the region. It wasn't helped by a false report in *The Weekly Journal* that spring, alleging that Roberts had captured and hanged the French governor of Martinique. To many, it looked as if the pirates now ruled the seas and the Navy had abandoned the West Indies to their fate.[20]

In fact, not only was Captain Whitney's HMS *Rose* out looking for them but another frigate, Captain Durrel's HMS *Seahorse*, and the sloop-of-war HMS *Shark* were also on patrol in the Leeward Islands. Individually, they were arguably no match for the two well-armed pirate brigs, but together they had a good chance of defeating Anstis and Roberts. That encounter, though, never took place. The merchants of Barbados also put five pirate-hunting privateers to sea, but despite a lot of searching, nobody could find Roberts. The Admiralty had also sent reinforcements in the shape of the large frigate HMS *Milford*, which had supported Woodes Rogers' expedition to New Providence, and another large 40-gun ship, HMS *Launceston*. The reason they couldn't find Roberts was that he wasn't there. Instead, as he was well aware that the Navy was gathering its forces, he put to sea again and shaped a course for Africa.[21]

In early April Roberts headed northwards from the Leeward Islands for the second time in six months, and on 9 April he overhauled the sloop *Jeremiah and Anne* of London to the south of Bermuda. She was bound for Williamsburg when she was stopped, and seven of her crew volunteered to join their captors. The *Royal Fortune* and *Good Fortune* then picked up the wind and current which would take them across the Atlantic. Eight days later they encountered a lone Dutch ship, the *Prinz Eugen*, which they pillaged. Then they continued on their way. However, somewhere in the mid-Atlantic the two pirate ships became separated – or more likely Thomas Anstis and his men in the *Good Fortune* decided to leave Roberts and go off hunting on their own account.[22]

So, for the second time in his career Roberts' deputy had deserted him. He was now left with the *Royal Fortune*, which was now armed with 42 guns of various sizes and a crew of around 150 men, including a number of former African slaves who had volunteered to join the pirates. In early May 1721, Roberts captured his first prize of the African cruise while he was approaching the Cape Verde Islands. The merchant galley *Norman* was pillaged, and three of her crew joined them. Then her owner, Captain Samuel Norman, was allowed to continue on his way. After making a successful landfall in the Cape Verde Islands, the *Royal Fortune* veered south and reached the African coast a little above the mouth of the Senegal River.[23]

Roberts got off to a good start by capturing two French patrol ships stationed in the Senegal River to protect the trading station of St Louis. The 16-gun and ten-gun corvettes came out to intercept the interloper, thinking her an unlicensed slave ship, and found themselves facing the guns of what amounted to a ship-of-the-line. Then, as Johnson put it, 'Their French hearts failed, and they both surrendered without any, or at least very little resistance.' Roberts decided to keep one of them with him as he continued on past the Gambia River to Fort Bunce and Sierra Leone. So, the former corvette *Compte de Tolouze* was duly renamed the *Ranger*.[24]

It was late June by the time they reached Sierra Leone. They found the river mouth empty. So, with nothing to fear from the Royal African Company and Fort Bunce, they spent the next six weeks careening their ships, including the French prizes, until 'the ships being cleaned and fitted, and the men weary of whoring and drinking, they bethought themselves of business.' It was the start of August when they returned to sea, and they came upon their first prizes a few days later. Three British slave ships were taken, all 'interlopers' or unregistered slave ships from Liverpool. However, only a handful of volunteers joined Roberts' crew. Roberts forcibly pressed many of the rest. Roberts knew the risk of disease in those waters, so he wanted as many men as he could find.[25]

Then, on 8 August they reached Little Cestos at the mouth of the Cestos River. Lying at anchor off the small trading port was the 400-ton three-masted Royal African Company ship *Onslow*, commanded by Captain William Gee. In theory she might possibly have stood her own in a fight with the *Royal Fortune*. However, most of her crew as well as her captain were ashore when the pirates arrived, and Roberts took them by surprise. The skeleton crew left aboard the *Onslow* had no chance, and so they wisely surrendered as the *Royal Fortune* ranged alongside them. So, Roberts decided to abandon his badly leaking ship, and 'trade up' for the *Onslow*.[26]

Once again, he set about moving guns, stores and provisions from one ship to the other, as Captain Gee and his men looked on impotently from the shore. By the time they were done the *Onslow* had been renamed the *Royal Fortune* and was armed with 40 guns. He left the old pirate ship behind for Captain Gee and his men, and after calling for volunteers, the pirates sailed off, leaving the crestfallen Gee to pick up the pieces. So, the cruise continued, with the new and improved *Royal Fortune* and the smaller but still powerful *Ranger* following the coast from Cape Palmas to the Bight of Benin. They captured several slave ships along the way – one French, two Dutch and a small Portuguese one, all taken off the Gold Coast, and then four British ones off Calabar.[27]

They reached Calabar on 1 October, and Roberts felt it might be an idea to take on supplies. However, the local ruler and his people – no friend of anyone who would upset business – proved hostile. An armed fracas began and several pirates were killed. They set the town ablaze and retreated back to their boats, chased by a small army of local warriors. So, a frustrated Roberts put to sea again. He cruised southwards as far as Cape Lopez, and captured a small Dutch slaver there before heading north-west past Príncipe to reach the Ivory Coast at Cap Lahou, 150 miles north-east of Cape Palmas.[28]

On 1 January 1722, they encountered a British slaver, the *Tarleton* of Liverpool, and took her – a perfect New Year's present. Six men were forced to join the pirates. Then, a little to the east it was the turn of the slaver *Elizabeth* of London. On board her was George Wilson, the young surgeon released from the slaver *Stanwich* which they'd captured in early August. Roberts clearly had an attraction for the young man, and it was later claimed that Roberts and Wilson became 'intimate'. So, the cruise continued to the east, and on 5 January they took a small Royal African Company ship, the *Diligence*, off Axim. This time the pirates sank the vessel and forced her crew to join them. Off Cape Appolonia, between Axim and Elmina, they captured another company ship, the 200-ton *King Solomon*, and a Dutch slaver, the *Flushingham*.[29]

Roberts was growing uneasy, as he'd learned there were at least two British warships out looking for him. Also, there seemed to be a growing friction between the crews and the new recruits, and between the men of the *Royal Fortune* and the *Ranger*. Still, Roberts decided on one last attack before quitting the area and possibly returning to Brazil. He settled on Whydah (now Ouidah), the busiest slave port on the West African coast. However, he'd veer out to sea first, to avoid Cape Coast Castle and the two patrolling warships. That meant that, depending on the winds, he'd appear off Whydah from seaward in a week's time.

In the end it was easy. He arrived off Whydah on 11 January. There wasn't a harbour there, or any port defences – just a long palm-fringed beach battered by a heavy surf. The town itself was a mile or so inland. It was the place Sam Bellamy's prestigious pirate ship had been named after as she began life as a British slaver. Clustered there at anchor off the coast were no fewer than 11 British, French and Portuguese slave ships. The two pirate ships captured the lot, and at least one, the British slaver *Porcupine*, was set on fire and burned to the waterline with her slave holds still full of chained-up humanity. This inhuman act of barbarity was carried out by a pirate, John Walden, against Roberts' orders. However, the other vessels were saved from destruction by their captains, who paid the pirates protection money in the form of bags of gold dust.[30]

The rest of the slave vessels were plundered, and one, a 20-gun former French privateer called the *St Agnes*, caught the pirates' eye. Roberts decided to keep her as a second consort, and she duly became the 32-gun *Great Ranger*. The original corvette *Ranger* then became the *Little Ranger*. Then, late on 13 January the pirates put to sea again. They were just in time. The following afternoon the 50-gun fourth-rate ship-of-the-line HMS *Swallow* arrived off Whydah, under the command of Captain Chaloner Ogle. A highly experienced officer, Ogle had been on Roberts' trail for weeks. Now, he knew he was close. So, on 19 January, Ogle put to sea again, determined to corner the elusive pirate.[31]

In fact, the pirate and the pirate-hunter missed each other somewhere in the Bight of Benin. Just hours after leaving Whydah, Roberts captured a Royal African Company sloop, the *Whydah*, ransacked her and burned the prize. A Liverpool slaver called the *Neptune* was nearby, and after running her down Roberts had the *Whydah* crew transferred to her. Then, with the *Neptune* with them, the three pirate vessels made for Cape Lopez, on the far side of the Bight. However, Captain Ogle was on their trail. He took the *Swallow* to Príncipe but found no sign of the pirates there. Next, Ogle explored the mouth of the Gabon River, near modern-day Libreville, but the river mouth was empty. Finally, at dawn on 5 February 1722, at around 6.30am, he found them. Three pirate vessels and a prize were lying at anchor off Cape Lopez. Captain Ogle let his men have their breakfast, then went to quarters – preparing for the tough battle to the death that lay ahead.[32]

The *Swallow* approached the cape from the north. In between it and the anchorage was a sandbank, forcing Ogle to alter a little to seaward to avoid it. The approaching ship was spotted by the pirates, who sounded the alarm. They thought that she had turned away to the west, into the Atlantic, as if she were shying away from a fight. This made them think she was a large armed merchantman rather than a warship. After all, the *Swallow* wasn't flying any colours. So, as audacious as ever, Roberts decided to pursue her. However, he sent the *Great Ranger* to catch her, as she was the fastest ship in his pirate squadron.[33]

Ogle pretended to evade her pursuer, and the chase continued over the horizon. The pirate captain of the *Great Ranger*, the Welshman James Skrym, was so eager to catch his prey that he took to waving and slashing with his cutlass in his impatience. Then, at around 10.30am, with Cape Lopez out of sight over the eastern horizon, Captain Ogle slowed his ship and let the *Great Ranger* approach him. When the pirates drew within easy gun range they opened up with the chase guns mounted in their bow and simultaneously hoisted the black flag. The idea was to encourage their prey to surrender. Instead, Ogle gave the orders to raise his own flags, and with that his gunport lids opened. Then the *Swallow* turned slowly around and presented her full port broadside to the pirate ship. Moments later Captain Ogle gave the order to fire.

It was utterly devastating. The *Great Ranger* was still bows-on to the *Swallow*, so it was a raking shot, which meant the solid iron roundshot smashed through the whole length of the pirate ship. The *Swallow* carried a dozen each of 18-pounders and 12-pounders in each broadside, plus six more 6-pounders on her upper deck. So, in those few seconds over 400 pounds of metal struck Captain Skrym's ship. Men were torn bodily apart, guns were overturned, and the ship's rigging was cut through, leaving sails flapping and untended. Dead and wounded pirates littered the deck, some screaming, as blood ran into the scuppers. The battered *Great Ranger* turned away, probably because there was nobody left standing to man her tiller. As her starboard guns bore, she offered a half-hearted broadside in reply, but it did little damage.

One young pirate, David Littlejohn, even tried to haul down the black flag, before his shipmates stopped him. Others, terrified by the blood and carnage, tried to hide below but were physically stopped by the pirate's boatswain, Israel Hynde, who forced them back to their posts. After that the two ships kept their distance, trying to avoid the other's broadsides, and exchanging fire at a longer range of a few hundred yards. Both Ogle and Skrym were trying to outmanoeuvre their opponent and deliver a telling blow. Some of the pirate crew wanted to board the enemy and go down fighting, while others begged Skrym to flee – even though the light winds made that virtually impossible. The two ships were locked in a fight neither could now run away from.

Captain Ogle's chance finally came at around 2pm. The *Great Ranger* tried to tack and missed her stays, so she lay in irons – all way off the ship, lying dead in the water, and completely becalmed in the light winds. Seizing the moment, Ogle closed in and was able to deliver another smashing close-range broadside, this time with his starboard guns. The shot slammed into the pirate ship, and the British seamen cheered as they watched her upper mainmast waver, topple and fall, crushing men below and covering the decks of the *Great Ranger* in fallen spars, canvas and rigging. The broadside had battered great holes in the corvette's side, and yet more men were killed and wounded. Captain Skrym had a foot blown off. By now, the pirates were able to reply with only a pitifully ragged fire. They were beaten, but still the fight dragged on for another hour, as Skrym and his more resolute followers refused to admit it.

At around 3pm, after yet more British shot slammed into their ship, they had finally had enough. The black flag was hauled down, and the pirates begged for quarter. Ogle ceased fire and closed in, ready to board. Then, there was a blinding flash from the pirate ship, followed by the sound of a muffled explosion. Some of the most determined of the crew had lived up to their threat to blow up their ship, but there wasn't enough powder left to do the job. All they did was damage her and maim themselves. Ogle sent his surgeon John Atkins with the boarding party, but many of the injured pirates refused to be treated. Captain Skrym was one of them. Atkins was kept busy treating the others.

In all, the British seamen took over a hundred prisoners, almost a quarter of whom were former slaves. They were taken aboard the *Swallow*, stripped naked and placed in irons in the orlop deck. Ogle's men spent two days patching up the two ships. Then, on 7 February, Captain Ogle sent the *Great Ranger* off to Príncipe with a prize crew, for further repairs, while he ordered the *Swallow* to head back to Cape Lopez and the waiting pirate ships. He still had an account to settle with Bartholomew Roberts. Two days later, on Monday 7 February 1722, the sun rose over Cape Lopez at around 6.30am. Captain Ogle had timed his arrival perfectly, and the sun broke over the flat-looking forest-covered coast just as Ogle came within sight of the pirate anchorage. The rising

Bartholomew Roberts, dressed in his finery, with his pirate flagship Royal Fortune, *together with the* Ranger *and the slave ships he captured off Whydah.*

sun revealed Roberts' flagship the *Royal Fortune* lying at anchor to the east of the *Swallow*, some ten miles away in the lee of the headland.

She was accompanied by two other vessels – a merchant ship, the *Neptune*, which had probably brought them provisions from the Gold Coast, and Roberts' smallest vessel, the *Little Ranger*. The night before the pirates had been drinking into the night with the crew of the *Neptune* and so were slow to spot the approaching ship. On board the *Royal Fortune*, Bartholomew Roberts was having breakfast with Thomas Hill, captain of the *Neptune*, when the alarm was raised. Many thought it was the *Great Ranger* heading back from her chase, but others were less certain. As a *ruse de guerre* the *Swallow* was flying a French flag as she approached, but in those waters that was a common-enough ruse. Roberts dressed carefully in 'a rich crimson damask waistcoat and breeches, a red feather in his hat, a gold chain around his neck, with a diamond cross hanging to it'. Then he went on deck.

It gradually became clear that the approaching ship-rigged three-master was a warship. One crewman, David Armstrong, a deserter from the *Swallow*, identified her as his old ship. So, leaving the other vessels at anchor, Roberts recovered his anchor and made sail, heading out to sea to meet the approaching warship. His plan, probably, was to exchange broadsides with her and then slip past her, out into the Atlantic. Then he had a good chance of getting away. A very light wind was blowing from the south that morning, which suited his plan well enough. The *Royal Fortune* performed well in light winds. Still, in those winds it took time for the two ships to come within range of each other.

At around 9.30am, when they were still a few miles apart, a tropical shower swept over the sea, briefly preventing either ship from seeing its foe. It passed, and they spotted each other, just over a mile apart. It was later claimed that the battle was fought amid thunder and lightning, but the *Swallow*'s log makes no mention of this, nor do the accounts of the participants. So, the chances are that the rain passed, and the dramatic weather was little more than a later literary invention. According to the log of the *Swallow* it was 11am when battle was finally joined. At that moment Captain Ogle ordered the French flag hauled down, and Britain's Union flag raised in its place. Then, at a range of around a hundred yards, the two ships exchanged their first broadsides.

It was the warship that fired first – a telling broadside which smashed into the larboard (port) side of the *Royal Fortune*. Moments later the pirate master gunner, Henry Dennis, gave the order to return fire. As the smoke cleared the *Royal Fortune* was still steering towards the open sea, while off her port quarter the *Swallow* was heading inshore. The warship had passed so close that she blocked the *Royal Fortune*'s wind for a few seconds. Moments later, once the breeze returned, the mizzen topmast of the pirate ship fell to the deck below. It had, presumably, been hit by the British broadside. As a result, the pirate's helmsman let go of the wheel – possibly the result of being hit by falling rigging – and the *Royal Fortune* began veering off course to larboard, heading into the wind. As she did, Ogle began turning the *Swallow* to larboard too, to begin his pursuit of Roberts.

That mizzen topmast snatched away the pirates' chance of escaping what followed. Roberts recovered control and turned his ship to starboard, back towards the open sea. There was almost no breeze, and the turn was agonizingly slow. The *Swallow* began drawing closer, and it looked as if there would be nothing for it but to lie yardarm to yardarm – a smashing match, with victory going to the ship which could deal out the most damage, or could survive the carnage the longest. That, of course, played into the hands of Chaloner Ogle, whose men were not only better trained, but whose ship also carried the bigger guns. On the *Royal Fortune*, both Bartholomew Roberts on the quarterdeck and Henry Davis on the main deck yelled at their men to stand to their guns. At that point the *Swallow* finally, slowly, ranged up on the pirates' starboard side and unleashed her second broadside. Once again, the range was less than a hundred yards – almost within pistol shot.

As before, the Royal Naval gunners fired a mixture of shot. The larger 18-pounders fired solid roundshot, while the 12-pounders used chain-shot – a split roundshot linked by chain, designed to scythe through an enemy's rigging. This time, though, the smaller 6-pounders on the upper deck fired grapeshot – bags of musket balls which would spread out and cut down men standing on the target's deck. Up in the fighting tops, marksmen in both ships fired down at the enemy deck, while on the rail, small swivel guns popped off, armed with more grapeshot. It was a devastating combination – and delivered by professionally trained gunners.

One of the pirates, John Atkins, thought they'd been struck by lightning, likening it to 'the rattling of 10,000 small arms within three yards of our heads.' This was where the stories of a battle in a thunderstorm originated. If so, it was a storm of fire, delivered with skill by the Royal Navy. When the smoke cleared, the sails and rigging of the pirate ship were in tatters. Men lay dead and wounded all over the deck. The men of the *Swallow* watched and cheered as the pirates' main topmast toppled overboard, meaning the *Great Fortune* was now virtually dead in the water. John Stephenson, a shipmate of Roberts since his days aboard the slaver *Princess*, had ducked behind a gun moments earlier and missed the worst of it.

When he stood up, he saw Bartholomew Roberts kneeling, with his left hand grasping the breeching rope of another gun, while his right held a sword. Stephenson thought Roberts had lost his nerve and stepped over to kick him, yelling 'Stand up and fight like a man!' It was only then that he saw the great gaping wound in his captain's throat. It had been an oversized musket ball from grapeshot that had struck him just seconds before. Roberts turned and fell forward, and his old friend caught him. Bartholomew Roberts was dead.

The fight seemed to go out of the pirates when they realized what had just happened. It was now about 1.30pm, and while some wanted to fight on, and others seemed determined to die in a last defiant blaze of glory, most dejectedly wanted no more of the battle. One of the pirates, James Philips, went down to the powder room, determined to blow the whole ship up with him, but the sentry there, Stephen Thomas, overpowered him and snatched the burning slow match from Philips' hand. Up on deck only a few guns were still firing, as the *Swallow* fired more full broadsides into the battered *Royal Fortune*. Inevitably, it couldn't go on. As the most senior survivor, it fell to the quartermaster William Magness to haul down the black flag and surrender the ship.

The victorious Ogle heaved to and boats were lowered from the *Swallow* filled with an armed prize crew. In the warship, gunners stood by their guns, now all charged with grapeshot, in case of any trouble. However, Magness had one last thing to do. Earlier, Roberts had told his men that if he were killed in battle, they should throw his body over the side so the authorities couldn't use his corpse as a grisly trophy of war. That, after all, is exactly what had happened to Blackbeard's head. So, Magness and Stephenson reverently carried Roberts' blood-soaked body to the opposite gunwale from the *Swallow* and pitched it into the sea. Bartholomew Roberts, still dressed in his finery, was destined to feed the sharks rather than swing on a noose and be hung up as a warning to others.

That dramatic final act brought the sea battle to an end – the greatest stand-up fight of the whole age. As the boarding parties took possession of the *Royal Fortune* and began rounding up their prisoners, few of the men there would have realized it at the time. This marked the finale of the great pirate menace. Certainly, there were loose ends to tie up, and other battles to fight, but the death of Bartholomew Roberts marked the end of the era. It also was the end of the chain of events that had started in September 1718 – three and a half years earlier – when Walter Kennedy and his fellow mutineers rose up and seized Woodes Rogers' sloop, the *Buck*. Now, all that remained was to very publicly hold the survivors of Roberts' crew to account for their crimes, and to hunt down any of their kind who still remained at large. The 'Great Pyrate', Bartholomew Roberts, had probably been lucky to have died the way he did, a defiant and unbowed pirate captain to the end.

SIXTEEN

The Enemies of Mankind

T HE DEATH OF BARTHOLOMEW Roberts marked the end of an era and gave the British authorities something to celebrate. Captain Chaloner Ogle was eventually rewarded with a knighthood, and he and his men earned prize money as their share of the spoils. It gave the newspapers and broadsheets a story which caught the public imagination from London to Boston, and made Captain Ogle a bona fide hero. Still, to make the most out of the defeat of 'The Great Pyrate', the victory also had to be something more. It had to be turned into a warning to others not to follow in the footsteps of men like Bartholomew Roberts, Edward Thatch, Charles Vane or Stede Bonnet. That meant that his pirate crew had to be brought to justice and made an example of.

Once that was done, the Admiralty and the colonial governors between them had the task of dealing with the last few scattered remnants of those who still followed the black flag. In the case of pirates, this effectively meant their death, whether in battle or at the end of a rope. Only then could the authorities claim that the pirate menace had finally been eradicated. Fortunately, thanks to the global reach of their navies, and their equally effective and extensive colonial administrations, Europe's maritime powers had the wherewithal to carry this out. It was the misfortune of the last remaining pirates that they were at large in one of those rare historical periods when these same European powers weren't fighting among themselves. That meant they could concentrate on hunting pirates.

This mission was supported by a general sense of righteousness, created by a mixture of religious and social intolerance of those who bucked the established order. In most European countries, church and state were united in their desire to punish anyone who opposed the status quo. Throughout the pirate menace, when given the chance to speak, pirates had railed against the injustice of society, the cruelties of ship captains to the common seaman, and the need to fight back against an uncaring world. Neither church nor state liked any of that, and so they dubbed anyone who voiced these sort of opinions 'the enemies of mankind', which gave the eradication of piracy a peculiarly missionary quality to it. So, for once, everyone seemed to be in accord. The last vestiges of the pirate menace had to be removed. That, more than anything, is why in its final stage, this war against the pirates moved from the carrot and stick policy of forgiveness and redemption to one of what amounted to extirpation. Only once the last pirate had been hunted down could the balance of the established moral and social order be restored. This explains why the end of the pirate menace was so complete. Without any more pirates at large, there could be no more pirate problem.

'Piracy doesn't pay' was the message the British authorities wanted to convey. The best way to do that was to bring pirates to justice. Essentially, that meant a well-publicized trial and, ideally, a mass execution. The capture of Bartholomew Roberts' crew, then, was a great coup for the British. The prisoners from the *Royal Fortune*, *Great Ranger* and *Little Ranger*, which was taken after the battle, were held in irons aboard the *Swallow* and taken to Cape Coast Castle, on West Africa's Gold Coast. Once taken ashore, the pirates were imprisoned there pending a well-publicized trial.

The first Cape Coast Castle was built by the Swedes in the mid-17th century as a fortified trading post, where slaves could be brought, held and traded before being shipped overseas, as part of the triangular trade linking Europe and West Africa to the colonies in the Americas. Effectively, then, it was a slave castle, designed as much to keep prisoners in as to keep attackers out. The fort changed from Swedish to Danish and then to Dutch hands. Finally, in 1662 it was captured by the English, who rebuilt it as an impressive and intimidating fortress. On 15 March 1722 a relieved Captain Ogle transported his prisoners into its stone-built underground cells.

Less than two weeks later, on 28 March, the pirates were put on trial. This was held in the castle's spacious chapel, with Captain Mungo Heardman of HMS *Weymouth* presiding over the Vice Admiralty court assisted by six commissioners. Most of them were officially of the Royal African Company and so would have little sympathy for the defendants. In all 254 pirates had been captured, but 19 of them had since died of their wounds, either in *Swallow* or in the cells. The 70 Africans among the pirate crew weren't put on trial. Instead, they were sold back into slavery. That left 165 defendants, five of whom were French and the rest British. Most of them had joined Roberts' crew after he'd arrived on the African coast, although some of them had joined earlier, either in the West Indies or off Newfoundland. Only nine of them had been around long enough to have served under Howell Davis.[1]

For the court, though, this didn't really matter. Unless proven otherwise, or if there were extenuating circumstances, then they were all equally guilty of piracy, and most would pay the price. The prisoners were brought up from their cells one at a time for their charging and the hearing of their plea. While most protested innocence or begged for mercy, a few remained defiant to the last. It took two days to process everyone, but on the third day the trial began in earnest. A batch of 16 men were tried that day, and all but two were found guilty. Six were condemned to death – all men the authorities considered ringleaders, or especially likely to incite some sort of rising. So, quartermaster William Magness, the master gunner Thomas Sutton, and Valentine Ashplant, Christopher Moody, Richard Hardy and David Simpson were all hanged from the ramparts on 3 April.

Afterwards, their pitch-coated bodies were hung in gibbets erected on the summits of the surrounding hills. Naturally these decomposed rapidly in the tropical heat. The rest of the pirates were tried in batches during the weeks that followed, with the trial concluding on 20 April.

In all, of the 165 defendants, 74 of them were acquitted, usually because there was evidence showing they'd been forced to join the pirate crew. Of the rest, 52 were executed and two more had their death sentence respited at the gallows, thanks to new evidence proving they had been among the forced men.

That left 37, who were deemed guilty but didn't warrant an execution. They fell into two groups. The luckiest were shipped back to London, where they were incarcerated in the notorious Marshalsea prison. Those 17 men at least had some chance of staying alive by the time they'd served their sentence. Less fortunate were the 20 pirates who were sentenced to work in the nearby gold mines, operated on behalf of the Royal African Company. That was a death sentence in all but name. Most of the condemned men were hanged in batches, the majority at Cape Coast Castle, but others from other Royal African Company forts along the West African coast. Eighteen of these bodies were then hung in gibbets, in the words of the fort commandant, 'to affright and deter others from pursuing such vile practices on this coast.' It was almost as if a mass hanging wasn't enough of a deterrent on its own without adding this final touch of humiliation.[2]

The business of hunting down the last of the pirates still at large was a complex and time-consuming process, but it actually began even before Bartholomew Roberts sailed for Africa. When he was betrayed by Walter Kennedy back in November 1719, there was a schism among the old *Buck* mutineers that saw Kennedy and Roberts go their separate ways. To understand what followed, we need to return to Cayenne in French Guiana, where Kennedy absconded with all of Roberts' plunder and most of his old crew. That created a breakaway pirate group, who forged their own path.

Walter Kennedy was born in London in 1695, the son of a poor Irish couple. As a youth he was reputedly a pickpocket and thief, but he eventually took to the sea and may, for a while, have served in the Royal Navy. In April 1718 he formed part of the small crew of the hired armed sloop *Buck* during Woodes Rogers' expedition to the Bahamas. That September he was the ringleader of the mutiny that saw the sloop's captain killed, and Kennedy briefly assumed command. However, when a leadership election was held among the small band of mutineers Howell Davis was selected to replace Kennedy as their pirate captain. From that point on, Kennedy sailed as part of Davis' crew. Then, in June 1719, after Davis' death on Príncipe off the West African coast, Kennedy stood for election again. This time his pirate shipmates opted for the relative newcomer Bartholomew Roberts.

Kennedy was a self-appointed 'lord' of the pirate crew – one of those like Thomas Anstis who was regarded as one of the company's founder members, having taken part in the *Buck* mutiny. As a trusted lieutenant, Kennedy had some real standing among Roberts' crew. So, his betrayal of Bartholomew Roberts wasn't taken lightly, although it was opportunistic. He wasn't particularly popular among the crew and he lacked Roberts' literacy and navigational skills. Instead, after leaving Roberts, he relied on fear and the threat of violence to hold his crew together. His first move was to hand the Portuguese prize *Sagrada Familia* over to Captain Cane of the recently captured *Princess*, who sailed off to Antigua in her with the Portuguese prisoners still aboard. Kennedy then took command of the *Royal Fortune* and headed towards the West Indies.

On 15 December, somewhere off Barbados, Kennedy captured his first prize, the snow *Sea Nymph* of New York. Then he headed north to the Leeward Islands and on to the Virginia Capes. He only captured one ship – the *West River Merchant* – and rather than recruiting volunteers from her, eight of his crew deserted. This wasn't a good sign for any pirate captain. He moved south again, and in early January 1720 he captured the six-gun sloop *Eagle* of New York. He kept her, and his crew were split between her and the *Royal Rover*. Those aboard Roberts' old ship sailed off to cruise on their own, leaving Kennedy with the *Eagle* and about 50 crew. It was almost as if he couldn't hold his crew together.

The *Royal Rover* with the remaining 24 pirates put in to the Danish island of St Thomas in the Virgin Islands, hoping to exchange their leaking ship for a small sloop. There the *Royal Rover* was identified as a pirate ship by a Major Holmes from Nevis, who led a group of men to capture her. The pirates abandoned the *Royal Rover* and hid ashore. Having captured the *Royal Rover*, Holmes tried to tow her to Nevis, where he could claim her as a prize. She proved hopelessly unseaworthy, and Holmes got as far as St Kitts, where he was forced to beach the ship before she foundered.

There they stripped the *Royal Rover* of anything valuable and abandoned her on the beach outside Basseterre. Captain John Rose of the 24-gun frigate HMS *Seaford* was sent to bring the pirate ship to Nevis but found the task impossible, as the ship was no longer seaworthy. So, the beached timbers of Roberts' old ship quietly rotted away. It was a dismal end to the pirate ship which Roberts had led into Bahía to cut out a Portuguese treasure galleon. Incidentally the *Sagrada Familia* reached Antigua safely, where she was handed over to the British authorities.

As for Walter Kennedy's *Eagle*, he decided to sail across the Atlantic. Most pirates would have headed for West Africa, but it seems Kennedy's navigational skills weren't up to the job. So, carried on the Gulf Stream, Kennedy headed for Ireland. He missed it, and instead got caught in a gale, and on 8 February ended up being driven ashore at the head of Loch Craignish in Argyllshire on the west coast of Scotland. The first the locals knew of it was when two disreputable-looking shipwrecked mariners knocked on the door of Berbreck House, at the head of the sea loch, begging for help. There, the suspicious Lady Campbell directed them to the magistrate at Inveraray, 40 miles to the west. Then, when they'd gone, she sent her son there over the hills, to warn the Sheriff Depute, James Campbell of Stonefield (the equivalent of a modern-day Summary Sheriff), before the pair of sailors arrived.[3]

By then a group of rough-looking seamen who paid for their drink in Portuguese coin had been reported in an Inveraray tavern. After hearing the news from Berbreck, the sheriff sent a group of armed deputies to arrest the sailors. More of them were rounded up over the next few days, all with pockets filled with Portuguese moidores, English guineas, bags of gold dust and jewels. Under interrogation a few agreed to talk, claiming they had been pressed, and their shipmates were pirates. Their snow the *Eagle* had been driven ashore. When the sheriff sent a mounted posse to investigate, the remaining pirates tried to put to sea but were driven back ashore and hard aground. The survivors were rounded up. In the end, 21 of them were caught and transported to Edinburgh to stand trial.

One of the prisoners turned out to be a fellow Scot, Archibald Murray, the surgeon of the *Buck*. He was able to prove he'd been held captive by the pirates, and in return for his freedom he willingly told the sheriff everything he knew. James Campbell learned that the pirates – around 40 of them in all – had split into two groups. The men he'd arrested had planned to head to England where they could blend in more easily. The rest, led by their pirate captain Walter Kennedy, had bypassed Inveraray and had set off for Edinburgh. So, after seeking the help of the local magnate, the Duke of Argyll, word was sent ahead to the Scottish capital, warning the authorities there to look out for the remaining pirates.

The trial of the crew of the *Eagle* began on 3 November 1720. Of the 21 prisoners, two were released for lack of evidence, and two more because they'd proved they'd been forced to join the pirate crew. One of these was Archibald Murray, whose evidence proved vital in the trial. After their pleas were heard, evidence was given which proved utterly damning. So, on 22 November the jury delivered their verdict. All 17 remaining defendants were guilty. The judge, Lord James Graham, delivered the death sentence, but the execution had to wait for ratification from London.

One of them was eventually pardoned due to his youth, but the rest were eventually hanged on the Sands of Leith outside Edinburgh. This was done in three batches, on 11 December 1720, and 1 and 8 January 1721, in front of cheering, jeering crowds of onlookers. Only one of them, John Clark, a *Buck* mutineer and one of Roberts' 'lords', confessed his guilt beneath the gallows. That still left Kennedy and the others. It seems they hadn't headed to Edinburgh at all but had taken the road to England. Of those pirates, only Walter Kennedy and one other were caught. It was claimed he used his money to purchase a thriving brothel in Deptford. One of his harlots accused him of robbery, and in spring 1721, he was arrested and convicted of the theft.

Then, in Bridewell Prison, another convict, a former mariner, identified Kennedy, as his ship had once been plundered by pirates and he remembered Kennedy due to his threatening manner. So, Kennedy was transferred to Marshalsea Prison, and in mid-July he was tried in a specially convened Admiralty court. It didn't take long to find Kennedy guilty, along with one of his crew from the *Eagle*, John Bradshaw, who had been arrested in Limehouse. They were both hanged at Execution Dock near Wapping Stairs on 21 July 1721. If he ever heard the news, Bartholomew Roberts would probably have taken a grim delight in it. His betrayal had been avenged. The Portuguese plunder, apart from the few thousand coins and jewels captured in Inveraray, had all gone – frittered away by men who revelled in living for the present rather than worrying about a future that almost certainly involved a noose.

Another of the original *Buck* mutineers was Thomas Anstis, who became one of Howell Davis' inner cabal of lieutenants. He was another of those pirates whose origins were obscure. However, it was claimed that he came from Bridgewater in Somerset. He first really surfaced in the historical record when he signed on to serve aboard the six-gun 75-ton sloop *Buck* when it sailed from Britain in March 1718 bound for the Bahamas. Then, in December he was named as one of the six mutineers who seized the sloop off Hispaniola and murdered her captain. Afterwards, under the black flag, he cruised with Howell Davis, and then with Bartholomew Roberts.[4]

After Walter Kennedy's betrayal of Roberts off Cayenne in late 1719, Anstis was with Roberts as his trusted deputy. That December he temporarily took over as pirate captain of the band when Roberts was deposed. In late spring 1720, after Roberts was re-elected, Anstis was given command of a captured 18-gun brig renamed the *Good Fortune*. For the rest of the year, he sailed in consort with Roberts and played his part in the stunningly successful cruise off Newfoundland. On 18 April 1721, when Bartholomew Roberts headed across the Atlantic towards West Africa, Anstis parted company. He and his men headed back towards the West Indies, to begin their own cruise.[5]

Anstis quickly developed a reputation for violence. Over the next few months he captured several vessels, from little coastal traders to large ocean-going merchantmen. One of these was the *Irwin*, a large merchant ship which Anstis captured in the Windward Passage in mid-June. Johnson alleged that the pirates took turns raping one of their prisoners, the wife of a Colonel Doyly of Montserrat, then killed her before throwing her body overboard. The colonel was beaten and injured himself after trying to defend his wife. Towards the end of the summer Anstis put into a secluded bay to careen the *Good Fortune*, possibly Samana Bay in Santo Domingo, the Spanish portion of Hispaniola.[6]

Later that summer they returned to sea, and somewhere between the Leeward Islands and Bermuda the pirates intercepted the slave ship *Morning Star* bound for Charles Town. Anstis liked the look of this fast ship and kept her for himself. Between the slaver and another prize captured a few days later, Anstis had enough captured ordnance to arm her with 32 guns. He preferred his fast-sailing brig *Good Fortune*, though, so he made the *Morning Star* his powerful consort and gave command of her to his master gunner, John Fenn. By this stage, Anstis and many of his crew felt it was time to get out of the pirate business. So, they drafted an open letter addressed to the British king, asking for a pardon, and handed it over to a merchant ship they encountered, the *Nightingale*, to be delivered.

Then they took themselves off to an uninhabited island off Cuba, where they could lie low until they received a reply. This was probably one of the smaller barrier islands off Cuba's south-western coast near the Isla de los Piños. According to Captain Johnson they lived off fish, turtles and fruit, and amused themselves by holding mock trials, where one of the pirates would play the part of the judge and dish out death sentences. Then, in August 1722, Anstis sent the *Good Fortune* to Jamaica to put ashore and find out if there was news of the pardon. They learned that the King hadn't even bothered answering their appeal, which meant there wouldn't be any reprieve for them. So, they put to sea again, with the *Morning Star* and the *Good Fortune* sailing together.[7]

The next day, though, John Fenn ran the *Morning Star* aground on a reef off the Grand Caymans. There was no saving her. The once-prestigious 32-gun pirate ship was a complete wreck. For once the *Good Fortune* lived up to its name and hauled off just in time. Anstis and his men spent the next few days ferrying men and stores from the wreck and a nearby island. Then, without warning, two Royal Naval frigates appeared, the 40-gun fifth-rate HMS *Adventure* and the 44-gun HMS *Hector*. So, with only half the *Morning Star*'s crew aboard, Anstis ordered his men to cut the *Good Fortune*'s anchor cable and they sped off, pursued by one of the pirate-hunters. The chase lasted for several hours, with the *Adventure*'s bow chase gun firing at them all the while. Eventually, though, when the wind dropped, they managed to pull away using their sweeps and escape their pursuers.[8]

Meanwhile, to the north-east of Grand Cayman, the crew of the *Hector* landed on the small island near the wreck and rounded up 40 of the pirates. All of them, unsurprisingly, claimed to have been pressed men. A few hid in the woods in the hope that they might be rescued later by someone who didn't plan to hang them. On board the *Good Fortune*, Anstis decided to head west to the Gulf of Honduras to careen the brig, as the recent chase had shown she'd lost some of her speed. There they captured three or four vessels, including a sloop from Rhode Island. To bolster his band, Anstis pressed almost all of their crews.[9]

The pirate crew of Thomas Anstis, amusing themselves ashore by holding a mock trial.

While they careened in the Gulf of Honduras, probably in one of the Bay Islands near Roatán, Captain Durfrey of the captured sloop and a handful of other prisoners managed to get away. Taking weapons and provisions with them, they stole a canoe and escaped ashore. When the pirates came after them, they held them off with musket fire and drove their pursuers off. Anstis left them to it. It was December 1722 when Anstis put to sea again and headed west, towards the Windward Passage. The cruise began well, as they captured a 24-gun merchantman. Again, Anstis decided to keep her, but once again he chose to keep the *Good Fortune* to himself. So, he gave the command of the new ship to John Fenn, who'd wrecked the *Morning Star.*

They cruised northwards through the passage, taking a couple of prizes on the way, and eventually reached the southern fringe of the Bahamas. It was now early February 1723. There, somewhere off Crooked Island they captured the sloop *Antelope* of Dublin. While they were stripping her of anything useful, Anstis learned that the Royal Navy was still out looking for him. At that point, some of his crew stole the sloop and deserted – a sure sign that morale was low among the pirate crew. So, Anstis rounded Hispaniola, headed south through the Mona Passage, and shaped a course south, keeping well to the east of the chain of the West Indies. The two pirate ships made landfall on the north-eastern coast of Tobago in early 1723. Once again, Anstis planned to put in to a suitable spot there – probably modern-day Bon Accord Lagoon – to careen his ships.

Sensibly, they did this one ship at a time. After unloading all the guns and stores from the *Morning Star*, she was beached, and the crew set about the task of scraping her lower hull. It was then, on 17 May, that the sixth-rate 24-gun frigate HMS *Winchelsey* appeared, standing into the bay. They were cornered. Fortunately for Anstis the *Good Fortune* was still riding at anchor, so for the second time in seven months, Anstis was forced to cut the anchor cable of the *Good Fortune* and she escaped out to sea. Captain Orm of the *Winchelsey* was hampered by the reef which covered most of the bay's seaward side. So, by the time he'd worked his way around it, the *Good Fortune* had slipped out of the bay into the open sea. Once there, Anstis' fast brig was able to outpace the slower *Winchelsey.*

Most of the *Morning Star*'s crew managed to flee with Anstis, but when the frigate returned to Tobago, after giving up the chase, Captain

Orm sent armed landing parties ashore, and Fenn and four of his stranded crew were caught. The rest escaped into the island's interior, and some, Johnson claimed, not only survived but eventually made it home to Britain. John Fenn, though, was less fortunate. He was shipped the 400 miles north to St John's in Antigua. There, in late June 1723, Fenn was found guilty by a Vice Admiralty court convened by John Hart, the new governor of the Leeward Islands. The following day, he and his four shipmates were hanged outside St John's. Fenn's body was wrapped in chains, covered in tar and suspended from a gibbet, reputedly off Fort James, overlooking the entrance to the harbour.

As for Thomas Anstis, this final disaster proved too much for what remained of his crew. Many of them were pressed men, while others had genuinely wanted to give up piracy. Their solution was to shoot Anstis in the head as he lay sleeping in his hammock aboard the *Good Fortune*, somewhere off the Venezuelan coast. Afterwards, the crew turned on the handful of pirates who wanted to continue and imprisoned them. They then sailed to the Dutch colony of Curaçao, where they turned themselves in. In the inevitable trial that followed, most of them were acquitted, having proved they'd been forced to join Anstis' crew. Anstis' quartermaster and three others were found guilty, and duly hanged that July.

There were, of course, other minor strands which continued. For instance, John Phillips, a carpenter who was captured by Anstis in 1721, escaped from the pirates aboard the merchantman *Nightingale*, which Anstis used to send his letter to King George I. Two years later he was working as a fisherman in Newfoundland but decided a return to piracy was preferable. In August 1723 he and a few accomplices stole a sloop, which they renamed the *Revenge*, and cruised the waters of New England, plundering as many as 30 vessels, most of them small fishing boats. In April 1724, he was overpowered by men he'd pressed, and was killed. His two surviving followers were duly handed over to stand trial in Boston and were executed in June 1724.[10]

Sensibly, though, the line has to be drawn somewhere. Phillips had no link to Nassau or its pirates, or to the sloop *Buck*. So, the death of Thomas Anstis in June 1723 effectively marked the end of that amazing chain of events that began one night off Hispaniola in late September 1718. The mutiny on board the armed sloop *Buck* led to a rolling pirate menace that moved around the Atlantic like a hurricane, from the Gulf of Honduras to Guinea, and from Newfoundland to Brazil. It involved shipwrecks as far apart as the Cayman Islands and the west coast of Scotland, and sea battles from as far afield as Barbados in the Windward Islands to Cape Lopez on the West African coast. Never before or since has one seemingly small pirate attack had such long-lasting and wide-ranging consequences.

The whole pirate menace had started with Benjamin Hornigold and Henry Jennings. The repercussions of their piratical careers lasted long after their own meek acceptance of the royal pardon. As a result, the subsequent fate of these two key men can easily be overlooked.

Following his surrender to Captain Pearse of HMS *Phoenix* in February 1717, Jennings remained true to his word. He accepted a provisional pardon, and then, even before Woodes Rogers appeared that summer, Jennings re-affirmed his stance by sailing his *Barsheba* to Bermuda, where he and 15 of his men were officially pardoned by Governor Benjamin Bennett. Afterwards he returned to New Providence and was there when Woodes Rogers arrived that summer.

His time there, though, had passed. He returned to his native Bermuda and his family estates there in the centre of the island, around the Flatts and Smith's Tribe. His family was one of the oldest in the colony, and he knew Governor Bennett and his leading advisers. So, Jennings had no problem whatsoever re-establishing himself in Bermudian society, and re-inventing himself as a gentleman and plantation owner, rather than a salvor and pirate. The family, according to one historian, also maintained a low-key smuggling operation based at the Flatts.[11]

The following March Jennings sailed to Jamaica, where it was claimed he'd been issued a Letter of Marque by William Keith, the deputy governor of the Pennsylvania colony, to operate against Spanish shipping during the brief conflict of the period. In 1719 he even captured three prizes, all of which were duly condemned in Philadelphia. Then, in 1723 he was supposedly captured by a small-time pirate called Evans, but Jennings and his men overpowered the pirates and took their sloop as a prize, which they sailed into Bermuda. It is unclear how long Jennings remained in business, either in Bermuda or as a shipowner. His name disappears from the records in the mid-1730s, although the family remained in both the plantation and shipping businesses until the later 18th century, if not later. More research needs to be done on Jennings' later years, in Barbados or elsewhere.[12]

As for Benjamin Hornigold, he too went down the road of accepting a pardon and landed up leading the pro-pardon faction within the Nassau pirate commune. He, more than anyone, put an end to this once lively pirate community, and encouraged its return to legality through the acceptance of a pardon. After this was verified by Governor Rogers in Nassau, Hornigold offered his services to the British governor. So, the poacher turned gamekeeper and became Rogers' main pirate-hunter. It was he who captured the sloop *Wolf* in September 1718 and brought in her crew of Vane's supporters so they could stand trial. After that, Governor Rogers wrote to his superiors in London to report, 'I am glad of this new proof that Captain Hornigold has given the word to wipe off the infamous name he has hitherto been known by.' He added that his own position in Nassau was boosted by Hornigold's support.[13]

The execution of the *Wolf* pirates in December 1718 cemented Rogers' authority in the Bahamas and marked a real turning point in the war against the pirates. That, as Rogers readily admitted, was largely due to the efforts of Benjamin Hornigold, the former pirate. He was now a vital element in Rogers' plans to bring order and prosperity to the archipelago. The colony, though, had problems. The most immediate of these was the Spanish. In August 1718 King Philip V of Spain decided to invade Italy, in an attempt to recover lost territories there. As a result, Europe was plunged into a fresh war, with, for once, France and Britain allied against Spain, together with the Dutch Republic and the Austrian Empire. In the Americas, this became a great excuse to settle old scores and to resume legal privateering.[14]

In Havana, Governor Gregorio Guazo y Calderón Fernández jumped on the bandwagon and began gathering an expedition to invade the Bahamas. With up to a dozen warships and 4,000 regular Spanish troops, the Spanish had more than enough military muscle to conquer the Bahamas. Instead, there was a last-minute change of plan, and the Spanish turned around and headed to Pensacola on the western side of Spanish Florida. The French had captured the place, and the Spanish expedition was redirected there. In the end the French held on until the end of the war, before ceding that corner of Florida to the Spanish in the peace negotiations which followed.

In February 1720, just as peace talks were nearing completion in the Hague, the Spanish decided to launch a strike against the Bahamas, to secure an extra bargaining chip in the negotiations. By then, Rogers had finished the rebuilding of Fort Nassau and placed other gun batteries to the east of the port. On 24 February, three Spanish frigates and a squadron of privateers appeared off Nassau. As well as the fort and the battery, Rogers had a small British sixth-rate frigate, the 24-gun HMS *Flamborough*, and his own *Delicia*. The Spanish landed on the seaward side of Hog Island and began ferrying troops and privateers across the harbour in longboats. Waiting for them on the beach in Nassau was Rogers' hastily assembled Bahamian militia, many of whom were former pirates. After a few ragged volleys, supported by the guns of *Flamborough*, the Spanish longboats turned back.[15]

The Spanish force was re-embarked, and this time the Spanish commander, Commodore Don Francisco Javier Cornejo, sailed round to the west of the island and tried landing there, at South-West Bay. Rogers was one step ahead of him, and once again the landing was opposed by the Bahamian militia. The Spanish withdrew in the face of a determined defence of the shore. Eventually, a storm blowing in from the west forced Cornejo to give up on the venture. The expedition returned to Havana on 1 March, minus one ship, the 20-gun frigate *San Cristóforo*, which grounded and was wrecked off Grand Bahama Island.

So, the islands were spared, but afterwards Governor Rogers faced another, even more serious threat. He had bankrolled the whole expedition to restore British government to the Bahamas from his own purse. It was now empty, and his debts were mounting. Through the years following his establishment in Nassau in the summer of 1718 the British government continued to starve the colony of funds. Officially, it saw this as a private venture, a bit like the Lords Proprietors' tenure over South Carolina. One by one, Rogers' creditors stopped lending him money. He repeatedly wrote to London asking for help, but his pleas were studiously ignored. By February 1722 Rogers had had enough. He turned over his governorship to his principal adviser, Sir William Fairfax, and took passage home. On his arrival he was only spared the ignominy of debtors' prison through the intervention of his creditors, who wrote off his debts.[16]

The British government's response was to appoint their own man, George Phenney, as the governor, giving him all the official support that they'd denied Woodes Rogers. Strangely, Rogers was saved by Captain Johnson. When his *A General History of the Pyrates* was first published in May 1724, Woodes Rogers was cast in the light of a hero and restored to national prominence. Two years later, following a petition to the King, Rogers was finally reimbursed for his Bahamian enterprise. Better still, after George II succeeded his father to the throne the following year, the new monarch proved an ally to the ageing former governor. So, in October 1728, Woodes Rogers was re-appointed to the governorship of the colony he'd created.[17]

From that point on the colony's motto became 'Piracy Expelled, Commerce Restored'. Woodes Rogers never fully recovered from his financial setbacks, largely because the Bahamas never flourished economically in the way that he'd once hoped. His health never fully recovered either. Woodes Rogers died in Nassau in July 1732, leaving behind a firmly established British colony, but an unprofitable one, which was generally viewed as something of a backwater. It was only really after Bahamas' independence in 1973 and the arrival of mass tourism that the islands finally turned the corner. This, and the development of the Bahamas as an offshore banking centre, have turned the archipelago into one of the richest parts of the Americas. One would like to think that Woodes Rogers would have been delighted by this long-awaited transformation.

As for Rogers' pirate-hunter Benjamin Hornigold, his position was assured in December 1718. However, he didn't live long enough to truly enjoy his newfound position as trusted lieutenant and naval commander to Governor Rogers. Britain and Spain were now at war, and so armed with a Letter of Marque from Rogers, Hornigold became a privateer. The aim, it seems, was to use the money from any prizes to boost the fragile economy of the Bahamas. However, at some point in late summer 1719, Hornigold's sloop was caught in a hurricane, probably somewhere to the west of Cuba, and was wrecked on an uncharted reef. As Captain Johnson told it, 'Captain Hornigold … was cast away upon rocks, a great way from land, and perished.' He added that 'five of his men got into a canoe and were saved'. So ended the life of the founder of the pirates of Nassau, and the man who helped bring about their demise.

A few other characters that feature in this story also deserve a mention. We last came across Sam Bellamy's friend Olivier Levasseur in the early summer of 1719 when he briefly joined forces with Howell Davis on the West African coast. Levasseur continued to cruise independently in West African waters for the remainder of the year, with Bellamy's other lieutenant Paulsgrave Williams acting as his quartermaster. Over the winter this culminated in a raid on Whydah in February 1720, where the French pirate and his crew seized control of the port for a few days. The presence of Royal Naval warships in the area forced him to seek fresh, less dangerous pastures. So, Levasseur and Williams headed south and rounded the Cape of Good Hope to enter the Indian Ocean.

They then headed north towards the promising hunting ground of the Mozambique Channel, but ran aground on the volcanic Johanna Island (now Anjouan, or Nzwani), part of the Comoros Islands, between Mozambique and the East African coast. However, by the autumn Levasseur had managed to make his way to the old pirate haven of St Mary's Island (the Île Sainte-Marie, or Nosy Boraha), off the north-eastern corner of Mozambique. There he teamed up with Edward England, the pirate who'd last been heard of operating off the West African coast. For the rest of 1720, England, Levasseur and Williams operated together, preying on shipping from the Red Sea to the Malabar coast, on the south-western tip of India.[18]

Edward England made his mark on 26 August when his Dutch-built brig the *Fancy* engaged a much larger East Indiaman, the *Cassandra*, off Johanna Island. Captain James Macrae of the *Cassandra* eventually ran his ship aground, and after a week hiding out on the island, he and his men surrendered. Surprisingly, England treated them well, and even gave them the *Fancy* to sail off in. England kept the *Cassandra*. This act of kindness drove a wedge in England's crew, and in early 1721 he was eventually deposed in favour of his quartermaster, John Taylor, and marooned on Mauritius. Eventually, England reached St Mary's, where he survived until at least 1724, when he disappeared from the historical record.[19]

As for John Taylor, he sailed in consort with Olivier Levasseur for a time, and gave the Frenchman command of his powerful second ship, the *Victory*. Then, off the French island of La Réunion they intercepted the Portuguese merchantman *Nossa Senhora de Cabo*. She was richly laden, making her a prize almost as worthy as the Portuguese *Sagrada Família* captured by Bartholomew Roberts off Brazil. Levasseur took the Portuguese prize for himself, abandoning the now-rotten *Victory*, a name which was transferred to his new ship. Taylor and Levasseur parted company after dividing the haul, and Taylor then sailed the *Cassandra* across the Pacific to Panama, which he reached in 1723.

There he abandoned his ship and disappeared. It was later claimed that he took service with the Spanish Navy.[20]

While Taylor sailed east, Levasseur headed west but found cruising in the Mozambique Channel again was too dangerous due to the presence of a Royal Naval squadron. After this force raided St Mary's Island, it was clear that without a secure haven of some sort, further operations were nigh-on impossible. So, he abandoned the Portuguese-built *Victory* somewhere, either on the coast of Mozambique or East Africa, and like Taylor he vanished from history. It was claimed that he took passage to France, but so far this has never been verified. It was also claimed that his quartermaster, Paulsgrave Williams, also took the opportunity to retire from piracy around the same time – the latter half of 1723.[21]

The demise of the Indian Ocean pirates – men like Levasseur, Williams and England, who had once operated in Nassau – represented the last major strand of the tale. They had once shipped alongside Henry Jennings, Benjamin Hornigold and Charles Vane. Now, some five years after the end of Nassau as a pirate haven, they had all retired from their old trade. They were also the last of Nassau's die-hard pirates – the men who refused to accept a pardon – and when they slipped from the pages of history, so too did the last vestiges of that now half-forgotten pirate commune.

Today, our view of piracy is coloured by centuries of romanticized flimflam. First, in 1724, came Captain Johnson's *General History*, which, while accurate in some parts, was also padded out with inaccuracies, half-truths and downright flights of fancy. The fact that the book is still in print today demonstrates just how popular these tales became. This was followed by the likes of Gilbert and Sullivan's *Pirates of Penzance*, the romanticized pirate fiction of Raphael Sabatini, and the Hollywood versions of piracy, featuring the likes of Errol Flynn and Johnny Depp.

Much of this took us even farther from the real pirates of the so-called Golden Age of Piracy. However, they also helped keep the flame of fascination with pirates alight for new generations. With luck, this book will also play its part in feeding our continued fascination with these pirates, but add a touch of historical grounding to their story. In many ways their tale remains more colourful and enthralling than anything Hollywood could create.

NOTES

PROLOUGE

1 This account of the entrance of Governor Rogers' squadron is primarily drawn from the *Log of HMS Rose January 1718 to May 1721* [ADM 51/801]. Also, *Log of HMS Milford, 16 January to December 1719* [ADM 51/606], *Log of HM Sloop-of-War Shark, January 1718 to August 1722* [ADM 51/892].

2 *Letter from Governor Woodes Rogers of the Bahamas to the Council of Trade, Nassau,* October 1718 [CO 23/1].

CHAPTER 1

1 This description is drawn from *Letter from Edmund Edyline to William Blathwayt,* June 1692 [John D. Rockefeller Jr. Library, Colonial Williamsburg Foundation]; William Blathwyt Papers, 1946.2.1459 [vol XXII f.5].

2 For a useful account of Cromwell's 'Western Design' see Sutton, *Cromwell's Jamaica Campaign* (Leigh-on-Sea, 1990).

3 John Taylor, writing in 1689, quoted in Pawson & Buisseret, *Port Royal, Jamaica* (1975). Also Marx, *Port Royal* (2003), p.12; Hamilton, *Pirates and Merchants*, in Skowrontek & Ewen, *X Marks the Spot* (2006), p.12; and Cordingly & Falconer, *Pirates: Fact & Fiction* (1992), pp.38–39.

4 This account of the earthquake is drawn primarily from Heath, *A Full Account of the Late Dreadful Earthquake at Port Royal* (1692). Also, Hamilton, *op. cit.*, pp.13–21 and Marx *op. cit.*, pp.11–26. Also see Boyle, *The Last Days of Port Royal* (2019) for a colourful description of the disaster.

5 Marx, *op. cit.*, pp.21–22.

6 Heath, *op. cit.*, pp.4–5.

7 Quoted in Marx, *op. cit.*, pp.25–26.

8 Exquemelin, *The Buccaneers of America*, Amsterdam, 1678 – English reprint London: The Folio Society, 1969, pp. 56–57. Also, Konstam, *Piracy: The Complete History* (2008), pp.98–102.

9 Apestegui, *Pirates of the Caribbean* (2002), p.153. This account of the rise of the Port Royal buccaneers is drawn from Exquemelin, Pawson and Buisseret, and Pope. Details of the governorship of Jamaica during this period is drawn from *Acts of the Privy Council of England, Colonial Series 1630–80* (6 vols), and from Bridges, *The Annals of Jamaica* (1837), pp.48–64.

10 'No peace beyond the line' referred to the meridian line used by the Spanish and Portuguese at the Treaty of Tordesillas (1494). It effectively bisected the

Atlantic, leaving Brazil in Portugal's eastern side, while Spain had control of everything west of the line. This is why they saw other Europeans as 'interlopers' and harried them when they tried to establish settlements 'beyond the line'. The sentiment was reciprocated by these Europeans, who happily waged an undeclared war against Spanish possessions in the New World.

11 Exquemelin, *op. cit.*, pp.145–49. Also, Pope, *op. cit.*, pp.235–37. The most detailed account of Morgan's Panama raid is found in Earle, *The Sack of Panama* (1981).

12 Bridges, *op. cit.*, p.58.

13 Pope, *op. cit.*, pp.291–95.

14 *Ibid.*, pp.310–21.

15 *Ibid.*, pp.319–20.

16 'An Act for Restraining and Punishing Privateers' (1681), published in McLaine, *Piracy Papers* (2020), pp.283–86.

17 Pope, *op. cit.*, pp.347–48.

18 *Ibid.*, p.349.

19 *Ibid.*, pp.373–80.

20 *Ibid.*, pp.380–81.

21 'A Proclamation for the more effectual reducing and suppressing of pirates and privateers' (1688) in McLaine, *op. cit.*, pp.287–90.

22 An excellent summary of this conflict and the subsequent War of the Spanish Succession is provided in Lynn, *The Wars of Louis XIX* (1999).

23 Bourne, Ruth, *Queen Anne's Navy in the West Indies* (1939), p.20; Chapin, *Privateer Ships and Sailors* (1927, reprinted 2017), pp.206–12.

24 For a discussion of the French privateering enterprise during this period see Jenkins, *A History of the French Navy* (1973), pp.100–05.

25 Apestegui, *op. cit.*, pp.199–200 provides a succinct account of this campaign. Also, Konstam, *op. cit.*, pp.147–49.

26 Quoted in Andrews, *The Colonial Period of American History* (1938), Vol. IV, p.323. Morley, *British-Colonial Privateering in the War of the Spanish Succession* (unpublished thesis, 2000) provides an excellent account of English (British from 1707) privateering efforts during this conflict.

27 Morley, *op. cit.*, provides a useful description of the organization of the Admiralty and Vice Admiralty court system in Britain's American colonies.

28 Bridges, *op. cit.*, p.71.

29 Morley, *op. cit.*, p.53.

30 *Letter from Governor Handasyd of Jamaica to Council of Trade, September 1704* [CSP Col. (1704–05) 566].

CHAPTER 2

1 Much of this account is based on the well-researched description of the voyage in Burgess & Clausen, *Florida's Golden Galleons* (1982), pp.5–41. Details of shipboard life and organization are drawn from Pérez-Mallaína, *Spain's Men of the Sea* (1998), which, although covering life in the treasure

flotas in the 16th century, is also generally relevant to this later period, in terms of shipboard organization and berthing.

2 *Ibid.*, pp.158–59. This provides a list of the fleets' ships, commanders and cargo.

3 Walton: *The Spanish Treasure Fleets* (1994), pp.44–64, contains a detailed description of the organization of these treasure *flotas*, and the routes they took.

4 Burgess & Clausen, *op. cit.*, pp.18–20.

5 *Ibid.*, pp.36–42. Also, *Letter from Don Miguel de Lima y Melo to the Duke de Linares*, Havana, October 1715 [*Translation of Spanish and Vatican Documents from the Archivas des Indies, Seville* – unpublished – Islamorada Public Library, FL, pp.31–35].

6 Burgess & Clausen, *op cit.*, pp.40–42.

7 *Letter from Don Miguel de Lima y Melo to the Duke de Linares*, Havana, October 1715 [*Translation of Spanish and Vatican Documents from the Archivas des Indies, Seville* – unpublished – Islamorada Public Library, FL, pp.31–35]. Also, Burgess & Clausen, *op. cit.*, pp.42–47.

8 *Ibid.* Much of this is drawn from the Spanish report of the disaster, contained in the letter by Don Miguel de Lima. Also see Wagner, *Pieces of Eight* (1966), pp.55–73. Information is also drawn from the unpublished files of the late Dr Eugene Lyon, in the archives of the Mel Fisher Maritime Museum, Key West, FL.

9 Brock, *The Official Letters of Alexander Spotswood* (1885), pp.39–41.

10 Hamilton, *An Answer to an Anonymous Libel* (1718), pp.42–44; *A List of Vessels Commissioned by Governor Hamilton of Jamaica, May 1716* [CO 137/12].

11 Matthew & Harrison, *Oxford Dictionary of National Biography* (2004), vol. 10.

12 *Representation of the Jamaica Assembly to the King*, Spring 1716 [CSP Col. (1716–17) 158 xi f.83–87].

13 *Ibid.*

14 Hamilton, *An Answer to an Anonymous Libel* (1718), p.43; *An Account of the maladministration in Jamaica under the government of Lord Hamilton*, Spring 1716 [CSP Col. (1716–17) 158 xii f.88–90].

15 Brooks, *op. cit.*, pp.221–25, provides a useful and well-researched account of Jennings' Bermudian origins.

16 Johnson, *A General History of the Pyrates* (1724) provides a brief but partly inaccurate account of Jennings and his early career (1998 reprint), pp.8–10.

17 Hamilton, *op cit.*, p.41; *A List of Vessels Commissioned by Governor Hamilton of Jamaica*, May 1716 [CO 137/12].

18 *Marquis de Cassa Torres to Governor Hamilton*, January 1716 [CO 137/12]; *Declarations of Pedro de la Vaga*, August 1716 [Consulado de Cadiz, leg. 853 AGI]; *Deposition of Joseph Lorrain*, August 1716 [Jamaica Council Minutes (1716) f. 110–115].

19 *Francisco Salmón to the King, Palmar de Ays*, September 1715 [*Translation of Spanish and Vatican Documents from the Archivas des Indies, Seville* – unpublished – Islamorada Public Library, FL, pp.6–7]; *Letter of Don Juan Francisco*

del Valle to the Marquis de Monteleon, March 1716 [CSP Col. (1716–17) 158 i f.78–79].

20 *Ibid.* Also *Declaration of Antonio Peralta*, Havana, summer 1716 [*Translation of Spanish and Vatican Documents from the Archivas des Indies, Seville* – unpublished – Islamorada Public Library, FL, pp.115–16].

21 *Ibid.* Also see Hamilton, *op. cit.*, pp.6–7.

22 *Deposition of Joseph Lorrain*, Jamaica, August 1716 [Jamaica Council Minutes (1716) f. 110–115]; *Deposition of Thomas Walker the Younger*, Charles Town, August 1716 [CO 5/1265 f.52].

23 *Marquis de Casa Torres to Governor Hamilton*, January 1716 [CO 137/12]; Hamilton, *op. cit.*, pp. 57–58.

24 Hamilton, *An Answer to an Anonymous Libel* (1718), p.43; *An Account of the maladministration in Jamaica under the government of Lord Hamilton, Spring 1716* [CSP Col. (1716–17) 158 xii f.88–90].

25 *Ibid.*

26 *Captain Balchen, HMS Diamond to the Admiralty*, May 1716 [ADM 1/1471 f.24].

27 *Deposition of Walter Adlington, Jamaica*, May 1716 [CSP Col. (1716–17) 158 vi f.81]; *Deposition of Samuel Liddell, Jamaica*, August 1716 and *Deposition of Allen Bernard, Jamaica*, August 1716 [Jamaica Council Minutes (1716) f.49–50, 60–64]; *Deposition of Joseph Eels, Jamaica*, December 1716 [CO 137/12].

28 Letter from *Captain D'Escoubet to Lord Hamilton, Bahía Honda*, May 1716 [Jamaica Council Minutes (1716) f.17–21]; *The Comte le Blenac to Governor Hamilton, Leogane*, July 1716 [Jamaica Council Minutes (1716) f.21–23].

29 *Governor Michon to Governor Hamilton, Leogane*, June 1717 [CO 137/12 21 iv].

30 *Peter Heywood to the Council of Trade, Jamaica*, August 1716 [CSP Col. (1716–17) 308 f.163–165]; *Royal Warrant revoking the commission of Governor Hamilton of Jamaica*, London, August 1716 [CSP Col. (1716–17) 159 i f.91].

31 Hamilton, *op. cit.*, lays out Lord Hamilton's own case against these charges.

32 *A Royal Proclamation concerning Pyrates* [Jamaica Council Minutes (1716) f.153–155].

CHAPTER 3

1 The following description of the Bahamas' early history is drawn from Michael Craton, *A History of the Bahamas* (1962), pp.42–54.

2 This account of both Nassau in the late 17th century and Henry Every's association with the island is drawn from Oldmixon, *The British Empire in America* (1741), pp. 428–35.

3 This account of Every's career is drawn from Rogoziński, *Honour among Thieves* (2000), pp.83–88.

4 *Ibid.*, pp.88–89.

NOTES

5 *Ibid.*, pp.89–91. Also see *The Case of Nicholas Trott*, October 1798 [CSP Col. (1697–98), f. 928, 506]; and Middleton, *Privateering and Piracy in the Colonial Period* (1923), p.172.

6 *The Case of Nicholas Trott*, October 1798 [CSP Col. (1697–98), f. 928, 506]. Also, Rogoziński, *op. cit.*, pp.90–91.

7 *Letter from John Moore to the Council of Trade*, September 1703 [CSP Col. (1702–03), f. 681]. Also Brooks, *Quest for Blackbeard* (2016), pp.79–80, deals with the attack in more detail, and Craton, *op. cit.*, pp.90–94.

8 John Graves, quoted in Craton, *op. cit.*, pp.93–94.

9 *Letter from Capt. Chadwell to Robert Holden*, October 1707 [CSP Col. (1706–08), f. 1128].

10 Chadwell, quoted in Brooks, *op. cit.*, p.82.

11 A. B., *The State of the Island of Jamaica* (1726), p.8.

12 This account of Hornigold's activities in the Bahamas during this period is primarily drawn from *Henry Pulleine to the Council of Trade*, April 1714 [CSP Col. (1712–14), f. 651]; *Boston News Letter*, April 1714. A useful summary of Hornigold's early career in the Bahamas is also provided in Woodard, *The Republic of Pirates* (2014), p.88.

13 *A List of the Men's Names that sailed from Ilitheria and committed Pyracies*, March 1715 [CSP Col. (1715–16), f. 1265]. In addition, [CSP Col. (1712–14), f. 651] hints at Hornigold's relationship with Thompson. Also see Woodard, *op. cit.*, pp.88–90.

14 *Ibid.* Also see *Deposition of John Vickers to Governor Spotswood, Virginia colony*, July 1716 [CSP Col. (1716–17) fl. 240 (i)]. Also see Woodard, *op. cit.*, p.98.

15 Woodard, *op. cit.*, p.97.

16 *Ibid.*, pp.98–99.

17 *Thomas Walker to the Council of Trade*, March 1715 [CSP Col. (1715–16) 5/1265 f.16 i]; *Thomas Walker to the Proprietors of the Bahamas*, March 1715 [CSP Col. (1715–16) 5/1265 f.17]. For Walker's background see Craton, *op. cit.*, p.91.

18 *Thomas Walker to the Council of Trade*, March 1715 [CSP Col. (1715–16) 5/1265 f.16 i].

19 *Ibid.*

20 *Thomas Walker to the Proprietors of the Bahamas*, March 1715 [CSP Col. (1715–16) 5/1265 f.17].

21 *Marquis de Cassa Torres to Thomas Walker*, February 1715 [CSP Col. (1715–16) 5/1265 f.17 iii].

22 *Deposition of John Vickers to Governor Spotswood, Virginia colony*, July 1716 [CSP Col. (1715–16) 5/1265 fl. 240 i].

23 *Ibid*

24 *Ibid.*

25 *Deposition of Thomas Walker the Younger, Charles Town, South Carolina colony*, 6 August 1716 [CSP Col. (1715–16) 5/1265 fl. 521].

26 *Council of Trade to the King*, 14 December 1715 [CSP Col. (1715–16) 5/1265 fl. 521 i]; *Pulleine to the Council of Trade*, 23 April 1714 [CSP Col. (1715–16) 5/1265 fl. 521 ii].

CHAPTER 4

1 *Thomas Walker to the Council of Trade, Charles Town*, August 1716 [Co 5/1265 f.52].

2 Woodard (2014), pp.122–23, provides a vivid description of the situation in New Providence in early 1716.

3 For a description of Hornigold's life before he turned to piracy, see Baylus (2016), p.58. He also provides a similar well-researched account of Jennings' origins, pp.221–25. Also, Konstam, *op cit.* (2008), pp.155–58.

4 *Deposition of John Vickers to Governor Spotswood, Virginia colony*, July 1716 [CSP Col. (1716–17) fl. 140].

5 Woodard, *op. cit.*, p.122.

6 *Deposition of Joseph Lorrain*, August 1716 [Jamaica Council Minutes (1716), fl. 110–111].

7 *Deposition of Samuel Liddell*, August 1716 [Jamaica Council Minutes (1716), fl. 49–50].

8 *Captain Ayala Escobar to Governor of Cuba*, February 1716 [Translation of documents from the Archive des Indies, Seville, in Islamorada Library, FL – compiled by treasure salvor Kip Wagner, pp.56, 69], quoted in Woodard, *op. cit.*, p.124.

9 *Deposition of Allen Bernard, Jamaica*, December 1716 [CSP Col. (1715–16) 137/12 fl. 411 i]; *Deposition of Joseph Eels*, December 1716 [Jamaica Council Minutes (1716), fl. 68–69].

10 *Ibid.* Also *Deposition of Samuel Liddell*, August 1716 [Jamaica Council Minutes (1716), fl. 49–50]; *Letter from the Comte de Blenac to Lord Hamilton*, July 1716 [CSP Col. 137/12 fl. 2 iii]; *French testimony to the Jamaica Assembly*, August 1716 [Jamaica Council Minutes (1716), fl. 17–23].

11 *Captain Ayala Escobar to Governor of Cuba*, February 1716 [Translation of documents from the Archive des Indioes, Seville, in Islamorada Library, FL – compiled by treasure salvor Kip Wagner, p.69]; *Deposition of John Vickers to Governor Spotswood, Virginia colony*, July 1716 [CSP Col. (1716–17) fl. 240 i].

12 *Deposition of John Vickers to Governor Spotswood, Virginia colony*, July 1716 [CSP Col. (1716–17) fl. 240 i].

13 *Ibid.*

14 *Letter from the Comte de Blenac to Lord Hamilton*, July 1716 [CSP Col. 137/12 fl. 2 iii]; *French testimony to the Jamaica Assembly*, August 1716 [Jamaica Council Minutes (1716), fl. 17–23].

15 *Deposition of Allen Bernard, Jamaica*, December 1716 [CSP Col. (1715–16) 137/12 fl. 411 i]; *Deposition of Joseph Eels*, December 1716 [Jamaica Council Minutes (1716), fl. 68–69].

16 *Ibid.*

17 Details of Bellamy's association with Hornigold and subsequent cruise are provided in *The Trials of Eight Persons indicted for* Piracy (1718), p.24. This contains the transcript of one of Bellamy's crew, Simon von Horst, who was tried in Boston two years after these events took place.

18 *Deposition of Jeremiah Higgins,* June 1717 [National Archives, Washington DC, Vice Admiralty Court Records, New York colony, 1701–14 – Gr.21.34.1 mf. M-948].

19 *Ibid.*

20 *The Trials of Eight Persons indicted for Piracy* (1718), pp.23–25, 154–155, contains the examination of Bellamy's crewmen Simon von Horst and Jeremiah Higgins.

21 *Ibid.*

22 *Ibid.*

23 *Deposition of Allen Bernard, Jamaica,* December 1716 [CSP Col. (1715–16) 137/12 fl. 411 i]; *Deposition of Joseph Eels,* December 1716 [Jamaica Council Minutes (1716), fl. 68–69].

24 *Deposition of Allen Bernard, Jamaica,* December 1716 [CSP Col. (1715–16) 137/12 fl. 411 i].

25 *Ibid.* Also, *Deposition of Joseph Eels,* December 1716 [Jamaica Council Minutes (1716), fl. 68–69].

26 *Deposition of John Cockrane in Jamaica,* August 1716 [Jamaica Council Minutes (1716), fl.68–69].

27 *Letter from the Comte de Blenac to Lord Hamilton,* July 1716 [CSP Col. 137/12 fl. 2 iii]; *French testimony to the Jamaica Assembly,* August 1716 [Jamaica Council Minutes (1716), fl. 17–23].

28 *A Royal Proclamation against Pyrates,* August 1716 [Jamaica Council Minutes (1716) fl. 153–155].

29 *Thomas Walker to the Council of Trade,* August 1716 [CSP Col. (1716–17) 328 fl. 176]; *Deposition of Robert Daniel, Charles town, South Carolina colony, July 1716* [CSP Col. (1716–17) 267 fl. 149].

30 *The Trials of Eight Persons indicted for Piracy* (1718), pp.23–25, 154–55, contains the examination of Bellamy's crewmen Simon von Horst and Jeremiah Higgins. See also, *Examination of Andrew Turbett and Robert Gilmore, Williamsburg, Virginia colony,* April 1717 [CSP Col. (1716–17) 5/1318 fl. 16 ii].

31 *The Trials of Eight Persons indicted for Piracy* (1718), pp.154–55; (*Examination of Jeremiah Higgins*).

32 *Ibid.*

CHAPTER 5

1 A discussion of sources can be found in Rediker, *op. cit.,* pp.19–37. See also Konstam, *Blackbeard* (2006), pp.41–44.

2 Unless noted, Johnson (1724, 2nd edition, reprinted 1998) is the version used throughout this book. In fact, there were two versions that year – the first being a two-volume set. The second edition incorporated several changes by the anonymous Captain Charles Johnson. The name was a *nom de plume*, and there have been several attempts to identify the author. These include the author and intelligence agent Daniel Defoe, author of *Robinson Crusoe*. A more likely candidate is Nathaniel Mist, a contemporary publisher and journalist. See Bialuschewski, Arne, 'Daniel Defoe, Nathaniel Mist and the General History of the Pyrates' in *The Papers of the Bibliographical Society of America*, v.98 (March 2004), p.26 et. seq. for a compelling case citing Mist as the book's author.

3 *Boston News Letter*, 29 March–5 April 1714. For a discussion of the rise of pirate attacks, see Rediker, *op. cit.*, pp.17–24, 57–59.

4 *Letter from Thomas Walker to the Lords Proprietors*, March 1715 [CO 5/1264 17i].

5 *Deposition of Mathew Musson*, July 1717 [CO 5/1265].

6 *James Logan to Robert Hunter*, October 1717 [Historical Society of Pennsylvania: James Logan Papers, misc. vol. 2 p.167]; *Governor Benjamin Bennett of Bermuda to the Council of Trade*, May 1718 [CSP Col. (1717–18) 551]; *Captain Vincent Pearse, HMS Phoenix to the Admiralty*, February 1718 [ADM 51/690].

7 Rediker, *op. cit.*, pp.29–30.

8 This theme is explored in Cordingly, *Under the Black Flag* (1995), pp.13–15.

9 *Ibid.*, p.10.

10 Konstam, *Piracy: The Complete History* (2008), p.268; Rediker, *op. cit.*, p.54; Johnson (1998 reprint) discusses the chain of events in his chapters on Edward England and Howell Davis.

11 Johnson, *op. cit.*, chapters on Roberts and Anstis. Also, Rediker, *op. cit.*, pp.45–49, and Konstam (2008), *op. cit.*, pp.246–48 for brief accounts of Phillips' connection with the others.

12 *Governor Bennett of Bermuda to the Council of Trade*, July 1717 [CSP Col. (1716–17) 677].

13 Johnson (1998 reprint), *op cit.*, pp.185–86.

14 *Ibid.*, pp. 333–34; Rediker, *op. cit.*, pp.29–30.

15 *Boston News Letter*, 29 March–5 April 1714.

16 Rediker, *op. cit.*, pp.52–56.

17 *Governor Nicholas Lawes of Jamaica to the Council of Trade*, July 1718 [CSP Col. (1717–18) 524 vi].

18 Rediker, *op. cit.*, pp.53–54.

19 Rediker, *op. cit.*, pp.49–50.

20 *Captain Pearse, HMS Phoenix to the Admiralty*, February 1718 [ADM 51/690]. For a discussion of nationality see Rediker, *op. cit.*, pp. 50–53.

21 Rediker, *op. cit.*, pp.52–53.

22 *Ibid.*, p.99.

23 For a discussion of the conditions of life aboard merchant ships of this period see Earle, *Sailors* (1998), pp.29–48.

24 Quoted in Rediker, *op. cit.*, pp.1–6.

25 *Ibid.*, pp.39–40.

26 Snelgrave, *A New Account* (1734), p.114. Also see Konstam (2008), *op. cit.*, p.50.

27 Konstam, *op. cit.*, pp.50–55.

28 Rediker, *op. cit.*, pp.60–85.

29 *Ibid.*, pp.39–40.

30 *Ibid.*, pp.66–88.

CHAPTER 6

1 For a detailed account of the Lords Proprietors' rule of the Carolinas, see Stiles (ed.), *The Colonizers* (1998), pp.296–324.

2 Albury, *The Story of the Bahamas* (1975), pp.47–51.

3 For a discussion of Trott's position, see Brooks (2016), pp.60–61. Also, Craton, *History of the Bahamas* (1962), p.62.

4 Governor William Beeston, quoted in Craton *op. cit.*, p. 71.

5 *Deposition of John Vickers to Governor Spotswood, Virginia colony*, July 1716 [CSP Col. (1716–17) fl. 240 (i)].

6 *Deposition of John Vickers to Governor Spotswood, Virginia colony*, July 1716 [CSP Col. (1716–17) fl. 240 (i); *Deposition of Allen Bernard, Jamaica*, December 1716 [CSP Col. (1715–16) 137/12 fl. 411 i]; *Deposition of Joseph Eels*, December 1716 [Jamaica Council Minutes (1716), fl. 68–69].

7 Hofenk de Graff, *The Colourful Past* (2004), p.235.

8 *Thomas Bannister to the Council of Trade and Plantations, July 1715* [CSP Col. (1714–15) fl. 508]; *The Proposal for Preventing the French South Sea Trade, October 1714* [CSP Col. (1714–15) fl. 129 ii].

9 Rhode Island section, in the *Boston News Letter*, 12 September 1715; New York section, in the *Boston News Letter*, 3 October 1715.

10 *Deposition of Simon Slocum, William Knock, Paul Gerish, John Tuffton and Thomas Porter, February 1716* [CSP Col. (1716–17) fl. 484 iii].

11 Alexander Spotswood to the Council of Trade, July 1716, reproduced in Brock (ed.), *The Official Letters of Alexander Spotswood* (Richmond VA, 1885), p.186; *The Tryals of Major Stede Bonnet and Other Pirates* (London, 1719), p.24.

12 Cordingly, *Spanish Gold* (2011), p.189, provides a description of Harbour Island. Details of Thompson's trading ventures are provided in *Thomas Walker's Account of Pirates and the State and Condition of the Bahamas*, March 1714 [CSP Col. (1714–15) fl. 241]; *Thomas Walker to the Council of Trade*, August 1716 [CSP Col. (1716–17) fl. 596].

13 For details of these trading voyages, see *Thomas Walker to the Council of Trade*, August 1716 [CO 5/1265 f.52]; *South Carolina Shipping Returns*,

1716–17 [CO 5/208 fl.1 6–23]; *Jamaica Shipping Returns*, 1716–17 [CO 142/14 fl. 70].

14 *Elias Haskett to the Council of Trade*, July 1701 [CSP Col. (1701–02) fl. 142].

15 For the defensive capability of the island in 1710, see *Report by Captain Smith of HMS Hazardous*, August 1710 [CSP Col. (1710–11) f. 421 i].

16 *Thomas Walker to the Council of Trade*, August 1716 [CSP Col. (1716–17) 328 fl. 176]; *Captain Chadewell, Flying Horse sloop, to Robert Holden*, October 1707 [CSP Col. (1706–07) fl. 555–579]. For the buildings of this period, see Craton & Saunders, *Islanders in the Stream* Vol. 1 (1992), pp.82–84.

17 *Thomas Walker to the Council of Trade*, August 1716 [CSP Col. (1716–17) 328 fl. 176].

18 Craton & Saunders, *op. cit.*, p.82.

19 *Deposition of Henry Timberlake of the Lamb, Jamaica*, December 1716 [Jamaica Council Minutes (1716) IB/5/3/8 f.426–427].

20 *Deposition of John Vickers to Governor Spotswood, Virginia colony*, July 1716 [CSP Col. (1716–17) fl. 240 (i)].

21 *Thomas Walker to the Council of Trade*, August 1716 [CSP Col. (1716–17) 328 fl. 176].

22 Woodard, *op cit.*, pp.112–14 *et seq.*

23 Johnson, *A General History of the Pyrates* (1724) 1st edn Vol 2. Chapter on Charles Misson.

24 Konstam (2008), p.271. For more on Sainte-Marie see Rogoziński, *Honour Among Thieves* (2000), which covers the history of the island in depth, and touches on it acting as a model for Libertalia.

25 Oldmixon (1741), *op. cit.*, p.356.

26 *Thomas Walker to the Council of Trade*, August 1716 [CSP Col. (1716–17) 328 fl. 176]; *Deposition of Allen Bernard, Jamaica*, December 1716 [CSP Col. (1715–16) 137/12 fl. 411 i]; *Deposition of Joseph Eels*, December 1716 [Jamaica Council Minutes (1716), fl. 68–69] (1716–17) 328 fl. 176].

27 Walker, *op. cit.*

28 *Ibid.*

29 For a deeper understanding of this, see Kropotkin, *Mutual Aid* (1902), esp. pp.140–72.

CHAPTER 7

1 *Deposition of Henry Timberlake, Jamaica*, December 1716 [Jamaica Council Minutes (1716) IB/5/3/8 f.426–427]. Details of sunset and coastal features are drawn from modern and near-contemporary navigational and pilot guides.

2 *Ibid.*

3 Johnson, *A General History of the Pyrates* (1724 – second edition – reprinted 1998), p.46.

4 Johnson; *A General History of the Pyrates* (1724 – first edition) Vol. 1., pp.62, 84.

5 The North Carolina origin story is opined in Lee, *Blackbeard the Pirate* (1974), p.1-9 and fleshed out in Duffus, *The Last Days of Blackbeard the Pirate* (2004), pp.180–93, and interestingly identifies him as Edward Beard, a scion of an established North Carolina family. Duffus also discusses the Bristol option. Brooks (2016), *op. cit.*, pp.143–70 provides convincing proof of the pirate's roots in Jamaica, where his surname is usually spelt 'Thache'. He also discusses the Gloucestershire link and settles on the Thache family of Sapperton, a village outside Gloucester.

6 Brooks, *op cit.*, pp. 187–88.

7 *Ibid.*, pp.181–201. Also see Lavery, *The Ship of the Line* (1983), p.163; Rogers, *The Wooden World* (1986) pp.119–23.

8 This argument about Thatch's training in piratical skills is mirrored by Brooks, *op. cit.*, pp.202–03.

9 *Letter from Captain Mathew Musson to the Council of Trade*, July 1717 [CSP Col. (1716–17) v.29 f. 635].

10 *Letter from Captain Mathew Musson to the Council of Trade*, July 1717 [CSP Col. (1716-17) v.29 f. 635].

11 Rediker (2005), *op. cit.*, p.7.

12 *A Proclamation concerning Pyrates*, August 1716 [Jamaica Assembly Minutes, f.153–55].

13 Johnson (reprinted 1998), p.60.

14 *Ibid.*, p.60.

15 Konstam (2006), *op. cit.*, pp.68–69; Woodard, pp.205–06, citing 'Indictment of William Howard, Williamsburg, October 1718', in Lee (1974), pp.101–04.

16 *Boston News Letter*, 24 October 1717 and 4–11 November 1717.

17 *Boston News Letter*, 24 October 1717; Barbados Shipping Returns, 1716–17 [CO 33/15 f.53–54], cited in Moore (2018), p.157. Moore is an expert on Blackbeard, and his article in the *North Carolina Historical Review* (2018) is a superb précis of Thatch's piratical career.

18 Johnson (1998 reprint), p.47; *Deposition of Thomas Knight*, November 1717 (CO 152/12]. For a discussion of the capture and conversion of *La Concorde*, see Moore, *op. cit.*, pp.163–64 and Konstam (2006), pp.80–82.

19 Johnson, *op cit.*, p.47; Moore, *op cit.*, pp.163–64.

20 *Deposition of Christopher Taylor*, January 1718 [CO 152/12 67 ii]; Moore, *op. cit.*, pp.165–66.

21 *Deposition of Henry Blackstock*, November 1717 [CSP Col. (1717–18) v.30 298 ii].

22 Johnson, *op. cit.*, p.47. Also, Konstam (2006), pp.124–25.

23 Johnson, *op. cit.*, p.47.

24 Johnson, *op. cit.*, p.47; *Boston News Letter*, 16 June 1718; *The Tryals of Major Stede Bonnet and Other Pirates* (1719), pp.44–45.

25 Johnson, *op. cit.*, p.48; *The Tryals of Major Stede Bonnet and Other Pirates* (1719), p.45.

26 *Ibid.* Also *Governor Robert Johnson to the Council of Trade*, June 1718 [CSP Col. (1717–18) 30 f.556].

27 *Ibid.*

28 *Ibid.* Also *Governor Robert Johnson to the Lords Proprietors,* June 1718 [CO 5/1265], *Boston News Letter,* 7 July 1718, *South Carolina Dispatch,* 6 June 1718, *Philadelphia Dispatch,* 26 June 1718.

29 Johnson, *op. cit.,* p.49; *Governor Robert Johnson to the Council of Trade,* June 1718 [CSP Col. (1717–18) 30 f.556].

30 *Ibid.*

31 Johnson, *op. cit.,* p.49. The syringe is now on display in the North Carolina Maritime Museum, Beaufort NC.

32 *Governor Robert Johnson to the Lords Proprietors,* June 1718 [CO 5/1265].

33 Thatch's motivation for breaking up his squadron is examined in detail in Konstam (2006), *op. cit.,* pp.147–51, and Woodard, *op. cit.,* pp.254–62.

34 Watkins-Kenney (2018), pp.186–88; Johnson, *op. cit.,* pp.49–50; *Deposition of David Herriot,* November 1718, in *The Tryals of Major Stede Bonnet* (1719), p.45; *Captain Ellis Brand to the Admiralty,* July 1718 [ADM 1/1472].

35 *Deposition of David Herriot,* November 1718, in *The Tryals of Major Stede Bonnet* (1719), p.45.

36 *Ibid.* Also see Konstam (2006), p.183.

37 *Governor Alexander Spotswood to the Admiralty,* August 1719 [ADM 1/1826]. Also Johnson, *op. cit.,* pp.65–66; Woodard, *op. cit.,* pp.255–59; Konstam, *op. cit.,* pp.196–99.

38 Johnson, *op. cit.,* p.66; Moore, *op. cit.,* pp.176–78.

39 Johnson, *op. cit.,* pp.50–51.

CHAPTER 8

1 The inter-relationship between pirates of this era is discussed in detail in Rediker, *Villains of All Nations* (2004), pp.79–82.

2 *The Trials of Eight Persons indicted for* Piracy (1718), pp.23–25, 154–55, contains the examination of Bellamy's crewmen Simon von Horst and Jeremiah Higgins.

3 *Ibid.*

4 Samuel Bellamy's background is discussed in Woodard, *op. cit.,* pp.28–30, 91–93, drawing on unpublished research by the late Kenneth J. Kinkor in the collection of the Whydah Museum, Provincetown, MA. Also see Clifford (ed.), *Real Pirates* (2007), which outlines research into Bellamy's origins, and his crew; and Clifford & Perry, *The Black Ship* (1999), p.98.

5 *Ibid.* Also see Woodard, *op. cit.,* pp.124–27.

6 *Deposition of Allen Bernard, Jamaica,* December 1716 [CSP Col. (1715–16) 137/12 fl. 411 i]; *Deposition of Joseph Eels,* December 1716 [Jamaica Council Minutes (1716), fl. 68–69].

7 *Examination of Richard Caverley, New York, June 1717* and *Examination of Jeremiah Higgins, New York,* June 1716 [*Records of the Vice Admiralty Court of the Province of New York, 1685–1838,* f. 36–39].

8 *Deposition of Abijah Savage, Antigua,* November 1716 [CO 137/11 f. 45 iii].

9 *The Trials of Eight Persons indicted for* Piracy (1718), pp.23–25, 154–55, contains the examination of Jeremiah Higgins; *Examination of Richard Caverley, New York,* June 1717 [*Records of the Vice Admiralty Court of the Province of New York, 1685–1838,* f. 36–39].

10 *The Trials of Eight Persons indicted for* Piracy (1718), pp.23–25, 154–55, contains the examination of Bellamy's crewmen Simon von Horst and Jeremiah Higgins.

11 This account of Paulsgrave Williams' origins and life is based on fairly sketchy evidence, recounted in Sandler, *The Whydah* (2017). Also Clifford, *op. cit.,* pp.54–55; and Dow and Edmonds, *Pirates of New England* (1923), pp.116–17, which claims Williams' usual name was Paul and was said to have been born on Nantucket before moving to Newport, Rhode Island. To complement this, Brooks, *op. cit.,* p.354, states he was the son of the attorney general for the Rhode Island colony, John Williams. Brooks adds that Williams was the suitor of Goody (or Mary) Hallett, whose son from Williams died soon after childbirth, while Bellamy and Williams were at sea.

12 *Governor Walter Hamilton to the Council of Trade,* December 1717 [CSP Col. (1716–17) 425 f.23]; *The Trials of Eight Persons indicted for Piracy* (1718), pp.23–25, 154–55, contains the *Examination of Jeremiah Higgins, New York, June 1717* [*Records of the Vice Admiralty Court of the Province of New York, 1685–1838,* f. 36–3].

13 *Governor Walter Hamilton to the Council of Trade,* December 1717 [CSP Col. (1716–17) 425 f.23].

14 *An Inventory of Goods taken from the Pirates at St Cruze by HMS Scarborough,* Summer 1717 [ADM 1/1689 f.5]; *HMS Scarborough Log Entries,* January 1717 [ADM 51/865]; Governor Walter Hamilton to the Council of Trade, March 1717 [CSP Col. (1716–17) 484]; *The Trials of Eight Persons indicted for Piracy* (1718), pp.23–25, 154–55, contains the *Examination of Jeremiah Higgins, New York, June 1717* [*Records of the Vice Admiralty Court of the Province of New York, 1685–1838,* f. 65–69]; *Governor Robert Lowther to the Council of Trade,* March 1717 [CSP Col. (1716–17) 204, 351].

15 Johnson, *op. cit.,* (1998 reprint), pp. 41–45, claims that Martel was a British pirate, but the surname is unreservedly French. There is also contemporary evidence he was a Frenchman, being cited as such in *The Boston News Letter* 12 November 1716, when he first began his piratical attacks. Also see Rogozinski, *Pirates!* (1996), p.216.

16 *Deputy Governor Hornby to Governor Walter Hamilton, March 1717* (CSP Col. (1716–17) 425v f.231]; *Captain Bartholomew Chandler, HMS Winchelsea to Secretary Burchett, Admiralty,* May 1717 [CSP Col. (1716–17) 639i f.339]; *The Trials of Eight Persons indicted for Piracy* (1718), pp.23–25, 154–55, contains the *Examination of Jeremiah Higgins, New York,* June 1717 [*Records of the Vice Admiralty Court of the Province of New York, 1685–1838,* f. 36–39].

17 Clifford & Turchi, *The Pirate Prince* (1993), pp.24–27 and Clifford & Perry (1999), *op. cit.*, pp. 246–54, outline the story of the *Whydah* and her capture. Also *Examination of Richard Caverley, New York*, June 1717 and *Examination of Jeremiah Higgins, New York*, June 1716 [*Records of the Vice Admiralty Court of the Province of New York, 1685–1838*, f. 36–39].

18 *Jamaican Shipping returns, September 1713–March 1715* [CO 142/14 58]; *Examination of Jeremiah Higgins, New York*, June 1716 [*Records of the Vice Admiralty Court of the Province of New York, 1685–1838*, f. 36–39]. Also Woodard, *op. cit.*, pp.156–58.

19 *The Trials of Eight Persons indicted for* Piracy (1718), pp.23–25, 154–55, contains the *Examination of Jeremiah Higgins, New York*, June 1717 [*Records of the Vice Admiralty Court of the Province of New York, 1685–1838*, f. 23–24].

20 *Ibid.*, f.23–25.

21 *Ibid.*, p.25. Also Woodard, *op. cit.*, pp.171–72.

22 *The Trials of Eight Persons indicted for* Piracy (1718), pp.23–25, 154–55, contains the *Examination of Jeremiah Higgins, New York*, June 1717 [*Records of the Vice Admiralty Court of the Province of New York, 1685–1838*, f. 23–24]. Also *The Boston News Letter*, 6 May 1717, *Rhode Island Dispatch*, 3 May 1717.

23 Johnson (original 1724 edition, 1st edn.), *op. cit.*, p.587. Also Rediker, *op. cit.*, p.69.

24 *The Trials of Eight Persons indicted for* Piracy (1718), pp.23–25, 154–55, contains the *Examination of Richard Caverley, New York*, June 1717 [*Records of the Vice Admiralty Court of the Province of New York, 1685–1838*, f. 23–24].

25 *Deposition of Andrew Turbett, Williamsburg*, April 1717 [CO 5/1318 fl. 16ii]; *The Trials of Eight Persons indicted for Piracy* (1718), pp.23–25.

26 *Deposition of Thomas Fitzgerald and Alexander Mackonichie, Boston*, May 1717, in Dow and Edmonds, *op. cit.*, pp.296–97; *The Trials of Eight Persons indicted for Piracy* (1718), p.9.

27 *Depositions of Ralph Merry and Samuel Roberts*, May 1717, cited in Jameson, *Privateering and Piracy in the Colonial Period* (1923), pp.296–97.

28 This account is drawn from *The Boston News Letter*, 29 April 1717; *Letter from Cyprian Southack to Governor Samuel Shute, Provincetown May 1717* [Massachusetts State Archives, 51 / 289]; *The Trials of Eight Persons indicted for Piracy* (1718), pp.23–25, 154–55, contains the *Examination of Thomas Fitzgerald and Alexander Mackonichie* [*Records of the Vice Admiralty Court of the Province of New York, 1685–1838*, f. 24]. Also see Woodard, *op. cit.*, pp.183–84 and Clifford & Perry, *op. cit.*, pp.9–10, for spirited accounts of the wrecking.

29 Mather, *Instructions to the Living, from the Condition of the Dead* (1717). A published tract outlining the circumstances of the wrecking, the fate of the pirate crew, and an account of the confessions extracted from some survivors during their subsequent trial. [Author's Collection]

30 Sandler, *op cit.*, pp.44–79.

31 Mather, *op. cit.*

32 *Boston News Letter*, 27 May 1717, *Deposition of Edward Sargeant, New York,*
    June 1717 *[Records of the Vice Admiralty Court of the Province of New York, 1685–*
    1838, f. 36/3*]*; *Deposition of Zachariah Hill, Boston,* May 1717 *[Massachusetts*
    State Archive, Sussex Court Files f. 11945]; *Deposition of Paul Mansfield, Salem,*
    May 1717 *[Massachusetts State Archive, Sussex Court Files f. 11945]*.

33 *Boston News Letter*, 27 May 1717, *Deposition Samuel Skinner, Salem,* May
    1717 *[Massachusetts State Archive, Sussex Court Files f. 11945]*.

34 Rediker, *op. cit.*, pp.29–31.

CHAPTER 9

1   See Richard Ford's *A New Map of the Island of Barbados, printed in London in*
    1674. Also Sanders, *Barbados Records* (1979), pp.37–38, and Parish Records,
    St Michael's Parish Barbados (1648–1739) in the collection of the Genealogy
    Society of Utah, cited in Woodard, *op. cit.*, p.197.

2   Johnson (1998 reprint), p.63.

3   *Barbadian shipping returns, 1716–17* [Co 33.15 f.53–54]. These record a
    35-ton sloop called the *Revenge* arriving in Barbados in December 1716.
    David Moore traced shipping records further, and discovered the sloop was
    originally registered in Newport in the Rhode Island colony, and had visited
    Jamaica, as she appeared in Jamaican shipping records. Before sailing for
    Barbados, she was operating in Charles Town, South Carolina colony, under
    the command of Captain Godfrey Malbone. See Moore, *op. cit.*, pp.156–57.

4   *Captain Bartholomew Chandler, HMS Winchelsey to Josiah Burnet, Secretary*
    of the Admiralty [ADM 1/1597], *Barbadian shipping returns, 1716–17* [Co
    33.15 f.53–54].

5   Johnson, *op. cit.*, p.63.

6   *Ibid.*, pp.63–64.

7   *Ibid.*, p.65. Also *Boston News Letter*, 28 October 1717.

8   *Ibid.*, p.64.

9   *Boston News Letter*, 11 November 1717; *Philadelphia Dispatch*, 24 October
    1717.

10 *Trial of William Howell, Nassau,* December 1721 [CO 23/1].

11 *Boston News Letter*, 11 November 1717.

12 Johnson, *op. cit.*, p.65.

13 *Ibid.*, p.65. Also, Cordingly (2011), p.170.

14 McLaine, *op. cit.*, p.319.

15 Johnson, *op. cit.*, pp.65–66.

16 *Ibid.*, p.66.

17 *Ibid.*, pp.66–67.

18 *Ibid.*, p.67; *The Tryals of Major Stede Bonnet and Other Pirates* (London, 1719),
    p.46.

19 *Ibid.*, pp.67–68; *The Tryals of Major Stede Bonnet and Other Pirates* (London,
    1719), pp.46–47.

20 Johnson, *op. cit.*, p.68.

21 *The Tryals of Major Stede Bonnet and Other Pirates* (London, 1719), p.46.

22 *Ibid.*, pp.46–47. Also, *Governor Robert Johnson of South Carolina colony to the Council of Trade, Charles Town*, 21 October 1718 [CSP Col. (1717–18) f.130 p.366–67]. The following account of the battle in the Cape Fear River is drawn primarily from these two sources. Also, *Information of William Rhett Jr. to Admiralty, London*, 28 September 1721 [HCA 1/55].

23 *The Tryals of Major Stede Bonnet and Other Pirates* (London, 1719), pp.46–47.

24 *Ibid.*, p.47; *Letter from Christopher Gale to Thomas Pitt, Charles Town*, 4 November 1718 [CO 23/1 f.121].

25 *Ibid.*, pp.47–48.

26 *Ibid.*, p.48.

27 This account of the trial is based on *The Tryals of Major Stede Bonnet and Other Pirates* (London, 1719), pp.48–54. Also, Johnson., *op. cit.*, pp.72–79; *Applebee's Original Weekly Journal*, London, 28 February 1719.

28 *The Tryals of Major Stede Bonnet and Other Pirates* (London, 1719), pp.53–54.

CHAPTER 10

1 *Governor Spotswood of Virginia to the Admiralty*, July 1716 in Brock, *op. cit.*, vol. 1, p.246.

2 *Letter from Virginia merchants*, quoted in Rediker, *op. cit.*, p. 32 and Brock, *op. cit.*, vol. 2, p.249.

3 *Letter from Governor Spotswood to the Admiralty*, May 1717, in Brock, *op. cit.*, vol. 1, p.249.

4 *Acting Governor Heywood of Jamaica to the Admiralty*, December 1716 [CSP Col. (1716–17) 411. f.29]; *Board of Trade to the Admiralty*, September 1717 [CSP Col. (1717–18) 331 and 331 i].

5 Cordingly (2011), *op. cit.*, pp.65–98.

6 Details of *An Act for Suppressing Pirates in West Indies* (1717) are drawn from a copy of the act itself, in McLaine (2020), *op. cit.*, pp.319–20.

7 A facsimile of the front page of this edition of *The London Gazette* (Saturday 14 to Tuesday 17 September 1717) is published in McLaine, *op. cit.*, p.321.

8 *Deposition of Henry Bostock, St Christopher* [St Kitts], December 1717 [CO 152/12 67 iii].

9 The *Boston News Letter*, 19 December 1717.

10 *Governor Bennett of Bermuda to the Council of Trade*, February 1718 [CSP Col. (1717–18) 345 f.170]. An account of the Bennetts' actions is also outlined in *The London Gazette*, 12–16 April 1718. Incidentally, before accepting his appointment in Bermuda, Bennett was a Burgess of the Scottish city of Glasgow. See Anderson, *Burgesses and Guild Brethren* (1925), p.225.

11 *Governor Bennett of Bermuda to the Council of Trade*, February 1718 [CSP Col. (1717–18) 345 f.170]. Also see Brooks, *op. cit.*, p.375.

12 *The British Gazetteer*, 7 June 1718; *The London Gazette*, 23 December 1718; *Deposition of Benjamin Sims, London*, September 1721 [HCA 1/54].

13 Johnson (1998 reprint), *op cit.*, p.15; Craton, *op. cit.*, p.100. Also *George Cammocke to Queen Mary of Modena, St Germaine*, March 1718 [Stuart Papers 29/45], cited in Woodard, *op. cit.*, p.230.

14 *Boston News Letter*, 17 March 1718; Earle, *The Pirate Wars* (2003), p.162.

15 *Boston News Letter*, 31 March 1718.

16 *Log of HMS Phoenix* [ADM 51/690]; *Captain Pearse, HMS Phoenix to the Admiralty*, February 1718 [ADM 1/2283 f.13].

17 *Ibid.*

18 *Ibid.*

19 *Captain Pearse, HMS Phoenix to the Admiralty*, June 1718 [ADM 1/2282 f.13]; *A List of the Names of Such Pirates as Surrendered themselves at Providence to Capt. Vincent Pearse, Nassau, Bahamas, 26 February to 11 March 1718* [ADM 1/2282 f.13 – appended list].

20 *Log of HMS Phoenix* [ADM 51/690].

21 *Ibid.*

22 *Log of HMS Phoenix* [ADM 51/590]; *Captain Pearse, HMS Phoenix to the Admiralty*, June 1718 [ADM 1/2282].

23 *Ibid.*

24 *The Trial of Captain Charles Vane, St Jago de la Vega*, March 1721, attached to *The Tryals of Captain Jack Rackam and other Pyrates* (Kingston, Jamaica, 1721), p.37.

25 The three deserters from the *Phoenix* were Robert Hudson, Thomas Kingston and John Warren [names listed in ADM 1/2282].

26 *Log of HMS Phoenix* [Adm 51/590]; *Captain Pearse, HMS Phoenix to the Admiralty*, June 1718 [ADM 1/2282].

27 *Ibid.*

CHAPTER 11

1 Johnson (1998 reprint), *op. cit.*, p.103.

2 Rediker, *op. cit.*, pp.51–52, contains a discussion of the geographical origins of British-born pirates. The supposition of Vane's age is based on details in the *Boston News Letter*, 27 February 1721.

3 For a discussion of this period in Vane's life, see Woodard, *op. cit.*, pp.84–85. Woodard links him with Jennings, claiming both were present when Jamaica was ravaged by a hurricane in August 1712. If this is true, then the association between Jennings and Vane predates the sinking of the Spanish Treasure Fleet by almost three years.

4 Woodard, *op. cit.*, p.129, suggests that Vane was present at the capture of the *St Marie*. This is based on the *Deposition of Samuel Liddell, Jamaica*, August 1716 [Jamaica Council Minutes f.49–50], although neither it nor the *Deposition of Allen Bernard, Jamaica*, August 1716 [Jamaica Council Minutes f.63–6] appears to mention Vane by name. This association with the *St Marie* capture is also proposed by historian Baylus Brooks on his blog (baylusbrooks.com).

5 Woodard, *op. cit.*, p.138, also suggests that Vane took part of the plundering of the *St Marie*. Again, a lack of evidence makes it hard to verify this supposition.

6 Konstam (2008), *op. cit.*, pp.157–58, contains a summary of Nassau during this period and of Vane's activities.

7 Woodard, *op. cit.*, pp.230–31, discusses this Jacobite sentiment among Vane and his fellow die-hards.

8 Brooks, *op. cit.*, pp.643–45, provides a copy of the list of surrendered pirates, taken from the addendum to Pearse's report to the Admiralty after leaving Nassau; *Capt. Pearse, HMS Phoenix to the Admiralty*, June 1718 [ADM 1/2282].

9 Woodard, *op. cit.*, p.244. Also see *Deposition of Samuel Cooper, Bermuda*, May 1718 [CO 37/10 f.10 i].

10 *The Trial of Captain Charles Vane, St Jago de la Vega*, March 1721, attached to *The Tryals of Captain Jack Rackam and other Pyrates* (Kingston, Jamaica, 1721), p.40.

11 *Ibid.*, p.38.

12 *Ibid.*

13 *Ibid.*, p.37. Also *Governor Bennett of Bermuda to the Council of Trade*, May 1718 [CSP Col. (1717–18) 551].

14 *Deposition of John Libby, Bermuda*, May 1718 [CO 37/10 f.10 viii]; *Deposition of Edward North, Bermuda*, May 1718 [CO 37/10 f.10 ii]; *Deposition of Nathaniel Catling, Bermuda*, May 1718 [CO 37/10 f.10 v].

15 *Ibid.* Also see Woodard, *op. cit.*, pp.244–46.

16 Johnson (1998 reprint), *op cit.*, pp.103–04. Johnson's timeline is somewhat inaccurate.

17 *Vice Admiralty Court Proceedings, Nassau*, August 1718 [ADM 1/2649 f.11]. This includes a manifest of her plundered cargo, which also included beef and flour.

18 *Ibid.* This includes the depositions of Captain Robert Brown of *Eagle*, Captain John Draper of *Drake*, and Captain John Fredd of *Ulster*. Also see Johnson (reprinted 1998), *op. cit.*, pp.103–04 for a somewhat inaccurate account of Vane's activities during this period.

19 *Ibid.* This includes the depositions of William Harris of *Dove* and Neal Walker of *Lancaster*.

20 Johnson (original 1724 edn, vol. 1), *op. cit.*, pp.141–43.

21 *Log of HMS Rose January 1718 to May 1721* [ADM 51/801]. Also, *Log of HMS Milford, 16 January to December 1719* [ADM 51/606]; *Log of HM Sloop-of-War Shark, January 1718 to August 1722* [ADM 51/892].

22 *Letter from Governor Woodes Rogers of the Bahamas to the Council of Trade, Nassau*, October 1718 [CO 23/1].

23 *Ibid.*

24 *Log of HMS Rose January 1718 to May 1721* [ADM 51/801]; *Log of HM Sloop-of-War Shark, January 1718 to August 1722* [ADM 51/892].

25 *Ibid.*

26 *Letter from Governor Woodes Rogers of the Bahamas to the Council of Trade, Nassau,* October 1718 [CO 23/1]; *Log of HMS Milford, 16 January to December 1719* [ADM 51/606].

27 *Letter from Governor Woodes Rogers of the Bahamas to the Council of Trade, Nassau,* October 1718 [CO 23/1]; *Log of HMS Rose January 1718 to May 1721* [ADM 51/801]; *Master and Commander George Pomeroy, HMS Sloop-of-War Shark to the Admiralty, New York,* September 1718 [ADM 1/2282 f.2].

28 This account is drawn from *Letter from Governor Woodes Rogers of the Bahamas to the Council of Trade, Nassau,* October 1718 [CO 23/1].

29 *Ibid.*

30 *Ibid.* Also, *Minutes of the Bahamian Governing Council, Nassau,* August 1718 [CO 23/1 f. 10 ii].

31 This account is drawn from *Letter from Governor Woodes Rogers of the Bahamas to the Council of Trade, Nassau,* October 1718 [CO 23/1].

32 *Ibid.*

33 *Log of HMS Rose January 1718 to May 1721* [ADM 51/801]; *Captain Chamberlaine, HMS Milford to the Admiralty, New York,* November 1718 [ASM 1/1597 f.11].

34 *Letter from Governor Woodes Rogers of the Bahamas to the Council of Trade, Nassau,* October 1718 [CO 23/1]. In his report, Rogers appended a request for 16 large guns, small arms, gunpowder and building tools.

35 *Ibid.*

36 *Deposition of Captain Joseph Aspinwall, London,* July 1719, in Coldham, *English Adventurers and Immigrants, 1661–1733* (1985), p.150.

37 *Ibid.* Also Johnson (1724 – 1st edition), *op. cit.,* pp.144–45.

38 Johnson (1724 – 1st edition), *op. cit.,* p.146.

39 Bahamian Governing Council Minutes, November 1718 [CO 23/1 f. 10 iv]

40 The following account is drawn from *The Tryal and Condemnation of Ten Persons for Piracy, Nassau,* December 1718 [CO 23/1 f.75–82].

41 *Governor Woodes Rogers to Secretary of State (Southern Department) James Craggs the Younger, Nassau,* December 1718 [CO 23/13 f.20]; Johnson (1724 – 1st edition), *op. cit.,* p.146.

42 The nine condemned men were John Augur, George Bendall, William Cunningham, William Dowling, William Lewis, William Ling, Dennis McCarthy, Thomas Morris and George Rounsivel.

CHAPTER 12

1 Dodson, *Alexander Spotswood* (1932); Havighurst, *Alexander Spotswood* (1967); and Dabney, *Virginia* (1983), all recount Spotswood's determination to counter the growing pirate menace in the Americas. For a detailed account of his correspondence on the matter, see Brock, *op. cit.,* pp.351–54.

2 *Governor Charles Eden to the North Carolina Assembly, Chowan,* December 1718, quoted in Saunders, *Colonial Records of North Carolina* (1882), p.322.

Also, *Captain Brand, HMS Lyme to the Admiralty, Virginia,* February 1719 [ADM 1/1472 f.11].

3 *Ibid.* For Thatch in Philadelphia, see Woodman, *op. cit.,* p.278. Brooks, *op. cit.,* pp.511–13, discusses the various unsubstantiated local legends about this visit to the city, but found no evidence that it actually happened.

4 Johnson (1998 reprint), *op. cit.,* p.51. Johnson claims this happened in June 1718 – a timeline which was roughly two months out.

5 *Ibid.,* p.51. Also *Governor Alexander Spotswood to the Council of Trade, Williamsburg,* May 1719, reprinted in Brock, *op. cit.,* pp.316–18.

6 *Boston News Letter,* 17 November 1718; Johnson (1998 reprint), *op. cit.,* p.51.

7 North Carolina Assembly Minutes, Chowan, May 1719, quoted in Saunders, *op. cit.,* p.341; *Governor Alexander Spotswood to the Council of Trade, Williamsburg,* May 1719, reprinted in Brock, *op. cit.,* pp.322–23.

8 Saunders, *op. cit.,* pp.341, 347–50, especially the Testimony of Tobias Knight, and Ellis Brand (pp.346–47). For a more detailed description of this arrangement, see Konstam (2006), *op. cit.,* pp.202–03.

9 Saunders, *op. cit.,* pp.347–50. For the meeting of the two pirate crews, see Johnson (1998 reprint), *op. cit.,* pp.106–07.

10 Johnson (1998 reprint), *op. cit.,* p,107; *Governor Alexander Spotswood to the Council of Trade, Williamsburg,* August 1719 [CSP COl. (1718–19) 357 f.207].

11 *The Log of HMS Lyme,* 1717–18 [ADM 51/4250]; *The Log of HMS Pearl,* 1717–18 [ADM L/32]. Also see Brock, *op. cit.,* p.317, and Lyon, *The Sailing Navy List* (2001) for details of the two frigates.

12 *Letter from Captain Ellis Brand, HMS Pearl to the Admiralty,* February 1719 [CSP Col. 1718–19 30 f.800].

13 *Ibid.*

14 *Ibid.* Also see Konstam (2006) *op. cit.,* pp.240–42.

15 *Letter from Lieutenant Maynard to Lieutenant Symonds, HMS Phoenix, December 1718,* abstracted and reprinted in the *Weekly Journal* or *British Gazette,* 25 April 1719.

16 Johnson (reprinted 1998), *op. cit.,* pp.53–54. Also see *Letter from Colonel Thomas Pollock to Governor Charles Eden of North Carolina,* December 1718 [North Carolina Colonial Records, Vol. II, pp.318–20].

17 *Report by Lieutenant Robert Maynard to Captain Ellis Brand, HMS Pearl, Kecoughtan,* December 1718 [ADM L f. P 32]; *Orders from Captain George Gordon to Lieutenant Robert Maynard* [ADM1/1826]. Also Konstam (2006), *op. cit.,* pp.244–45.

18 *Letter from Lieutenant Maynard to Lieutenant Symonds, HMS Phoenix,* December 1718, abstracted and reprinted in the *Weekly Journal* or *British Gazette,* 25 April 1719.

19 Johnson (reprinted 1998), *op. cit.,* p.54.

20 The following account of the action between Maynard and Thatch is drawn from a compilation of several sources: *The Log of HMS Lyme,* 1717–18 [ADM 51/4250]; *The Log of HMS Pearl,* 1717–18 [ADM L/32]; *Report by Lieutenant Robert Maynard to Captain Ellis Brand, HMS Pearl, Kecoughtan,*

December 1718 [ADM L f. P 32]; *Letter from Captain Ellis Brand, HMS Pearl to the Admiralty,* February 1719 [CSP Col. 1718–19 30 f.800]; *Letter from Lieutenant Maynard to Lieutenant Symonds, HMS Phoenix,* December 1718, abstracted and reprinted in the *Weekly Journal* or *British Gazette,* 25 April 1719; *Letter from Captain George Gordon, HMS Lyme to the Admiralty,* February 1719 [ADM 1/1826], and Johnson (reprinted 1998), *op. cit.,* pp.54–59.

21 *Ibid.*

22 *Ibid.*

23 *Ibid.* Also extracts from various artillery manuals, listed in Blackmore, *Ordnance* (1976), pp.396–405.

24 *Letter from Lieutenant Maynard to Lieutenant Symonds, HMS Phoenix,* December 1718, abstracted and reprinted in the *Weekly Journal* or *British Gazette,* 25 April 1719.

25 *Ibid.* Also *Boston News Letter,* 16–23 February 1719.

26 *Ibid.*

27 *Letter from Lieutenant Maynard to Lieutenant Symonds, HMS Phoenix,* December 1718, abstracted and reprinted in the *Weekly Journal* or *British Gazette,* 25 April 1719.

28 *Ibid.* Also *Boston News Letter,* 16–23 February 1719 and Johnson (reprinted 1998), *op. cit.,* p.59.

29 *Ibid.* Also *Report by Lieutenant Robert Maynard to Captain Ellis Brand, HMS Pearl, Kecoughtan,* December 1718 [ADM L f. P 32].

30 *Letter from Lieutenant Maynard to Lieutenant Symonds, HMS Phoenix,* December 1718, abstracted and reprinted in the *Weekly Journal* or *British Gazette,* 25 April 1719.

31 *Boston News Letter,* 16–23 February 1719.

32 *Ibid.*

33 *Ibid.* Also *Report by Lieutenant Robert Maynard to Captain Ellis Brand, HMS Pearl, Kecoughtan,* December 1718 [ADM L f. P 32]; *Letter from Lieutenant Maynard to Lieutenant Symonds, HMS Phoenix,* December 1718, abstracted and reprinted in the *Weekly Journal* or *British Gazette,* 25 April 1719.

34 *Report by Lieutenant Robert Maynard to Captain Ellis Brand, HMS Pearl, Kecoughtan,* December 1718 [ADM L f. P 32]; *Letter from Captain Ellis Brand, HMS Pearl to the Admiralty,* February 1719 [CSP Col. 1718–19 30 f.800]; *Letter from Captain George Gordon, HMS Lyme to the Admiralty,* February 1719 [ADM 1/1826].

35 *Ibid.*

36 *Letter from Captain Ellis Brand, HMS Pearl to the Admiralty,* December 1718 [ADM 1/1472]; Johnson (reprinted 1998), *op. cit.,* 57–58.

37 *Ibid.*

38 *Letter from Captain Gordon, HMS Lyme to the Admiralty,* February 1719 [ADM 1/1826]; *Report by Lieutenant Robert Maynard to Captain Ellis Brand, HMS Pearl, Kecoughtan,* December 1718 [ADM L f. P 32].

39 *Letter from Captain Ellis Brand, HMS Pearl to the Admiralty*, December 1718 [ADM 1/1472]; *Letter from Colonel Thomas Pollock to Governor Charles Eden*, December 1718 [North Carolina Colonial Records, Vol. II, pp.318–20]. Also see North Carolina Colonial Records Vol. II, pp.341–49, and British Privy Council Register [1721 2/87 f.293] for details of this legal exchange.
40 For a discussion of Spotswood's situation during this period see Dodson, *op. cit.*, and Havighurst, *op. cit.*
41 *Log of HMS Lyme*, 1717–18 [ADM 51/1420]; *Letter from Captain Gordon, HMS Lyme to the Admiralty*, February 1719 [ADM 1/1826]; *Report by Lieutenant Robert Maynard to Captain Ellis Brand, HMS Pearl, Kecoughtan*, December 1718 [ADM L f. P 32].
42 *Report by Lieutenant Robert Maynard to Captain Ellis Brand, HMS Pearl, Kecoughtan*, December 1718 [ADM L f. P 32].
43 Johnson (reprinted 1998), *op. cit.*, p. 62. The original trial transcripts have been lost. However, see *North Carolina Colonial Records* Vol. II, pp.328, 341–49 for extracts. Also Konstam (2006), *op. cit.*, pp.267–68 for a discussion of the evidence.
44 *Ibid.* Also see Lee, *Blackbeard the Pirate* (1974), pp.136–38 for a legal perspective.
45 For a lively discussion of the fate of Blackbeard's skull see Lee, *op. cit.*, pp.124–25. Also see the curatorial notes for the Peabody-Essex Museum, Salem MA, and the Mariners' Museum, Newport News, VA. Legend has it that the skull was used as a drinking vessel in the Raleigh Tavern in Williamsburg, VA, and was later ornamented with silver fittings. An object purporting to be the skull now forms part of the Edward Rowe collection of the Peabody-Essex Museum. There is no way of authenticating it, and so it remains a curiosity, rather than an answer to the mystery.
46 Details of Maynard's subsequent career were provided to the author by the late David Lyon, curator at the National Maritime Museum, Greenwich. See Konstam (2006), *op. cit.*, p.274.

CHAPTER 13

1 *Governor Woodes Rogers to the Council of Trade, Nassau*, October 1718 [CSP Col. (1717–18) 737 f.372]. Also see *Governor Alexander Spotswood to the Council of Trade, Williamsburg*, May 1717 [CO 5/1318] for a discussion of the potential risks of offering pardons to pirates. Also see Jameson, *op cit.*, p.315.
2 An Act for Supressing Pirates in the West Indies (1717), in McLaine (2020), *op. cit.*, pp.319–20.
3 *Ibid.*, pp.323–25.
4 Johnson (1998 reprint), *op. cit.*, p.103. Also see Woodman, *op. cit.*, p.272.
5 *British Gazetteer* or *Weekly Journal*, 27 December 1718, includes the report given from one of the ships, which subsequently reported the attack while in Charles Town, in the South Carolina colony.
6 *Ibid.*

NOTES

7 *Boston News Letter*, 20 October 1718. Also see *Governor Robert Johnson of South Carolina to the Council of Trade, Charles Town*, October 1718 [CSP Col. (1717–18) 730 f.366]. *South Carolina Colony Shipping Records, 1717–19* [CO 5/508 f.68].

8 *Boston News Letter*, 20 October 1718. According to the newspaper, cross-referenced with the shipping records from the *Dorothy*, at the time Yeats was carrying 70 slaves, taken off one of Vane's prizes. Also see Johnson (1998 reprint), *op. cit.*, p.105.

9 *Governor Woodes Rogers to the Council of Trade, Nassau*, October 1718 [CSP Col. (1717–18) 737 f.372].

10 *Letter from Governor Robert Johnson of South Carolina to the Council of Trade*, October 1718 [CSP Col. (1717–18) 730 f.366]; Johnson (1998 reprint), *op. cit.*, pp.69–71.

11 Johnson (1998 reprint), *op. cit.*, pp.106–07.

12 *Governor Woodes Rogers to the Council of Trade, Nassau*, October 1718 [CSP Col. (1717–1718) 737 f.372].

13 *The Tryals of Captain Jack Rackam and other Pyrates*, addendum; *The Trial of Charles Vane, St Jago de la Vega*, 22 March 1720, p.39.

14 *Ibid.*, p.24

15 *Ibid.* Also Johnson (1998 reprint), *op. cit.*, p.107.

16 *The Tryals of Captain Jack Rackam and other Pyrates*, addendum; *The Trial of Charles Vane, St Jago de la Vega*, 22 March 1720, pp.24–25. Also Johnson (1998 reprint), *op. cit.*, p.107–08.

17 Johnson (1998 reprint), *op. cit.*, p. 108.

18 *Ibid.* Also *The Tryals of Captain Jack Rackam and other Pyrates*, addendum; *The Trial of Charles Vane, St Jago de la Vega*, 22 March 1720, p.39.

19 *Ibid.*, p.25; Johnson (2009 reprint), *op. cit.*, pp.107–08.

20 *Ibid.*

21 Johnson (1998 reprint); *op. cit.*, p.109.

22 *Ibid.*

23 *Ibid.*

24 The brief account of the trial of Charles Vane is drawn from *The Tryals of Captain Jack Rackam and other Pyrates*, addendum; *The Trial of Charles Vane, St Jago de la Vega*, 22 March 1720, pp.36–40. An account of it was also published in the *American Weekly Mercury*, 4 May 1721, in its New York Despatch section. The *Mercury* was published in Philadelphia.

25 *Governor Nicholas Lawes of Jamaica to the Council of Trade, Kingston*, January 1719 [CSP Col. (1718–19) 34 f.18].

26 *Ibid.*

27 Johnson (1998 reprint), *op. cit.*, pp.111–12.

28 *Governor Nicholas Lawes of Jamaica to the Council of Trade, Kingston*, March 1719 [CSP Col. (1719–20) 132 f.64]; *Weekly Jamaica Courant*, Kingston, 11 February 1719.

29 Woodard, *op. cit.*, pp.315–16.

30 *Ibid.*, p.316.

31 Almost everything we know about Anne Bonny's background comes from Johnson. Attempts have been made to verify this account, or to augment it, but so far these attempts lack convincing documentary support. So, until these appear, we only have his account of her life. See Johnson (1998 reprint), *op. cit.*, pp.125–30.

32 *Ibid.*

33 *Ibid.*, pp.117–21.

34 Descriptions of the two women are provided in *The Tryals of Captain Jack Rackam and other Pyrates, op. cit.*, pp.18–19.

35 *Ibid.*, p.123. Also Governor Woodes Rogers' Proclamation, published in the *Boston Gazette*, 17 October 1720.

36 *Lieutenant Joseph Lawes to Captain Edward Vernon, HMS Mary*, October 1720 [CSP Col. (1720–21) 527 xxxiv f.344].

37 *Ibid.*

38 *Ibid.* Also New Providence Dispatch, dated 4 September, in the *Boston Gazette*, 17 October 1720.

39 Deposition of Dorothy Thomas, in *The Tryals of Captain Jack Rackam and other Pyrates, op. cit.*, p. 18.

40 Johnson (1998 reprint), *op. cit.*, p.113; *The Tryals of Captain Jack Rackam and other Pyrates, op. cit.*, pp.8–9.

41 *Ibid.*, pp.9–10.

42 *Ibid.*, pp.10–11.

43 *Ibid.*, p.11.

44 *Ibid.*, pp.11–12.

45 *Ibid.*, p.11.

46 *Ibid.*

47 *Ibid.*

48 *Ibid.*

49 *Ibid.* Also Johnson (1998 reprint), *op. cit.*, p.116. The bodies of two other pirates hanged alongside Rackam, John Davies and John Howell, were buried in unmarked graves, as were the four hanged in Kingston on 19 November (Patrick Carty, James Dobbin, Thomas Earl and John Fenwick), plus the two hanged on Gallows Point near Port Royal on 21 November (Thomas Brown and John Fenwick).

50 *The Tryals of Captain Jack Rackam and other Pyrates, op. cit.*, pp.15–19.

51 *Ibid.*, p.19.

52 Woodman, *op. cit.*, p.320; Konstam (2008), *op. cit.*, pp.186–88.

53 *Letter from Captain Edward Vernon, HMS Mary to the Admiralty, Jamaica,* April 1721 [ADM 1/2624 f.6].

CHAPTER 14

1 Details of the sloop *Buck* are contained in the *Memorial from the Co-Partners for Carrying Trade and Settling the Bahamas to the Council of Trade*, May 1721 [CO 23/1 f.2].

NOTES

2 *Governor Woodes Rogers of Bahama to the Council of Trade, Nassau,* October 1718 [CSP Col. (1717–18) 737 f.372].

3 *Log of HMS Rose January 1718 to May 1721* [ADM 51/801]; *Captain Chamberlaine, HMS Milford to the Admiralty, New York,* November 1718 [ASM 1/1597 f.11].

4 *Captain Peter Chamberlaine, HMS Milford to the Admiralty, New York,* November 1718 [ADM 1/1597 f.11].

5 Rediker, *op. cit.,* p.37. Also see Johnson (1724 2nd edition), *op. cit.,* p.288.

6 Johnson (1998 reprint), *op. cit.,* p.134. Local legend in Boca de Yumurí has it that English buccaneers used this narrow and easily defended anchorage during the late 17th century, and later, early 18th-century pirates used the same hideaway. The name Coxen's Hole, like Coxen's Hole in Roatán in the Gulf of Honduras, is likely to be a reference to the Jamaican buccaneer John Coxen, active in the Caribbean during the 1670s and 1680s.

7 Johnson (1998 reprint), *op. cit.,* p.132.

8 *Ibid.* Also see Woodard, *op. cit.,* p.232.

9 Woodard, *op. cit.,* p.232; Earle (2003), *op. cit.,* p.162.

10 Johnson (1998 reprint), *op. cit.,* pp.132–33.

11 *Ibid.,* pp.134–35; Sanders, *If a Pirate I must be* (2007), pp.29–30.

12 Johnson (1998 reprint), *op. cit.,* p.136.

13 *Ibid.,* p.137. The following description of Howell Davis' sojourn in the Cape Verde Islands is drawn from Johnson's account of it, on pp.136–42.

14 *Ibid.,* p.140–42, for Johnson's account of the capture of the Portuguese governor, his mansion and the fort.

15 This account of Davis' actions in the Gambia River is based on Johnson (1998 reprint), *op. cit.,* pp.141–42. Also Konstam (2008) *op. cit.,* pp.230–31 and Sanders, *op. cit.,* pp.30–31.

16 Rogozinski (1995), *op. cit.,* p.188; Gosse, *The Pirates' Who's Who* (reprinted 1988), pp.58–59.

17 Hostin, *The Pirate of Cotinga Island* (2019), contains a description of the rediscovery of Levasseur's pirate ship.

18 *Letter from Governor Walter Hamilton of the Leeward Islands to the Council of Trade, St Christopher,* December 1718 [CSP Col. (1718–1719) 797].

19 *Deposition of John Bois, Wade frigate,* January 1719 [CSP Col. (1717–18) 797 ii].

20 *Letter from Governor Walter Hamilton of the Leeward Islands to the Council of Trade, St Christopher,* December 1718 [CSP Col. (1717–18) 797]; *Deposition of Captain Robert Leonard of the Eagle, Antigua,* February 1719 [CSP Col. (1718–19) 797 vi]; *Deposition of Captain Robert Leathes of the Upton, Antigua,* March 1719 [CSP Col. (1718–19) 797 vi]. Cordingly (1995), *op. cit.,* p.251, lists the Royal Naval reinforcements sent to the Americas in late 1719, many of which were earmarked for anti-piracy duties, primarily in the West Indies.

21 Johnson (1998 reprint), *op. cit.,* p.142; Rediker, *op. cit.,* p.80.

22 Sanders, *op. cit.,* p.52. This well-researched book is the source for most of the following account of the pirates in Príncipe, and the death of Davis. Also see Johnson (1998 reprint), *op. cit.,* pp.157–60.

23 A full copy of Bartholomew Roberts' pirate code is found in Johnson (1998 reprint), *op. cit.*, pp.180–81 or Konstam (2008), *op. cit.*, pp.226–27.

CHAPTER 15

1 *Captain John Balchen, HMS Diamond to the Admiralty, Jamaica,* May 1717 [CSP Col. (1717–18) 271].

2 Johnson (1998 reprint), *op. cit.*, p.184 (although he misidentifies both the ship and the location of her capture), and Sanders, *op. cit.*, p.92.

3 For a discussion of the involvement of the French pirate in all this, see Burl, *Black Barty* (1997), pp.119–24.

4 The location of Roberts' careening spot was proposed by a Dominican historian, Edward Scobie, during a chance encounter with the author in 1982, while the latter was part of a naval party helping to restore a colonial British fort on the island. This proposal was based on long-established local folklore.

5 *British Gazetteer,* or *Weekly Journal,* 26 November 1720; Johnson (2008 reprint), *op. cit.*, pp.185–86; Burl, *op. cit.*, pp.133–36; Sanders, *op. cit.*, pp.106–09; Konstam (2008), *op. cit.*, p.238. .

6 *Boston News Letter,* 13 July 1720.

7 Johnson (1998 reprint), *op. cit.*, pp.187–88.

8 *Ibid.* Also Sanders, *op. cit.*, pp.123–24; Burl, *op. cit.*, p.129.

9 *Ibid.*, pp.188–89. Deposition of Captain Robert Dunn, October 1720 [CSP Col. (1720–21) 251 f.15 i]. Also see Sanders, *op. cit.*, pp.122–23.

10 Deposition of Captain Robert Dunn, October 1720 [CSP Col. (1720–21) 251 f.15 i]. Also Sanders, *op. cit.*, p.130.

11 Johnson (1998 reprint), *op. cit.*, pp.192–93.

12 Sanders, *op. cit.*, pp.133–34.

13 Quoted in full in Sanders, *op. cit.*, p.135.

14 Sanders, *op. cit.*, pp.140–41.

15 Johnson (1998 reprint), *op. cit.*, p.193; *The Weekly Journal,* or *Saturday Post,* 1 April 1721.

16 *Governor Benjamin Bennet of Bermuda to the Council of Trade,* February 1721 [CSP Col. (1720–21) 42/17]; Johnson (1998 reprint), *op. cit.*, pp.193–94; Sanders, *op. cit.*, p,148.

17 *The Weekly Journal,* or *British Gazetteer,* 14 May 1721; *Deposition of Captain Richard Simes of the Fisher, St Lucia,* January 1721 [CO 31/14].

18 *Post Boy* newspaper of London, 7 April 1721. Also Sanders, *op. cit.*, p.156.

19 *Ibid.*, pp.160–61.

20 *The Weekly Journal,* or *British Gazetteer,* 29 July 1721; Correspondence between Captain Whitney, HMS *Rose* and Governor Walter Hamilton of the Leeward Islands, March–April 1721 [CO 152/14 f.23].

21 Cordingly, *op. cit.*, p.252; Sanders, *op. cit.*, pp.158–62.

22 Johnson (1998 reprint), *op. cit.*, p.195.

23 *Ibid.*, p.195. Also Sanders, *op. cit.*, pp.167–68; Burl, *op. cit.*, p.205.

24 Johnson (1998 reprint), *op. cit.*, p.196.

25 Sanders, *op. cit.*, pp.184–85.

26 *Ibid.*, p.198.

27 *The Weekly Journal, or Saturday Post,* 7 April 1722; Johnson (1998 reprint), *op. cit.*, p.199.

28 Sanders, *op. cit.*, pp.205–07.

29 *Ibid.*, pp.207–08.

30 Johnson (1998 reprint), *op. cit.*, pp.203–04.

31 *The Log of HMS Swallow, 1721–1723* [ADM 1/2242].

32 *Ibid.*

33 This account is based on *The Log of HMS Swallow, 1721–1723* [ADM 1/2242], and the testimonies and depositions given in *Trial at Cape Coast Castle, Africa, 1722* [HCA 49 104]. Also see Johnson (1998 reprint), *op. cit.*, pp.208–15, although Johnson was mistaken about the location of the battles; Sanders, *op. cit.*, pp.212–26 and Burl, *op. cit.*, pp.225–41.

CHAPTER 16

1 The following account of the trial and subsequent sentences is drawn primarily from *Trial at Cape Coast Castle, Africa, 1722* [HCA 49 104]. Also see Johnson (1998 reprint), *op. cit.*, pp.225–59; Sanders, *op. cit.*, pp.228–40; Burl, *op. cit.*, pp.245–59.

2 *Letter from Governor Phipps of Cape Coast Castle to the Royal African Company,* May 1722, quoted in Sanders, *op. cit.*, p.238.

3 This description of the fate of the *Eagle*'s crew in Argyllshire and Edinburgh is drawn primarily from Graham, *Seawolves* (2005), pp.47–60, which contains the first thoroughly researched account of the arrest of the pirate crew, and their subsequent trial and execution.

4 For details of the *Buck*, see Cordingly (2011), *op. cit.*, pp.138–40.

5 Johnson (1998 reprint), *op. cit.*, p.260.

6 *Ibid.*, pp. 261–62.

7 *Ibid.*, p.262

8 *Ibid.*, pp.262–63.

9 *Ibid.*, p.263.

10 *Ibid.*, pp.313–24.

11 Brooks, *op. cit.*, pp.224–25; *Governor Benjamin Bennett to the Council of Trade,* August 1718 [CSP Col. (1717–18) 30 f.168].

12 *American Weekly Mercury,* Philadelphia, 18 August 1720; Brooks, *op. cit.*, p.225.

13 *Governor Woodes Rogers of the Bahamas to James Craggs the Younger, Secretary of State for the South, Nassau,* December 1718 [CO13/1 i].

14 The War of the Quadruple Alliance (mid-1718 to early 1720) was largely waged in Europe – for the most part in Italy. However, it also saw a Spanish landing in Scotland, in support of the Jacobites, and fighting between the French and the Spanish in the Pyrenees.

15 The account of the Spanish operation is drawn from Cordingly (2012), *op. cit.*, pp.179–80. Also see the *Log of HMS Flamborough, 1719–1721* [ADM 51/357 viii]; *Governor Woodes Rogers of the Bahamas to James Craggs the Younger, Secretary of State for the South, Nassau,* March 1719 [CO 23/13].

16 For examples of this correspondence, see *Governor Woodes Rogers of the Bahamas to James Craggs the Younger, Secretary of State for the South, Nassau,* January 1719 [CSP Col. (1719–20) 28 f.9]; *Governor Woodes Rogers of the Bahamas to James Craggs the Younger, Secretary of State for the South, Nassau,* November 1720 [CSP Col. (1720–21) 302 f.201]; *Governor Woodes Rogers of the Bahamas to the Council of Trade, Nassau,* April 1720 [CSP Col. (1720–21) 47 f.30].

17 *Petition from Governor Woodes Rogers of the Bahamas to King George I of Britain,* July 1726 [CO 23/12/2]. Rogers also wrote a similar letter praising Hornigold to the Council of Trade.

18 Konstam (2008), *op. cit.*, pp.268–70.

19 *Ibid.*, p.270.

20 *Ibid.*, p.271.

21 *Ibid.*

BIBLIOGRAPHY

PRIMARY SOURCES
ADM Admiralty Records
CO Colonial Office Records
CSP Col. Calendar of State Papers (Colonial Series)
HC ADM High Court of the Admiralty Records
AGI Archivo General de las Indies, Seville

PUBLISHED PRIMARY SOURCES

Exquemelin, Alexandre, *The Buccaneers of America*, Amsterdam, 1678 – English
 reprint London: The Folio Society, 1969
Hamilton, Lord Alexander, *An Answer to an Anonymous Libel* (pamphlet),
 London, 1718
Heath, Dr Emmanuel, *A Full Account of the Late Dreadful Earthquake at Port
 Royal* (pamphlet), London, 1692
Jameson, John F., *Privateering and Piracy in the Colonial Period: Illustrative
 Documents*, New York: Macmillan, 1923
Mather, Rev. Cotton, *Instructions to the Living, from the Condition of the Dead*,
 Boston: John Allen, 1717
McLaine, Matt (ed.), *Piracy Papers: Primary Source Documents from the Golden Age
 of Piracy*, Great Britain: Amazon, 2020
Middleton, John (ed.), *Privateering and Piracy in the Colonial Period: Illustrative
 Documents*, New York: Macmillan, 1923
The Trials of Eight Persons indicted for Pyracy, Boston: John Edwards, 1718
The Tryals of Captain Jack Rackam and other Pyrates, Kingston, Jamaica: Robert
 Baldwin, 1721
The Tryals of Major Stede Bonnet and Other Pirates, London: Benjamin Cowes,
 1719

SECONDARY SOURCES

Anon, *The State of the Island of Jamaica*, London: Henry Whitridge, 1726
Albury, Paul, *The Story of the Bahamas*, Nassau: Macmillan Caribbean, 1975
Anderson, James R. (ed.), *The Burgesses and Guild Brethren of Glasgow, 1573–
 1750*, Edinburgh: Scottish Records Society, 1925
Andrews, Charles, *The Colonial Period in American History; England's Commercial
 and Colonial Policy*, 5 vols, New Haven, CT: Yale University Press, 1938

Apestegui, Cruz, *Pirates of the Caribbean: Buccaneers, Privateers, Freebooters and Filibusters, 1493–1720*, London: Conway Maritime Press, 2002

Blackmore, Howard L., *The Armouries of the Tower of London: Vol. 1 – Ordnance*, London: HMSO, 1976

Bourne, Ruth, *Queen Anne's Navy in the West Indies*, London: H. Milford on behalf of Oxford University Press, 1939

Boyle, David, *The Last Days of Port Royal: The Destruction of the Home of the Pirates of the Caribbean*, Horsham: The Real Press, 2019

Bridges, G. W., *The Annals of Jamaica*, London: John Murray, 1837

Brock, R. A., *The Official Letters of Alexander Spotswood, Lieutenant-Governor of the Colony of Virginia, 1710–1722*, vol. 2, Richmond, VA: The Virginia Historical Society, 1885

Brooks, Baylus C., *Quest for Blackbeard: The True Story of Edward Thache and his World*, Lulu Press (self-published), 2016

Burgess, Robert F. & Clausen, Carl J., *Florida's Golden Galleons: The Search for the 1715 Treasure Fleet*, Port Salerno, FL: Florida Classics Library, 1982

Burl, Aubrey, *Black Barty: The Real Pirate of the Caribbean*, Port Talbot: Alun Books, 1997

Chapin, Howard M., *Privateer Ships and Sailors: The First Century of American Colonial Privateering, 1625–1725*, first published Toulon, 1926; New York, 2017

Clifford, Barry & Turchi, Peter, *The Pirate Prince: Discovering the Priceless Treasures of the Sunken Ship Whydah*, New York: Simon & Schuster, 1993

Clifford, Barry & Perry, Paul, *The Black Ship: The Quest to Recover an English Pirate Ship and its Lost Treasure*, London: Headline Book Publishing, 1999

Clifford, Barry (ed.), *Real Pirates: The Untold Story of the Whydah from Slave Ship to Pirate Ship*, Washington DC: National Geographic, 2007

Coldingham, Peter W. (ed.), *English Adventurers and Immigrants, 1661–1733*, Baltimore: Genealogical Publishing Inc., 1985

Cordingly, David & Falconer, John, *Pirates: Fact & Fiction*, London: Collins & Brown Ltd., 1992

Cordingly, David, *Under the Black Flag: The Romance and the Reality of Life Among the Pirates*, London: Random House, 1995

Cordingly, David, *Spanish Gold: Captain Woodes Rogers and the Pirates of the Caribbean*, London: Bloomsbury Publishing, 2011

Craton, Michael, *A History of the Bahamas*, London: Collins, 1962

Craton, Michael & Saunders, Gail, *Islanders in the Stream: A History of the Bahamian People Vol. 1 From Aboriginal Times to the Ending of Slavery*, Athens GA: University of Georgia Press, 1992

Dabney, Virginius, *Virginia: The New Dominion – A History from 1607 to the Present Day*, Charlottesville, VA: University of Virginia Press, 1983

Dodson, Leonidas, *Alexander Spotswood: Governor of Colonial Virginia*, Philadelphia: University of Pennsylvania Press, 1932

Dow, George F. & Edmonds, John H., *The Pirates of the New England Coast 1630–1730*, Salem MA: Marine Research Society, 1923

Earle, Peter, *The Sack of Panama*, London: Jill, Norman & Hobhouse, 1981

Earle, Peter, *Sailors: English Merchant Seamen, 1650–1775*, London: Methuen, 1998

Earle, Peter, *The Pirate Wars*, London: Methuen, 2003

Graham, Eric C., *Seawolves: Pirates & The Scots*, Edinburgh: Birlinn, 2005

Gosse, Philip, *The Pirates' Who's Who: Giving the Particulars of the Lives and Deaths of the Pirates and Buccaneers*, Glorieta, NM: Rio Grande Press, 1988; first published 1924

Havinghurst, Walter, *Alexander Spotswood: A Portrait of a Governor*, New York, NY: Holt, Rinehart and Winston, 1967

Hofenk de Graff, Judith, *The Colourful Past: Chemistry and Identification of Natural Dyestuffs*, London: Archetype Books, 2004

Hostin, Geraldo, *The Pirate of Cotinga Island, 1718: A Historical and Archaeological Study of a Mysterious Shipwreck in the South of Brazil*, MPA thesis, Perth, Australia: University of Western Australia, 2019

Jenkins, E. H., *A History of the French Navy*, London: Macdonald & Jane's, 1973

Johnson, Captain Charles, *A General History of Pyrates*, 2 vols, London: Charles Rivington, 1724

Johnson, Captain Charles, *A General History of the Pyrates*, London: Conway Maritime Press, 1998; reprint of 1724 original (Vol. 1), with additional introduction and commentary

Konstam, Angus, *Blackbeard: America's Most Notorious Pirate*, Hoboken, NJ: Wiley & Sons, 2006

Konstam, Angus, *Piracy: The Complete History*, Oxford: Osprey Publishing, 2008

Kropotkin, Petr, *Mutual Aid: A Factor of Evolution*, New York: McClure Phillips & Co., 1902

Lavery, Brian, *The Ship of the Line: Vol. 1 The Development of the Battlefleet, 1650–1850*, London: Conway Maritime Press, 1983

Lee, Robert E., *Blackbeard the Pirate: A Reappraisal of his Life and Times*, Winston-Salem, NC: John F. Blair, 1975; reprinted 2002

Lynn, John A., *The Wars of Louis XIV, 1667–1714*, London: Addison Wesley Longman Ltd., 1999

Lyon, David, *The Sailing Navy List: All the Ships of the Royal Navy, Built, Purchased and Captured, 1688–1720*, London: Conway Maritime Press, 2001

Marx, Robert F., *Port Royal The Sunken City*, Southend-on-Sea: AquaPress, 2003

Matthew, Colin & Harrison, Brian (eds.), *The Oxford Dictionary of National Biography*, Oxford: Oxford University Press, 2004

Moore, David, 'Primary source documents concerning the notorious Blackbeard' in *The North Carolina Historical Review*, Vol. XCV No. 2, April 2018

Morley, Nicholas, *British-Colonial Privateering in the War of the Spanish Succession*, M.Phil thesis, University of Glasgow, 2000 (available online)

Oldmixon, John, *The British Empire in America*, London: John Brotherton, 1741

Pawson, Michael & Buisseret, David, *Port Royal, Jamaica*, Oxford: Oxford University Press, 1975

Pérez-Mallaína, Pablo E., *Spain's Men of the Sea: Daily Life on the Indies Fleets in the Sixteenth Century*, Baltimore: Johns Hopkins University Press, 1998

Pope, Dudley, *Harry Morgan's Way: A Biography of Sir Henry Morgan, 1635–1684*, London: House of Stratus, 1977

Rediker, Marcus, *Villains of All Nations: Atlantic Pirates in the Golden Age*, Boston, MA: Beacon Press, 2004

Rogers, N. A. M., *The Wooden World: An Anatomy of the Georgian Navy*, William Collins, 1986

Rogoziński, Jan, *Pirates! An A–Z Encyclopaedia*, New York: Da Capo Press, 1996

Rogoziński, Jan, *Honour Among Thieves: Captain Kidd, Henry Every and the Story of Pirate Island*, London: Conway Maritime Press, 2000

Sanders, Joanne McRee, *Barbados Records: Wills and Administrations*, Vol. 1 (1639–1680), Marceline, WI: Sanders Historical Publications, 1979

Sanders, Richard, *If a Pirate I must be: The True Story of Bartholomew Roberts, King of the Caribbean*, London: Aurum Press, 2007

Sandler, Martin W., *The Whydah: A Pirate Ship Feared, Wrecked and Found*, Somerville, MA: Candlewick Press, 2017

Saunders, William L., *Colonial Records of North Carolina*, Vol. 2, Raleigh, NC: P. M. Hale Publisher, 1886

Skowrontek, Russell K. & Ewen, Charles R. (eds.), *X Marks the Spot: The Archaeology of Piracy*, Gainesville, FL: University of Florida Press, 2006

Snelgrave, William, *A New Account of Some Parts of Guinea and the Slave Trade*, London: J. Wrenn, 1734

Stephen, Sir Leslie (ed.), *Dictionary of National Biography*, London: Smith, Elder & Co., 1885

Stiles, T. (ed.), *The Colonizers: Early European Settlers and the Shaping of North America*, Hoboken, NJ: Prentice Hall, 2002

Sutton, Paul, *Cromwell's Western Design: The Attack on the West Indies, 1654–55*, Leigh-on-Sea: Partizan Press, 1990

Wagner, Kip, *Pieces-of-Eight: Recovering the Riches of a Lost Spanish Treasure Fleet*, New York: E. P. Dutton & Co., 1966

Walton, Timothy R., *The Spanish Treasure Fleets*, Sarasota, FL: Pineapple Press, 1994

Watkins-Kennedy, Sarah, 'A Tale of One Ship with Two Names' in *The North Carolina Historical Review*, Vol. XCV No. 2, April 2018

INDEX

References to illustrations are in **bold**